Who Else

writes like ...

A readers' guide to fiction authors

Seventh edition

Edited by
Ian Baillie

A LISU publication

Loughborough University

BAILLE, Ian, Editor

Who Else Writes Like ...? A readers' guide to fiction authors

First published 1993, 7th edition 2012

ISBN: 978-1-905499-41-0

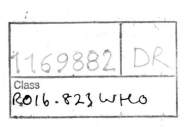
Cover design by
Clarissa Musson, Design and Print Services, Loughborough University

Inside pages designed and typeset in Verdana and Arial by
Mary Ashworth & Sharon Fletcher, LISU

Printed by
Sterling, Sterling House, Kettering Venture Park, Kettering NN15 6XU

Published and distributed by
LISU
Loughborough University, Loughborough, LE11 3TU
Tel: +44 (0)1509 635680 Fax: +44 (0)1509 635699
E-mail: lisu@lboro.ac.uk
Web: www.lboro.ac.uk/microsites/infosci/lisu

Contents

Acknowledgements

I am extremely grateful to this edition's team of advisors, five of whom have assisted in earlier editions. A special mention to Jennie Bolitho and her colleagues from Melbourne, without whose advice I would have deleted an unacceptably high number of Australian authors, thus making the book less relevant to that country. Their meticulous and thoughtful contribution throughout the process was much appreciated. The full list of advisors is as follows:

Daniel Andrews	Wandsworth Borough Council
Terri Beckett	Flintshire County Council
Jennie Bolitho and team	Bayside Libraries, Melbourne
Rose Child	Bristol Grammar School
Paul Cowan	North Ayrshire Libraries
Jill Currie	Plymouth City Council
Tim Davies	North Lincolnshire Council
Carolyn Huckfield	Herefordshire Libraries
Susannah Leigh	Norfolk County Council
Michael Maxwell	Formerly of Leicester Libraries
Jack Meadows	Loughborough University
Jennifer Morley	Brighton and Hove Libraries
Jeremy Preston	Richmond-on-Thames Libraries

I owe a huge debt of gratitude to my friend and former West Dunbartonshire Libraries colleague, Arthur Jones. Without Arthur's regular consultations I shudder to think what damage I might have inflicted on the project, given my ineptitude on the computer. As for LISU, it has been a real pleasure to work directly with Mary and Sharon, and I'd like to thank them for their constant support and for always being there when I needed advice. Thanks, too, to Director, Claire Creaser, for her trust in my suggestions!

From the beginning Public Lending Right has been the arbiter for the core collection of authors that form the basis of the book. I therefore greatly appreciate the help I receive from Dr Jim Parker, the Registrar of Public Lending Right, and his colleagues.

I must also praise my editorial predecessors, Roy and Jeanne Huse. Having edited only one edition, I can scarcely imagine the stamina and dedication required to cope with six! I have been privileged to get to know Roy and Jeanne over the years, and their friendship is greatly valued.

I am also most grateful to Viv Warren and Mary Yardley, the editors of *Who Next ...? A guide to children's authors,* for their expertise in identifying suitable authors for young adult readers.

Finally, my wife, Claire, deserves a medal for 'living' with 'phrase *Who Else Writes Like...?*' for the past year and a bit. Fortunately she likes books!

Ian Baillie

Alexandria
October 2012

Introduction

Who Else Writes Like...? first appeared in 1993, since when it has gone through six editions, and has, for several years, also been available in electronic form. Its main purpose is to act as a guide for readers who find an author they really like, read all of that person's output, and then want to find someone similar whose work they might also enjoy. Obviously, no two authors write in an identical manner, but *Who Else Writes Like...?* offers a range of alternatives (between 6 and 12) which at the very least provides the reader with a starting point among the bewildering array of authors normally found on library shelves and in bookshops. A handy aspect of the paper version of the book is its portability, which means that the reader or library assistant can carry it around with them, thus making the task of browsing that much easier.

As with all previous editions, the starting point in choosing which authors to feature has been the 400 most borrowed writers in UK libraries as provided by the Registrar of Public Lending Right (minus those who write solely for children). This year a decision was taken to remove 'classic' and many 'modern classic' writers from the main section of the book, thus giving it a more contemporary feel and also freeing up much-needed space for the hundreds of new authors who have emerged since the 6th edition. However, those who have been removed feature in a separate list at the back of the book as they are still well worth seeking out.

This edition features over 2,000 authors, the largest number of any edition so far. Many have been added from the quarterly updates to the electronic version, while others have been suggested by our team of advisors. Self evidently, we cannot feature everyone who deserves to be included, but I believe that the book represents an excellent cross section of what is available in libraries and bookshops throughout the UK and Australia. As previously, the main criterion for inclusion is that the author should have written at least three books, though that rule is flexible in certain circumstances.

Inevitably, with a new edition, there are a few changes, but these have been kept to a minimum as Roy and Jeanne Huse have refined the book so effectively over the years. Genres remain largely untouched, but one obvious change is that we no longer feature authors' websites as these can be easily found via Google or a similar search engine. However, the electronic version will continue to feature links to authors' websites, while the list of book-related websites at the back of the paper edition has been expanded. In addition, there is a section offering a selection of fiction-related reference books, a list of environments in which some authors' works are most usually set, and an updated list of Literary Prizes.

In short, the guide aims to open up the amazing world of literature available in libraries and bookshops. Happy reading!

How to use this Guide

The Reader's Guide - An Alphabetical List

Authors are listed in alphabetical order, followed by a list of suggested alternatives. So pick out an author whose books you like, and see which other writers are recommended underneath. For instance, if you like Bryce Courtenay, you might also like Nick Brownlee, Frank Coates and so on.

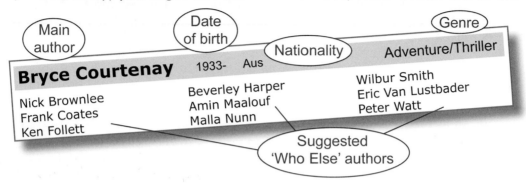

Additional information is given, where known:

- Dates of birth and death
- Nationality (or place of birth) of authors who are not English — see page vi for a list of abbreviations used
- Genre and, in some cases, subgenre, or type of novel (unless 'general')
- Pseudonyms
- Characters ⚐ and/or Environment, Occupation
- Prize winners ♟
- Crossover (may be suitable for young adults) ⌓
- Also writes for children ☺

Genre

For a list of authors who write in a particular category or genre, such as Crime or Saga, go straight to the Genre listings, beginning on page 278. Some of these are further divided into subgenre, e.g. Crime: Historical - Medieval; Fantasy: Humour.

An increasing number of authors are writing in alternative genres and have separate entries in the main listing for each.

Authors who usually write in one category may occasionally produce a book in a quite different genre, so if genre is important to you, check the jacket details of a book before you read it.

Where there is no genre given, this is because an author's work is considered to be 'general' rather than in a specific genre.

Pseudonym(s)   Also writes/wrote as and is/was

Many writers use pseudonyms and some write under several different names. Please go to page 269 for an index of the alternative names used by authors in the main A-Z listing, for which there is no separate entry.

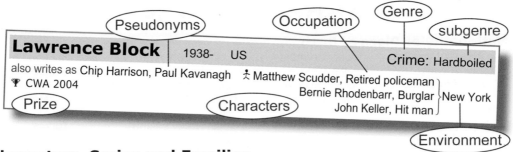

Characters, Series and Families
In the main section these are identified by ☧. If you know a character's name but have no idea of the author's name, go to page 294 for an alphabetical list of Characters, Sagas, Series and Families, which gives the relevant author.

Environments
If you are interested in reading novels that take place in a particular setting or location, or you can't remember the name of an author who writes about a ficticious place, eg Midsomer Worthy, go to page 318 for an alphabetical list of environments.

Literary Prizes and Awards
Where an author has won a literary prize or award, this is shown by ☫ followed by an abbreviated form of the prize and the year(s) won — see page vi for a list of abbreviations used. Most are listed in full, with their descriptions, in the list of Literary Prizes and Awards (pages 329–343).

Classic Authors
A list of classic authors with selected titles can be found on pages 344-345. As explained in the introduction, these authors do not appear in the main A-Z section of this edition although they can be found in the online version at www.whoelsewriteslike.com.

Crossover Authors
Authors who have also written books for children are identified by a ☺, as they may offer an easy crossover for readers (although in some cases the children's books are written for a much younger age range). Suggestions for authors to introduce older teenagers to adult fiction are indicated by ⌒. More details and a list of authors are provided on pages 346-348.

Further Reading
There is an increasing number of guides to novelists and their works. Some information about these can be found on page 349.

Websites
A list of useful websites can be found on pages 350-351.

Abbreviations

Nationality or Place of Birth

Afg	Afghanistan	Ger	Germany	Leb	Lebanon	Sco	Scotland
Alb	Albania	Gre	Greece	Malay	Malaysia	Sing	Singapore
Arg	Argentina	Guy	Guyana	Mex	Mexico	Sri Lan	Sri Lanka
Aus	Australia	Ice	Iceland	Neth	Netherlands	Swe	Sweden
Belg	Belgium	Ind	India	Nor	Norway	Trin	Trinidad
Braz	Brazil	Ire	Ireland	NZ	New Zealand	Tur	Turkey
Can	Canada	Isr	Israel	Pak	Pakistan	Ukr	Ukraine
Col	Columbia	It	Italy	Pol	Poland	US	United States
Den	Denmark	Ja	Japan	Por	Portugal		of America
Fin	Finland	Jam	Jamaica	Rus	Russia	Zam	Zambia
Fr	France	Kor	Korea	SA	South Africa	Zan	Zanzibar
Fr-Maur	French Mauritius						

Literary Prizes and Awards

Authors	Authors' Club First Novel Award
Black	James Tait Black Memorial Prizes
Bollinger	Bollinger Everyman Wodehouse Prize
Booker	Man Booker Prize for Fiction
Best of Booker	Best of Booker
Harry Bowling	Harry Bowling Prize for New Writing
British Fantasy	British Fantasy Awards
BSFA	British Science Fiction Association Awards
Arthur C Clarke	Arthur C Clarke Award
Commonwealth	Commonwealth Writers' Prize
Costa	Costa Book Awards (formerly Whitbread)
CWA	Crime Writers' Association
Encore	Encore Award
Faber	Geoffrey Faber Memorial Prize
Miles Franklin	Miles Franklin Literary Award
Guardian	Guardian Fiction Prize / First Book Award
Hawthornden	Hawthornden Prize
Higham	David Higham Prize for Fiction
Holtby	Winifred Holtby Memorial Prize
IMPAC	International IMPAC Dublin Literary Award
Independent Foreign Fiction	Independent Foreign Fiction Award
Irish Times	Irish Times International Fiction Prize
JLR	John Lewellyn Rhys Prize (formerly Mail on Sunday)
Man Booker	Man Booker Prize for Fiction
Man Booker Int	Man Booker International Prize
S Maugham	Somerset Maugham Awards
McKitterick	McKitterick Prize
Nathan	Melissa Nathan Award for Comedy Romance
Ondaatje	Ondaatje Prize (formerly Winifred Holtby)
Orange	Orange Prize
Pulitzer	Pulitzer Prize for Fiction
Romantic	Romantic Novel of the Year
Saga for Wit	Saga Award for Wit
Sagittarius	Sagittarius Prize
Saltire	Saltire Society Scottish Book of the Year Award
WHSmith	WHSmith Literary Award
Sunday Times	Sunday Times Young Writer of the Year Award
TGR	Thumping Good Read Book Award
Theakston's	Theakston's Old Peculier Crime Novel of the Year
Betty Trask	Betty Trask Awards
Whitbread	Whitbread Book of the Year and Literary Awards
Patrick White	Patrick White Award
Wingate	Jewish Quarterly / Wingate Literary Prize for Fiction

Prizes listed in previous editions can also be found in full at www.whoelsewriteslike.com

The Readers' Guide
An Alphabetical List

Jeff Abbott 1963- US Adventure/Thriller: Legal/financial

🏃 Whit Mosley, Judge - Texas

Russell Andrews	Harlan Coben	Matt Hilton
Adam Baron	Robert Crais	Elisabeth Hyde
Brett Battles	James Grippando	Simon Kernick
Sam Bourne	Raymond Haigh	George P Pelecanos

Megan Abbott 1971- US Crime: Hardboiled

Hollywood - C20th

Raymond Chandler	Dennis Lehane	Denise Ryan
James Ellroy	Ross Macdonald	Jim Thompson
Dashiell Hammett		

Joe Abercrombie 1974- Fantasy: Epic

Jacqueline Carey	Robin Hobb	Brandon Sanderson
Mike Carey	Tom Lloyd	Adrian Tchaikovsky
Stephen Donaldson	Scott Lynch	Brent Weeks
Raymond E Feist	Naomi Novik	Chris Wooding

Dan Abnett 1965- Science Fiction: Space opera

Lois McMaster Bujold	David A Drake	Tanith Lee
Ben Counter	Mercedes Lackey	Philip Palmer

Leila Aboulela 1964- Sudan

Roddy Doyle	Yasmina Khadra	Sarah Waters
Khaled Hosseini	Zadie Smith	Irvine Welsh

Chinua Achebe ⌒ 1930- Nigeria

🏆 Man Booker Int 2007

Chimamanda	Helon Habila	Yasmina Khadra
Ngozi Adichie	Khaled Hosseini	Ben Okri
Thalassa Ali	Barbara &	Markus Zusak
Nadeem Aslam	Stephanie Keating	

Peter Ackroyd ⌒ 1949-

🏆 S Maugham 1984 Guardian 1985 Whitbread 1985

Martin Amis	John Fowles	Robert Nye
John Banville	Maggie Gee	Iain Sinclair
Julian Barnes	Benjamin Markovits	Colm Toibin
Sebastian Barry	James Meek	Jill Paton Walsh

Simon Acland
Historical: C11th

♟ Hugh de Verdon, Crusader knight

Cora Harrison	Sharan Newman	Kate Sedley
Pat McIntosh	C J Sansom	Peter Tremayne

Gilbert Adair   1944-2011   Sco

Julian Barnes	Patrick Gale	Ian McEwan
A S Byatt	Alan Hollinghurst	Blake Morrison

Crime: Amateur sleuth

🏆 Authors 1988   ♟ Evadne Mount, Author • CI Trubshawe, Retired policeman

Catherine Aird	Gyles Brandreth	Christopher Fowler
James Anderson	Agatha Christie	Mark Gatiss
Marian Babson	Carola Dunn	Susan Kandel
M C Beaton	Jasper Fforde	Mike Ripley

Paul Adam   1958-
Adventure/Thriller

Paul Carson	Robert Harris	Mark Mills
Robin Cook	Roy Lewis	Eliot Pattison
Len Deighton	Ken McClure	Jon Stock
Ken Follett		

Douglas Adams   ☎   1952-2001
Science Fiction: Humour

♟ Hitch-Hikers Guide to the Galaxy Series

Karl Alexander	Jasper Fforde	Sharyn McCrumb
Robert Asprin	Neil Gaiman	Robert Rankin
Lois McMaster Bujold	Rob Grant	Andy Secombe
Eoin Colfer	Tom Holt	

Jane Adams   1960-
Crime: Psychological

♟ DI Mike Croft • DS Ray Flowers - Norfolk • Naomi Blake, Blind ex-policewoman

Lisa Appignanesi	Frances Fyfield	Danuta Reah
Hilary Bonner	P D James	Margaret Yorke
Deborah Crombie	Ed O'Connor	

Jessica Adams   1964-   Aus
Chick Lit

Cecelia Ahern	Eve Makis	Melissa Nathan
Susie Boyt	Chris Manby	Alexandra Potter
Megan Crane	Carole Matthews	Fiona Walker
Serena Mackesy		

Will Adams
Adventure/Thriller

♟ Daniel Knox, Underwater archaeologist

Sam Bourne	David Gibbins	Tom Knox
Dan Brown	Tom Grace	Chris Kuzneski
Paul Christopher	Thomas Greanias	James Rollins
William Dietrich	Tom Harper	

Gil Adamson   Can

Richard Bausch	Emma Donoghue	Jane Smiley
Geraldine Brooks	Lawrence Hill	Jane Urquhart

Debra Adelaide   Aus

Jennifer Donnelly	David Guterson	Lawrence Hill
Helen Garner	Jane Hamilton	Meg Rosoff

Chimamanda Ngozi Adichie   1977-   Nigeria

🏆 Commonwealth 2005   Orange 2007

Chinua Achebe	Helon Habila	Rohinton Mistry
Thalassa Ali	Kathryn Harrison	V S Naipaul
Nathacha Appanah	Khaled Hosseini	Helen Oyeyemi
Abdulrazak Gurnah	M J Hyland	Roma Tearne

Aravind Adiga   1974-   Ind

🏆 Man Booker 2008

Vikram Chandra	Rohinton Mistry	Vikram Seth
Amit Chaudhuri	Toni Morrison	Vikas Swarup
Anita Desai	Arundhati Roy	Adam Williams
Kiran Desai	Salman Rushdie	

Elizabeth Adler   Crime: Romantic suspense

also writes as Ariana Scott

Charlotte Bingham	Anita Burgh	Carol Rivers
Rose Boucheron	Elizabeth Edmondson	Penny Vincenzi
Barbara Taylor Bradford	Judith Gould	

Jussi Adler-Olsen   Den   Crime: Police work - Denmark

🏃 Det Carl Mørck

Karin Alvtegen	Karin Fossum	Stieg Larsson
Ake Edwardson	Arnaldur Indridason	Henning Mankell
Kjell Eriksson	Mari Jungstedt	Jo Nesbo

Katie Agnew   1972-   Sco   Chick Lit

Cecelia Ahern	Jane Costello	Lisa Jewell
Louise Bagshawe	Olivia Darling	Marian Keyes
Tilly Bagshawe	Emily Giffin	Adele Parks
Jo Carnegie	Jane Green	Tasmina Perry

Cecelia Ahern   1981-   Ire   Chick Lit

Jessica Adams	Claudia Carroll	Sinead Moriarty
Katie Agnew	Niamh Greene	Morag Prunty
Meg Cabot	Julia Llewellyn	Melanie Rose
Rebecca Campbell	Pauline McLynn	Cathy Woodman

Catherine Aird 1930- Crime: Police work - UK

is Kinn Hamilton McIntosh ☆ DI Sloan & DS Crosby - 'Calleshire'

Gilbert Adair	Pauline Bell	Chris Collett
Vivien Armstrong	W J Burley	Roderic Jeffries
A C Baantjer	Agatha Christie	Katherine John
M C Beaton	Ann Cleeves	Robin Paige

Rennie Airth 1935- SA Crime: Police work - UK

☆ Insp John Madden - Surrey

Boris Akunin	Deborah Crombie	Peter James
Stephen Booth	Carola Dunn	Peter Robinson
Agatha Christie	Ann Granger	Charles Todd

Boris Akunin 1956- Rus Crime: Historical - C19th

is Grigory Chkhartishvili ☆ Erast Fandorin, Tsarist agent • Sister Pelagia, Nun

Rennie Airth	Jason Goodwin	R N Morris
Tom Bradby	Clio Gray	Michael Pearce
Gyles Brandreth	Michael Gregorio	Barrie Roberts
George Macdonald Fraser	Andrey Kurkov	Frank Tallis

Brian W Aldiss ⌒ 1925- Science Fiction: Space and time

🏆 BSFA 1982 & 1985

Isaac Asimov	Joe Haldeman	Frank Herbert
Greg Bear	Robert A Heinlein	Kurt Vonnegut
Arthur C Clarke	Brian Herbert	John Wyndham
Harlan Ellison		

Karl Alexander 1944- US

Douglas Adams	Rob Grant	Audrey Niffenegger
Jasper Fforde	David Mitchell	Robert Rankin

Monica Ali ⌒ 1967-

Michel Faber	Andrea Levy	Zadie Smith
Roopa Farooki	Arundhati Roy	Meera Syal
Abdulrazak Gurnah	Salman Rushdie	Alex Wheatle
Hanif Kureishi		

Thalassa Ali US Historical

☆ Mariana Givens - C19th India and Afghanistan

Chinua Achebe	Barbara Cleverly	Yasmina Khadra
Chimamanda Ngozi Adichie	Chitra Banerjee Divakaruni	Rohinton Mistry
Nadeem Aslam	Khaled Hosseini	Paul Scott
		Carolyn Slaughter

⌒ may be suitable for young adults

Ted Allbeury   1917-2005   Adventure/Thriller

also wrote as Richard Butler, Patrick Kelly

Len Deighton	Brian Freemantle	Tom Rob Smith
Clive Egleton	John Lawton	Robin White
Colin Forbes		

Sarah Addison Allen   US

also writes as Katie Gallagher

Connie May Fowler	Sue Monk Kidd	Curtis Sittenfeld
Laurie Graham	Lorna Landvik	Miriam Toews
Alice Hoffman	Alison Lurie	

Isabel Allende   1942-   Chile

Gail Anderson-Dargatz	Laura Esquivel	Elif Shafak
Alessandro Baricco	Carlos Fuentes	Patrick Suskind
Roberto Bolano	Gabriel Garcia Márquez	Mario Vargas Llosa
Louise Erdrich	Shifra Horn	Jeanette Winterson

Catherine Alliott   Mature Chick Lit

Jane Fallon	Carole Matthews	Fiona Walker
Cathy Kelly	Tasmina Perry	Polly Williams
Sue Margolis	Patricia Scanlan	Isabel Wolff

Karin Alvtegen   1966-   Swe   Crime: Psychological

Ake Edwardson	Arnaldur Indridason	Jo Nesbo
Kjell Eriksson	Mari Jungstedt	Häkan Nesser
Karin Fossum	Camilla Läckberg	Maj Sjöwall & Per Wahlöö
Anne Holt	Stieg Larsson	Johan Theorin

Martin Amis   1949-

Peter Ackroyd	David Flusfeder	Vladimir Nabokov
J G Ballard	Tobias Hill	D B C Pierre
Iain Banks	Benjamin Markovits	Adam Thirlwell
Justin Cartwright	Blake Morrison	Virginia Woolf

Niccolo Ammaniti   1966-   It

Andrea Camilleri	Jonathan Franzen	Nicole Krauss
Jonathan Safran Foer	Khaled Hosseini	Ian McEwan

Kevin J Anderson   ☺   1962-   US   Science Fiction: Space opera

also writes jointly with Brian Herbert   ⚗ Dune Saga

Iain M Banks	Brian Herbert	Alastair Reynolds
Christie Golden	Frank Herbert	Kristine Kathryn Rusch
Simon Green	Larry Niven	Dan Simmons
Peter F Hamilton		

Lin Anderson   Sco   Crime: Forensic

♟ Rhona MacLeod, Forensic scientist - Glasgow

Simon Beckett	Gillian Galbraith	Ian Rankin
Benjamin Black	Alex Gray	Manda Scott
Karen Campbell	Nigel McCrery	Louise Welsh
Beverly Connor	Caro Ramsay	

Lyn Andrews   1943-   Saga

is Lynda M Andrews   Liverpool Irish

Anne Baker	Noëlle Harrison	Maureen Lee
Dilly Court	Joan Jonker	Lynda Page
June Francis	Mary A Larkin	Rowena Summers
Ruth Hamilton		

Virginia Andrews   ☞   1923-86   US

also wrote as V C Andrews (with Andrew Neiderman)   ♟ DeBeers Family Series

Daphne Du Maurier	Gwen Hunter	Kate Morton
Susan Hill	Judith Kelman	Nora Roberts

Manette Ansay   1964-   US

Amy Bloom	Maggie O'Farrell	Anne Rivers Siddons
Karen Joy Fowler	Jodi Picoult	Anne Tyler

Nathacha Appanah   1973-   Fr-Maur

Chimamanda Ngozi Adichie	Lloyd Jones	V S Naipaul
Kiran Desai	Barbara Kingsolver	Helen Oyeyemi

Lisa Appignanesi   1946-   Pol

Jane Adams	Jonathan Safran Foer	Lesley Glaister
Michael Chabon	Clare Francis	Cynthia Ozick
Helen Dunmore	Nicci French	Philip Roth

Diana Appleyard   Aga Saga

Charlotte Bingham	Sarah Grazebrook	Elizabeth Palmer
Elizabeth Buchan	Sandra Howard	Joanna Trollope
Victoria Clayton	Linda Kelsey	Jane Elizabeth Varley
Annabel Dilke		

Geoffrey Archer   1944-   Adventure/Thriller

♟ Sam Packer - MI6

Stephen Coonts	Stephen Leather	Tim Sebastian
Graham Hurley	Chris Ryan	Craig Thomas
Philip Kerr	Julian Jay Savarin	

Jeffrey Archer 1940- Adventure/Thriller

Harry Bingham	Michael Dobbs	Colin Harrison
Tom Cain	Gavin Esler	Philip Hensher
Nicholas Coleridge	Joseph Finder	Sidney Sheldon
Stephen Coonts	Frederick Forsyth	

Michael Arditti

Vikram Chandra	Michel Faber	Armistead Maupin
Michael Cunningham	Jonathan Franzen	Jonathan Tropper

Aileen Armitage 1930- Saga

also writes as Aileen Quigley; is Ruth Fabian   🕏 Eva Bower • Hawksmoor Series - Yorkshire

Jessica Blair	Helen Cannam	Rosie Goodwin
Philip Boast	Catherine Cookson	Kay Stephens
Rita Bradshaw	Glenice Crossland	

Campbell Armstrong 1944- Sco Adventure/Thriller

is Campbell Black   🕏 DS Lou Perlman - Glasgow

Russell Andrews	Stuart MacBride	Julian Jay Savarin
Brett Battles	Glenn Meade	Tim Sebastian
Harold Coyle	David Morrell	Gerald Seymour
Colin Forbes		

David Armstrong Crime: Police work - UK

🕏 DI Frank Kavanagh & DC Jane Salt - Shropshire

Marjorie Eccles	J M Gregson	Dorothy Simpson
Kate Ellis	Patricia Hall	Sally Spencer
Geraldine Evans	Louise Penny	Charles Todd

Kelley Armstrong 1968- Can Paranormal

Keri Arthur	Christine Feehan	Suzanne McLeod
Rachel Caine	Lori Handeland	Richelle Mead
Cassandra Clare	Barb & J C Hendee	J R Ward
Mary Janice Davidson	Sherrilyn Kenyon	Kim Wilkins

Vivien Armstrong Crime: Police work - UK

🕏 DI Ian Preston & DS Judith Pullen - Great Yarmouth
DS Roger Hayes & Sgt Prentice - Oxfordshire

Catherine Aird	Ken Bruen	P D James
Lindsay Ashford	Brian Cooper	Susan B Kelly
Stephen Booth	Geraldine Evans	David Lawrence

Go to back for lists of
Pseudonyms • Authors by Genre • Characters and Series • Environments
Prize Winners • Classic Authors • Crossover Authors • Further Reading • Websites

Jake Arnott   1961-   Crime: Hardboiled

♆ CWA 2005

Glenn Chandler	Ken McCoy	Mark Timlin
Mark Gatiss	Adrian McKinty	Louise Welsh
Toby Litt	David Peace	John Williams

Suzanne Arruda   US   Crime: Amateur sleuth

⚐ Jade del Cameron - Africa 1920s

Barbara Cleverly	Michael Pearce	Deanna Raybourn
Carola Dunn	Anne Perry	Jill Paton Walsh

Keri Arthur   Aus   Paranormal

⚐ Riley Jensen, Half vampire

Lara Adrian	Mary Janice Davidson	Tanya Huff
Kelley Armstrong	Christine Feehan	J R Ward

Neal Asher   1961-   Science Fiction: Near future

Tony Ballantyne	Gary Gibson	Philip Palmer
John Birmingham	Peter F Hamilton	Alastair Reynolds
Hal Duncan	Sergei Lukyanenko	Andrzej Sapkowski
Jaine Fenn	Larry Niven	Tricia Sullivan

Trisha Ashley   Aga Saga

Victoria Clayton	Gil McNeil	Nicky Pellegrino
Lucy Dawson	Holly McQueen	Victoria Routledge
Louise Harwood	Sarah Mason	Linda Taylor
Dorothy Koomson	Adele Parks	Julia Williams

David Ashton   1941-   Sco   Crime: Historical - C19th

⚐ Insp James McLevy - Edinburgh

Joyce Holms	James McGee	Anne Perry
Arnaldur Indridason	Edward Marston	Deanna Raybourn
Alanna Knight	Amy Myers	

Sherry Ashworth   ☺   1953-   Chick Lit

Zoë Barnes	Helen Fielding	Kathy Lette
Emily Barr	Niamh Greene	Kate O'Riordan
Martina Devlin	Milly Johnson	Arabella Weir
Anne Dunlop		

Isaac Asimov   1920-92   US   Science Fiction: Space and time

Brian W Aldiss	Ben Bova	Robert A Heinlein
Poul Anderson	Arthur C Clarke	Larry Niven
Gregory Benford	Philip K Dick	John Wyndham

Judy Astley — Aga Saga

Raffaella Barker
Anne Doughty
Rebecca Gregson
Veronica Henry

Cathy Kelly
Santa Montefiore
Charlotte Moore

Sinead Moriarty
Annie Sanders
Madeleine Wickham

Kate Atkinson 1951-

🏆 Whitbread 1995   Saltire 2005

Beryl Bainbridge
Matthew D'Ancona
Laura Esquivel
Lissa Evans

Margaret Forster
Nick Laird
Charlotte Mendelson
Kate Muir

Tim Pears
Alice Sebold
Roma Tearne
James Wilson

 Crime: PI

🏃 Det Jackson Brodie

Giles Blunt
Arnaldur Indridason
Laura Lippman

Alexander McCall Smith
Elizabeth McGregor
Irene Nemirovsky

Häkan Nesser
Peter Robinson
R D Wingfield

Margaret Atwood 1939- Can

🏆 Arthur C Clarke 1987   Booker 2000

Joan Barfoot
Clare Chambers
Robb Forman Dew
Miranda Glover

Gail Godwin
Nadine Gordimer
Sarah Hall
Shaena Lambert

Valerie Martin
Clare Morrall
Rachel Seiffert
Marcel Theroux

Bernardo Atxaga 1951- Spain

is Jose Irazu Garmendia

E M Forster
Nadine Gordimer

Ernest Hemingway
Amin Maalouf

Javier Marias
Arturo Pérez-Reverte

Jean M Auel 1936- US — Historical

is Jean Marie Untinen Auel

Louise Cooper
Diana Gabaldon
Kathleen O'Neal Gear

Christian Jacq
Tamara McKinley
Juliet Marillier

Edward Rutherfurd
Manda Scott
Jules Watson

Paul Auster 1947- US

Nicola Barker
Julian Barnes
E L Doctorow
Dave Eggers

Nathan Englander
Ben Faccini
Jonathan Safran Foer
Denis Johnson

Jayne Anne Phillips
Thomas Pynchon
Geoff Ryman
Adam Thorpe

Trezza Azzopardi 1961- Wales

🏆 Faber 2001

Stevie Davies
Anne Enright
Maggie Gee

Denis Johnson
Ian McEwan
Ann Patchett

Rachel Seiffert
Carol Shields
Zadie Smith

Marian Babson   1929-   US   Crime: Amateur sleuth

is Ruth Stenstreem

🏃 Trixie Dolan & Evangeline Sinclair, Actresses
Douglas Perkins & Gerry Tate, PR consultants } London

Gilbert Adair	Lilian Jackson Braun	Anthea Fraser
Gyles Brandreth	Simon Brett	Alison Joseph

David Baddiel   ◠   1964-

Mark Barrowcliffe	Rob Grant	Matt Thorne
Peter Ho Davies	Andrew Holmes	Nigel Williams
Ben Elton		

Louise Bagshawe   1972-   Chick Lit

Katie Agnew	Christina Jones	Robyn Sisman
Celia Brayfield	Susan Lewis	Lulu Taylor
Olivia Darling	Lesley Lokko	Jane Elizabeth Varley
Imogen Edwards-Jones	Tasmina Perry	Cathy Woodman

Tilly Bagshawe   Glitz & Glamour

also writes as Sidney Sheldon

Katie Agnew	Jane Green	Carole Matthews
Jo Carnegie	Cathy Kelly	Fiona O'Brien
Jackle Colllns	Lesley Lokko	Tasmina Perry
Olivia Darling	Jill Mansell	Lulu Taylor

Beryl Bainbridge   ◠   1934-2010

🏆 Guardian 1974   Whitbread 1977 & 1996   Black 1998   WHSmith 1999   Man Booker 2011

Kate Atkinson	Giles Foden	Bernice Rubens
Pat Barker	Linda Grant	Fiona Shaw
Penelope Fitzgerald	Simon Mawer	Fay Weldon

Anne Baker   Saga

Liverpool

Lyn Andrews	Jean Fullerton	Margaret Mayhew
Dilly Court	Rosie Harris	Elizabeth Murphy
Tania Crosse	Audrey Howard	Rowena Summers
Katie Flynn	Maureen Lee	

Jo Baker   1973-

Geraldine Brooks	Barbara Erskine	Kate Morton
Daphne Du Maurier	Susan Hill	Kate Mosse

Sam Baker   Crime: Romantic suspense

Beverly Barton	Louise Kean	Sharon Sala
Lisa Jackson	Anna Maxted	Lauren Weisberger

David Baldacci ⌒ 1960- US   Adventure/Thriller

🏆 TGR 1997   🏃 Sean King & Michelle Maxwell, ex-Secret Service agents
                                          Camel Club - Washington, DC

Linwood Barclay	Joseph Finder	Mike Lawson
Ted Bell	Mark Gimenez	Brad Meltzer
Julie Compton	Craig Holden	Michael Robotham
Nelson DeMille	Gregg Hurwitz	Brad Thor

B

Tom Bale 1966-   Crime: Police work - UK

is David Harrison   🏃 Joe Clayton, ex-CID officer

Lisa Gardner	Val McDermid	Craig Russell
M R Hall	Mark Pearson	Jon Stock
Peter James		

Tony Ballantyne   Science Fiction: Near Future

Neal Asher	Peter F Hamilton	Jeff Noon
John Birmingham	Richard Morgan	Neal Stephenson
Gary Gibson		

J G Ballard ⌒ 1930-2009

was James Graham Ballard

Martin Amis	Tobias Hill	Will Self
Peter Carey	Gunnar Kopperud	Edward St Aubyn
Romesh Gunesekera		

⌒   Science Fiction: Technical

🏆 BSFA 1979   Black 1984   Guardian 1984

Steve Aylett	William Gibson	Jack O'Connell
Ray Bradbury	Joe Haldeman	Christopher Priest
Philip K Dick	James Lovegrove	Kurt Vonnegut
Michael Jan Friedman		

Iain Banks ⌒ 1954- Sco

also writes as Iain M Banks

John Aberdein	Ian McEwan	Alan Warner
Martin Amis	Yann Martel	Jeanette Winterson
Douglas Coupland	Will Self	

Iain M Banks ⌒ 1954- Sco   Science Fiction: Space opera

also writes as Iain Banks   🏆 BSFA 1994 & 1996

Kevin J Anderson	Peter F Hamilton	Charles Stross
Neal Asher	Sergei Lukyanenko	Tricia Sullivan
Greg Bear	Ken MacLeod	Jack Vance
Steven Gould	Philip Palmer	Chris Wooding

⌒ may be suitable for young adults

11

Ray Banks   1977-   Sco   Crime: PI

♁ Cal Innes

Ken Bruen	Alex Gray	Caro Ramsay
Karen Campbell	Allan Guthrie	Ian Rankin

Russell Banks   1940-   US

T C Boyle	F Scott Fitzgerald	Cormac McCarthy
Louis de Bernières	Charles Frazier	Sue Miller
Pete Dexter	David Guterson	

B

Jo Bannister   1951-   Crime: Police work - UK

♁ DI Liz Graham & DS Cal Donovan - Castlemere • DCI Frank Shapiro
Brodie Farrell, PI - South Coast, England • Clio Rees, Doctor

Simon Brett	Liz Evans	Priscilla Masters
Deborah Crombie	Adrian Magson	Peter Turnbull
Marjorie Eccles	Barry Maitland	

John Banville   1945-   Ire

also writes as Benjamin Black   ♆ Guardian 1981   Man Booker 2005

Peter Ackroyd	James Hamilton-Paterson	Vladimir Nabokov
Sebastian Barry	Ismail Kadare	José Saramago
Richard Bausch	John McGahern	William Trevor
Dermot Bolger	Martin Malone	Barry Unsworth

Muriel Barbery   1969-   Fr

Geraldine Brooks	James Hamilton-Paterson	Richard Mason
Faïza Guène	Nicole Krauss	Claire Messud

Alex Barclay   1974-   Ire   Adventure/Thriller

♁ Det Joe Lucchesi - NYPD • Ren Bryce, FBI agent

Mark Billingham	Kathryn Fox	Michael Marshall
Ann Cleeves	David Hosp	Glenn Meade
Elena Forbes	J A Kerley	Chris Mooney

James Barclay   1965-   Fantasy: Epic

Stephen Donaldson	Greg Keyes	Caiseal Mor
Steven Erikson	Juliet E McKenna	Robert Newcomb
Jude Fisher	John Marco	Stan Nicholls
David Gemmell	George R R Martin	Freda Warrington

Go to back for lists of
Pseudonyms • Authors by Genre • Characters and Series • Environments
Prize Winners • Classic Authors • Crossover Authors • Further Reading • Websites

Linwood Barclay   Can   Adventure/Thriller

David Baldacci   Mark Gimenez   Patrick Lennon
Adam Baron   George Dawes Green   Rick Mofina
Harlan Coben   Gregg Hurwitz   Michael Robotham
Tess Gerritsen   Greg Iles

Crime: Humour
🏃 Zack Walker, Journalist - 'Oakwood', Canada

Christopher Brookmyre   Kinky Friedman   Denise Mina
Tim Dorsey   Douglas Lindsay   Malcolm Pryce

Tessa Barclay   1928-   Sco   Saga

is Jean Bowden   🏃 Craigallan, Corvill & Tramont Families
Emma Blair   Frances Paige   T R Wilson
Pamela Oldfield   Nicola Thorne   Janet Woods

Joan Barfoot   1946-   Can

Margaret Atwood   Margaret Drabble   Miriam Toews
Isla Dewar   Carol Shields   Anne Tyler

Clive Barker   ⌒   ☺   1952-   Horror

Jonathan Carroll   Neil Gaiman   Bentley Little
Simon Clark   Richard Laymon   David Moody
Christopher Fowler   John Ajvide Lindqvist Dan Simmons

Nicola Barker   1966-

🏆 Higham 1993   JLR 1996   IMPAC 2000   Hawthornden 2008
Paul Auster   Jenny Diski   Lloyd Jones
Julian Barnes   Edward Docx   Marcia Muller
Saul Bellow   Tessa Hadley   J D Salinger

Pat Barker   ⌒   1943-

🏆 Guardian 1993   Booker 1995
Beryl Bainbridge   Gunnar Kopperud   Fiona Shaw
Louis Begley   Valerie Martin   Charles Todd
Louis de Bernières   Irene Nemirovsky   Jonathan Tulloch
Linda Grant   Bernhard Schlink

Raffaella Barker   ⌒   ☺   1964-

Judy Astley   Kate Fenton   Mary Lawson
Victoria Clayton   Julie Highmore   Isabel Wolff
Louise Doughty   India Knight

Robert Barnard 1936- Crime: Police work - UK

also writes as Bernard Bastable ♛ Det Supt Oddie & DC Charlie Peace - Yorkshire
☠ CWA 2003 Supt Perry Trethowan - London

Pauline Bell	Jonathan Gash	Nicholas Rhea
Glenn Chandler	Patricia Hall	Pauline Rowson
Chris Collett	John Harvey	Peter Turnbull
Colin Dexter	Stuart Pawson	R D Wingfield

Julian Barnes 1946-

also writes as Dan Kavanagh ☠ S Maugham 1981 Faber 1985 Man Booker 2011

Peter Ackroyd	Nicola Barker	Rachel Seiffert
Gilbert Adair	Blake Morrison	Graham Swift
Paul Auster	Tim Parks	A N Wilson

Linda Barnes 1949- US Crime: PI

☠ Carlotta Carlyle - Boston, Mass

Nancy Cohen	Lauren Henderson	S J Rozan
Stella Duffy	Marcia Muller	Dana Stabenow
Janet Evanovich	P J Parrish	Sarah Strohmeyer
Meg Gardiner	Rick Riordan	

Zoë Barnes 1957-2009 Chick Lit

Cheltenham

Maggie Alderson	Donna Hay	Carole Matthews
Sherry Ashworth	Cathy Kelly	Elizabeth Noble
Maria Beaumont	Serena Mackesy	Lesley Pearse

Adam Baron Crime: Hardboiled

☠ Billy Rucher, PI - London

Jeff Abbott	Brett Battles	Matt Hilton
Linwood Barclay	Lee Child	Dennis Lehane

Sam Barone US Historical: Ancient

Richard Blake	Christian Jacq	Simon Scarrow
Conn Iggulden	Robert Low	John Stack
Glyn Iliffe	Scott Oden	

Emily Barr Mature Chick Lit

☠ WHSmith 2001

Sherry Ashworth	India Knight	Fiona Walker
Suzanne Bugler	Adele Parks	Jennifer Weiner
Jenny Colgan	Lisa Tucker	

Andrea Barrett 1954- US

T C Boyle	Penelope Fitzgerald	Ann Patchett
Sylvia Brownrigg	Daniel Kehlmann	Richard Russo
Anne Enright	Matthew Kneale	

B

Robert G Barrett
1943- Aus   Crime: Amateur sleuth

🚶 Les Norton, Bondi Beach lifeguard - Sydney

Peter Corris	Shane Maloney	Ian Rankin
Carl Hiaasen	Armistead Maupin	Peter Temple

Sebastian Barry
1955- Ire

🏆 Black 2008   Costa 2008

Peter Ackroyd	Andrew Greig	Martin Malone
John Banville	Claire Kilroy	Benjamin Markovits
Peter Ho Davies	John McGahern	Joseph O'Connor
Damon Galgut	Deirdre Madden	William Trevor

Beverly Barton
1946-2011 US   Crime: Romantic suspense

Sam Baker	Gwen Hunter	Nora Roberts
Allison Brennan	Lisa Jackson	Karen Rose
Heather Graham	Jennifer McMahon	Karin Slaughter
Linda Howard	J D Robb	

Jefferson Bass
US   Crime: Forensic

is Dr Bill Bass and Jon Jefferson   🚶 Dr Bill Brockton & Miranda, Forensic anthropologist
Body Farm Series - Tennessee

Simon Beckett	James Grippando	Michael Palmer
Aaron Elkins	Jonathan Kellerman	Kathy Reichs
Leonard Goldberg	Keith McCarthy	

Bateman
🌈 ☺ 1962- Ire   Crime: Humour

also writes as Colin Bateman; is Colin Bateman   🚶 Mystery Man Series, Bookseller - Belfast

Robert Barnard	Alan Bradley	Christopher Brookmyre
M C Beaton	Simon Brett	Mark Gatiss

Colin Bateman
🌈 ☺ 1962- Ire

also writes as Bateman   🏆 Betty Trask 1994   🚶 Dan Starkey, Journalist - Belfast

Peter Guttridge	Toby Litt	Zane Radcliffe
Danny King	Jason Pinter	Mike Ripley
Robert Lewis	Malcolm Pryce	Ian Sansom
Douglas Lindsay		

Brett Battles
US   Adventure/Thriller

🚶 Jonathan Quinn, Freelance operative

Jeff Abbott	Simon Conway	Matt Hilton
Campbell Armstrong	Clive Cussler	Robert Ludlum
Adam Baron	Barry Eisler	Alistair MacLean
Tom Cain	Jack Higgins	Daniel Silva

☺ also writes children's books

Belinda Bauer   1962-   Crime: Psychological

♟ CWA 2010   ☖ PC Jonas Holly - Exmoor

Jane Adams	Sophie Hannah	Jo Nesbo
Jane Casey	John Harvey	Daniel Silva
Carol Anne Davis	Simon Lelic	Erica Spindler

Richard Bausch   1945-   US

Gil Adamson	Richard Ford	Helen Simpson
John Banville	Simon Mawer	William Trevor
Sebastian Faulks	Alice Munro	

Lily Baxter   Saga

also writes as Dilly Court

Emma Blair	Annie Groves	Annie Murray
Dilly Court	Rosie Harris	Janet Tanner
Katie Flynn	Anna Jacobs	Dee Williams

Stephen Baxter ⌒ ☺ 1957-   Adventure/Thriller: Historical

also writes jointly with Terry Pratchett

Conn Iggulden	William Napier	Edward Rutherfurd
James H Jackson	Steven Pressfield	Tim Severin
James A Michener		

⌒ ☺   Science Fiction: Technical

♟ BSFA 1995

Poul Anderson	Gary Gibson	Sophia McDougall
Ben Bova	Wil McCarthy	China Miéville
Arthur C Clarke	Jack McDevitt	Robert Reed
Susanna Clarke	Ian McDonald	Charles Stross

Louis Bayard   US   Crime: Historical

Charles Cumming	Alanna Knight	James McGee
James Fleming	James McCreet	Andrew Pepper
Ariana Franklin		

Greg Bear ⌒ 1951- US   Science Fiction: Technical

Brian W Aldiss	C J Cherryh	Wil McCarthy
Iain M Banks	Arthur C Clarke	Kim Stanley Robinson
Gregory Benford	Harlan Ellison	Karen Traviss
David Brin	Peter F Hamilton	Sean Williams

G S Beard   Sea: Historical - C19th

☖ John Fury, Midshipman - Nelson's navy

Bernard Cornwell	Jonathan Lunn	Dudley Pope
David Donachie	Allan Mallinson	Peter Smalley
C S Forester	Patrick O'Brian	Julian Stockwin

M C Beaton 1936- Sco   Crime: Police work - UK

is Marion Chesney

PC Hamish MacBeth - Scotland
Agatha Raisin, Retired advertising executive

Gilbert Adair	Clare Curzon	Suzette Hill
Catherine Aird	Margaret Duffy	Joyce Holms
James Anderson	Gerald Hammond	Lis Howell
Pauline Bell	Patricia Harwin	Susan Kandel

Sally Beauman 1944-   Glitz & Glamour

also writes as Vanessa James

Jude Deveraux	Sara MacDonald	Una-Mary Parker
Susan Lewis	Judith Michael	Célestine Hitiura Vaite
Lesley Lokko	Hilary Norman	Penny Vincenzi

Matt Beaumont   Lad Lit

Mark Barrowcliffe	Tim Lott	Jonathan Tropper
Matt Dunn	William Sutcliffe	Matt Whyman
Mike Gayle		

Carrie Bebris US   Crime: Amateur sleuth

Mr & Mrs Darcy Series

Alanna Knight	Catriona McPherson	Nicola Upson
Alexander McCall Smith	Ian Sansom	Jacqueline Winspear

James Becker   Adventure/Thriller

Chris Bronson

Steve Berry	Glenn Cooper	Chris Kuzneski
Michael Byrnes	Tom Harper	James Rollins

Simon Beckett 1960-   Crime: Forensic

Dr David Hunter, Forensic anthropologist

Lin Anderson	Kathryn Fox	Nigel McCrery
Jefferson Bass	Tess Gerritsen	Louise Penny
Patricia D Cornwell	M R Hall	Kathy Reichs
Matthew D'Ancona	Peter James	Nick Stone

Louis Begley 1933- US

Irish Times 1991

Pat Barker	Anne Michaels	Bernhard Schlink
Sebastian Barry	Irene Nemirovsky	Rachel Seiffert

Nina Bell   Mature Chick Lit

Jo Carnegie	Veronica Henry	Jill Mansell
Lucy Diamond	Rachel Johnson	Penny Vincenzi

Ted Bell   1947-   US   Adventure/Thriller

♁ Alexander Hawke, British intelligence agent

David Baldacci	Vince Flynn	Daniel Silva
Clive Cussler	Jack Higgins	Brad Thor
Ian Fleming	Robert Ludlum	

B

Gregory Benford   1941-   US   Science Fiction: Technical

also writes as Sterling Blake   🏆 BSFA 1980

Poul Anderson	Ben Bova	Wil McCarthy
Isaac Asimov	C J Cherryh	Brian Stableford
Greg Bear	Paul J McAuley	Sean Williams

James Benn   1949-   US   Crime

♁ Billy Boyle

Gordon Ferris	Barbara Nadel	Andrew Taylor
Edward Marston	Craig Russell	Laura Wilson

Alan Bennett   ⌒   1934-   Humour

Jessica Duchen	John Lanchester	Lynne Truss
Stephen Fry	Magnus Mills	Nigel Williams
Laurie Graham	Sue Townsend	P G Wodehouse

Anne Bennett   1949-   Saga

Birmingham

Elizabeth Bailey	Tania Crosse	Margaret Mayhew
Benita Brown	Hilary Green	Kay Stephens
Julia Bryant	Rosie Harris	Janet Woods
Jean Chapman		

Robert Jackson Bennett   US

Ray Bradbury	Stephen Hunt	Adam Nevill
Neil Gaiman	China Miéville	John Steinbeck

Ronan Bennett   1956-   Ire   Adventure/Thriller

Robert Harris	John Le Carré	Henry Porter
Joseph Kanon	Edna O'Brien	Martin Cruz Smith
Philip Kerr	Andrew O'Hagan	Robert Wilson

Vanora Bennett   Historical

Barbara Erskine	Philippa Gregory	Fiona Mountain
Barbara Ewing	Jane Harris	Giles Waterfield
Ken Follett	Richard Mason	Alison Weir
C W Gortner	Jude Morgan	

⌒ may be suitable for young adults

18

Alex Berenson   1973-   US   Adventure/Thriller

☨ John Wells, CIA Agent

James Barrington	Dan Fesperman	Henry Porter
Simon Conway	Ian Fleming	Stella Rimington
Clive Egleton	David Ignatius	Theresa Schwegel
Gavin Esler	Adrian McKinty	E V Seymour

Elizabeth Berg   1948-   US

Suzanne Berne	Linda Gillard	Sue Miller
Liz Byrski	Laurie Graham	Jacquelyn Mitchard
Fannie Flagg	Ann Hood	Anita Shreve
Patricia Gaffney	Lorna Landvik	Adriana Trigiani

William Bernhardt   1960-   US   Crime: Legal/financial

☨ Ben Kincaid, Defense attorney - Oklahoma

Stephen L Carter	John Hart	Phillip Margolin
James Grippando	John Le Carré	Lisa Scottoline
John Grisham	John T Lescroart	

A L Berridge   Historical: Ancient

is Anne Louise Berridge   ☨ Andre de Roland • Harry Ryder

Bernard Cornwell	Ben Kane	M C Scott
Conn Iggulden	Robert Low	Tim Severin
Christian Jacq	Scott Oden	Harry Sidebottom

Steve Berry   1955-   US   Adventure/Thriller

☨ Cotton Malone, ex-US Justice Dept, now antiquarian book dealer - Copenhagen

James Becker	David Gibbins	Matthew Reilly
Sam Bourne	Tom Knox	James Rollins
John Case	Chris Kuzneski	Paul Sussman
Michael Cordy	Mike Lawson	James Twining

Mark Billingham   1961-   Crime: Police work - UK

also writes as Will Peterson   ♛ Theakston's 2005 & 2009   ☨ DI Tom Thorne - London

Alex Barclay	Stuart MacBride	Caro Ramsay
Garry Disher	Brian McGilloway	Chris Simms
Peter James	Barry Maitland	Nick Stone
David Lawrence	Mark Pearson	Neil White

Rachel Billington   1942-

Jane Austen	Penelope Fitzgerald	Bernardine Kennedy
Rachel Cusk	Margaret Forster	Penelope Lively
Anne Fine	Elizabeth Jane Howard	Alison Lurie

Chris Binchy   1970-   Ire

Roddy Doyle	Patrick McCabe	John O'Farrell
Nick Hornby	David Nicholls	Tony Parsons

Maeve Binchy   1940-2012   Ire   Aga Saga

Ireland

Marita Conlon-McKenna	Adèle Geras	Jojo Moyes
Anne Doughty	Noëlle Harrison	Geraldine O'Neill
Rose Doyle	Jan Karon	Imogen Parker
Leah Fleming	Kate Kerrlgan	Llz Ryan

Tim Binding   1947-   Adventure/Thriller

also writes as T J Middleton

Raymond Benson	Louis de Bernières	David Lodge
Jonathan Coe	William Golding	Tim Pears
Francis Cottam		

Charlotte Bingham   1942-   Aga Saga

Romantic 1995

Elizabeth Adler	Elizabeth Buchan	Sarah Harrison
Diana Appleyard	Elizabeth Elgin	Rosy Thornton
Barbara Taylor Bradford	Maeve Haran	

Harry Bingham   1967-   Adventure/Thriller: Legal/financial

Jeffrey Archer	John McLaren	Christopher Reich
Reg Gadney	Steve Martini	Michael Ridpath
John T Lescroart		

Carol Birch   1951-

Higham 1988   Faber 1991

Louise Doughty	Margaret Forster	Nell Leyshon
Helen Dunmore	Kate Grenville	Deborah Moggach

John Birmingham   1964-   Aus   Science Fiction: Near future

Neal Asher	Tom Clancy	Richard Powers
Tony Ballantyne	James Lovegrove	Neal Stephenson

Patrick Bishop   War

WW2

Francis Cottam	Andy McNab	Chris Ryan
David Fiddimore	Derek Robinson	Gerald Seymour

Go to back for lists of
Pseudonyms • Authors by Genre • Characters and Series • Environments
Prize Winners • Classic Authors • Crossover Authors • Further Reading • Websites

Benjamin Black
1945- Ire   Crime: Police work - Ireland

is John Banville   ⚐ Quirke, Pathologist - Dublin 1950s • Insp Hackett

Lin Anderson   Gene Kerrigan   Adrian McKinty
Simon Beckett   Laura Lippman   Andrew Nugent
Alex Gray   Nigel McCrery   Andrew Taylor
Peter James   Brian McGilloway   Peter Temple

Cara Black
US   Crime: PI

                                                   ⚐ Aimée Leduc - Paris

Liz Evans   Sara Paretsky   Zoë Sharp
Sue Grafton   Ian Rankin   Cath Staincliffe
Marcia Muller

Helen Black
                                                      Crime: Hardboiled

                                          ⚐ Lilly Valentine, Childcare lawyer

Kimberley Chambers   Roberta Kray   Louise Welsh
Martina Cole   Kevin Lewis   John Williams
Heather Graham   Denise Ryan

Sean Black
Sco   Adventure/Thriller

                                          ⚐ Ryan Lock, Bodyguard - New York

Raymond Haigh   Gregg Hurwitz   Christopher Reich
Matt HIlton   Stephen Leather   Olen Steinhauer

Tony Black
Sco   Crime: PI

                                              ⚐ Gus Dury - Edinburgh

Christopher Brookmyre Allan Guthrie   Ian Rankin
Gordon Brown   Simon Kernick   Craig Russell
Karen Campbell   Denise Mina

Emma Blair
1942- 2011 Sco   Saga

was Iain Blair   ⚐ Drummond Family - Scotland

Tessa Barclay   Christine Marion Fraser Lesley Pearse
Maggie Bennett   Hilary Green   Eileen Ramsay
Dilly Court   Elisabeth McNeill   Jessica Stirling

Jessica Blair
1923-   Saga

is Bill Spence   C19th Yorkshire

Rosemary Aitken   Jess Foley   Eileen Ramsay
Aileen Armitage   Iris Gower   Margaret Thornton
Helen Cannam   Annie Groves   Valerie Wood
Margaret Dickinson

Richard Blake

Historical: Ancient

♁ Aelric, Investigator - Roman Empire

Sam Barone	Glyn Iliffe	Robert Low
Lindsey Davis	Douglas Jackson	Simon Scarrow
Robert Graves		

B Lawrence Block   1938-   US   Crime: Hardboiled

also writes as Chip Harrison, Paul Kavanagh   ♁ Matthew Scudder, Retired policeman ⎫
🏆 CWA 2004   Bernie Rhodenbarr, Burglar ⎬ New York
                                        John Keller, Hit man ⎭

Raymond Chandler	Ross Macdonald	Peter Spiegelman
Loren D Estleman	Reggie Nadelson	Richard Stark
Dashiell Hammett	Robert B Parker	Darryl Wimberley
Elmore Leonard	Thomas Perry	

Amy Bloom   1953-   US

Manette Ansay	Gail Godwin	Haven Kimmel
Fannie Flagg	Kent Haruf	Mary Lawson

Anna Blundy   1970-   Adventure/Thriller

♁ Faith Zanetti, Journalist

Janet Evanovich	Allison Pearson	Tom Sharpe
Simon Kernick	Alexei Sayle	Carol Smith
Sara Paretsky		

Giles Blunt   1952-   Can   Crime: Police work - Canada

🏆 CWA 2001   ♁ Det John Cardinal & Det Lisa Delorme - 'Algonquin Bay', Canada

John Dunning	Jonathan Nasaw	Dana Stabenow
Donald Harstad	Ridley Pearson	Peter Temple
Archer Mayor	Louise Penny	Jess Walter
Theresa Monsour	Medora Sale	

Roberto Bolano   1953-2003   Chile

Isabel Allende	Javier Marias	Thomas Pynchon
Gordon Burn	Haruki Murakami	José Saramago
Gabriel Garcia Márquez	Per Petterson	Mario Vargas Llosa
Panos Karnezis		

Dermot Bolger   1959-   Ire

John Banville	Patrick McCabe	Joseph O'Connor
Roddy Doyle	Colum McCann	David Park
Anne Enright	Brian Moore	Glenn Patterson
James Joyce	Edna O'Brien	Niall Williams

S J Bolton 1961- Crime: Psychological

is Sharon J Bolton

Karin Fossum	Elly Griffiths	James Rollins
Nicci French	Sophie Hannah	Fred Vargas
Elizabeth George	Val McDermid	

Xavier-Marie Bonnot Fr Crime: Police work - France

B

♣ Commd't Michel de Palma - Marseilles

Cara Black	Pierre Magnan	Allan Massie
Colin Dexter	Guillermo Martinez	Fred Vargas

Stephen Booth 1952- Crime: Psychological

♣ DC Ben Cooper & DS Diane Fry - Peak District

Rennie Airth	M R Hall	Barry Maitland
Vivien Armstrong	Ken McCoy	Priscilla Masters
Carla Banks	Iain McDowall	Louise Penny
Tana French	John Macken	Andrew Pyper

Sam Bourne 1987- Adventure/Thriller

is Jonathan Freedland

Will Adams	Glenn Cooper	Chris Kuzneski
Steve Berry	Michael Cordy	Mike Lawson
Michael Byrnes	Raymond Haigh	Scott Mariani
John Case	Raymond Khoury	James Twining

C J Box US Crime: Amateur sleuth

♣ Joe Pickett, National warden - 'Saddlestring', Wyoming

Nevada Barr	Loren D Estleman	Tony Hillerman
James Lee Burke	Steve Hamilton	Michael McGarrity
Harlan Coben	Donald Harstad	Dana Stabenow

William Boyd 1952-

🏆 Whitbread 1981   JLR 1982   S Maugham 1982   Black 1990   Costa 2006

Nicholas Drayson	Christopher Hope	Simon Mawer
Margaret Elphinstone	Matthew Kneale	Tim Parks
Giles Foden	Nick Laird	Richard Powers
Philip Hensher	Alistair MacLeod	James Robertson

T C Boyle 1948- US

is Thomas Coraghessan Boyle

Russell Banks	Jonathan Coe	Benjamin Markovits
Andrea Barrett	Jonathan Franzen	Philip Roth

John Boyne ☺ 1971- Ire Historical

Geraldine Brooks	Irene Nemirovsky	Robert Louis Stevenson
Sebastian Faulks	Bernhard Schlink	Carlos Ruiz Zafón

23

Malcolm Bradbury 1932-2000

Kingsley Amis	David Lodge	Paul Torday
Melvyn Bragg	John Mortimer	Keith Waterhouse
Michael Frayn	Piers Paul Read	Evelyn Waugh
Howard Jacobson	Nicholas Shakespeare	A N Wilson

B

Ray Bradbury 1920- 2012   US   Science Fiction: Space and time

Poul Anderson	Harlan Ellison	Aldous Huxley
J G Ballard	Robert A Heinlein	Ken MacLeod

Tom Bradby   1967-   Adventure/Thriller

Boris Akunin	Kate Furnivall	Robert Ludlum
Daniel Easterman	Andrey Kurkov	Tim Sebastian
Clive Egleton	Stephen Leather	Gerald Seymour

Barbara Taylor Bradford   1933-   Saga

also writes as Sally Bradford   ⚡ Emma Harte • Ravenscar Series • Deravenel Series

Elizabeth Adler	Catherine King	Danielle Steel
Charlotte Bingham	Una-Mary Parker	Rosie Thomas
Rebecca Dean	Luanne Rice	Nicola Thorne
Jennifer Donnelly	Sidney Sheldon	Penny Vincenzi

Alan Bradley Can   Crime: Amateur sleuth

🏆 CWA 2007   ⚡ Flavia de Luce - 1950s

Bateman	Imogen Robertson	L C Tyler
Elizabeth George	Dorothy L Sayers	Jacqueline Winspear
Ngaio Marsh		

Marion Zimmer Bradley 1930-1999   US   Fantasy: Epic

Cecilia Dart-Thornton	Tanith Lee	Caiseal Mor
Barbara Hambly	Holly Lisle	Melanie Rawn
Robert Holdstock	Morgan Llywelyn	Sheri S Tepper
Helen Hollick	Julian May	Liz Williams

Rita Bradshaw   1950-   Saga

also writes as Helen Brooks   NE England

Aileen Armitage	Hilary Green	Meg Hutchinson
Josephine Cox	Annie Groves	Freda Lightfoot
Margaret Dickinson	Ruth Hamilton	Annie Murray
Jean Fullerton	Una Horne	Lynda Page

 may be suitable for young adults

Melvyn Bragg   1939-

🏆 WHSmith 2000

Malcolm Bradbury	Billy Hopkins	Julian Rathbone
A S Byatt	Sadie Jones	Owen Sheers
Margaret Drabble	Stanley Middleton	Alan Sillitoe
Sarah Hall	Andrew O'Hagan	Alan Titchmarsh

Gyles Brandreth   1948-   Crime: Amateur sleuth

🚶 Oscar Wilde - C19th

Gilbert Adair	Simon Brett	Arthur Conan Doyle
James Anderson	David Dickinson	Peter Lovesey
Marian Babson		

Ann Brashares   1967-   US

Douglas Kennedy	David Nicholls	Lionel Shriver
Richelle Mead	Audrey Niffenegger	Nicholas Sparks

Celia Brayfield   1945-   Glitz & Glamour

Louise Bagshawe	Barbara Delinsky	Katie Price
Jackie Collins	Judith Michael	Victoria Routledge
Jilly Cooper	Hilary Norman	

Chaz Brenchley   1959-   Fantasy: Epic

🏆 British Fantasy 1998

Jim Butcher	Stephen Gallagher	David Martin
Simon Clark	Andrew Klavan	K J Parker
Sara Douglass	Scott Lynch	Patrick Rothfuss

Allison Brennan   US   Crime: Romantic suspense

Beverly Barton	Lisa Jackson	J D Robb
Heather Graham	P D Martin	Karen Rose
Linda Howard	Theresa Monsour	Sharon Sala

Simon Brett   1945-   Crime: Amateur sleuth

🚶 Charles Paris, Actor • Mrs Pargeter - Sussex
Carole Seddon - 'Fethering', Sussex • Blotto & Twinks - 1930s

Marian Babson	W J Burley	Carolyn G Hart
Jo Bannister	Kate Charles	Veronica Heley
Bateman	Ruth Dudley Edwards	L C Tyler
Gyles Brandreth	Kate Ellis	Jill Paton Walsh

Patricia Briggs   1965-   US   Paranormal

🚶 Mercy Thompson, Car mechanic

Lara Adrian	Christine Feehan	Suzanne McLeod
Rachel Caine	Lori Handeland	Richelle Mead
Karen Chance	Kim Harrison	Naomi Novik
Cassandra Clare	Katie MacAlister	Michelle Rowen

Joanna Briscoe

Diane Chamberlain	Margaret Leroy	Maggie O'Farrell
Rachel Hore	Charlotte Mendelson	Rosie Thomas

Poppy Z Brite   1967-   US   Horror

Kelley Armstrong	Brian Lumley	Anne Rice
Tanya Huff	Kim Newman	Kim Wilkins
Joe R Lansdale		

B

William Brodrick   1960-   Crime: Amateur sleuth

🏆 CWA 2009   🚶 Father Anselm

Benjamin Black	Nicole Krauss	Andrew Nugent
Andrew M Greeley	Mary Lawson	Andrew Taylor
Alison Joseph	John Le Carré	

Frances Brody   Crime: Amateur sleuth

🚶 Kate Shackleton - Yorkshire

Simon Brett	Martin Edwards	Charles Todd
Barbara Cleverly	Catriona McPherson	Nicola Upson
Lesley Cookman	David Roberts	Jill Paton Walsh
Carola Dunn	Betty Rowlands	Jacqueline Winspear

Amanda Brookfield   1960-   Aga Saga

Anne Doughty	Kate Long	Robin Pilcher
Adèle Geras	Santa Montefiore	Jennie Rooney
Erica James	Elizabeth Palmer	Madeleine Wickham

Christopher Brookmyre   1968-   Sco   Crime: Humour

🏆 Bollinger 2006   🚶 Jack Parlabane, Journalist - Scotland

Linwood Barclay	Joolz Denby	Adrian Magson
Bateman	Christopher Fowler	Malcolm Pryce
Tony Black	Carl Hiaasen	Kevin Sampson
James Brownley	Douglas Lindsay	Ian Sansom

Anita Brookner ⌒   1928-

🏆 Booker 1984

A S Byatt	Ian McEwan	Bernice Rubens
Mavis Cheek	Charlotte Mendelson	Muriel Spark
Anne Enright	Gwendoline Riley	Salley Vickers
Penelope Fitzgerald		

Geraldine Brooks   1955-   Aus   Historical

🏆 Pulitzer 2006

Gil Adamson	Will Davenport	Melanie Gifford
Jo Baker	Kiran Desai	Christopher Koch
Muriel Barbery	Anita Diamant	Marilynne Robinson
Tracy Chevalier	E L Doctorow	James Wilson

Terry Brooks ⌒ 1944- US   Fantasy: Epic

James Clemens	Maggie Furey	Mickey Zucker Reichert
Kate Elliott	David Gemmell	Brandon Sanderson
David Farland	John Marco	Margaret Weis
Raymond E Feist	Elizabeth Moon	Tad Williams

Benita Brown   Saga

C19th Tyneside

Anne Bennett	Rosie Harris	Beryl Matthews
Catherine Cookson	Joan Jonker	Elizabeth Murphy
Dilly Court	Margaret Kaine	Mary Jane Staples

Dale Brown 1956- US   Adventure/Thriller

also writes with Jim Felice   ⚑ Patrick McLanahan - Aviation
Major Jason Richter - Special Operations Unit, FBI

Richard Herman	John J Nance	Eric Van Lustbader
Graham Hurley	Patrick Robinson	Robin White
Gordon Kent	Julian Jay Savarin	
Kyle Mills	James Siegel	

Dan Brown ⌒ 1964- US   Adventure/Thriller

also writes as Danielle Brown   ⚑ Professor Robert Langdon - Harvard University

Will Adams	Michael Cordy	Tom Knox
Michael Byrnes	William Dietrich	Chris Kuzneski
Lincoln Child	David Gibbins	Scott Mariani
Glenn Cooper	Raymond Khoury	Douglas Preston

Gordon Brown 1962- Sco   Crime: Hardboiled

Tony Black	Alex Gray	Denise Mina
Karen Campbell	Allan Guthrie	Caro Ramsay
Gillian Galbraith	Stuart MacBride	Craig Russell

Sandra Brown 1948- US   Crime: Romantic suspense

also writes as Laura Jordan, Rachel Ryan, Erin St Claire

Millenia Black	Olivia Goldsmith	Harold Robbins
Suzanne Brockmann	Lisa Jackson	Nora Roberts
Candace Bushnell	Jayne Ann Krentz	Penny Vincenzi
Jackie Collins	Karen Robards	

Nick Brownlee 1967-   Adventure/Thriller

⚑ Jake Moore & Insp Daniel Journa - Kenya

Bryce Courtenay	Stephen Leather	Gerald Seymour
Nelson DeMille	Julian Jay Savarin	Wilbur Smith

James Brownley

Crime: Amateur sleuth

🚶 Alison Glasby, Journalist

Lilian Jackson Braun	Edna Buchanan	Denise Mina
Christopher Brookmyre	Liza Marklund	Chris Niles

Sylvia Brownrigg

US

Andrea Barrett	Alice Munro	Jane Urquhart
Charlotte Mendelson	Carol Shields	Salley Vickers

Alison Bruce

Crime: Police work - UK

🚶 DC Gary Goodhew - Cambridge

Kate Atkinson	Deborah Crombie	Patrick Lennon
Ann Cleeves	Sophie Hannah	Aline Templeton

Ken Bruen   1951-   Ire

Crime: Hardboiled

🚶 DCI Roberts & DS Brant - London • Jack Taylor, Former policeman - Galway

Vivien Armstrong	Allan Guthrie	Simon Kernick
Ray Banks	Patricia Hall	David Peace
Paul Charles	Declan Hughes	Olen Steinhauer
Barry Eisler	Bill James	Mark Timlin

Julia Bryant

Saga

🚶 Forrest Family - Portsmouth

Anne Bennett	June Francis	Margaret Thornton
Rose Boucheron	Anna Jacobs	Janet Woods
Elizabeth Elgin	June Tate	

Elizabeth Buchan   1948-

Aga Saga

🏆 Romantic 1994

Diana Appleyard	Eileen Goudge	Mary Stanley
Charlotte Bingham	Angela Huth	Lou Wakefield
Kate Fenton	Anna Maxted	Fay Weldon

Jonathan Buckley   1956-

Ronald Frame	Lesley Glaister	Sophie Hannah
Nicci French	Robert Goddard	Kate Morton

Suzanne Bugler   ☺

Emily Barr	Lesley Glaister	Dorothy Koomson
Nicci Gerrard	Sophie Hannah	Jodi Picoult

Go to back for lists of
Pseudonyms • Authors by Genre • Characters and Series • Environments
Prize Winners • Classic Authors • Crossover Authors • Further Reading • Websites

Lois McMaster Bujold   1949-   US   Science Fiction: Space opera

🏃 Lord Miles Vorkosigan

Dan Abnett	Colin Greenland	Adam Roberts
Douglas Adams	Peter F Hamilton	Charles Stross
Orson Scott Card	Anne McCaffrey	Karen Traviss
Ben Counter	Elizabeth Moon	Liz Williams

John Burdett   Adventure/Thriller: Legal/financial

🏃 Sonchai Jitpleecheep, Thai American detective

Tom Clancy	Robert Ludlum	Gerald Seymour
Colin Cotterill	R N Morris	Martin Cruz Smith
Barry Eisler	Christopher Reich	Olen Steinhauer
John Le Carré		

Anita Burgh   1937-   Saga

also writes as Annie Leith

Elizabeth Adler	Winston Graham	Carol Rivers
Rosemary Aitken	Shena Mackay	Sue Sully
Rose Boucheron	Una-Mary Parker	Rowena Summers

Alafair Burke   1909-   US   Adventure/Thriller: Legal/financial

🏃 DDA Samantha Kincaid - Portland, Oregon

Brett Battles	Sue Grafton	Nancy Taylor Rosenberg
Edna Buchanan	Steve Martini	John Sandford
Linda Fairstein	Perri O'Shaughnessy	

Crime: Police work - US

🏃 Det Ellie Hatcher - NYPD

Michael Connelly	Faye Kellerman	John Sandford
Jilliane Hoffman	Jonathan Kellerman	Karin Slaughter

James Lee Burke   1936-   US   Crime: Hardboiled

🏆 CWA 1998   🏃 Dave Robicheaux, Policeman - New Iberia, Louisiana
Billy-Bob Holland, Attorney - Texas; Montana

C J Box	Tony Hillerman	George P Pelecanos
James Crumley	J A Kerley	Thomas Perry
Barry Eisler	Michael Malone	Richard Stark
James W Hall	Leonardo Padura	Darryl Wimberley

Jan Burke   1953-   US   Crime: Amateur sleuth

🏃 Irene Kelly, Journalist - California

Edna Buchanan	Denise Hamilton	Claire McNab
Caroline Carver	Faye Kellerman	Liza Marklund
Meg Gardiner	Laurie R King	Margaret Maron
Sue Grafton	Laura Lippman	Chris Niles

W J Burley 1914-2002 Crime: Police work - UK

was William John Burley

🏃 Supt Wycliffe - Cornwall

Catherine Aird	Kate Ellis	Ruth Rendell
Simon Brett	Caroline Graham	June Thomson
Ann Cleeves	Peter James	

B Gordon Burn 1948-2009

Sebastian Barry	Andrew Greig	Dennis Lehane
Roberto Bolano	Denis Johnson	David Peace

John Burnside 1955- Sco

🏆 Encore 2000

Ron Butlin	Janice Galloway	A L Kennedy
Michael Cannon	Jackie Kay	Ali Smith

Mary Burton US Adventure/Thriller

Lisa Gardner	Tami Hoag	Karin Slaughter
Tess Gerritsen	Iris Johansen	P J Tracy
Mo Hayder	Karen Rose	

Candace Bushnell ⌒ 1958- US Glitz & Glamour

Sandra Brown	Olivia Goldsmith	Katie Price
Jackie Collins	Niamh Greene	Nora Roberts
Barbara Delinsky	Jayne Ann Krentz	Plum Sykes
Imogen Edwards-Jones		

Jim Butcher 1971- US Paranormal

🏃 Harry Dresden, Wizard - Chicago

Chaz Brenchley	Lori Handeland	J K Rowling
Mike Carey	Kim Harrison	Liz Williams
Pamela Freeman	Barb & J C Hendee	

A S Byatt ⌒ 1936-

🏆 Booker 1990   Irish Times 1990   Black 2010

Gilbert Adair	Patricia Duncker	Benjamin Markovits
Melvyn Bragg	Arabella Edge	Francine Prose
Anita Brookner	Penelope Fitzgerald	Kate Pullinger
Margaret Drabble	Penelope Lively	Jill Paton Walsh

Michael Byrnes Adventure/Thriller

James Becker	Dan Brown	Thomas Greanias
Steve Berry	John Case	James Rollins
Sam Bourne	Lee Child	

Armand Cabasson ⌒ 1970- Fr · Adventure/Thriller: Historical

♀ Captain Quentin Margont

John Boyne
Andrea Camilleri

Claude Izner
Andrew Pepper

Arturo Perez-Reverte
Julian Rathbone

Meg Cabot ⌒ ☺ 1967- US · Chick Lit

also writes as Patricia Cabot & Jenny Carroll;
is Meggin Patricia Cabot

♀ Princess Mia Diaries Series
Heather Wells Series

Cecelia Ahern
Maggie Alderson
Hester Browne
Megan Crane

Kathy Lette
Chris Manby
Jill Mansell

Andrea Semple
Sara Shepard
Paige Toon

C

Colette Caddle Ire · Chick Lit

Claudia Carroll
Martina Devlin
Sabine Durrant

Monica McInerney
Sinead Moriarty
Anita Notaro

Kate O'Riordan
Morag Prunty
Kate Thompson

Chelsea Cain US · Crime: Police work - US

♀ Archie Sheridan, Detective • Gretchen Lowell, Serial killer

Thomas Harris
Mo Hayder
Tami Hoag
Jilliane Hoffman

Paul Johnston
Michael Koryta
Richard Kunzmann
Colleen McCullough

Michael Marshall
Richard Montanari
Chris Mooney
Karin Slaughter

Tom Cain · Adventure/Thriller

is David Thomas

♀ Samuel Carver, ex SAS

James Barrington
Brett Battles
Frederick Forsyth

Peter James
Robert Ludlum
Andy McNab

Chris Ryan
Jon Stock
Robin White

Rachel Caine ⌒ ☺ US · Paranormal

is Roxanne Longstreet Conrad

Kelley Armstrong
Patricia Briggs
P C & Kristin Cast

Charlaine Harris
Kim Harrison
Richelle Mead

Stephenie Meyer
Lilith Saintcrow

Brian Callison 1934- Sco · Sea: Modern

James H Cobb
Alexander Fullerton
Duncan Harding

Philip McCutchan
James Pattinson
Douglas Reeman

Justin Scott
Terence Strong

☺ also writes children's books

Christian Cameron   1962-   US   Historical: Ancient

also writes as Gordon Kent jointly with Kenneth Cameron   ⚲ Kineas, Athenian cavalry officer
                                                                Srayanka, Warrior & priestess

Bernard Cornwell	Christian Jacq	Harry Sidebottom
Robert Graves	Allan Massie	Paul Waters
Conn Iggulden	Manda Scott	Robyn Young
Glyn Iliffe		

Kenneth Cameron   US   Crime: Historical - C20th

also writes as Gordon Kent with Christian Cameron   ⚲ Denton, US novelist - Edwardian England

Arthur Conan Doyle	Laurie R King	R N Morris
Carola Dunn	Brian McGilloway	Dorothy L Sayers

Lindy Cameron   Aus   Crime: PI

⚲ Kit O'Malley - Melbourne

Janet Evanovich	Lauren Henderson	Denis Lehane
Helen Fitzgerald	Laurie R King	Sara Paretsky

Stella Cameron   1943-   US   Adventure/Thriller

Patricia D Cornwell	Tess Gerritsen	Jilliane Hoffman
Lisa Gardner	Mo Hayder	Karin Slaughter

Andrea Camilleri   1925-   It   Crime: Police work - Italy

🏆 CWA 2012   ⚲ Insp Salvo Montalbano - Sicily

Gianrico Carofiglio	Martin O'Brien	Olen Steinhauer
Michele Giuttari	Leonardo Padura	Ronald Tierney
Donna Leon	Jeffrey Siger	Michael Walters
Carlo Lucarelli	Georges Simenon	Anne Zouroudi

Karen Campbell   1967-   Sco   Crime: Police work - UK

⚲ Sgt Anna Cameron - Glasgow

Lin Anderson	Helen Fitzgerald	Frederic Lindsay
Ray Banks	Gillian Galbraith	Stuart MacBride
Tony Black	Alex Gray	Caro Ramsay
Gordon Brown	Allan Guthrie	Craig Russell

Ramsey Campbell   1946-   Horror

🏆 British Fantasy 1991, 1994 & 2008

Jonathan Carroll	Christopher Fowler	Whitley Strieber
Simon Clark	Stephen Laws	T M Wright
Douglas Clegg	John Saul	

Rebecca Campbell   Chick Lit

Cecelia Ahern	Lisa Jewell	Shari Low
Lynne Barrett-Lee	Josie Lloyd & Emlyn Rees	Jane Wenham-Jones
Louise Candlish		

Trudi Canavan ⌒ ☺ 1969- Aus Fantasy: Epic

Jacqueline Carey	Ursula K Le Guin	Naomi Novik
Sara Douglass	Juliet Marillier	Christopher Paolini
Terry Goodkind	William Nicholson	Brent Weeks
Lian Hearn	Garth Nix	

Louise Candlish Mature Chick Lit

Rebecca Campbell	Sophie Hannah	Dorothy Koomson
Sue Gee	Sophie King	Kate Long
Nikki Gemmell		

Helen Cannam Saga

Aileen Armitage	Elizabeth Elgin	Elvi Rhodes
Jessica Blair	Sheelagh Kelly	Kay Stephens

Stephen J Cannell 1941-2010 US Adventure/Thriller

⚐ Det Shane Scully - Los Angeles Police Dept

Nelson DeMille	John Lawton	James Long
Ken Follett	Robert Littell	Martin Cruz Smith

Michael Cannon 1958- Sco

John Burnside	Andrew Greig	A L Kennedy
Janice Galloway	Robin Jenkins	Andrew O'Hagan

Anthony Capella 1962-

Elizabeth Edmondson	Joanne Harris	Lily Prior
Imogen Edwards-Jones	Sarah Kate Lynch	Martin Walker
Susan Fletcher		

Lorenzo Carcaterra 1954- US Adventure/Thriller

Massimo Carlotto	David Peace	Boston Teran
Adrian McKinty	Mario Puzo	John Williams
Chuck Palahniuk	Sidney Sheldon	

Orson Scott Card ⌒ 1951- US Science Fiction: Space opera

Lois McMaster Bujold	John Scalzi	Charles Stross
Alan Dean Foster	Dan Simmons	David Zindell
Joe Haldeman		

Jacqueline Carey 1964- US Fantasy: Epic

Joe Abercrombie	Karen Chance	Laurell K Hamilton
Patricia Briggs	Sara Douglass	Robin Hobb
Trudi Canavan	Jennifer Fallon	Sheri S Tepper

C

Mike Carey   1959-   Paranormal

⚐ Felix Castor, Freelance exorcist

Joe Abercrombie	Lori Handeland	Ursula K Le Guin
Jim Butcher	Kim Harrison	China Miéville

Peter Carey   ⌒   1943-   Aus

🏆 Booker 1988 & 2001   Commonwealth 1998 & 2001   Miles Franklin 1998

Murray Bail	Gabriel Garcia Márquez	Hari Kunzru
Steven Carroll	Kate Grenville	David Leavitt
Robert Drewe	Lloyd Jones	David Malouf
Richard Flanagan	Thomas Keneally	Tim Winton

C

Isobelle Carmody   ⌒   ☺   1958-   Aus   Fantasy: Epic

Lian Hearn	George R R Martin	Garth Nix
Ursula K Le Guin	Stephenie Meyer	J K Rowling

Jo Carnegie   Glitz & Glamour

Katie Agnew	Jilly Cooper	Tasmina Perry
Tilly Bagshawe	Milly Johnson	Fiona Walker
Nina Bell		

Gianrico Carofiglio   1961-   It   Crime: Psychological

⚐ Guido Guerrieri, Lawyer - Bari

Andrea Camilleri	John Grisham	Donna Leon
Michael Dibdin	Patricia Highsmith	Andy Oakes

Amelia Carr   Saga

is Janet Tanner

Rosie Harris	Judith Lennox	Janet Tanner
Rachel Hore	Annie Murray	Marcia Willett

Claudia Carroll   Ire   Chick Lit

Cecelia Ahern	Sophie Kinsella	Patricia Scanlan
Colette Caddle	Carole Matthews	Tess Stimson
Maeve Haran	Morag Prunty	Lauren Weisberger
Marian Keyes		

Jonathan Carroll   1949-   US   Fantasy: Dark

🏆 British Fantasy 1992

Ben Counter	Neil Gaiman	Michael Moorcock
Stephen Donaldson	Katherine Kurtz	Janny Wurts

Go to back for lists of
Pseudonyms • Authors by Genre • Characters and Series • Environments
Prize Winners • Classic Authors • Crossover Authors • Further Reading • Websites

Steven Carroll
1949- Aus

🏆 Miles Franklin 2008

Murray Bail	Kate Grenville	David Malouf
Peter Carey	Pam Jenoff	Tim Winton

Chris Carter
Braz   Crime: Police work - US

🏃 Det Robert Hunter - Los Angeles

Tania Carver	Scott Frost	Chris Mooney
Jane Casey	Gregg Hurwitz	John Rickards
Brian Freeman	J A Kerley	

Justin Cartwright
1945- SA

🏆 Whitbread 1998   Hawthornden 2005

Martin Amis	Damon Galgut	David Leavitt
J M Coetzee	Christopher Hope	William Nicholson
Jennifer Egan	Pamela Jooste	John Updike

Caroline Carver
1959-   Crime: Amateur sleuth

also writes as C J Carver   🏃 India Kane, Journalist - Australia • Jay McCaulay, ex-Army officer
🏆 CWA 1999

Jan Burke	Denise Hamilton	Sarah Rayne
Jodi Compton	Hazel Holt	Peter Temple
Sarah Diamond	Adrian Magson	Martin Walker
G M Ford		

Tania Carver
Crime: Psychological

is Martyn and Linda Waites   🏃 DI Philip Brennan - Colchester, Essex

Chris Carter	Carol Goodman	Cody McFadyen
Jane Casey	Sophie Hannah	Gillian White

John Case
1943- US   Adventure/Thriller

also writes as James Eliot; is Jim & Carolyn Hougan

Steve Berry	Michael Cordy	Chris Kuzneski
Sam Bourne	Daniel Easterman	Scott Mariani
Michael Byrnes	Jean-Christophe Grangé	Bill Napier
Glenn Cooper	Raymond Khoury	Gareth O'Callaghan

Jane Casey
Ire   Crime: Psychological

Chris Carter	Sophie Hannah	Steve Mosby
Claudia Carroll	Mo Hayder	Louise Penny
Tana French	Chris Mooney	Neil White

P C & Kristin Cast
🎧 ☺ US   Paranormal

Lara Adrian	Charlaine Harris	J K Rowling
Rachel Caine	Richelle Mead	Lilith Saintcrow
Karen Chance	Stephenie Meyer	J R Ward

C

Linda Castillo   US   Crime: Police work - US

♁ Kate Burkholder, Chief of Police - 'Painter's Creek', Ohio

Tess Gerritsen	Ridley Pearson	P J Tracy
John Hart	Erica Spindler	Lisa Unger

Lucy Cavendish   Mature Chick Lit

Marita Conlon-McKenna	Jane Fallon	Allison Pearson
Sarah Duncan	Milly Johnson	Polly Williams

Margaret Cezair-Thompson   1956-   Jam

Jill Dawson	Victoria Hislop	Katharine McMahon
Roopa Farooki	Rachel Hore	Monique Roffey
Julia Gregson	Andrea Levy	Sara Sheridan

Michael Chabon   1963-   US

♛ Pulitzer 2001

Saul Bellow	Allegra Goodman	David Leavitt
Michael Cunningham	Howard Jacobson	Jonathan Lethem
Nathan Englander	Denis Johnson	Claire Messud
Jonathan Safran Foer	Daniel Kehlmann	Amos Oz

Mark Chadbourn   1960-   Fantasy: Contemporary

Charles de Lint	Terry Goodkind	Brent Weeks
Stephen Donaldson	Guy Gavriel Kay	David Zindell
David Eddings	Katharine Kerr	

Elizabeth Chadwick   Historical: Medieval

also writes as Nancy Herndon

Elizabeth Aston	Dorothy Dunnett	Anne Herries
Will Davenport	Barbara Erskine	Georgette Heyer
Christie Dickason	Barbara Ewing	Rosalind Laker
Jennifer Donnelly	Posie Graeme-Evans	Sharon Penman

Sarah Challis   Aga Saga

Maeve Binchy	Patricia Fawcett	Santa Montefiore
Claire Calman	Rebecca Gregson	Jojo Moyes
Marika Cobbold	Julie Highmore	Rosamunde Pilcher
Jennifer Donnelly	Sara MacDonald	Jane Yardley

Diane Chamberlain   US

Pat Conroy	Giselle Green	Marcia Preston
Kim Edwards	Margaret Leroy	Anita Shreve
Nicci Gerrard	Jodi Picoult	Curtis Sittenfeld

Holly Chamberlin   US   Mature Chick Lit

Rowan Coleman	Emily Giffin	Clare Morrall
Jill Dawson	Sue Miller	Nicholas Sparks
Patricia Duncker		

Clare Chambers   1966-   Aga Saga

♛ Romantic 1999

Sarah Challis	Rebecca Gregson	Amanda Eyre Ward
Katie Fforde	Sarah Jackman	Mary Wesley
Elizabeth Flock		

Joy Chambers   Aus   War: Historical

Elizabeth Darrell	Mark Mills	Kate Morton
Julie Garwood	Di Morrissey	Wilbur Smith
Mary Lawson		

Kimberley Chambers   1967-   Crime: Hardboiled

♀ Mitchell family & O'Hara family - East End of London

Helen Black	June Hampson	Roberta Kray
Martina Cole	Jessie Keane	Denise Ryan

Karen Chance   US   Paranormal

♀ Cassandra Palmer, Clairvoyant • Dorina Basarab, Dhampir

Lara Adrian	P C & Kristin Cast	Barb & J C Hendee
Patricia Briggs	Laurell K Hamilton	Suzanne McLeod
Jacqueline Carey	Kim Harrison	Stephenie Meyer

Rebecca Chance   Glitz & Glamour

Tilly Bagshawe	Tasmina Perry	Sasha Wagstaff
Olivia Darling	Katie Price	Fiona Walker
Veronica Henry	Karen Swan	

Raymond Chandler   1888-1959   US   Crime: PI

♀ Philip Marlowe - Los Angeles • John Delmas - Los Angeles

Megan Abbott	Declan Hughes	Leonardo Padura
Lawrence Block	Stuart M Kaminsky	Robert B Parker
James Hadley Chase	Ross Macdonald	James Sallis
Peter Corris	Reggie Nadelson	John Shannon

Vikram Chandra   1961-   Ind

♛ Higham 1995

Aravind Adiga	Rohinton Mistry	Vikas Swarup
Michael Arditti	V S Naipaul	Christos Tsiolkas
Amit Chaudhuri	R K Narayan	Alex Wheatle
Anita Desai	Vikram Seth	

Kate Charles   1950-   US   Crime: Amateur sleuth

is Carol A Chase   ⚲ Callie Anson, Female curate • David Middleton-Brown, Solicitor

Simon Brett	Veronica Heley	P D James
Ann Cleeves	Susan Hill	M R D Meek
Andrew M Greeley	Lis Howell	Keith Miles

Paul Charles   Crime: Police work - UK

⚲ DI Christy Kennedy - London • Insp Starrett - Irish Serious Crime Unit

Ken Bruen	Colin Dexter	Graham Ison
Gwendoline Butler	Georgie Hale	Susan B Kelly
Brian Cooper	Patricia Hall	Maureen O'Brien
Judith Cutler	Graham Hurley	Martyn Waites

James Hadley Chase   1906-85   US   Crime: Hardboiled

also wrote as James L Docherty, Ambrose Grant,   ⚲ Dave Fenner • Vic Malloy
Raymond Marshall; was René Brabazon Raymond   Steve Harmas • Frank Terrell
Mark Girland • Helga Rolfe

Lawrence Block	Dashiell Hammett	Ross Macdonald
Raymond Chandler	Stuart M Kaminsky	Robert B Parker

Amit Chaudhuri   1962-   Ind

🏆 Betty Trask 1991   Encore 1994

Aravind Adiga	R K Narayan	Vikram Seth
Vikram Chandra	Arundhati Roy	Zadie Smith
Rohinton Mistry	Salman Rushdie	Vikas Swarup

Mavis Cheek   Humour

Melissa Bank	Sue Limb	Lynne Truss
Isla Dewar	Shena Mackay	Arabella Weir
Jane Green	Lily Prior	Nigel Williams
Marina Lewycka	Ben Richards	

C J Cherryh   1942-   US   Fantasy: Myth

is Carolyn Janice Cherry

Kate Elliott	Tanith Lee	L E Modesitt Jr
Barbara Hambly	George R R Martin	Sheri S Tepper
Stephen R Lawhead		

Marion Chesney   1936-   Sco   Historical Romance

also writes as M C Beaton

Mary Balogh	Jude Deveraux	Stephanie Laurens
Anne Barbour	Emily Hendrickson	Fenella-Jane Miller
Catherine Coulter	Eloisa James	Julia Quinn
Elizabeth Darrell		

🏠 may be suitable for young adults

Tracy Chevalier ⌒ 1962- US   Historical

Geraldine Brooks	Maureen Freely	Jude Morgan
Will Davenport	Lee Langley	Maureen Peters
Sarah Dunant	Michelle Lovric	James Runcie
Marina Fiorato	Andrew Miller	Susan Vreeland

Elise Chidley SA   Chick Lit

Catherine Alliott	Katie Fforde	Carole Matthews
Harriet Evans	Melissa Hill	Polly Williams

Lee Child ⌒ ☺ 1954-   Adventure/Thriller

is Jim Grant   ⚐ Jack Reacher, ex-Military policeman - Florida
♛ TGR 1999   Theakston's 2011

Adam Baron	Eric Jerome Dickey	Declan Hughes
Robert Gregory Browne	John Gilstrap	Grant McKenzie
Michael Byrnes	Raymond Haigh	Scott Mariani
Simon Conway	James W Hall	Marcus Sakey

Lincoln Child 1957- US   Adventure/Thriller

also writes jointly with Douglas Preston

Dan Brown	Vince Flynn	Douglas Preston
Daniel Easterman	Andy McDermott	Matthew Reilly

Cinda Williams Chima US   Fantasy: Epic

Joe Abercrombie	Karen Miller	Rick Riordan
Fiona McIntosh	Christopher Paolini	Brandon Sanderson

P F Chisholm 1958-   Crime: Historical - Medieval

is Patricia Finney   ⚐ Sir Robert Carey - London

Rory Clements	Philip Gooden	John Pilkington
Michael Clynes	Shirley McKay	C J Sansom
Patricia Finney	Fidelis Morgan	Kate Sedley

Agatha Christie ⌒ 1890-1976   Crime: Amateur sleuth

also wrote as Mary Westmacott   ⚐ Miss Marple • Hercule Poirot

Gilbert Adair	Dolores Gordon-Smith	Catriona McPherson
Catherine Aird	Kerry Greenwood	Martin O'Brien
Rennie Airth	Claude Izner	Dorothy L Sayers
Carola Dunn	Susan Kandel	Anne Zouroudi

Paul Christopher 1949- Can   Adventure/Thriller

is Christopher Hyde   ⚐ Finn Ryan, Archaeologist • Templar Series

Will Adams	John Twelve Hawks	Scott Mariani
Richard Doetsch	Tobias Hill	Kate Mosse
Tom Harper	Greg Loomis	James Rollins
A J Hartley		

Tom Clancy ⌒ 1947- US Adventure/Thriller

🏃 Jack Ryan • Net Force Explorers

Michael Asher	John Burdett	Glenn Meade
James Barrington	Duncan Falconer	Kyle Mills
Raymond Benson	Brian Haig	John J Nance
John Birmingham	Gordon Kent	Brad Thor

Alys Clare 1944- Crime: Historical - Medieval

also writes as Elizabeth Harris 🏃 Abbess Helewise & Josse D'Acquin - C12th Kent
'Hawkenlye Abbey'

C

Simon Beaufort	Cora Harrison	Ian Morson
Cassandra Clark	Bernard Knight	Mary Reed and Eric Mayer
Paul Doherty	Pat McIntosh	Candace Robb
Margaret Frazer	The Medieval Murderers	Kate Sedley

Cassandra Clare ☺ US Paranormal

Kelley Armstrong	Christine Feehan	Stephenie Meyer
Patricia Briggs	Barb & J C Hendee	Darren Shan
Justin Cronin		

Lucy Clare 1949- Aga Saga

Rowan Coleman	Katie Fforde	Sara MacDonald
Patricia Fawcett	Sarah Jackman	Rosamunde Pilcher
Kate Fenton	Erica James	Kate Saunders

Candida Clark 1970-

Patricia Gaffney	Roma Tearne	Rosie Thomas
Libby Purves	Paul Theroux	Louise Voss

Carol Higgins Clark 1956- US Crime: PI

🏃 Regan Reilly - Missouri

Sue Grafton	Marcia Muller	Rick Riordan
Laura Lippman	Sara Paretsky	Nancy Taylor Rosenberg
Margaret Maron		

Cassandra Clark Crime: Historical - C14th

🏃 Abbess of Meaux - York

Alys Clare	Ariana Franklin	Ellis Peters
Michael Clynes	Susanna Gregory	Candace Robb
Paul Doherty	Michael Jecks	C J Sansom

Clare Clark 1967- Historical: C18th & C19th

Philippa Gregory	Fiona Mountain	Jane Stevenson
Jude Morgan	Edward Rutherfurd	Sarah Waters

Mary Higgins Clark 1929- US Adventure/Thriller: Psychological

Lara Adrian	Katy Gardner	Hilary Norman
Thomas H Cook	Carol Goodman	Julie Parsons
Joy Fielding	Sophie Hannah	Liz Rigbey
Clare Francis	Karen Harper	Christina Schwarz

Simon Clark 1958- Horror

🏆 British Fantasy 2002

Clive Barker	Douglas Clegg	Gregory Maguire
Chaz Brenchley	Shaun Hutson	Mark Morris
Ramsey Campbell	Bentley Little	Koji Suzuki

Arthur C Clarke 1917-2008 Science Fiction: Technical

also wrote as E G O'Brien, Charles Willis 🏆 BSFA 1973

Brian W Aldiss	Greg Bear	Robert Reed
Isaac Asimov	Ben Bova	Robert Silverberg
Stephen Baxter	Jack McDevitt	Dan Simmons

Susanna Clarke 1959- Fantasy

Stephen Baxter	Elizabeth Garner	Jack O'Connell
G W Dahlquist	Amanda Hemingway	Terry Pratchett
Barbara Ewing	Stephen Hunt	Scarlett Thomas
Neil Gaiman	David Mitchell	

Victoria Clayton Aga Saga

Diana Appleyard	Rowan Coleman	Imogen Parker
Trisha Ashley	Anne Doughty	Rosamunde Pilcher
Raffaella Barker	Elizabeth Jane Howard	Linda Taylor
Claire Calman	Elizabeth Palmer	

Chris Cleave 1974-

🏆 S Maugham 2006

Nick Hornby	Ian McEwan	Mark Mills
Barbara &	Jon McGregor	William Nicholson
Stephanie Keating	Andrei Makine	Paul Torday
David Lodge	Joe Meno	

Ann Cleeves 1954- Crime: Police work - UK

🏆 CWA 2006   DI Stephen Ramsay • DI Vera Stanhope ⎱ Northumberland
George & Molly Palmer-Jones, Ornithologists ⎰
Det Jimmy Perez - Shetland Isles

Catherine Aird	John Connor	Lesley Horton
Alex Barclay	Judith Cutler	Louise Penny
W J Burley	Kate Ellis	Pauline Rowson
Kate Charles	Elly Griffiths	Andrew Taylor

Rory Clements
Historical: C16th

🏆 CWA 2010 🚶 John Shakespeare, Intelligence officer

P F Chisholm	Philip Gooden	John Pilkington
Michael Clynes	S J Parris	C J Sansom

Barbara Cleverly
Crime: Historical - C20th

🏆 CWA 2004 🚶 Insp Joe Sandilands - 1920s India • Laetitia Talbot, Archaeologist - 1920s

Conrad Allen	Martha Grimes	Louise Penny
Suzanne Arruda	Graham Ison	Elizabeth Peters
David Dickinson	Ngaio Marsh	Jacqueline Winspear
Carola Dunn	Michael Pearce	Anne Zouroudi

Frank Coates
Aus

Adventure/Thriller

Jon Cleary	Tamara McKinley	Judy Nunn
Bryce Courtenay	Di Morrissey	Wilbur Smith
Beverley Harper		

James H Cobb
1953- US

Sea: Modern

🚶 Com Amanda Lee Garrett - Destroyer USS Cunningham

Brian Callison	Richard Herman	Douglas Reeman
Jonathan Carroll	Christopher Nicole	Patrick Robinson
Duncan Harding	James Pattinson	Justin Scott

Marika Cobbold
Swe

Aga Saga

Sarah Challis	Santa Montefiore	Lou Wakefield
Rachel Cusk	Elizabeth Noble	Amanda Eyre Ward
Jessica Duchen	Robin Pilcher	Jane Yardley
Kate Long	Ann Purser	Elizabeth Wrenn

Harlan Coben
☎ ☺ 1962- US

Crime: Amateur sleuth

🏆 TGR 2003 🚶 Myron Bolitar, Sports agent - New York

Jeff Abbott	Robert Crais	George Dawes Green
Linwood Barclay	Eric Jerome Dickey	Sam Hayes
C J Box	Loren D Estleman	Grant McKenzie
Jodi Compton	Scott Frost	Robert B Parker

Michael Cobley
1959-

Science Fiction: Space opera

Kevin J Anderson	Peter F Hamilton	Caiseal Mor
Gary Gibson	Paul J McAuley	Alastair Reynolds

Jonathan Coe
☎ 1961-

Humour

🏆 Bollinger 2001 JLR 1994

Guy Bellamy	John Lanchester	David Nicholls
Tim Binding	Jon McGregor	Tim Pears
T C Boyle	Magnus Mills	Henry Sutton
Joseph Connolly	David Mitchell	Nigel Williams

Paulo Coelho 1947- Braz

Mitch Albom	Mark Haddon	Elif Shafak
Alessandro Baricco	Eve Makis	Patrick Suskind
Umberto Eco	Audrey Niffenegger	Carlos Ruiz Zafón
Gabriel Garcia Márquez		

J M Coetzee 1940- SA

♟ Faber 1981   Booker 1983 & 1999   Irish Times 1995   Commonwealth 2000

André Brink	Nadine Gordimer	Doris Lessing
Justin Cartwright	Romesh Gunesekera	Francine Prose
Richard Flanagan	Christopher Hope	Kate Pullinger
Damon Galgut	Pamela Jooste	Gillian Slovo

C

Julie Cohen   US   Chick Lit

Jenny Colgan	Jill Mansell	Alexandra Potter
Katie Fforde	Carole Matthews	Polly Williams
Jane Green		

Nancy Cohen   US   Crime: Humour

is Nancy Cane   ⚉ Bad Hair Day Mysteries

Linda Barnes	Sparkle Hayter	Sarah Strohmeyer
Janet Evanovich	Carl Hiaasen	Donald Westlake

Martina Cole 1958-   Crime: Hardboiled

⚉ DI Kate Burrows - East End, London

Helen Black	Jessie Keane	Ken McCoy
June Hampson	Roberta Kray	Hilary Norman
Sam Hayes	Lynda La Plante	Sheila Quigley
Mandasue Heller	Kevin Lewis	Denise Ryan

Rowan Coleman   Mature Chick Lit

⚉ Ruby Parker

Maria Beaumont	Jenny Colgan	Kate Jacobs
Holly Chamberlin	Patricia Fawcett	Milly Johnson
Lucy Clare	Kate Fenton	Anna McPartlin
Victoria Clayton	Jane Green	Sheila O'Flanagan

Nicholas Coleridge   1957-

Jeffrey Archer	Douglas Kennedy	David Nicholls
Rachel Johnson	Jojo Moyes	Sidney Sheldon

Eoin Colfer ☺ 1965- Ire   Fantasy: Epic

⚉ Artemis Fowl

Douglas Adams	William Nicholson	Philip Pullman
Louise Cooper	Terry Pratchett	J K Rowling
Sam Llewellyn		

Jenny Colgan ⌒ 1972- Sco Chick Lit

♈ Nathan 2012

Maggie Alderson	Imogen Edwards-Jones	Milly Johnson
Emily Barr	Linda Green	Fiona Neill
Rowan Coleman	Alison Penton Harper	Tina Reilly
Lucy Dillon	Louise Harwood	Jane Wenham-Jones

Chris Collett Crime: Police work - UK

🏃 DI Tom Mariner - Birmingham

Catherine Aird	Marjorie Eccles	Stuart Pawson
Robert Barnard	Ann Granger	Peter Robinson
Deborah Crombie	John Harvey	R D Wingfield

Catrin Collier 1948- Wales Saga

also writes as **Katherine John** 🏃 Heart of Gold Series - Pontypridd, Wales

Elizabeth Daish	Rosie Goodwin	Anna Jacobs
Elizabeth Elgin	Iris Gower	Grace Thompson
Sara Fraser	Rosie Harris	

Jackie Collins 1941- Glitz & Glamour

🏃 Lucky Santangelo - California

Tilly Bagshawe	Candace Bushnell	Katie Price
Millenia Black	Lesley Lokko	Harold Robbins
Celia Brayfield	Fern Michaels	Madge Swindells
Sandra Brown	Fiona O'Brien	Penny Vincenzi

Michael Collins 1964- Ire

Clare Boylan	Richard Ford	Laura Lippman
Michael Cunningham	Alice Hoffman	Tim O'Brien
Louise Erdrich		

Jodi Compton US Crime: Police work - US

🏃 Det Sarah Pribek - Minneapolis • Hailey Cain - Chicago

Caroline Carver	Robert Crais	Laura Lippman
Harlan Coben	Linda Fairstein	John Sandford

Julie Compton US Crime: Legal/financial

David Baldacci	Steve Martini	David Morrell
Mark Gimenez	Brad Meltzer	Scott Turow

Marita Conlon-McKenna 1956- Ire Mature Chick Lit

Maeve Binchy	Jane Fallon	Joan O'Neill
Lucy Cavendish	Linda Kelsey	Liz Ryan
Anne Doughty	Geraldine O'Neill	Sue Welfare
Rose Doyle		

Michael Connelly 1956- US Crime: Police work - US

🏃 Harry Bosch
Terry McCaleb, Retired FBI Agent } Los Angeles
Mickey Haller, Attorney • Jack McEvoy, Crime reporter - Denver

Alafair Burke	Richard Kunzmann	Rick Mofina
G M Ford	Thomas Laird	Reggie Nadelson
Scott Frost	Peter Leonard	Thomas Perry
Andrew Gross	Grant McKenzie	Ayelet Waldman

Victoria Connelly Chick Lit

Trisha Ashley	Sophie Kinsella	Carole Matthews
Harriet Evans	Jill Mansell	Alexandra Potter

C

Tom Connery 1944- Sea: Historical

is David Donachie 🏃 George Markham, Lieut of Marines - C18th

David Donachie	Alexander Kent	Patrick O'Brian
Iain Gale	Allan Mallinson	Dudley Pope

John Connolly 1968- Ire Crime: Psychological

🏃 Charlie 'Bird' Parker, Retired policeman - New England

Thomas H Cook	Joy Fielding	Jefferson Parker
Carol Anne Davis	Mo Hayder	Boris Starling
Jeffery Deaver	Jonathan Kellerman	Nick Stone
Robert Ellis	Dennis Lehane	P J Tracy

Joseph Connolly 1950- Humour

Kingsley Amis	Charles Higson	Geoff Nicholson
Guy Bellamy	Liz Jensen	Tom Sharpe
Jonathan Coe	Iain McDowall	Evelyn Waugh

Alexandra Connor Saga

Lancashire

Glenice Crossland	Anna Jacobs	Annie Murray
Margaret Dickinson	Joan Jonker	Kay Stephens
Jean Fullerton	Freda Lightfoot	Margaret Thornton
Ruth Hamilton		

Beverly Connor US Crime: Forensic

🏃 Diane Fallon, Forensic archaeologist } Georgia
Lindsay Chamberlain, Archaeologist

Lin Anderson	Jeffery Deaver	Tess Gerritsen
Patricia D Cornwell	Lisa Gardner	Kathy Reichs
Colin Cotterill		

John Connor

Crime: Police work - UK

also writes as Tom Winship

🕈 DC Karen Sharpe - West Yorkshire

Ann Cleeves	Lesley Horton	Priscilla Masters
Brian Cooper	Lynda La Plante	Ed O'Connor
R J Ellory	David Lawrence	Danuta Reah
Patricia Hall	Iain McDowall	Cath Staincliffe

Joseph Conrad   1857-1924

John Buchan	Ernest Hemingway	Jack London
James Hamilton-Paterson	Denis Johnson	Malcolm Lowry

C

Storm Constantine   1956-

Fantasy: Dark

Mary Gentle	Michael Moorcock	Judith Tarr
Tim Lebbon	Anne Rice	Freda Warrington
Juliet Marillier		

Simon Conway

Adventure/Thriller

🏆 CWA 2010

🕈 Jonah Said

Brett Battles	Lee Child	John Le Carré
Alex Berenson	Philip Kerr	Gerald Seymour

Gloria Cook

Historical

🕈 Harvey Series - Cornwall • Pengarron Series - Cornwall

Rosemary Aitken	Winston Graham	Susan Sallis
Iris Gower	Elizabeth Ann Hill	E V Thompson

Robin Cook   1940-   US

Adventure/Thriller: Medical

🕈 Dr Jack Stapleton & Dr Laurie Montgomery - New York

Paul Adam	Kathryn Fox	John Macken
Paul Carson	Leonard Goldberg	Michael Palmer
Michael Crichton	Ken McClure	Scott Sigler

Thomas H Cook   1947-   US

Crime: Psychological

🕈 Frank Clemons, PI

Robert Gregory Browne	Thomas Harris	John Sandford
Mary Higgins Clark	Michael Malone	Martin Cruz Smith
John Connolly	Chris Mooney	Betsy Tobin
R J Ellory		

Lesley Cookman

Crime: Amateur sleuth

🕈 Sarjeant Libby

Simon Brett	Carola Dunn	Betty Rowlands
Frances Brody	Catriona MacPherson	Jacqueline Winspear
Barbara Cleverly		

Catherine Cookson   1906-1998   Saga

also wrote as Catherine Marchant   ♁ Mary Ann Shaughnessy • Tilly Trotter • Bill Bailey
NE England

Aileen Armitage	Tania Crosse	Denise Robertson
Rita Bradshaw	Rosie Goodwin	Grace Thompson
Benita Brown	Una Horne	Janet MacLeod Trotter
Irene Carr	Sheila Newberry	Annie Wilkinson

Stephen Coonts   1946-   US   Adventure/Thriller

also writes jointly with Jim DeFelice   ♁ Rear Admiral Jake Grafton, Naval pilot
& Tommy Carmellini, ex-Burglar now CIA operative

Geoffrey Archer	Vince Flynn	Chris Mooney
Jeffrey Archer	David Hagberg	Matthew Reilly
James Barrington	Richard Herman	Julian Jay Savarin

C

Glenn Cooper   US   Adventure/Thriller

Sam Bourne	Raymond Khoury	Scott Mariani
Dan Brown	Tom Knox	James Rollins
John Case		

Jilly Cooper   ⌢   1937-   Glitz & Glamour

Louise Bagshawe	Olivia Darling	Christina Jones
Tilly Bagshawe	Judith Gould	Lesley Pearse
Celia Brayfield	Veronica Henry	Fiona Walker
Jo Carnegie	Rachel Johnson	

Louise Cooper   ⌢   ☺   1952-2009   Fantasy: Epic

Jean M Auel	Robert Jordan	Melanie Rawn
Eoin Colfer	L E Modesitt Jr	Janny Wurts
Barbara Hambly	Michael Moorcock	

Natasha Cooper   1951-   Crime: Amateur sleuth

also writes as Clare Layton, Kate Hatfield,
N J Cooper; is Daphne Wright   ♁ Willow King, Civil servant ⎫
Trish Maguire, Barrister ⎬ London
Karen Taylor, Forensic psychologist ⎭

Agatha Christie	Susan B Kelly	Veronica Stallwood
Frances Fyfield	Betty Rowlands	Aline Templeton
Joyce Holms	Catherine Sampson	Leslie Thomas

Michael Cordy   Adventure/Thriller

Steve Berry	Michael Crichton	Chris Kuzneski
Sam Bourne	Daniel Easterman	Bill Napier
Dan Brown	Philip Kerr	Douglas Preston
John Case	Raymond Khoury	James Rollins

Vena Cork — Adventure/Thriller: Psychological

✦ Rosa Thorn, Amateur sleuth

Elizabeth Corley	P D James	Sarah Rayne
Joanna Hines	Julie Parsons	Karen Rose

Elizabeth Corley — Crime: Police work - UK

✦ DCI Andrew Fenwick - Sussex

Ingrid Black	Vena Cork	Karen Rose
Victoria Blake	Val McDermid	Claire Seeber
Alice Blanchard	Grace Monroe	Paullina Simons

Bernard Cornwell ◡ 1944- — Historical

also writes as Susannah Kells ✦ Grail Quest Series - C14th • Alfred the Great - C9th
King Arthur - C6th

Christian Cameron	Giles Kristian	Tim Severin
Tom Harper	Robert Low	Pip Vaughan-Hughes
M K Hume	William Napier	Jack Whyte
Douglas Jackson	Scott Oden	Robyn Young

◡ — War: Historical

✦ Richard Sharpe - Napoleonic Wars • Nathaniel Starbuck - American Civil War

G S Beard	C C Humphreys	Steven Pressfield
Roger Carpenter	Garry Kilworth	Patrick Rambaud
Iain Gale	Sam Llewellyn	Edward Rutherfurd
Richard Howard	Allan Mallinson	John Wilcox

Patricia D Cornwell ◡ 1956- US — Crime: Forensic

⚑ CWA 1990 & 1993   ✦ Kay Scarpetta, Pathologist ⎫ Virginia
Judy Hammer & Andy Brazil, State Police ⎭
Winston Garano

Lin Anderson	Kathryn Fox	Nigel McCrery
Simon Beckett	Leonard Goldberg	Jonathan Nasaw
Beverly Connor	Iris Johansen	P J Parrish
Colin Cotterill	Keith McCarthy	Kathy Reichs

Peter Corris 1942- Aus — Crime: PI

✦ Cliff Hardy - Sydney • Richard Browning • Ray Crawley

Robert G Barrett	Carl Hiaasen	Peter Temple
Raymond Chandler	Gabrielle Lord	Robert Wilson
Robert Crais	Elliot Perlman	

Jane Costello — Chick Lit

is Jane Wolstenholme

Katie Agnew	Lisa Jewell	Jill Mansell
Harriet Evans	Milly Johnson	Carole Matthews
Emily Giffin	Lindsey Kelk	Adele Parks
Linda Green	Holly McQueen	Sue Welfare

F G Cottam   1957-   Crime: Psychological

is Francis Cottam

Carol Goodman   Adam Nevill   Sarah Waters
John Harwood   Phil Rickman   Gillian White
Martin Malone

Francis Cottam   1957-   War: Modern

also writes as F G Cottam

Frank Barnard   Andrew Greig   Derek Robinson
Tim Binding   David L Robbins   Patrick Bishop
Peter Ho Davies

C

Colin Cotterill   1952-   Crime: Forensic

♛ CWA 2009   ⚓ Dr Siri Paiboun, Coroner - Laos • Jimm Juree, Crime reporter - Thailand

Lin Anderson   Garry Disher   Alexander McCall Smith
John Burdett   Nicholas Drayson   Pierre Magnan
Beverly Connor   Kathryn Fox   Peter May
Patricia D Cornwell   Luiz Alfredo Garcia-Roza Nury Vittachi

Jack Coughlin   1966-   US   Adventure/Thriller

⚓ Kyle Swanson, Gunnery sniper

James Barrington   Stephen Hunter   Andy McNab
Alex Berenson   Matt Lynn   Chris Ryan
Tom Clancy

Douglas Coupland   ✍   1961-   Can

Iain Banks   Will Ferguson   Ben Richards
Don DeLillo   Alex Garland   Scarlett Thomas
Bret Easton Ellis   Chuck Palahniuk   Rupert Thomson

Dilly Court   Saga

Lyn Andrews   Leah Fleming   Anna Jacobs
Anne Baker   Jess Foley   Catherine King
Benita Brown   Jean Fullerton   Kitty Neale
Tania Crosse   Rosie Harris   Janet Tanner

Bryce Courtenay   1933-   Aus   Adventure/Thriller

Nick Brownlee   Beverley Harper   Wilbur Smith
Frank Coates   Amin Maalouf   Eric Van Lustbader
Ken Follett   Malla Nunn   Peter Watt
Diana Gabaldon

Go to back for lists of
Pseudonyms • Authors by Genre • Characters and Series • Environments
Prize Winners • Classic Authors • Crossover Authors • Further Reading • Websites

Josephine Cox 1941- Saga

also writes as Jane Brindle

Rose Boucheron	Katie Flynn	Kitty Neale
Rita Bradshaw	Sara Fraser	Joan O'Neill
Tania Crosse	Rosie Goodwin	Wendy Robertson
Leah Fleming	Ruth Hamilton	Annie Wilkinson

Harold Coyle 1952- US Adventure/Thriller

Campbell Armstrong	Jack Higgins	Douglas Preston
Clive Cussler	Stephen Leather	Matthew Reilly
W E B Griffin	Andy McDermott	Craig Thomas

Jim Crace 1946-

🏆 Guardian 1986   Higham 1986   Whitbread 1986 & 1997   Holtby 1994

André Brink	Alistair MacLeod	Geoff Ryman
E L Doctorow	Yann Martel	Rupert Thomson
Damon Galgut	David Mitchell	Barry Unsworth

Amanda Craig 1959- Aga Saga

Domenica de Rosa	Laurie Graham	Nicky Pellegrino
Janice Galloway	A L Kennedy	Amanda Prantera
Jane Gardam	Allison Pearson	Barbara Trapido

Maggie Craig Sco Saga

Scotland

Tania Crosse	Evelyn Hood	Jessica Stirling
Doris Davidson	Betty McInnes	Reay Tannahill
Margaret Thomson Davis	Eileen Ramsay	Mary Withall
Meg Henderson		

Robert Crais 1953- US Crime: PI

🏃 Elvis Cole - Los Angeles • Joe Pike - Los Angeles

Jeff Abbott	G M Ford	Robert B Parker
Harlan Coben	Scott Frost	Theresa Schwegel
Jodi Compton	Chuck Hogan	Richard Stark
Peter Corris	Reggie Nadelson	Don Winslow

Megan Crane US Chick Lit

Jessica Adams	Emily Giffin	Paige Toon
Meg Cabot	Alexandra Potter	Madeleine Wickham
Harriet Evans		

Adam Creed Crime: Police work - UK

🏃 DI Will 'Staffe' Wagstaffe - London

Stephen Booth	Alex Gray	Mark Pearson
Nicci French	Camilla Läckberg	Neil White

C

Candida Crewe   1964-

Kim Edwards	Alice Hoffman	Deborah Moggach
Kate Grenville	Hilary Mantel	Anne Tyler

Michael Crichton   1942-2008   US

also wrote as Jeffrey Hudson, John Lange

Dan Brown	Thomas Harris	Michael Palmer
Robin Cook	Ken McClure	Douglas Preston
Michael Cordy	Rick Mofina	Kim Stanley Robinson
William Gibson	Richard Morgan	Scott Sigler

Deborah Crombie   1952-   US   Crime: Police work - UK

DS Duncan Kincaid & DI Gemma James - London

Jane Adams	Margaret Duffy	Cynthia Harrod-Eagles
Rennie Airth	Elena Forbes	Susan Hill
Jo Bannister	Paula Gosling	Priscilla Masters
Chris Collett	Martha Grimes	R D Wingfield

Justin Cronin   1962-   US   Paranormal

Lara Adrian	Cassandra Clare	Stephen King
Patricia Briggs	Lori Handeland	Michelle Rowen

Neil Cross   1969-

Mark Haddon	Tim Lott	Lionel Shriver
Sarah Hall	Julie Parsons	Matt Thorne
Mick Jackson	Tony Parsons	

Tania Crosse   Saga

Anne Baker	Dilly Court	Maggie Craig
Anne Bennett	Josephine Cox	Katie Flynn
Catherine Cookson		

Glenice Crossland   Saga

Aileen Armitage	Pamela Evans	Annie Groves
Alexandra Connor	Katie Flynn	Freda Lightfoot
Margaret Dickinson	June Francis	Margaret Thornton

James Crumley   1939-2008   US   Crime: PI

🏆 CWA 2002   C W Sughrue - Texas • Milo Milodragovitch - Montana

James Lee Burke	Ross Macdonald	Boston Teran
James Ellroy	George P Pelecanos	Jim Thompson
Robert Ferrigno	Jason Starr	

may be suitable for young adults

Charles Cumming　1971-　Sco　　　　Adventure/Thriller

🏃 Alec Milius - Spy

Louis Bayard	Juan Gómez-Jurado	E V Seymour
Alex Dryden	David Ignatius	Daniel Silva
Barry Eisler	Nick McDonell	Martin Cruz Smith
Alan Furst	Henry Porter	Robert Wilson

Michael Cunningham　🔊　1952-　US

🏆 Pulitzer 1999

Michael Arditti	Richard Ford	Sam Lipsyte
Michael Chabon	Jonathan Franzen	Tim O'Brien
Michael Collins	Alan Hollinghurst	Jonathan Tropper
Helen Dunmore		

Clare Curzon　1922-　　　　Crime: Police work - UK

also writes as Rhona Petrie;　🏃 Supt Mike Yeadings & DS Angus Mott - Thames Valley
is Marie Buchanan　　　　　　　　　Lucy Sedgwick - Early C20th England

M C Beaton	Caroline Graham	Elizabeth Peters
Rhys Bowen	Patricia Hall	Dorothy Simpson
Martin Edwards	Veronica Heley	

Rachel Cusk　1967-

🏆 S Maugham 1998　　Whitbread 1993

Rachel Billington	Jill Dawson	Tessa Hadley
Liz Byrski	Anne Fine	Prue Leith
Marika Cobbold	Esther Freud	Hilary Mantel

Clive Cussler　🔊　1931-　US　　　　Adventure/Thriller

also writes jointly with Grant Blackwood,　🏃 Dirk Pitt • Kurt Austin • Numa Files Series
Dirk Cussler, Craig Dirgo, Jack Du Brul,　Oregon Files Series • Isaac Bell, PI - early C20th
Paul Kemprecos, Justin Scott　　　　　　　　　　　　　　　　　Fargo Series

Brett Battles	Tom Grace	Julian Jay Savarin
Ted Bell	David Hagberg	Justin Scott
Harold Coyle	Andy McDermott	Brad Thor
Duncan Falconer	James Pattinson	James Twining

Judith Cutler　1946-　　　　Crime: Police work - UK

🏃 Sophie Rivers, Lecturer - Birmingham • DS Kate Power - Birmingham
DS Frances Harman - Kent • Lina Townend, Antiques Dealer

Paul Charles	Priscilla Masters	Catherine Sampson
Ann Cleeves	Rose Melikan	Michelle Spring
Martin Edwards	Nick Oldham	Cath Staincliffe
Hope McIntyre	Barrie Roberts	Stella Whitelaw

C

Matthew D'Ancona 1968-

Kate Atkinson	Sophie Hannah	Mark Mills
Simon Beckett	Natsuo Kirino	Toni Morrison

Janet Dailey 1944- US Saga

✗ Calder Family

Jayne Ann Krentz	Nora Roberts	LaVyrle Spencer
Joan Medlicott	Judith Saxton	Barbara Wood
Belva Plain	Anne Rivers Siddons	

Elizabeth Daish Saga

✗ Emma - London • Coppins Bridge Series - Isle of Wight

Catrin Collier	Harriet Hudson	Sally Stewart
Elizabeth Darrell	Joan Jonker	Sally Worboyes
Lilian Harry		

D

Olivia Darling 1977- Glitz & Glamour

Katie Agnew	Jackie Collins	Danielle Steel
Louise Bagshawe	Jilly Cooper	Lulu Taylor
Tilly Bagshawe		

Elizabeth Darrell Historical Romance

also writes as Emma Drummond ✗ Sheridan Family

Anne Barbour	Marion Chesney	Amanda Quick
Joy Chambers	Elizabeth Daish	

War: Modern

✗ Max Rydal & Tom Black - Royal Military Police

Frank Barnard	James Holland	Alan Savage
David Fiddimore	David L Robbins	Guy Walters

Cecilia Dart-Thornton Aus Fantasy: Myth

Marion Zimmer Bradley	Robin Hobb	Juliet Marillier
James Clemens	Katharine Kerr	Caiseal Mor
Amanda Hemingway	Tanith Lee	J R R Tolkien

Emma Darwin Historical: C18th & C19th

Tracy Chevalier	Kathleen Kent	Fidelis Morgan
Erica James	Katharine McMahon	Kate Morton

Doris Davidson 1922-2012 Sco Saga

Scotland

Maggie Craig	Gwen Kirkwood	Frances Paige
Margaret Thomson Davis	Betty McInnes	Eileen Ramsay
Elizabeth Elgin	Elisabeth McNeill	Jessica Stirling
Harriet Evans		

Mary Janice Davidson ⌒ 1969- US Paranormal

🕴 Betsy Taylor, Vampire

Lara Adrian	Christine Feehan	Sherrilyn Kenyon
Kelley Armstrong	Lori Handeland	Sara Reinke
Keri Arthur	Tanya Huff	J R Ward

Caitlin Davies

Lucy Diamond	Barbara &	Deborah Lawrenson
Margaret Forster	Stephanie Keating	Anna Quindlen
Susanna Kearsley		

Katharine Davies

🏆 Romantic 2005

Margaret Forster	Alice Hoffman	Anna Jacobs
Philippa Gregory	Angela Huth	Joyce Carol Oates
Cynthia Harrod-Eagles		

Linda Davies 1963- Adventure/Thriller: Legal/financial

🕴 Sarah Jensen, City trader

John Grisham	Mark Mills	Michael Ridpath
Craig Holden	Carol O'Connell	Stella Rimington
Brad Meltzer	Perri O'Shaughnessy	

Martin Davies Historical

Geraldine Brooks	Elizabeth Edmondson	Nicole Krauss
Cassandra Clark	Dave Eggers	Iain Pears

Peter Ho Davies 1966- Wales

🏆 JLR 1998

David Baddiel	Sebastian Faulks	Owen Sheers
Sebastian Barry	Andrew Greig	Lionel Shriver
Francis Cottam	Ian McEwan	Mark Slouka
Murray Davies		

Anna Davis

Susannah Bates	Harriet Evans	Kathleen Tessaro
Rebecca Dean	Sadie Jones	Lauren Weisberger

Lindsey Davis ⌒ 1949- Crime: Historical - Ancient

🏆 Authors 1989   CWA 1999 & 2011   🕴 Marcus Didius Falco - Ancient Rome

Richard Blake	Giulio Leoni	Steven Saylor
Margaret Doody	John Maddox Roberts	Harry Sidebottom
R S Downie	Rosemary Rowe	Marilyn Todd
Ben Kane	Laura Joh Rowland	David Wishart

Margaret Thomson Davis   1926-   Sco   Saga

🚶 Andrina McPherson • Monkton Family • Breadmakers Series
Scotland

Maggie Bennett	Harriet Evans	Alexandra Raife
Maggie Craig	Christine Marion Fraser	Eileen Ramsay
Doris Davidson	Meg Henderson	Jessica Stirling

Jill Dawson   1962-

Liz Byrski	Rachel Cusk	Rani Manicka
Margaret	Shirley Hazzard	Deborah Moggach
Cezair-Thompson	Zoë Heller	Anne Tyler
Holly Chamberlin	Liz Jensen	Salley Vickers

Lucy Dawson   Chick Lit

D

Trisha Ashley	Debbie Macomber	Tess Stimson
India Knight	Clare Naylor	Paige Toon
Julia Llewellyn	Adele Parks	Jennifer Weiner

Louis de Bernières   🕿   1954-

🏆 Commonwealth 1995

Russell Banks	Victoria Hislop	David Mitchell
Pat Barker	Panos Karnezis	Orhan Pamuk
Tim Binding	Yann Martel	Nicholas Shakespeare
James Hamilton-Paterson	James Meek	Mario Vargas Llosa

Mark de Castrique   US   Crime: Amateur sleuth

🚶 Barry Clayton, Undertaker - Charlotte, North Carolina • Buryin' Barry Mystery Series
Sam Blackman - North Carolina

James Lee Burke	Jesse Kellerman	Michael Malone
Tony Hillerman	Dennis Lehane	Margaret Maron

Michelle de Kretser   1958-   Aus

🏆 Encore 2004

Arthur Golden	Daniel Mason	Michael Ondaatje
Romesh Gunesekera	Timothy Mo	Jennie Rooney
Kazuo Ishiguro	Haruki Murakami	Salman Rushdie

Charles de Lint   1951-   Can   Fantasy: Contemporary

also writes as Samuel M Key

Mark Chadbourn	Robert Holdstock	Juliet Marillier
Sara Douglass	Guy Gavriel Kay	Caiseal Mor
Neil Gaiman	Morgan Llywelyn	Tim Powers

Domenica de Rosa   1963-   Aga Saga

Amanda Craig	Tamara McKinley	Tim Parks
Elizabeth Edmondson	Santa Montefiore	Nicky Pellegrino

Louise Dean
🏆 Betty Trask 2004

Ronald Frame	Ann Patchett	Rose Tremain
Patrick Gale	Nicholas Shakespeare	Jane Urquhart

Rebecca Dean
Historical

is Margaret Pemberton

Barbara Taylor Bradford	Ann Hood	Lesley Lokko
Anna Davis	Kate Jacobs	Tasmina Perry
Kate Furnivall	Judith Lennox	Penny Vincenzi
Laurie Graham		

Stephen Deas
Fantasy: Epic

R Scott Bakker	Robin Hobb	Karen Miller
Lian Hearn	Anne McCaffrey	Chris Wooding

Jeffery Deaver 1950- US
Crime: Forensic

🏆 TGR 2001
CWA 2004

🕺 Lincoln Rhyme, Forensic scientist
Rune, Film maker - New York • John Pellam, Film location scout
Kathryn Dance, Interrogator • James Bond

John Connolly	Michael Marshall	Jason Pinter
Beverly Connor	Jonathan Nasaw	Paullina Simons
Brian Freeman	Jean François Parot	Lee Weeks
John Katzenbach	Ridley Pearson	Stephen White

Len Deighton 1929-
Adventure/Thriller

🕺 Bernard Samson • Harry Palmer

Paul Adam	David Downing	John Lawton
Ted Allbeury	Clive Egleton	Stella Rimington
Michael Asher	Alexander Fullerton	Nigel West
Charles Cumming		

Frank Delaney 1942- Ire
Saga

also writes as Francis Bryan

🕺 Kane Family

Rose Doyle	D M Purcell	William Trevor
Mary A Larkin	Edward Rutherfurd	Jonathan Tropper
Joan O'Neill	Liz Ryan	

Don DeLillo 1936- US

also writes as Cleo Birdwell

🏆 Irish Times 1989

Saul Bellow	Ben Faccini	Chuck Palahniuk
Dave Eggers	Jonathan Safran Foer	Richard Powers
Brent Easton Ellis	Denis Johnson	Thomas Pynchon
Nathan Englander	Joe Meno	Tobias Wolff

James Delingpole 1965- Lad Lit: Humour

♰ Lt Dick Coward & Sgt Tom Price - WW2

George Macdonald Fraser	James Holland	John O'Farrell
Iain Gale	Nick Hornby	Mark Watson
John Harding	Mil Millington	

Barbara Delinsky 1945- US Aga Saga

also writes as Billy Douglass, Bonnie Drake

Celia Brayfield	Penny Jordan	Marcia Preston
Candace Bushnell	Judith McNaught	Luanne Rice
Therese Fowler	Una-Mary Parker	LaVyrle Spencer
Eileen Goudge	Belva Plain	Lisa Tucker

Nelson DeMille 1943- US Adventure/Thriller

D

also writes as Jack Cannon, Kurt Ladner, Brad Matthews   ♰ Det John Corey & Kate Mayfield

David Baldacci	Daniel Easterman	Tom Rob Smith
Suzanne Brockmann	Ken Follett	Wilbur Smith
Nick Brownlee	Robert Littell	James Webb
Stephen J Cannell	Stanley Pottinger	

Joolz Denby 1955-

♛ CWA 1998

Christopher Brookmyre	Tess Gerritsen	Karin Slaughter
Daphne Du Maurier	David Mitchell	Louise Tondeur

Jo Dereske 1947- US Crime: Amateur sleuth

♰ Miss Zukas, Librarian - Washington State

Nevada Barr	Paula Gosling	Ayelet Waldman
Stephen Donaldson	Hazel Holt	Don Winslow
Earlene Fowler	Jim Kelly	

Anita Desai 🌰 1937- Ind

Aravind Adiga	Amitav Ghosh	R K Narayan
Vikram Chandra	Ruth Prawer Jhabvala	Salman Rushdie
Chitra Banerjee Divakaruni	Amulya Malladi	Amy Tan

Kiran Desai 1971- Ind

♛ Betty Trask 1998   Man Booker 2006

Aravind Adiga	Kate Grenville	Vikram Seth
Nathacha Appanah	Helen Oyeyemi	Kamila Shamsie
James Fleming	Annie Proulx	Vikas Swarup
Amitav Ghosh	Arundhati Roy	Farahad Zama

🌰 may be suitable for young adults

57

Jude Deveraux 1947- US Glitz & Glamour

Sally Beauman
Marion Chesney
Lucy Diamond

Johanna Lindsey
Fern Michaels
Belva Plain

Nora Roberts
Danielle Steel

Isla Dewar Sco

Joan Barfoot
Mavis Cheek
Kate Fenton
Linda Gillard

Carole Matthews
Anna Maxted
Kate Muir

Maggie O'Farrell
Zoë Strachan
Lynne Truss

Colin Dexter 1930- Crime: Police work - UK

CWA 1979, 1981, 1989 & 1992   Theakston's 2012   DI Morse - Oxford

Robert Barnard
Paul Charles
Brian Cooper
Shamini Flint

Susan B Kelly
Iain McDowall
Guillermo Martinez
Häkan Nesser

Peter Robinson
Pauline Rowson
Fred Vargas
Jill Paton Walsh

Pete Dexter 1943- US

Russell Banks
Pat Conroy

Richard Ford
David Guterson

Cormac McCarthy
Jonathan Tropper

Anita Diamant 1951- US

Geraldine Brooks
Christie Dickason
Jenny Diski

Elisabeth Hyde
Alice Sebold
Salley Vickers

Susan Vreeland
Sarah Willis

Lucy Diamond Chick Lit

is Sue Mongredien

Nina Bell
Jude Deveraux
Wendy Holden

Jane Moore
Carmen Reid
Olivia Ryan

Arabella Weir
Deborah Wright

Sarah Diamond 1976- Crime: Psychological

Ingrid Black
Caroline Carver
Carol Anne Davis

Babs Horton
Julie Parsons
Sarah Rayne

Carol Smith
Gillian White
Laura Wilson

Michael Dibdin 1947-2007 Crime: Police work - Italy

CWA 1988 & 1990   Aurelio Zen

Gianrico Carofiglio
Dan Fesperman
Michele Giuttari
David Hewson
Donna Leon

Carlo Lucarelli
Manuel Vázquez
  Montalbán
Magdalen Nabb

Barbara Nadel
Jeffrey Siger
Olen Steinhauer
Ronald Tierney

Philip K Dick ⌒ 1928-82 US Science Fiction: Space and time

🏆 BSFA 1978

Poul Anderson
Isaac Asimov
J G Ballard
Robert A Heinlein

Todd McCaffrey
Michael Moorcock
Tim Powers
Christopher Priest

Adam Roberts
Kurt Vonnegut
John Wyndham

Christie Dickason 1942- US Historical: C17th

🚶 Francis Quoynt

Elizabeth Chadwick
Anita Diamant
Philippa Gregory

Edward Marston
Fidelis Morgan
Jean Plaidy

Edward Rutherfurd
Alison Weir

Eric Jerome Dickey 1961- US Adventure/Thriller

🚶 Gideon, Hit man

D

Lee Child
Harlan Coben

Meg Gardiner
Carol O'Connell

Robert B Parker
Dana Stabenow

David Dickinson Ire Crime: Historical - C20th

🚶 Lord Francis Powerscourt - Edwardian England

Rhys Bowen
Gyles Brandreth
John Buchan
Barbara Cleverly

Robin Paige
Anne Perry
Elizabeth Peters

David Pirie
Barrie Roberts
Imogen Robertson

Margaret Dickinson 1942- Saga

also writes as Everatt Jackson

🚶 Kate Hilton - Lincolnshire

Jessica Blair
Rita Bradshaw
Alexandra Connor
Glenice Crossland

Lilian Harry
Elizabeth Jeffrey
Jeannie Johnson
Joan Jonker

Mary Mackie
Sharon Owens
Linda Sole
T R Wilson

Miranda Dickinson US Chick Lit

Trisha Ashley
Lucy Dillon

Katie Fforde
Lindsey Kelk

Carole Matthews
Amy Silver

William Dietrich 1951- US Historical: C18th

🚶 Ethan Gage, Sharpshooter - C18th & C19th

Will Adams
Dan Brown

George Macdonald Fraser
Raymond Khoury

Kate Mosse
Matthew Reilly

Annabel Dilke Aga Saga

Diana Appleyard
Elizabeth Edmondson
Rachel Hore

Elizabeth Jane Howard
Sara MacDonald
Rosamunde Pilcher

Nicola Thorne
Penny Vincenzi
Ann Widdecombe

Des Dillon 1960- Sco

| Anne Donovan | Laura Marney | Alan Warner |
| James Kelman | Alan Spence | Irvine Welsh |

Lucy Dillon 1974- Chick Lit

♈ Romantic 2010

Jenny Colgan	Lindsey Kelk	Melanie Rose
Sarah Duncan	Lorna Landvik	Julia Williams
Harriet Evans	Kate Long	

Garry Disher 1949- Aus Crime: Police work - Australia

🏃 Insp Hal Challis - Victoria

| Mark Billingham | Val McDermid | Martin Cruz Smith |
| Colin Cotterill | Shane Maloney | Peter Temple |

D

Jenny Diski 1947-

Nicola Barker	Maggie Gee	Frances Hegarty
Anita Diamant	Lesley Glaister	Joyce Carol Oates
David Flusfeder		

Michael Dobbs 1948-

🏃 Tom Goodfellow, MP • Francis Urquhart Trilogy, MP • Winston Churchill, MP

Jeffrey Archer	Philip Hensher	Quintin Jardine
Gavin Esler	Sandra Howard	Allan Massie
Robert Harris		

Cory Doctorow 🌈 ☺ 1971- Can Science Fiction: Near future

| Greg Egan | William Gibson | Neal Stephenson |
| Neil Gaiman | John Scalzi | Charles Stross |

E L Doctorow 1931- US

Paul Auster	F Scott Fitzgerald	Hari Kunzru
Geraldine Brooks	Craig Holden	John Updike
Jim Crace	Thomas Keneally	Willy Vlautin

Edward Docx 1972-

♈ Faber 2007

| Nicola Barker | Jhumpa Lahiri | Adam Thirlwell |
| Howard Jacobson | Philip Roth | A N Wilson |

Go to back for lists of
Pseudonyms • Authors by Genre • Characters and Series • Environments
Prize Winners • Classic Authors • Crossover Authors • Further Reading • Websites

Paul Doherty
1946-   **Crime: Historical**

also writes as Vanessa Alexander, Anna Apostolou, Michael Clynes, P C Doherty, Ann Dukthas, C L Grace, Paul Harding

🏃 Alexander the Great & Telamon, Physician - C3rd BC Greece
Amerotke - Ancient Egypt
Sir Hugh Corbett & Brother Athelstan - C13th England
Mathilde of Westminster, Physician - C14th England
The Templars - C11th • Claudia, Spy - Ancient Rome

Simon Beaufort	Susanna Gregory	Simon Levack
Alys Clare	Michael Jecks	The Medieval Murderers
Cassandra Clark	Ben Kane	Ellis Peters
R S Downie	Bernard Knight	Lynda S Robinson

David Donachie
1944-   Sco   **Sea: Historical**

also writes as Tom Connery, Jack Ludlow

🏃 Harry Ludlow, Privateer
John Pearce - Napoleonic Wars

G S Beard	Alexander Kent	Dudley Pope
Tom Connery	James L Nelson	Peter Smalley
John Drake	Patrick O'Brian	Julian Stockwin
C S Forester		

Angus Donald
1965-   **Historical: C13th**

🏃 Robin Hood - Crusades

Elizabeth Chadwick	Tom Harper	Jack Ludlow
Bernard Cornwell	Robert Low	Adam Thorpe

Stephen Donaldson
☎   1947-   US   **Crime: PI**

also writes as Stephen R Donaldson, Reed Stephens

🏃 Ginny Fistoulari & Mick Axbrewder

Jo Dereske	Carolyn G Hart	Chuck Palahniuk
James Ellroy	Walter Mosley	Ayelet Waldman

☎   **Fantasy: Epic**

🏃 Thomas Covenant

Joe Abercrombie	Ian C Esslemont	Scott Lynch
James Barclay	Ian Irvine	Karen Miller
Mark Chadbourn	Paul Kearney	Robert Newcomb
Steven Erikson	Tom Lloyd	Sean Russell

Sara Donati
           Historical

is Rosina Lippi

Daphne Du Maurier	Kathleen O'Neal Gear	Victoria Holt
Barbara Erskine	Susan Hill	Kate Mosse
Diana Gabaldon		

Stephen Done
           Crime: Historical - C20th

🏃 DI Charles Vignoles - 1940s Railways

James Benn	Barbara Nadel	Andrew Taylor
Gordon Ferris	Craig Russell	Nicola Upson
Edward Marston	Sara Sheridan	Laura Wilson
Andrew Martin		

Jennifer Donnelly ☺ 1963- US Historical

Debra Adelaide	Ken Follett	Kate Morton
Barbara Taylor Bradford	David Guterson	Jojo Moyes
Elizabeth Chadwick	Jane Hamilton	Ben Richards
Sarah Challis	Haven Kimmel	Meg Rosoff

Emma Donoghue 1969- Ire

Gil Adamson	Anne Haverty	Alice Walker
Jennifer Egan	Sarah Kate Lynch	Sarah Waters
Allegra Goodman	Michèle Roberts	Jeanette Winterson
Joanne Harris	Betsy Tobin	

Anne Donovan Sco

Des Dillon	Laura Marney	Zoë Strachan
Suzannah Dunn	Alan Spence	

Tim Dorsey 1961- US Crime: Humour

🏃 Serge Storms - Florida

Linwood Barclay	Joe R Lansdale	Malcolm Pryce
Kinky Friedman	Elmore Leonard	Donald Westlake
Carl Hiaasen	Douglas Lindsay	

Anne Doughty Ire Saga

🏃 Hamilton Family - 'Ballydown', Ireland

Judy Astley	Victoria Clayton	Kate Fenton
Maeve Binchy	Marita Conlon-McKenna	Kate Long
Amanda Brookfield	Patricia Fawcett	Joanna Trollope

Louise Doughty

Raffaella Barker	Lesley Glaister	Jane Wenham-Jones
Carol Birch	Caroline Graham	Meg Wolitzer
Janet Evanovich	Marge Piercy	Margaret Yorke

Louise Douglas

Daphne Du Maurier	Esther Freud	Julie Myerson
Elizabeth Edmondson	Emily Giffin	Alice Sebold

Sara Douglass 1957-2011 Aus Fantasy: Epic

Carol Berg	Charles de Lint	R A Salvatore
Chaz Brenchley	Jennifer Fallon	Harry Turtledove
Trudi Canavan	Terry Goodkind	Freda Warrington
Jacqueline Carey	Gwyneth Jones	

☺ also writes children's books

Clare Dowling   1968-   Ire   Chick Lit

Harriet Evans	Marian Keyes	Sheila O'Flanagan
Melissa Hill	Shari Low	Sarah Webb
Cathy Kelly	Monica McInerney	

R S Downie   Crime: Historical - Ancient

is Ruth S Downie   ⚥ Gaius Petreius Ruso & Tilla, Army doctor & slave girl - Roman Empire

Lindsey Davis	Allan Massie	Paul Waters
Paul Doherty	Steven Saylor	David Wishart
Ariana Franklin	Simon Scarrow	

David Downing   Adventure/Thriller: Historical

⚥ John Russell, Journalist - Germany WW2

Len Deighton	Jack Higgins	Alistair MacLean
Ken Follett	Philip Kerr	Henry Porter
Alexander Fullerton	John Le Carré	Robert Wilson
Alan Furst		

D

Arthur Conan Doyle   ⌒   1859-1930   Crime: PI

⚥ Sherlock Holmes & Dr John Watson

Gyles Brandreth	Laurie R King	David Pirie
Kenneth Cameron	Alanna Knight	Norman Russell
David Stuart Davies	Catriona McPherson	June Thomson
Peter J Heck	Anne Perry	M J Trow

Roddy Doyle   ⌒   ☺   1958-   Ire   Humour

🏆 Booker 1993   ⚥ Henry Smart

Leila Aboulela	Stephen Fry	Magnus Mills
Chris Binchy	Niall Griffiths	David Nobbs
Dermot Bolger	Claire Kilroy	Joseph O'Connor
Catherine Dunne	Patrick McCabe	Irvine Welsh

Rose Doyle   Ire   Aga Saga

Maeve Binchy	Jennifer Johnston	D M Purcell
Marita Conlon-McKenna	Mary A Larkin	Elizabeth Wrenn
Frank Delaney	Joan O'Neill	

Margaret Drabble   ⌒   1939-

Nadeem Aslam	A S Byatt	Frederic Raphael
Joan Barfoot	Blake Morrison	Bernice Rubens
Melvyn Bragg	Ann Patchett	Graham Swift

Nick Drake   1961-   Crime: HIstorical - Ancient

⚥ Rai Rahotep, Chief Detective - Thebes, Ancient Egypt

Philip Boast	Lauren Haney	Lynda S Robinson
Margaret Doody	John Maddox Roberts	Marilyn Todd

Nicholas Drayson

William Boyd
Colin Cotterill
Catriona McPherson
Magnus Mills
Owen Sheers
Alexander McCall Smith
Farahad Zama

Robert Drewe 1943- Aus

Peter Carey
Janette Turner Hospital
Thomas Keneally
Matthew Kneale
David Malouf
Elliot Perlman
Peter Watt
Tim Winton

Alex Dryden Adventure/Thriller

Finn, Spy - Russia

Charles Cumming
Dan Fesperman
Joseph Finder
Brian Freemantle
Michael Harvey
Olen Steinhauer

D

Daphne Du Maurier 1907-89

Jo Baker
Joolz Denby
Sara Donati
John Harwood
Susan Hill
Joanna Hines
Susan Howatch
Susanna Kearsley
Elizabeth Kostova
Rose Melikan
Mark Mills
Adam Nevill

Brendan Dubois US Adventure/Thriller

Lewis Cole

Murray Davies
Robert Harris
Robert Ludlum
Kyle Mills
James Siegel
Daniel Silva

Jessica Duchen Aga Saga

Marika Cobbold
Sandra Howard
Elisabeth Hyde
Sarah Jackman
Santa Montefiore
Joanna Trollope

Margaret Duffy 1942- Crime: Police work - UK

Insp James Carrick • Ingrid Langley, Novelist
Patrick Gillard • Joanna Mackenzie, PI
} Bath

M C Beaton
Deborah Crombie
Caroline Graham
Stuart MacBride
Adrian Magson
Priscilla Masters

Stella Duffy 1963- NZ Crime: PI

Saz Martin - London

Linda Barnes
Sparkle Hayter
Lauren Henderson
Claire McNab
Marcia Muller
Ayelet Waldman

Sarah Dunant 1950- Historical

Tracy Chevalier
Umberto Eco
Marina Fiorato
Philippa Gregory
Joanne Harris
Michelle Lovric
Rose Tremain
Salley Vickers
Susan Vreeland

Glen Duncan   1965-

Tobias Hill	A L Kennedy	Tim Pears
Nick Hornby	Andrew O'Hagan	Will Self
Denis Johnson		

Sarah Duncan   Mature Chick Lit

Lucy Cavendish	Jane Green	Melanie Rose
Lucy Dillon	Sarah May	Joanna Trollope
Harriet Evans	Imogen Parker	Isabel Wolff
Katie Fforde		

Patricia Duncker   1951-
♛ McKitterick 1997

A S Byatt	Graham Greene	Salley Vickers
Holly Chamberlin	Manju Kapur	Jeanette Winterson
William Golding	Pauline Melville	

D

Anne Dunlop   1969-   Ire   Chick Lit

Sherry Ashworth	Sarah Mason	Kathleen Tessaro
Christina Jones	Anita Notaro	Sarah Webb
Monica McInerney	Carmen Reid	Jane Wenham-Jones

Helen Dunmore   ◠ ☺   1952-
♛ McKitterick 1994   Orange 1996

Lisa Appignanesi	Suzannah Dunn	Nell Leyshon
Carol Birch	Nikki Gemmell	James Meek
Louise Candlish	Linda Gillard	Helen Simpson
Michael Cunningham	Panos Karnezis	Gillian White

Alan Dunn   Crime: Hardboiled
⚸ Billy Oliphant, Security consultant - NE England

Massimo Carlotto	Ken McCoy	Catherine Sampson
Robert Edric	Mike Ripley	Martyn Waites
Brian Freeman		

Carola Dunn   1946-   Crime: Historical - C20th
⚸ Daisy Dalrymple, Journalist - 1920s

Gilbert Adair	Rhys Bowen	Catriona McPherson
Rennie Airth	Kenneth Cameron	Robin Paige
Conrad Allen	Barbara Cleverly	Caro Peacock
Suzanne Arruda	Patricia Harwin	R T Raichev

Matt Dunn   Lad Lit

Mark Barrowcliffe	Mike Gayle	Mil Millington
Matt Beaumont	Nick Hornby	Tony Parsons
Paul Burke		

Suzannah Dunn 1963-

| Anne Donovan | Susan Fletcher | Rupert Thomson |
| Helen Dunmore | Esther Freud | Anne Tyler |

Historical: C16th

C W Gortner	Katie Hickman	Robin Maxwell
Posie Graeme-Evans	Jeanne Kalogridis	Jude Morgan
Philippa Gregory	Katharine McMahon	Alison Weir

Dorothy Dunnett 1923-2001 Sco Historical

also wrote as Dorothy Halliday   ⚐ Francis Crawford of Lymond - C15th England

Elizabeth Chadwick	Margaret Pemberton	Edward Rutherfurd
Margaret Elphinstone	Sharon Penman	Jane Stevenson
Posie Graeme-Evans	Jean Plaidy	Reay Tannahill
Robert Low	Julian Rathbone	Nigel Tranter

Daniel Easterman 1949- Adventure/Thriller

also writes as Jonathan Aycliffe; is Denis McEoin

Michael Asher	Lincoln Child	Jack Higgins
Tom Bradby	Michael Cordy	Amin Maalouf
John Case	Nelson DeMille	

Sam Eastland 1963- Crime: Police work - Russia

is Paul Watkins   ⚐ Insp Pekkala - 1950s Siberia

Charles Cumming	Andrey Kurkov	Tom Rob Smith
Elizabeth George	R N Morris	Olen Steinhauer
Philip Kerr		

Will Eaves 1967-

Julian Barnes	Penelope Fitzgerald	Iris Murdoch
William Boyd	John Lanchester	Edward St Aubyn
Justin Cartwright		

Marjorie Eccles 1927- Crime: Police work - UK

also writes as Judith Bordill, Jennifer Hyde   ⚐ DI Abigail Moon & Supt Gil Mayo - Midlands
DI Tom Richmonds - Yorkshire

David Armstrong	Pauline Bell	Elizabeth George
A C Baantjer	Chris Collett	Priscilla Masters
Jo Bannister	Geraldine Evans	Betty Rowlands

Umberto Eco 1932- It

Paulo Coelho	Andrew M Greeley	Arturo Perez-Reverte
Sarah Dunant	Amin Maalouf	Jill Paton Walsh
Jostein Gaarder	Orhan Pamuk	Carlos Ruiz Zafón
William Golding		

David Eddings ⌒ 1931-2009 US   Fantasy: Epic

also wrote jointly with Leigh Eddings

Sarah Ash	Ian Irvine	Mickey Zucker Reichert
David Bilsborough	Fiona McIntosh	Robert Silverberg
Mark Chadbourn	Stan Nicholls	Tad Williams
Elizabeth Haydon	Christopher Paolini	Sarah Zettel

Arabella Edge   Aus   Historical

A S Byatt	Maggie Gee	Rose Tremain
Sarah Dunant	Elizabeth Kostova	Susan Vreeland

Elizabeth Edmondson   Aga Saga

also writes as Elizabeth Aston; is Elizabeth Pewsey

Elizabeth Adler	Rachel Hore	Robin Pilcher
Domenica de Rosa	Christobel Kent	Marcia Willett
Annabel Dilke	Prue Leith	Elizabeth Wrenn
Julia Gregson	Sara MacDonald	

Robert Edric   1956-   Crime: PI

E

is Gary Edric Armitage   ⚐ Leo Rivers - Hull

Ken Bruen	Graham Hurley	Philip Kerr
Reg Gadney	Simon Kernick	Martyn Waites
Kerry Greenwood		

       Historical

🏆 Black 1985

Alan Dunn	James H Jackson	Tim Pears
Giles Foden	Chris Paling	Barry Unsworth

Kim Edwards   US

Diane Chamberlain	Victoria Hislop	Lori Lansens
Helen Garner	Linda Holeman	Prue Leith
Giselle Green	Sadie Jones	Valerie Martin
Kate Grenville	Nicole Krauss	Kate Morton

Martin Edwards   1955-   Crime: Amateur sleuth

⚐ Harry Devlin, Solicitor - Liverpool • DCI Hannah Scarlett - Lake District

Jeffrey Ashford	Kate Ellis	Ken McCoy
Clare Curzon	Bill James	M R D Meek
Judith Cutler	Jim Kelly	Barrie Roberts

Ruth Dudley Edwards   1944-   Ire   Crime: Amateur sleuth

⚐ Robert Amiss & Baroness Troutbeck

Simon Brett	Lis Howell	Tom Sharpe
Bartholomew Gill	M R D Meek	Jill Paton Walsh
Veronica Heley	Gwen Moffat	Patricia Wentworth

Imogen Edwards-Jones 1959-   Chick Lit

Louise Bagshawe	Jenny Colgan	Arabella Weir
Lynne Barrett-Lee	Melissa Hill	Jane Wenham-Jones
Candace Bushnell	Tina Reilly	

Ake Edwardson 1953- Swe   Crime: Police work - Sweden

♁ Erik Winter, Detective - Gothenburg

Karin Alvtegen	Matti Joensuu	Häkan Nesser
Anne Holt	Mari Jungstedt	Ruth Rendell
Arnaldur Indridason	Åsa Larsson	Yrsa Sigurdardottir
P D James	Stieg Larsson	Jan Costin Wagner

Greg Egan 1961- Aus   Science Fiction: Near future

Ben Bova	Ken MacLeod	Neal Stephenson
Jon Courtenay Grimwood	Robert Reed	Sean Williams
Ian McDonald	Nick Sagan	

Jennifer Egan 1962- US

🏆 Pulitzer 2011

Justin Cartwright	Jhumpa Lahiri	Edward St Aubyn
Emma Donoghue	Claire Messud	David Szalay
Allegra Goodman		

Tom Egeland 1959- Nor   Adventure/Thriller

Will Adams	Dan Brown	Kate Mosse
Steve Berry	Raymond Khoury	James Rollins

Dave Eggers 1970- US

Paul Auster	Jonathan Safran Foer	John Harding
Don DeLillo	Jonathan Franzen	Philip Roth
Ben Faccini		

Clive Egleton 🔗 1927-2006   Adventure/Thriller

also wrote as Patrick Blake, John Tarrant   ♁ Peter Ashton

Ted Allbeury	Len Deighton	Brian Freemantle
Alex Berenson	Colin Forbes	Gerald Seymour
Tom Bradby	Frederick Forsyth	

Thomas Eidson 1944- US

🏆 TGR 1995

Nicholas Evans	Larry McMurtry	Annie Proulx
Charles Frazier	Mark Mills	Jane Smiley
Kathleen O'Neal Gear	Stewart O'Nan	Jane Urquhart

E

Barry Eisler　1964-　US　　　　　　　　Adventure/Thriller

🏃 John Rain, Assassin

Brett Battles	Charles Cumming	Jefferson Parker
Ken Bruen	Ian Fleming	Robert Ryan
John Burdett	Mike Lawson	Olen Steinhauer
James Lee Burke	Andy McNab	

Elizabeth Elgin　　　　　　　　　　　　Saga

🏃 Sutton Family - Yorkshire

Charlotte Bingham	Doris Davidson	Wendy Robertson
Julia Bryant	Anna Jacobs	Susan Sallis
Helen Cannam	Beryl Matthews	Kay Stephens
Catrin Collier	Margaret Mayhew	June Tate

Kate Elliott　1958-　US　　　　　　　Fantasy: Epic

is Alis A Rasmussen

Ashok K Banker	Maggie Furey	Katharine Kerr
Terry Brooks	J V Jones	Holly Lisle
C J Cherryh	Paul Kearney	Elizabeth Moon
Jennifer Fallon		

Bret Easton Ellis　1964-　US

Douglas Coupland	Haruki Murakami	Will Self
Don De Lillo	Chuck Palahniuk	Peter Straub
Jay McInerney	Tim Parks	Tom Wolfe

David Ellis　US　　　　　　　　　Adventure/Thriller

Joseph Finder	John Grisham	Scott Turow
Sue Grafton	John Hart	Stephen White

Kate Ellis　1953-　　　　　　　Crime: Police work - UK

🏃 DS Wesley Peterson - West Country • DI Joe Plantagenet - 'Eborby', North Yorkshire

David Armstrong	Ann Cleeves	P D James
Jeffrey Ashford	Martin Edwards	Roy Lewis
Simon Brett	Aaron Elkins	R D Wingfield
W J Burley		

Robert Ellis　US　　　　　　　Crime: Police work - US

🏃 Det Lena Gamble - LAPD

John Connolly	Ed McBain	Thomas Perry
Andrew Gross	P D Martin	J D Robb
Jonathan Kellerman	James Patterson	Nick Stone

E

Go to back for lists of
Pseudonyms • Authors by Genre • Characters and Series • Environments
Prize Winners • Classic Authors • Crossover Authors • Further Reading • Websites

Harlan Ellison 1934- Science Fiction: Space and time

Brian W Aldiss
Poul Anderson
Greg Bear

Ray Bradbury
Joe Haldeman

Connie Willis
David Zindell

R J Ellory 1965- Crime: Psychological

♔ Theakston's 2010

John Connor
Thomas H Cook
Carol Anne Davis

Karin Fossum
Jim Kelly
Patrick Lennon

Jeff Lindsay
Andy Oakes
George P Pelecanos

James Ellroy 1948- US Crime: Hardboiled

♁ DS Lloyd Hopkins - Los Angeles

Megan Abbott
James Crumley
Stephen Donaldson
Loren D Estleman

John Hart
Stuart M Kaminsky
Chuck Palahniuk
Jason Starr

Jim Thompson
Joseph Wambaugh
John Williams
Edward Wright

E Margaret Elphinstone 1948- Sco Historical

Dorothy Dunnett
Barbara Erskine
Julie Garwood

Sandra Gulland
Matthew Kneale
Ursula K Le Guin

Margaret Pemberton
James Robertson
Rebecca Stott

Ben Elton 1959-

♔ CWA 1996

David Baddiel
Stephen Fry

Rob Grant
James Hawes

Charles Higson
Keith Waterhouse

Marina Endicott 1958- Can

Mary Lawson
Penelope Lively

Alice Munro
Carol Shields

Lionel Shriver
Anne Tyler

Leif Enger 1961- US

Kate Atkinson
Louise Erdrich
Nicholas Evans

Charles Frazier
Kent Haruf
Haven Kimmel

Jhumpa Lahiri
Adriana Trigiani
Carlos Ruiz Zafón

Anne Enright 1962- Ire

♔ Booker 2007   Encore 2001

Trezza Azzopardi
Andrea Barrett
Dermot Bolger
Anita Brookner

Maggie Gee
Jennifer Johnston
Edna O'Brien

Graham Swift
Gerard Woodward
Louisa Young

Louise Erdrich 1954- US

Isabel Allende	Chang-rae Lee	Annie Proulx
Michael Collins	Alison Lurie	Geoff Ryman
Leif Enger	Stewart O'Nan	Rebecca Wells
Barbara Kingsolver	Jayne Anne Phillips	

Steven Erikson 1959- Can   Fantasy: Epic

is Steve Rune Lundin

R Scott Bakker	Ian C Esslemont	John Marco
James Barclay	Raymond E Feist	Patrick Rothfuss
David Bilsborough	Jude Fisher	Brian Ruckley
Stephen Donaldson	David Gemmell	Adrian Tchaikovsky

Kjell Eriksson 1953- Swe   Crime: Police work - Sweden

🕴 Insp Ann Lindell

Karin Alvtegen	Matti Joensuu	Ed McBain
Anne Holt	Mari Jungstedt	Henning Mankell
Arnaldur Indridason	Åsa Larsson	Häkan Nesser

Barbara Erskine 🔗 1944-   Historical

is Barbara Hope-Lewis

Elizabeth Aston	Sara Donati	Kate Mosse
Jo Baker	Margaret Elphinstone	Fiona Mountain
Vanora Bennett	Helen Hollick	Rebecca Stott
Elizabeth Chadwick	Jane Johnson	Reay Tannahill

Gavin Esler 1953-   Adventure/Thriller

Jeffrey Archer	Jon Evans	Tim Sebastian
Alex Berenson	Robert Harris	Gerald Seymour
Michael Dobbs	Stella Rimington	

Laura Esquivel 1951- Mex

Isabel Allende	Gabriel García Márquez	Patrick Suskind
Kate Atkinson	Shifra Horn	Célestine Hitiura Vaite
Alessandro Baricco	Lily Prior	Jeanette Winterson

Ian C Esslemont 1962- Can   Fantasy: Epic

Joe Abercrombie	Steven Erikson	Scott Lynch
Stephen Donaldson	Tom Lloyd	R A Salvatore

Loren D Estleman 1952- US   Crime: PI

🕴 Amos Walker - Detroit • Peter Macklin, Hitman

Lawrence Block	Steve Hamilton	Reggie Nadelson
C J Box	Dashiell Hammett	Rick Riordan
Harlan Coben	Hari Kunzru	Ronald Tierney
James Ellroy	Joe R Lansdale	Don Winslow

E

Jeffrey Eugenides   1960-   US

🏆 Pulitzer 2003

Michel Faber	Siri Hustvedt	Richard Powers
Jonathan Franzen	Joe Meno	Donna Tartt
Andrew Sean Greer	Rick Moody	John Updike

Janet Evanovich   🕮   1943-   US   Crime: Humour

also writes as Steffie Hall   🏃 Stephanie Plum, Bail bondswoman - Newark, New Jersey
🏆 CWA 1995 & 1997   Max Holt • Alexandra Barnaby & Sam Hooker, Racing drivers
Lizzy Tucker & Diesel - Marblehead

Linda Barnes	Liz Evans	Pauline McLynn
Lindy Cameron	Helen Fitzgerald	P D Martin
Nancy Cohen	Joanne Fluke	Zoë Sharp
Louise Doughty	Kerry Greenwood	Sarah Strohmeyer

Chris Evans   Can   Fantasy: Epic

Joe Abercrombie	Terry Brooks	Stan Nicholls
R Scott Bakker	C S Friedman	Adrian Tchaikovsky

E Geraldine Evans   1953-   Crime: Police work - UK

also writes as Geraldine Hartnett   🏃 DI Joe Rafferty & Sgt D Llewellyn
DCI Casey & Thomas Catt

David Armstrong	Marjorie Eccles	J M Gregson
Vivien Armstrong	Caroline Graham	Reginald Hill
Brian Cooper	Ann Granger	Peter Turnbull

Harriet Evans   1974-   Chick Lit

Jane Costello	Clare Dowling	Pauline McLynn
Megan Crane	Sarah Duncan	Annie Sanders
Anna Davis	Emily Giffin	Bernadette Strachan
Lucy Dillon	Louise Harwood	Julia Williams

Lissa Evans   ☺

Kate Atkinson	Nick Hornby	Tom Sharpe
Rachel Hore	John O'Farrell	Meera Syal

Liz Evans   Crime: PI

is Patricia Grey   🏃 Grace Smith - 'Seatoun', South Coast, England

Jo Bannister	Sparkle Hayter	Michelle Spring
Cara Black	Joyce Holms	Sarah Strohmeyer
Janet Evanovich	Pauline McLynn	Rebecca Tope
Sue Grafton	Zoë Sharp	Stella Whitelaw

🕮 may be suitable for young adults

Nicholas Evans 🕶 1950-

Pat Conroy	Molly Gloss	Paullina Simons
Thomas Eidson	Jules Hardy	Nicholas Sparks
Leif Enger	Stuart Harrison	Robert James Waller
Charles Frazier	Larry McMurtry	Daniel Woodrell

Pamela Evans   Saga
London

Glenice Crossland	Elizabeth Lord	Elizabeth Waite
Hilary Green	Victor Pemberton	Jeanne Whitmee
Annie Groves	Carol Rivers	

Barbara Ewing   NZ   Historical

Vanora Bennett	Elizabeth Garner	Diana Norman
Elizabeth Chadwick	Deborah Moggach	James Runcie
Susanna Clarke		

Michel Faber   1960-   Neth

Monica Ali	Alasdair Gray	Jack Kerouac
Michael Arditti	James Kelman	Patrick McGrath
Jeffrey Eugenides	A L Kennedy	Dan Rhodes
Elizabeth Garner		

Linda Fairstein   1947-   US   Crime: Legal/financial

🚶 Alexandra Cooper, Assistant DA - New York • Det Mike Chapman - New York

Lindsay Ashford	John T Lescroart	Nancy Taylor Rosenberg
Alafair Burke	Steve Martini	Lisa Scottoline
Jodi Compton	Perri O'Shaughnessy	Susan R Sloan
Lisa Gardner	Kathy Reichs	Robert K Tanenbaum

Duncan Falconer   Adventure/Thriller

🚶 John Stratton, Special Boat Service Operative

Tom Clancy	Paul Henke	Chris Ryan
Clive Cussler	Andy McNab	Terence Strong
Murray Davies		

Ildefonso Falcones   1959-   Spain   Historical

Juan Gómez-Jurado	Matthew Pearl	C J Sansom
Manuel Vázquez Montalbán	Arturo Pérez-Reverte	Carlos Ruiz Zafón

Jane Fallon   Mature Chick Lit

Catherine Alliott	Noëlle Harrison	Julia Llewellyn
Lucy Cavendish	Linda Kelsey	Lauren Weisberger
Marita Conlon-McKenna	Kate Lawson	Polly Williams
Therese Fowler		

Jennifer Fallon
Aus   Fantasy: Epic

Sarah Ash	Kate Elliott	Naomi Novik
Jacqueline Carey	Terry Goodkind	Brandon Sanderson
Sara Douglass	Fiona McIntosh	

David Farland
1957-   US   Fantasy: Epic

is Dave Wolverton

Terry Brooks	Robert Jordan	John Marco
Jude Fisher	Mercedes Lackey	Harry Turtledove
Maggie Furey	Juliet E McKenna	Jane Welch
J V Jones		

Roopa Farooki
1974-   Pak

Margaret Cezair-Thompson	Sharon Maas	Ben Okri
Vikram Chandra	Amulya Malladi	Monique Roffey
Ha Jin	Anita Nair	Arundhati Roy
Jhumpa Lahiri	Preethi Nair	Thrity Umrigar

Sebastian Faulks
1953-

Richard Bausch	Sadie Jones	Lorrie Moore
John Boyne	Daniel Mason	Irene Nemirovsky
Peter Ho Davies	Richard Mason	Chris Paling
James Fleming	Simon Mawer	Andrew Rosenheim

Patricia Fawcett
Aga Saga

Sarah Challis	Anne Doughty	Charlotte Moore
Lucy Clare	Adèle Geras	Rebecca Shaw
Rowan Coleman		

Christine Feehan
US   Paranormal

Lara Adrian	Cassandra Clare	Sherrilyn Kenyon
Kelley Armstrong	Mary Janice Davidson	Sara Reinke
Keri Arthur	Lori Handeland	Susan Sizemore
Patricia Briggs	Tanya Huff	J R Ward

Raymond E Feist
1945-   US   Fantasy: Epic

Joe Abercrombie	Steven Erikson	Scott Lynch
David Bilsborough	Maggie Furey	John Marco
Terry Brooks	Paul Kearney	Karen Miller
James Clemens	Russell Kirkpatrick	Christopher Paolini

Ellen Feldman
1941-   US

also writes as Amanda Russell, Elizabeth Villars

Jane Fallon	Catherine Ryan Hyde	Joyce Carol Oates
Gail Godwin	Alison Lurie	Rosie Thomas

Jaine Fenn
Science Fiction: Near future

Neal Asher	China Miéville	Alastair Reynolds
Peter F Hamilton	Richard Morgan	Charles Stross
Scott Lynch		

Kate Fenton
1954-
Aga Saga

Raffaella Barker	Rowan Coleman	Katie Fforde
Elizabeth Buchan	Isla Dewar	Sue Limb
Lucy Clare	Anne Doughty	Sue Welfare

Zoë Ferraris
1970- US
Crime

Saudi Arabia

Belinda Bauer	Alison Joseph	Anne Perry
Ariana Franklin	Barbara Nadel	Phil Rickman

Robert Ferrigno
1948- US
Crime: Hardboiled

🏃 Jimmy Gage, Reporter - Los Angeles

Massimo Carlotto	James W Hall	Michael McGarrity
James Crumley	Tony Hillerman	Boston Teran
Murray Davies	Jonathon King	

Gordon Ferris
Sco
Adventure/Thriller: PI

🏃 Douglas Brodie, Reporter - 1940s Glasgow • Danny McRae - London

Kate Atkinson	Stephen Done	Ian Rankin
John Buchan	Alan Furst	Craig Russell
Charles Cumming	Andrew Martin	Sara Sheridan

F

Dan Fesperman
US
Adventure/Thriller

🏆 CWA 1999 & 2003 🏃 Vlado Petric - Bosnia

Alex Berenson	Jon Evans	Chris Petit
Michael Dibdin	Joseph Kanon	Stella Rimington
Alex Dryden	Gayle Lynds	Robert Wilson

Jasper Fforde
☎ ☺ 1961- Wales
Crime: Humour

🏆 Bollinger 2004 🏃 Thursday Next, Literary detective - Swindon
DI Jack Spratt & DS Mary Mary - Reading Police Dept

Gilbert Adair	Mark Gatiss	Malcolm Pryce
Karl Alexander	Tom Holt	Robert Rankin
Robert Asprin	Paul Magrs	Andy Secombe
Christopher Fowler	Terry Pratchett	Connie Willis

Katie Fforde
1952-
Mature Chick Lit

Trisha Ashley	Kate Fenton	Holly McQueen
Clare Chambers	Debby Holt	Sharon Owens
Lucy Clare	Prue Leith	Tasmina Perry
Sarah Duncan	Debbie Macomber	Alan Titchmarsh

David Fiddimore 1944- War: Modern

♟ Charlie Bassett, ex RAF, now spy

Frank Barnard	Andrew Greig	Derek Robinson
Patrick Bishop	James Holland	Alan Savage
Elizabeth Darrell	Henry Porter	Terence Strong
Alan Furst	Robert Radcliffe	Guy Walters

Helen Fielding ⌒ 1959- Chick Lit

♟ Bridget Jones

Sherry Ashworth	Serena Mackesy	Lynne Truss
Joanne Harris	Alexandra Potter	Jennifer Weiner
Veronica Henry	Robyn Sisman	

Joy Fielding 1945- Can Crime: Psychological

Mark Billingham	Sophie Hannah	Judith Kelman
Mary Higgins Clark	Karen Harper	Margaret Murphy
John Connolly	Sam Hayes	Christina Schwarz
Katy Gardner	Faye Kellerman	

Joseph Finder 1958- US Adventure/Thriller

♟ Nick Heller, Corporate Investigator - Washington DC

Jeffrey Archer	Vince Flynn	Matthew Klein
David Baldacci	Andrew Gross	Robert Ludlum
Alex Dryden	Chuck Hogan	Michael Marshall
David Ellis	Simon Kernick	Gareth O'Callaghan

F

Anne Fine ⌒ ☺ 1947-

Rachel Billington	Bernardine Kennedy	Liz Rigbey
Rachel Cusk	Joan Lingard	Meg Rosoff
Catherine Dunne	Kate Long	Mary Stanley
Zoë Heller	Libby Purves	Louise Tondeur

Patricia Finney ☺ 1958- Crime: Historical - C16th

also writes as P F Chisholm, Grace Cavendish
🏆 Higham 1977

♟ David Becket & Simon Ames - Elizabethan England

P F Chisholm	Shirley McKay	C J Sansom
Michael Clynes	Edward Marston	Martin Stephen
Philip Gooden	John Pilkington	Peter Tonkin
C C Humphreys		

Marina Fiorato Historical

C16th Italy

Geraldine Brooks	Sarah Dunant	Susan Vreeland
Tracy Chevalier	Lee Langley	Alison Weir

Conor Fitzgerald
1964- Ire   **Crime:** Police work - Italy

♁ Alec Blume, Commisario - Rome

Andrea Camilleri	Karin Fossum	Daniel Silva
Gianrico Carofiglio	Michele Giuttari	Marco Vichi
Vince Flynn	Denise Mina	Martin Walker

F Scott Fitzgerald
1896-1940   US

Russell Banks	Carson McCullers	John Updike
E L Doctorow	Jay McInerney	Tom Wolfe
Craig Holden	John Steinbeck	Tobias Wolff
John Irving		

Helen Fitzgerald
1966- Aus   **Crime:** Psychological

Mark Billingham	Karen Campbell	Joanne Fluke
Lindy Cameron	Janet Evanovich	Stuart MacBride

Penelope Fitzgerald
1916-2000

♔ Booker 1979

Jane Austen	Anita Brookner	Penelope Lively
Beryl Bainbridge	A S Byatt	Fiona Shaw
Andrea Barrett	Jane Gardam	Emma Tennant
Rachel Billington	Helen Garner	Edith Wharton

Fannie Flagg
1944- US

is Patricia Neal

Elizabeth Berg	Haven Kimmel	Ann B Ross
Amy Bloom	Lorna Landvik	Adriana Trigiani
Laurie Graham	Jojo Moyes	Rebecca Wells
Jan Karon	Annie Proulx	

Richard Flanagan
1961- Aus

♔ Commonwealth 2002

Peter Carey	Cormac McCarthy	Daniel Silva
J M Coetzee	David Malouf	Peter Spiegelman
Laura Lippman	Salman Rushdie	

Ian Fleming
1908-64   Adventure/Thriller

♁ James Bond

Boris Akunin	Alex Berenson	Brian Freemantle
Brett Battles	John Buchan	Stella Rimington
Ted Bell	Barry Eisler	Daniel Silva
Raymond Benson	James Follett	

James Fleming
1944-   Historical

♁ Charlie Doig - Russian Revolution

Louis Bayard	Sebastian Faulks	Bernhard Schlink
Harlan Coben	Matthew Kneale	Barry Unsworth
Kiran Desai		

F

Leah Fleming Saga

Maeve Binchy	June Francis	Noëlle Harrison
Dilly Court	Giselle Green	Kitty Neale
Josephine Cox	Annie Groves	Lesley Pearse
Katie Flynn		

Susan Fletcher 1979-

🏆 Whitbread 2004   Betty Trask 2005   Authors 2004

Anthony Capella	Giselle Green	Maggie O'Farrell
Suzannah Dunn	Charlotte Mendelson	Lionel Shriver
Catherine Dunne	Julie Myerson	

Shamini Flint 1969-   Sing Crime: Police work - Asia

🚶 Insp Singh - Asia

Colin Cotterill	Margaret Doody	Farahad Zama
Colin Dexter	Alexander McCall Smith	Anne Zouroudi

Joanne Fluke 1943-   US Crime: Amateur sleuth

🚶 Hannah Swensen, Bakery owner - Minnesota

Lilian Jackson Braun	Catriona McPherson	Ian Sansom
Janet Evanovich	Margaret Maron	Sarah Strohmeyer
Helen Fitzgerald	Mike Ripley	

David Flusfeder 1960-   US

🏆 Encore 1997

Martin Amis	Sue Gee	Toby Litt
Jenny Diski	Graham Greene	Glenn Patterson
Helen Dunmore		

Gillian Flynn US Adventure/Thriller: Psychological

🏆 CWA 2007

Sara Gran	Julie Parsons	Lisa Unger
Sophie Hannah	Liz Rigbey	Don Winslow
Jennifer McMahon		

Katie Flynn 1936- Saga

also writes as Judy Turner; is Judith Saxton 🚶 Lilac Larkin - Liverpool

Anne Baker	Rosie Goodwin	Catherine King
Dilly Court	Ruth Hamilton	Elizabeth Murphy
Tania Crosse	Rosie Harris	Kitty Neale
Leah Fleming	Anna Jacobs	Lynda Page

Go to back for lists of
Pseudonyms • Authors by Genre • Characters and Series • Environments
Prize Winners • Classic Authors • Crossover Authors • Further Reading • Websites

Vince Flynn 1966- US   Adventure/Thriller

ᛧ Mitch Rapp - CIA Washington

Ted Bell	Joseph Finder	Mike Lawson
Suzanne Brockmann	David Hagberg	John J Nance
Lincoln Child	Brian Haig	Brad Thor
Stephen Coonts	Lynne Heitman	

Giles Foden 1967-

🏆 Whitbread 1998   Holtby 1998   S Maugham 1999

Beryl Bainbridge	Robert Edric	Andrew O'Hagan
William Boyd	Pamela Jooste	Paul Theroux
James Clavell		

Jonathan Safran Foer 1977- US

🏆 Guardian 2002

Niccolo Ammaniti	Don DeLillo	Nicole Krauss
Lisa Appignanesi	Dave Eggers	Richard Powers
Paul Auster	Jonathan Franzen	Lynne Sharon Schwartz
Michael Chabon	Kate Kerrigan	Colson Whitehead

Jess Foley 1934-   Saga

is Bernard Taylor

Jessica Blair	Audrey Howard	Wendy Robertson
Dilly Court	Ken McCoy	Valerie Wood
Rosie Harris	Kitty Neale	

James Follett 🌰 1939-   Adventure/Thriller

Raymond Benson	Charles Higson	Justin Scott
Ian Fleming	Alistair MacLean	Craig Thomas
Colin Forbes	Matthew Reilly	

Ken Follett 🌰 1949-   Adventure/Thriller

also writes as Simon Myles

Paul Adam	David Downing	Lynne Heitman
Carla Banks	Tom Gabbay	John Lawton
Nicholas Coleridge	Lucretia Grindle	Robert Littell
Nelson DeMille	Humphrey Hawksley	Michael White

🌰   Historical

Vanora Bennett	Linda Holeman	Jack Whyte
Tracy Chevalier	Edward Rutherfurd	Adam Williams
Jennifer Donnelly	Salley Vickers	

🌰 may be suitable for young adults

Colin Forbes 1923-2006   Adventure/Thriller

also wrote as Richard Raine, Raymond Sawkins;   ⚡ Tweed, Bob Newman & Paula Grey - SIS
was Raymond Harold Sawkins

Ted Allbeury	Clive Egleton	Jack Higgins
Campbell Armstrong	James Follett	Charles Higson
Jon Cleary	Frederick Forsyth	Tom Rob Smith

Elena Forbes   Crime: Police work - UK

⚡ DI Mark Tartaglia & DS Sam Donovan - West London

Alex Barclay	Tana French	Mark Pearson
Deborah Crombie	Elizabeth George	Caro Ramsay

G M Ford 1945- US   Crime: Hardboiled

⚡ Frank Corso, Journalist - Seattle • Leo Waterman, Amateur sleuth

Robert Gregory Browne	James W Hall	Dennis Lehane
Caroline Carver	Steve Hamilton	Kevin Lewis
Michael Connelly	J A Jance	Liza Marklund
Robert Crais	Jim Kelly	Richard Stark

Richard Ford 1944- US

🏆 Pulitzer 1996   ⚡ Frank Bascombe

Richard Bausch	Jim Lynch	Richard Russo
Michael Collins	Tim O'Brien	Jonathan Tropper
Michael Cunningham	Richard Powers	Robert James Waller
Pete Dexter	Marilynne Robinson	Tobias Wolff

C S Forester ⌒ 1899-1966   Sea: Historical

⚡ Horatio Hornblower - C18th/19th England

G S Beard	Jonathan Lunn	Dudley Pope
David Donachie	James L Nelson	Peter Smalley
Seth Hunter	Patrick O'Brian	Julian Stockwin
Alexander Kent		

E M Forster ⌒ 1879-1970

Henry James	Paul Scott	Edith Wharton
Ruth Prawer Jhabvala	H G Wells	Colson Whitehead
Anthony Powell		

Margaret Forster ⌒ 1938-

Kate Atkinson	Sue Gee	Anna Quindlen
Rachel Billington	Linda Grant	Louise Tondeur
Carol Birch	Sarah Hall	Fay Weldon
Katharine Davies	Charlotte Mendelson	Ann Widdecombe

F

Frederick Forsyth 1938- Adventure/Thriller

🏆 CWA 2012

James Barrington	Paul Henke	Kyle Mills
Tom Cain	James Long	Alex Scarrow
Clive Egleton	Robert Ludlum	Gerald Seymour
Colin Forbes	Glenn Meade	

Karin Fossum 1954- Nor Crime: Police work - Norway

🚶 Insp Konrad Sejer & Jacob Skarre - Oslo

Karin Alvtegen	Mari Jungstedt	Yrsa Sigurdardottir
S J Bolton	Camilla Läckberg	Johan Theorin
R J Ellory	Liza Marklund	Linn Ullmann
Arnaldur Indridason	Häkan Nesser	Jan Costin Wagner

Alan Dean Foster 1946- US Science Fiction: Space opera

Robert Asprin	C J Cherryh	Colin Greenland
David Brin	Michael Jan Friedman	Elizabeth Haydon
Orson Scott Card	Simon Green	Elizabeth Moon

Christopher Fowler 1953- Crime: Humour

🚶 Arthur Bryant & John May, Policemen - London

Peter Ackroyd	Jasper Fforde	Malcolm Pryce
Gilbert Adair	Andrey Kurkov	Iain Sinclair
Christopher Brookmyre	Louise Penny	

F

Horror

🏆 British Fantasy 2004

Clive Barker	Graham Joyce	Malcolm Pryce
Ramsey Campbell	Graham Masterton	Michael Marshall Smith
Jonathan Carroll	Kim Newman	

Connie May Fowler 1958- US

Sarah Addison Allen	Carson McCullers	Joyce Carol Oates
Therese Fowler	Sue Miller	Jodi Picoult
Sue Monk Kidd		

Karen Joy Fowler 1950- US

Manette Ansay	Elinor Lipman	Anne Tyler
Patricia Gaffney	Jodi Picoult	Rebecca Wells
William Kowalski	Anne Rivers Siddons	

John Fowles 1926-2005

Peter Ackroyd	Victoria Hislop	Graham Swift
Maggie Gee	Nick McDonell	D J Taylor
William Golding	Robert Nye	Rupert Thomson

Kathryn Fox 1966- Aus Crime: Forensic

⚥ Dr Anya Crichton, Forensic pathologist

Alex Barclay	Frances Fyfield	Chris Mooney
Simon Beckett	Tess Gerritsen	Kathy Reichs
Patricia D Cornwell	Nigel McCrery	Karin Slaughter
Colin Cotterill	Richard Montanari	Lisa Unger

Ronald Frame 1953- Sco

🏆 Betty Trask 1984

Jonathan Buckley	Robin Jenkins	Allan Massie
Robert Goddard	A L Kennedy	William Trevor
Kazuo Ishiguro	Bernard MacLaverty	

Clare Francis 1946- Adventure/Thriller: Psychological

Lisa Appignanesi	Paula Gosling	John Harvey
Carla Banks	Sophie Hannah	Hilary Norman
Ken Follett	Karen Harper	Christina Schwarz
Lesley Glaister		

Dick Francis 1920-2010 Wales Crime: Amateur sleuth

also wrote jointly with Felix Francis ⚥ Sid Halley & Kit Fielding - Horse racing

🏆 CWA 1979

John Francome	Robert B Parker	Graeme Roe
Elizabeth George	Jenny Pitman	Lyndon Stacey
Gerald Hammond	Richard Pitman	

F

June Francis 1941- Saga

Liverpool

Lyn Andrews	Glenice Crossland	Sheila Newberry
Elizabeth Bailey	Leah Fleming	June Tate
Julia Bryant	Jeannie Johnson	Margaret Thornton
Jean Chapman	Gwen Madoc	

John Francome 1952- Crime: Amateur sleuth

also writes jointly with James MacGregor Horse racing

Dick Francis	Jenny Pitman	Graeme Roe
Gerald Hammond	Richard Pitman	Lyndon Stacey

Ariana Franklin 1935-2011 Crime: Historical - Medieval

was Diana Norman ⚥ Adelia Aguiler, Female doctor

🏆 CWA 2007 & 2010

Louis Bayard	Susanna Gregory	Sharan Newman
Cassandra Clark	Cora Harrison	Ellis Peters
R S Downie	Michael Jecks	Candace Robb
Margaret Frazer	The Medieval Murderers	Kate Sedley

Tom Franklin   US   Adventure/Thriller

🏆 CWA 2011

Charles Cumming	Jim Kelly	John Rector
William Faulkner	Ron Rash	Daniel Woodrell
Charles Frazier		

Jonathan Franzen   ⌂   1959-   US

🏆 Black 2002

Michael Arditti	Jeffrey Eugenides	Elliot Perlman
T C Boyle	Jonathan Safran Foer	Annie Proulx
Michael Cunningham	A M Homes	Donna Tartt
Dave Eggers	Nicole Krauss	Brady Udall

Anthea Fraser   1930-   Crime: Police work - UK

also writes as Vanessa Graham   ⟡ DCI David Webb & DS Ken Jackson
'Broadshire', Home Counties • Rona Parish, Author

Marian Babson	Veronica Heley	Catherine Sampson
Elizabeth Ferrars	Hope McIntyre	June Thomson
Ann Granger	Barry Maitland	

Caro Fraser   Sco

⟡ Leo Davies, QC • Caper Court Series - London Inner Temple Legal Chambers

| Liz Byrski | David Lodge | John Mortimer |
| Cynthia Harrod-Eagles | John McLaren | Joanna Trollope |

F

George Macdonald Fraser   ⌂   1925-2008   Sco   War: Historical

⟡ Sir Harry Flashman

Boris Akunin	William Dietrich	Garry Kilworth
Roger Carpenter	Joseph Heller	Tom Sharpe
James Delingpole	Tom Holt	Leslie Thomas

Michael Frayn   ⌂   1933-   Humour

🏆 Bollinger 2002   Whitbread 2002

Kingsley Amis	Patrick Gale	Simon Mawer
Guy Bellamy	Howard Jacobson	Barry Pilton
Malcolm Bradbury	David Lodge	Paul Torday

Margaret Frazer   US   Crime: Historical - Medieval

also writes as Mary Monica Pulver; is Gail Frazer   ⟡ Sister Frevisse - C15th England
Joliffe Players Series

Alys Clare	Michael Jecks	Ellis Peters
Ariana Franklin	The Medieval Murderers	Mary Reed and Eric Mayer
Philip Gooden	Sharan Newman	Peter Tremayne
Cora Harrison		

Charles Frazier 1950- US

Russell Banks	David Guterson	Joseph O'Connor
Thomas Eidson	Thomas Keneally	Stewart O'Nan
Leif Enger	Larry McMurtry	Michael White
Nicholas Evans	Tim O'Brien	Daniel Woodrell

Maureen Freely 1952- US

Tracy Chevalier	Graham Greene	Paul Theroux
Gabriel Garcia Márquez	Orhan Pamuk	Mario Vargas Llosa

Brian Freeman 1963- US   Crime: Police work - US

⚂ Det Jonathan Stride & Det Serena Dial - Minnesota

Harlan Coben	Scott Frost	Chris Mooney
Jeffery Deaver	Gregg Hurwitz	John Rickards
Alan Dunn	Patrick Lennon	P J Tracy

Pamela Freeman Aus   Fantasy: Epic

Jim Butcher	Karen Miller	Patrick Rothfuss
Fiona McIntosh	Elizabeth Moon	Adrian Tchaikovsky

Brian Freemantle 1936-   Adventure/Thriller

also writes as John Maxwell,   ⚂ Charlie Muffin - MI6
Jonathan Evans, Jack Winchester   Sebastian Holmes, Son of Sherlock - early C20th

Ted Allbeury	Ian Fleming	Patrick Lennon
Alex Dryden	John Le Carré	James Patterson
Clive Egleton		

Nicci French 1958-   Adventure/Thriller: Psychological

is Nicci Gerrard writing with Sean French   ⚂ Dr Samantha Laschen
Frieda Klein, Psychotherapist - London

S J Bolton	Sam Hayes	Elizabeth McGregor
Jonathan Buckley	Frances Hegarty	Andrew Pyper
Sophie Hannah	Jane Hill	Patrick Redmond
Karen Harper	Joanna Hines	Sally Spedding

Tana French 1973- Ire   Crime: Psychological

⚂ Det Rob Ryan - Garda police force - Dublin • Det Cassie Maddox

Stephen Booth	Camilla Läckberg	Val McDermid
Elena Forbes	Stieg Larsson	Denise Mina
Gene Kerrigan	Laura Lippman	Andrew Nugent

Esther Freud 1963-

Rachel Cusk	Terry McMillan	Meera Syal
Suzannah Dunn	Deborah Moggach	Emma Tennant
Alex Garland	Gwendoline Riley	

C S Friedman 1957- US   Fantasy: Epic

is Celia S Friedman

Joe Abercrombie	C J Cherryh	Scott Lynch
R Scott Bakker	Ian C Esslemont	Brandon Sanderson
Lois McMaster Bujold	Chris Evans	

Kinky Friedman 1944- US   Crime: Humour

♣ Kinky Friedman, Country & Western singer - New York

Linwood Barclay	James Hawes	Rosemary Martin
Tim Dorsey	Sparkle Hayter	Robert B Parker
Dashiell Hammett	Elmore Leonard	

Scott Frost   Adventure/Thriller

♣ Det Alex Delillo - Los Angeles

Harlan Coben	Brian Freeman	Gregg Hurwitz
Michael Connelly	George Dawes Green	John Sandford
Robert Crais		

Stephen Fry 1957-   Humour

Alan Bennett	Charles Higson	Barry Pilton
Paul Burke	Tim Lott	Nigel Williams
Roddy Doyle	Geoff Nicholson	P G Wodehouse
Ben Elton		

Carlos Fuentes 1928-2012 Mex

Isabel Allende	Milton Hatoum	Patrick Suskind
Alessandro Baricco	Tomas Eloy Martinez	Mario Vargas Llosa
Gabriel Garcia Márquez		

Alexander Fullerton 1924-   Adventure/Thriller

♣ Nicholas Everard

Brian Callison	Hammond Innes	Allan Mallinson
Len Deighton	Alexander Kent	James Pattinson
David Downing	Philip McCutchan	Douglas Reeman
Duncan Harding		

Jean Fullerton   Saga

🏆 Harry Bowling 2006   London East End

Anne Baker	Alexandra Connor	Rosie Goodwin
Rita Bradshaw	Dilly Court	Valerie Wood

Maggie Furey 1955-   Fantasy: Epic

Terry Brooks	Raymond E Feist	Paul Kearney
Kate Elliott	Terry Goodkind	George R R Martin
David Farland	J V Jones	Harry Turtledove

F

Kate Furnivall ⌒ Wales Historical

Tom Bradby	Anchee Min	Sara Sheridan
Rebecca Dean	Vladimir Nabokov	Amy Tan
Kathryn Harrison	Lisa See	Adam Williams
Katie Hickman		

Alan Furst 1941- US Adventure/Thriller

Charles Cumming	Philip Kerr	Robert Ryan
David Downing	John Lawton	Tom Rob Smith
David Fiddimore	Robert Littell	Olen Steinhauer
David Ignatius	Stella Rimington	Robert Wilson

Frances Fyfield 1948- Crime: Amateur sleuth

is Frances Hegarty   🚶 Helen West, Lawyer, & DS Geoffrey Bailey - London
🏆 CWA 1990, 1991 & 2008   Sarah Fortune, Lawyer

Jane Adams	Kathryn Fox	Margaret Murphy
Lindsay Ashford	Joanna Hines	Robert K Tanenbaum
Natasha Cooper	M R D Meek	

Jostein Gaarder ⌒ ☺ 1952- Nor

Umberto Eco	Mark Haddon	Iris Murdoch
Gabriel Garcia Márquez	Peter Hoeg	Orhan Pamuk

F
G

Diana Gabaldon 1952- US Historical

is Diana Jean Gabaldon Watkins   🚶 Outlander Series • Lord John Grey, Soldier - C18th

Bryce Courtenay	Kathleen O'Neal Gear	Audrey Niffenegger
Sara Donati	Katie Hickman	Reay Tannahill
Dorothy Dunnett	Judith Lennox	Jack Whyte
Julie Garwood	James Long	

Patricia Gaffney US Aga Saga

Elizabeth Berg	Barbara Kingsolver	Jodi Picoult
Karen Joy Fowler	Sue Miller	Libby Purves
Ann Hood	Maggie O'Farrell	Adriana Trigiani

Neil Gaiman ⌒ ☺ 1960- Fantasy: Contemporary

🏆 British Fantasy 2006

Douglas Adams	Cory Doctorow	Jack O'Connell
Clive Barker	John Ajvide Lindqvist	Tim Powers
Jonathan Carroll	Christopher Moore	Andy Remic
Susanna Clarke	Adam Nevill	Jack Vance

Gillian Galbraith 1957- Sco Crime: Police work - UK

🚶 Alice Rice - Edinburgh

Lin Anderson	Frederic Lindsay	Caro Ramsay
Karen Campbell	Denise Mina	Ian Rankin
Quintin Jardine		

Iain Gale 1959- Sco   War: Historical

🏃 Lt Jack Steel - Scottish Grenadiers • Peter Lamb - WW2

Roger Carpenter	James Holland	Edward Marston
Tom Connery	Garry Kilworth	William Napier
Bernard Cornwell	James McGee	Simon Scarrow
James Delingpole	Allan Mallinson	John Wilcox

Patrick Gale ⌒ 1962-

Gilbert Adair	Lee Langley	Mark Slouka
Louise Dean	Katharine McMahon	Edward St Aubyn
Alan Hollinghurst	Armistead Maupin	Giles Waterfield
Lloyd Jones	Carol Shields	Edmund White

Damon Galgut 1963- SA

Sebastian Barry	Jim Crace	Christopher Hope
Justin Cartwright	Nadine Gordimer	Pamela Jooste
J M Coetzee		

Janice Galloway 1955- Sco

John Burnside	Jackie Kay	Ali Smith
Ron Butlin	A L Kennedy	Alan Spence
Michael Cannon	Hari Kunzru	Zoë Strachan
Amanda Craig	Andrew O'Hagan	Alice Thompson

Gabriel Garcia Márquez ⌒ 1928- Col

Isabel Allende	Maureen Freely	Ismail Kadare
Roberto Bolano	Carlos Fuentes	Javier Marias
Paulo Coelho	Jostein Gaarder	Tomas Eloy Martinez
Laura Esquivel	Milton Hatoum	Ben Okri

G

Jane Gardam ⌒ ☺ 1928-

🏆 Higham 1975   Whitbread 1991

Amanda Craig	Susan Hill	Jill Paton Walsh
Penelope Fitzgerald	Joan Lingard	Mary Wesley
James Hamilton-Paterson	Fiona Shaw	

Meg Gardiner 1957- US   Crime: PI

🏃 Evan Delaney - Santa Barbara, California
Dr Jo Beckett, Forensic psychiatrist - San Francisco

Linda Barnes	Lynn Hightower	Marcia Muller
Jan Burke	Laurie R King	Carol O'Connell
Eric Jerome Dickey	Theresa Monsour	Dana Stabenow

Craig Shaw Gardner 1949- US   Fantasy: Humour

also writes as Peter Garrison

Robert Asprin	Tom Holt	Terry Pratchett
Mary Gentle	Christopher Moore	Martin Scott

Katy Gardner   Adventure/Thriller: Psychological

| Suzanne Berne | Joy Fielding | Joanna Hines |
| Mary Higgins Clark | Lisa Gardner | Barbara Vine |

Lisa Gardner   US   Adventure/Thriller

also writes as Alicia Scott   ☩ Pierce Quincy, FBI Special Agent
                          Kimberly Quincy, FBI Special Agent • Det Sgt D D Warren - Boston

Stella Cameron	Katy Gardner	Karin Slaughter
Beverly Connor	Tess Gerritsen	Erica Spindler
Linda Fairstein	Iris Johansen	Lee Weeks

Alex Garland ⌒ 1970-

☙ Betty Trask 1997

Douglas Coupland	Jack Kerouac	Timothy Mo
Esther Freud	Tim Lott	William Sutcliffe
James Hamilton-Paterson		

Elizabeth Garner   Historical

| Joan Aiken | Susanna Clarke | Michel Faber |
| Angela Carter | Barbara Ewing | Philip Pullman |

Helen Garner   1942-   Aus

Debra Adelaide	Valerie Martin	Anita Shreve
Kim Edwards	Ann Packer	Rose Tremain
Penelope Fitzgerald	Ann Patchett	Tim Winton
Zoë Heller		

G

Jonathan Gash   1933-   Crime: Amateur sleuth

also writes as Jonathan Grant; is John Grant   ☩ Lovejoy, Antique dealer - London
☙ CWA 1977   Dr Clare Burtonall

| Robert Barnard | Gerald Hammond | John Malcolm |
| Earlene Fowler | Alison Joseph | Catherine Sampson |

Mark Gatiss ⌒ 1966-   Crime: Amateur sleuth

                    ☩ Lucifer Box, Painter & secret agent - Edwardian England

Gilbert Adair	Jeremy Dyson	David Roberts
James Anderson	Jasper Fforde	Dorothy L Sayers
Jake Arnott	Malcolm Pryce	Charles Todd
Bateman		

Anna Gavalda   1970-   Fr

| Muriel Barbery | Barbara Kingsolver | Ann Patchett |
| Susan Fletcher | Maggie O'Farrell | Colin Thubron |

Mike Gayle 1970-   Lad Lit

Mark Barrowcliffe   Sam Holden   Tony Parsons
Matt Beaumont   Mick Jackson   Matt Whyman
Matt Dunn

Kathleen O'Neal Gear 1954- US   Historical

also writes with **Michael Gear** (husband)   ⚐ First North American Series

Jean M Auel   Diana Gabaldon   Edward Rutherfurd
Sara Donati   James A Michener   Judith Tarr
Thomas Eldson

Maggie Gee 1948-

Peter Ackroyd   Anne Enright   Rachel Seiffert
Trezza Azzopardi   John Fowles   Graham Swift
Jenny Diski   Doris Lessing   Rose Tremain

Maurice Gee 1931- NZ

🏆 Black 1978

Murray Bail   Robin Jenkins   David Malouf
Nadine Gordimer   Thomas Keneally   Rose Tremain

Sue Gee 1947-

🏆 Romantic 1997

Louise Candlish   Pam Jenoff   Charlotte Mendelson
David Flusfeder   Joan Lingard   Deborah Moggach
Margaret Forster   Penelope Lively   Salley Vickers

David Gemmell ⌂ 1948-2006   Fantasy: Epic

also wrote as **Ross Harding**

James Barclay   Paul Kearney   Brian Ruckley
Terry Brooks   Tom Lloyd   Alex Rutherford
Steven Erikson   Stan Nicholls   Jane Welch
Simon Green   Andy Remic

Nikki Gemmell 1967- Aus

Louise Candlish   Zoë Heller   Clare Morrall
Helen Dunmore   Sue Miller   Anita Shreve

Mary Gentle 1956-   Fantasy: Epic

🏆 BSFA 2000

Storm Constantine   Ursula K Le Guin   Philip Pullman
Craig Shaw Gardner   China Miéville   Steph Swainston
Colin Greenland   Michael Moorcock   Sheri S Tepper
Gwyneth Jones   Tim Powers   Harry Turtledove

G

Elizabeth George ⌒ 1949- US   Crime: Police work - UK
🏃 DCI Thomas Lynley & DS Barbara Havers - London

S J Bolton	Elly Griffiths	Declan Hughes
Marjorie Eccles	Martha Grimes	Colleen McCullough
Elena Forbes	Erin Hart	Matt Rees
Dick Francis	Susan Hill	Jill Paton Walsh

Margaret George 1943- US   Historical

Will Davenport	Michelle Moran	Jean Plaidy
Christian Jacq	Edith Pargeter	Gore Vidal
Colleen McCullough		

Ciara Geraghty Ire   Chick Lit

Rowan Coleman	Lisa Jewell	Sinead Moriarty
Lucy Diamond	Lindsey Kelk	Patricia Scanlan

Adèle Geras ⌒ ☺ 1944-   Aga Saga

Maeve Binchy	Rebecca Gregson	Jojo Moyes
Amanda Brookfield	Audrey Howard	Rosamunde Pilcher
Patricia Fawcett	Sandra Howard	Eileen Ramsay
Linda Gillard	Sara MacDonald	Marcia Willett

Nicci Gerrard ⌒ 1958-
also writes as Nicci French when writing with Sean French

Suzanne Bugler	Jules Hardy	Julie Myerson
Diane Chamberlain	Shirley Hazzard	Marcia Preston
Lesley Glaister	Siri Hustvedt	Sarah Rayner
Tessa Hadley	Mary Alice Monroe	Liz Rigbey

Tess Gerritsen ⌒ 1953- US   Crime: Medical
🏃 Det Jane Rizzoli & Dr Maura Isles, Detective & Pathologist - New York

Linwood Barclay	Joolz Denby	Jesse Kellerman
Stella Cameron	Kathryn Fox	Ken McClure
Linda Castillo	Lisa Gardner	Michael Palmer
Beverly Connor	Jilliane Hoffman	Jason Pinter

Amitav Ghosh 1956- Ind   Historical
🏆 Arthur C Clarke 1997

Anita Desai	Rohinton Mistry	Vikram Seth
Kiran Desai	Arundhati Roy	Vikas Swarup
Daniel Mason	Geoff Ryman	

Camilla Gibb 1968-

Monica Ali	Andrea Levy	Zadie Smith
Liz Jensen	Elif Shafak	Miriam Toews

G

David Gibbins   1962-   Can   Adventure/Thriller

Jack Howard, Marine Archaeologist

Will Adams
Steve Berry
Dan Brown
Thomas Greanias

Tom Harper
Douglas Preston
Matthew Reilly

James Rollins
Paul Sussman
James Twining

Fiona Gibson   Sco   Mature Chick Lit

Lisa Jewell
Rachel Johnson
Kate Lawson
Kathy Lette

Kate Long
Laura Marney
Elizabeth Noble

John O'Farrell
Carmen Reid
Sue Townsend

Gary Gibson   Sco   Science Fiction: Space opera

Neal Asher
Tony Ballantyne
Stephen Baxter

Peter F Hamilton
Paul J McAuley

Tim Powers
John Scalzi

William Gibson   1948-   Can   Science Fiction: Near future

Steve Aylett
J G Ballard
Eric Brown
Cory Doctorow

John Twelve Hawks
Jack O'Connell
Justina Robson
Andrzej Sapkowski

Lucius Shepard
Michael Marshall Smith
Kurt Vonnegut
Connie Willis

Emily Giffin   1972-   US   Chick Lit

Katie Agnew
Holly Chamberlin
Jane Costello
Megan Crane

Harriet Evans
Lindsey Kelk
Anna McPartlin

Tess Stimson
Kathleen Tessaro
Laura Zigman

G

Melanie Gifford   Historical

Geraldine Brooks
Sandra Gulland

Victoria Holt
Rosalind Laker

Robin Maxwell
James Runcie

Elizabeth Gill   1950-   Saga

also writes as Elizabeth Hankin

Irene Carr
Jean Chapman
Una Horne

Audrey Howard
Freda Lightfoot

Elvi Rhodes
Janet MacLeod Trotter

Linda Gillard

Elizabeth Berg
Isla Dewar
Helen Dunmore

Adèle Geras
Sue Miller

Kate Muir
Maggie O'Farrell

Mark Gimenez   US   Crime: Legal/financial

David Baldacci	David Hosp	Steve Martini
Linwood Barclay	Gregg Hurwitz	Michael Robotham
Julie Compton	Patrick Lennon	Scott Turow
John Grisham		

Michele Giuttari   1950-   It   Crime: Police work - Italy

🚶 Chief Sup Michele Ferrara - Florence

Andrea Camilleri	Philip Kerr	Guillermo Martinez
Michael Dibdin	Donna Leon	Magdalen Nabb
David Hewson	Carlo Lucarelli	

Lesley Glaister   1956-   Adventure/Thriller: Psychological

🏆 S Maugham 1991

Carol Birch	Nicci Gerrard	Joanna Hines
Jonathan Buckley	Sophie Hannah	Aline Templeton
Suzanne Bugler	Sam Hayes	Gillian White
Louise Doughty	Shirley Hazzard	James Wilson

Julia Glass   1956-   US

Russell Banks	Ann Patchett	Vendela Vida
Claire Messud	Edward St Aubyn	Alice Walker

Matthew Glass   Aus   Adventure/Thriller

David Baldacci	Michael Crichton	Matt Lynn
Dale Brown	Graham Hurley	Jon Stock

Molly Gloss   1944-   US

Nicholas Evans	Marge Piercy	Nicholas Sparks
Kate Grenville	Jane Smiley	Robert James Waller

Alan Glynn   1960-   Ire   Adventure/Thriller

James Crumley	James Ellroy	Gene Kerrigan
Bret Easton Ellis	Loren D Estleman	Roslund and Hellström

Robert Goddard   ⌒ 1954-   Adventure/Thriller

🏆 TGR 1992   🚶 Harry Barnett

Hilary Bonner	Erin Hart	Kate Morton
Stephen Booth	Susanna Kearsley	Patrick Redmond
Jonathan Buckley	Elizabeth Kostova	Pauline Rowson
Ronald Frame	Mark Mills	

⌒ may be suitable for young adults

G

Arthur Golden   1957-   US

Alma Alexander	Catherine Lim	Su Tong
Michelle de Kretser	Anchee Min	Amy Tan
Kazuo Ishiguro	Timothy Mo	Xinran

Christie Golden   1963-   US   Science Fiction: Space and time

| Kevin J Anderson | Brian Herbert | Alastair Reynolds |
| Harry Harrison | Larry Niven | Kristine Kathryn Rusch |

William Golding   1911-93

🏆 Black 1979   Booker 1980

Tim Binding	John Fowles	José Saramago
Patricia Duncker	Alex Garland	Linn Ullmann
Umberto Eco	Karen Maitland	Barry Unsworth

Adrian Goldsworthy   War: Historical - C19th

🏃 Hamish Williams - Napoleonic wars

| Bernard Cornwell | Edward Marston | Patrick Rambaud |
| Richard Howard | Patrick Mercer | Peter Smalley |

Juan Gómez-Jurado   1977-   Spain   Crime: PI

🏃 Father Anthony Fowler, Priest & CIA operative - Vatican

| Charles Cumming | Chris Kuzneski | Daniel Silva |
| Ildefonso Falcones | Matthew Pearl | James Twining |

Philip Gooden   Crime: Historical - C16th

also writes as Philippa Morgan,   🏃 Nick Revill, Shakespearean actor
The Medieval Murderers (with Susanne Gregory,   C16th
Michael Jecks, Bernard Knight, Karen Maitland, Ian Morson, C J Sansom)

P F Chisholm	Margaret Frazer	S J Parris
Rory Clements	C C Humphreys	Iain Pears
Michael Clynes	Shirley McKay	John Pilkington
Patricia Finney	Edward Marston	Peter Tonkin

G

Terry Goodkind   1948-   US   Fantasy: Epic

🏃 Richard Cypher

Carol Berg	Sara Douglass	Russell Kirkpatrick
Trudi Canavan	Jennifer Fallon	Robert Newcomb
Mark Chadbourn	Maggie Furey	Mickey Zucker Reichert
James Clemens	Ian Irvine	Brent Weeks

Allegra Goodman   1967-   US

| Michael Chabon | Jennifer Egan | Toni Morrison |
| Emma Donoghue | Howard Jacobson | Lionel Shriver |

Jason Goodwin   1964-   Crime: Historical - C19th

‡ Yashim Tagalu - Istanbul

Boris Akunin	H R F Keating	Matt Rees
Clio Gray	R N Morris	James Runcie
Michael Gregorio	Barbara Nadel	Elif Shafak
Katie Hickman	Michael Pearce	Jenny White

Rosie Goodwin   Saga

Aileen Armitage	Katie Flynn	Rosie Harris
Maggie Bennett	Jean Fullerton	Audrey Howard
Catrin Collier	Iris Gower	Judith Lennox
Josephine Cox	Pip Granger	Valerie Wood

Nadine Gordimer   1923-   SA

♛ Black 1971   Booker 1974

Margaret Atwood	Christopher Hope	Doris Lessing
André Brink	Pamela Jooste	Rani Manicka
J M Coetzee	Barbara &	Paul Scott
Damon Galgut	Stephanie Keating	
Maurice Gee		

Dolores Gordon-Smith   1958-   Crime: Amateur sleuth

‡ Jack Haldean - 1920s England

Agatha Christie	Edward Marston	Patricia Wentworth
Catriona McPherson	Dorothy L Sayers	P G Wodehouse

C W Gortner   US   Historical

G

also writes as Christopher Gortner

Vanora Bennett	Philippa Gregory	Jean Plaidy
Suzannah Dunn	Jeanne Kalogridis	Alison Weir

Paula Gosling   1939-   US   Crime: Police work - US

also writes as Ainslie Skinner   ‡ Sheriff Matt Gabriel, Lt Jack Stryker & Prof Kate Trevorne
♛ CWA 1978 & 1985   'Blackwater Bay', Michigan

Lilian Jackson Braun	Clare Francis	Laurie R King
Deborah Crombie	Martha Grimes	Archer Mayor
Jo Dereske		

Eileen Goudge   1950-   US   Glitz & Glamour

Elizabeth Buchan	Elizabeth Jane Howard	Nora Roberts
Barbara Delinsky	Joan Lingard	Danielle Steel
Judith Gould	Fern Michaels	

Judith Gould 1952- US Glitz & Glamour

also writes as W R Gallaher; is Nicholas Bienes & Rhea Gallaher

Elizabeth Adler
Jilly Cooper
Eileen Goudge
Rachel Johnson
Jayne Ann Krentz
Susan Lewis
Judith McNaught
Judith Michael
Madge Swindells

Iris Gower 1939-2010 Wales Saga

was Iris Davies

⚲ Cordwainer Series - South Wales • Sweet Rosie Series
Firebird Series • Drovers Series • Palace Theatre Series - South Wales

Jessica Blair
Catrin Collier
Gloria Cook
Rosie Goodwin
Rosie Harris
Catherine King
Joan O'Neill
Jack Sheffield
Grace Thompson
Barbara Whitnell
Barbara Wood

Tom Grace US Adventure/Thriller

⚲ Nolan Kilkenny - US Navy Seal

Will Adams
Clive Cussler
Tom Harper
Jack Higgins
Chris Kuzneski
Scott Mariani
James Twining

Posie Graeme-Evans 1952- Aus Historical

Elizabeth Chadwick
Suzannah Dunn
Dorothy Dunnett
Philippa Gregory
Jeanne Kalogridis
Sarah Waters
Alison Weir

Sue Grafton 1940- US Crime: PI

CWA 2008

⚲ Kinsey Millhone - 'Santa Teresa', California

Cara Black
Edna Buchanan
Alafair Burke
Jan Burke
Carol Higgins Clark
David Ellis
Liz Evans
Earlene Fowler
Steve Hamilton
Theresa Schwegel
Zoë Sharp
Ayelet Waldman

G

Caroline Graham 1931- Crime: Police work - UK

⚲ DCI Tom Barnaby & DS Troy - 'Midsomer Worthy'

A C Baantjer
W J Burley
Clare Curzon
Louise Doughty
Margaret Duffy
Geraldine Evans
J M Gregson
Lis Howell
Pierre Magnan
Ann Purser
Roger Silverwood
Sally Spencer

Heather Graham US Crime: Hardboiled

also writes as Shannon Drake; is Heather Graham Pozzessere

Helen Black
June Hampson
Tami Hoag
James Patterson
J D Robb
Martyn Waites

Crime: Romantic Suspense

Beverly Barton
Allison Brennan
Linda Howard
Lisa Jackson
Sharon Sala
Madge Swindells

Laurie Graham 1947-

Sarah Addison Allen
Elizabeth Berg
Amanda Craig
Rebecca Dean

Fannie Flagg
Jennifer Haigh
Sue Monk Kidd
Lorna Landvik

Elinor Lipman
Jojo Moyes
Sue Townsend
Arabella Weir

Winston Graham 🕭 1909-2003 Historical

🏃 Poldark Series

Rosemary Aitken
Anita Burgh
Gloria Cook

Joanna Hines
Reay Tannahill
E V Thompson

Nigel Tranter
Kate Tremayne

Sara Gran 1971- US Adventure/Thriller

Lawrence Block
Alafair Burke
Jennifer Egan

Gillian Flynn
Tana French

Robert B Parker
Ron Rash

Jean-Christophe Grangé 1961- Fr Adventure/Thriller

🏃 Pierre Niemans & Abdouf

John Case
Karin Fossum

Alan Furst
Paul Henke

Henry Porter
Wilbur Smith

Ann Granger 1939- Crime: Police work - UK

also writes as Ann Hulme
🏃 Det Supt Alan Markby & Meredith Mitchell - Cotswolds
Fran Varady, PI ⎫
Lizzie Martin & Insp Ben Ross, C19th ⎬ London

Chris Collett
Geraldine Evans
Anthea Fraser
J M Gregson

Hazel Holt
Lis Howell
Ann Purser
Betty Rowlands

Sally Spencer
Ronald Tierney
Rebecca Tope
Jacqueline Winspear

Pip Granger Saga

🏆 Harry Bowling 2000
🏃 Zelda Fluck - Soho London, 1940s

Rosie Goodwin
Connie Monk
Gilda O'Neill

Carol Rivers
Mary Jane Staples
Elizabeth Waite

Dee Williams
Sally Worboyes

Linda Grant 1951-

🏆 Higham 1996   Orange 2000

Beryl Bainbridge
Pat Barker
Suzanne Berne

Margaret Forster
David Grossman
Anna Quindlen

Zadie Smith
David Szalay

Go to back for lists of
Pseudonyms • Authors by Genre • Characters and Series • Environments
Prize Winners • Classic Authors • Crossover Authors • Further Reading • Websites

Rob Grant

Science Fiction: Humour

also writes as Grant Naylor (with Doug Naylor)

Douglas Adams	Harry Harrison	Terry Pratchett
David Baddiel	Tom Holt	Robert Rankin
Ben Elton		

Alasdair Gray   1934-   Sco

♛ Guardian 1992   Whitbread 1992

John Aberdein	A L Kennedy	Ali Smith
Michel Faber	Will Self	Graham Swift
John Fowles	Iain Sinclair	Kurt Vonnegut
James Kelman		

Alex Gray   1950-   Sco

Crime: Police work - UK

⚐ DCI William Lorimer & Dr Solomon Brightman, Psychologist - Glasgow

Lin Anderson	Allan Guthrie	Caro Ramsay
Benjamin Black	Quintin Jardine	Ian Rankin
Gordon Brown	John Macken	Manda Scott
Karen Campbell	Denise Mina	Aline Templeton

Clio Gray

Crime: Historical - C19th

♛ Harry Bowling 2004   ⚐ Whilbert Stroop, Finder of missing persons

Boris Akunin	Michael Gregorio	Frank Tallis
Jason Goodwin	R N Morris	Alison Weir

Sarah Grazebrook

Diana Appleyard	Kate Long	M J Trow
Rebecca Gregson	Robin Pilcher	Jane Elizabeth Varley

Thomas Greanias   US

Adventure/Thriller

Will Adams	David Gibbins	James Rollins
Michael Byrnes	Greg Loomis	James Twining

Andrew M Greeley   1928-   US

Crime: Amateur sleuth

⚐ Blackie Ryan, Bishop - Chicago

William Brodrick	Alison Joseph	Ellis Peters
Kate Charles	Andrew Nugent	Peter Tremayne
Umberto Eco		

George Dawes Green   1954-   US

Crime

Linwood Barclay	Scott Frost	Andrew Klavan
Harlan Coben	John Grisham	Richard Montanari

G

Giselle Green

Diane Chamberlain	Leah Fleming	Margaret Leroy
Kim Edwards	Susan Fletcher	Jodi Picoult

Hilary Green — Saga

WW2

Anne Bennett	Annie Groves	Margaret Mayhew
Emma Blair	Pam Jenoff	Annie Murray
Rita Bradshaw	Beryl Kingston	Lynda Page
Pamela Evans		

Jane Green 1968- — Mature Chick Lit

Katie Agnew	Sarah Duncan	Karen Quinn
Tilly Bagshawe	Milly Johnson	Kathleen Gilles Seidel
Mavis Cheek	Pauline McLynn	Lynne Truss
Rowan Coleman	Allison Pearson	Polly Williams

Linda Green 1970- — Chick Lit

Jenny Colgan	Milly Johnson	Tess Stimson
Jane Costello	Belinda Jones	Gemma Townley

Simon Green 1955- — Fantasy: Dark

also writes as Simon R Green

Kevin J Anderson	L E Modesitt Jr	Andy Remic
Alan Dean Foster	Naomi Novik	Martin Scott
David Gemmell	Terry Pratchett	Jane Welch
Holly Lisle		

G

Graham Greene 1904-91

Justin Cartwright	Alan Furst	Brian Moore
Patricia Duncker	Denis Johnson	Nicholas Shakespeare
David Flusfeder	Nick McDonell	Jonathan Tulloch
Maureen Freely	Pauline Melville	Morris West

Niamh Greene Ire — Chick Lit

Cecelia Ahern	Candace Bushnell	Sophie Kinsella
Sherry Ashworth	Marian Keyes	Adele Parks

Colin Greenland 1954- — Science Fiction: Space opera

 BSFA 1990   Arthur C Clarke 1991

Lois McMaster Bujold	Mary Gentle	Brian Herbert
C J Cherryh	Peter F Hamilton	Brian Stableford
Alan Dean Foster	Harry Harrison	Karen Traviss

Kerry Greenwood   1954-   Aus   Crime: PI

is Isabelle Lewis   ⚵ Hon Phryne Fisher - Melbourne, 1920s

Kate Atkinson   Janet Evanovich   J D Robb
Robert Edric   Anne Perry   Michelle Spring

Michael Gregorio   Crime: Historical - C19th

is Michael G Jacob & Daniela De Gregorio   ⚵ Hanno Stiffeniis, Magistrate - C19th Prussia

Boris Akunin   Stuart M Kaminsky   R N Morris
Jason Goodwin   Andrey Kurkov   Michael Pearce
Clio Gray   David Liss   Frank Tallis

Philippa Gregory   ⌒ ☺   1954-   Historical

🏆 Romantic 2002   ⚵ Wideacre Trilogy

Vanora Bennett   Suzannah Dunn   Katharine McMahon
Clare Clark   Posie Graeme-Evans   Jude Morgan
Katharine Davies   Caroline Harvey   Kate Saunders
Christie Dickason   Jane Johnson   Alison Weir

Susanna Gregory   1958-   Crime: Historical

also writes as Simon Beaufort,   ⚵ Matthew Bartholomew - C14th ⎫ England
The Medieval Murderers (with Philip Gooden,   Thomas Chaloner, Spy - C17th ⎭
Michael Jeck, Bernard Knight, Karen Maitland,
Ian Morson, C J Sansom); is Elizabeth Cruwys

Cassandra Clark   Michael Jecks   S J Parris
Paul Doherty   Bernard Knight   Ellis Peters
Ariana Franklin   Giulio Leoni   Candace Robb
C S Harris   Pat McIntosh   Kate Sedley

J M Gregson   1934-   Crime: Police work - UK

also writes as Jim Gregson;   ⚵ DCI Percy Peach & DS Lucy Blake - East Lancashire
is James Michael Gregson   Det John Lambert & Det Bert Hook

David Armstrong   Caroline Graham   Nicholas Rhea
Jeffrey Ashford   Ann Granger   Sally Spencer
Geraldine Evans

Julia Gregson   1947-

🏆 Romantic 2009

Margaret Cezair-Thompson   Mary Lawson   Kate Morton
Elizabeth Edmondson   Katharine McMahon   Sara Sheridan
Victoria Hislop

Andrew Greig   1951-   Sco

John Aberdein   Francis Cottam   Simon Mawer
Sebastian Barry   Peter Ho Davies   Robert Radcliffe
John Buchan   David Fiddimore   Owen Sheers
Michael Cannon   Robin Jenkins   Alan Spence

G

Kate Grenville 1950- Aus

🏆 Orange 2001   Commonwealth 2006

Murray Bail	Kiran Desai	Lloyd Jones
Carol Birch	Jessica Duchen	Andrew McGahan
Peter Carey	Kim Edwards	Imogen Parker
Candida Crewe	Molly Gloss	Jane Smiley

W E B Griffin 1929- US   Crime: Police work - US

also writes as Alex Baldwin; is William E Butterworth III   Philadelphia

Donald Harstad	Ed McBain	Ridley Pearson
Jack Higgins	Margaret Maron	Joseph Wambaugh

War: Modern

🏃 Corps Series • Badge of Honour Series • Brotherhood of War Series

Harold Coyle	Matthew Reilly	Terence Strong
Graham Hurley	David L Robbins	James Webb
Gordon Kent	Derek Robinson	

Elly Griffiths   Crime: Police work - UK

🏃 Dr Ruth Galloway, Forensic archaeologist - Norfolk • DCI Harry Nelson

S J Bolton	Elizabeth George	Dana Stabenow
Ann Cleeves	Louise Penny	Charles Todd
Kate Ellis		

Martha Grimes 1931- US   Crime: Police work - UK

🏃 DCI Richard Jury - London

Lilian Jackson Braun	Elizabeth George	Maureen O'Brien
Barbara Cleverly	Paula Gosling	Dorothy L Sayers
Deborah Crombie	Graham Ison	Charles Todd

G

Jon Courtenay Grimwood   Science Fiction: Near future

🏆 BSFA 2003 & 2006   🏃 Ashraf Bey

Greg Egan	Jeff Noon	Neal Stephenson
Ian McDonald	Justina Robson	Tad Williams
John Meaney	Lucius Shepard	

Lucretia Grindle US   Adventure/Thriller: Psychological

Suzanne Berne	Mari Jungstedt	Julie Parsons
Ken Follett	Christobel Kent	Gillian White

James Grippando 1958- US   Crime: Legal/financial

🏃 Jack Swyteck, Lawyer - Miami

Jeff Abbott	John T Lescroart	Peter Spiegelman
Jefferson Bass	Steve Martini	Robert K Tanenbaum
William Bernhardt	Richard North Patterson	Scott Turow
Joseph Garber	Michael Ridpath	Stuart Woods

John Grisham ☎ ☺ 1955- US Crime: Legal/financial

♟ Theodore Boone, Amateur Lawyer - 'Strattenburg'

William Bernhardt	Mark Gimenez	Craig Holden
Gianrico Carofiglio	George Dawes Green	Barbara Parker
Linda Davies	John Hart	Christopher Reich
David Ellis	Jilliane Hoffman	Michael Ridpath

Andrew Gross 1952- US Adventure/Thriller

also writes jointly with James Patterson

Michael Connelly	Steve Martini	James Siegel
Robert Ellis	James Patterson	Karin Slaughter
Joseph Finder		

David Grossman 1954- Isr

🏆 Wingate 2004 & 2011

Saul Bellow	Chang-rae Lee	Philip Roth
Linda Grant	Amos Oz	Salman Rushdie
Howard Jacobson	Jonathan Raban	

Annie Groves Saga

is Penny Jordan   ♟ Pride Family - Preston • Campion Family - Liverpool

Maggie Bennett	Pamela Evans	Margaret Mayhew
Jessica Blair	Leah Fleming	Carol Rivers
Rita Bradshaw	Hilary Green	Dee Williams
Glenice Crossland	Maureen Lee	

Heather Gudenkauf US

Diane Chamberlain	Giselle Green	Margaret Leroy
Laura Elliott	Dorothy Koomson	Jodi Picoult

Romesh Gunesekera 1954- Sri Lan

J G Ballard	Michael Ondaatje	Roma Tearne
J M Coetzee	Kamila Shamsie	Paul Theroux
Michelle de Kretser		

Xiaolu Guo 1974- China

Ha Jin	Anchee Min	Qiu Xiaolong
Hanif Kureishi	Andy Oakes	Lisa See
Yiyun Li	Caryl Phillips	Xinran

Abdulrazak Gurnah 1948- Zan

Chimamanda Ngozi Adichie	Joseph Conrad	Rohinton Mistry
Monica Ali	Khaled Hosseini	V S Naipaul
	Ruth Prawer Jhabvala	Paul Theroux

G

David Guterson 1956- US

Debra Adelaide	Lawrence Hill	Marilynne Robinson
Pete Dexter	Michael Kimball	Jane Urquhart
Jennifer Donnelly	William Kowalski	James Wilson
Charles Frazier	Alistair MacLeod	Daniel Woodrell

Allan Guthrie 1965- Sco   Crime: Hardboiled

♥ Theakston's 2007   ⚲ Pearce, ex-Con - Edinburgh

Ray Banks	Alex Gray	Denise Mina
Tony Black	Quintin Jardine	Charlie Owen
Ken Bruen	Stuart MacBride	Ian Rankin
Karen Campbell		

Helon Habila 1967- Nigeria

Chinua Achebe	J M Coetzee	Ben Okri
Chimamanda	Rohinton Mistry	Helen Oyeyemi
Ngozi Adichie	V S Naipaul	

Mark Haddon ☺ 1962-

♥ McKitterick 2004   Whitbread 2003

Neil Cross	Marti Leimbach	Dan Rhodes
Jostein Gaarder	Marina Lewycka	Alice Sebold
Matt Haig	Yann Martel	Miriam Toews
M J Hyland	Rick Moody	Jonathan Tropper

Tessa Hadley

Nicola Barker	Nicci Gerrard	Maggie O'Farrell
Jill Barnett	Alison Jameson	Rachel Seiffert
Rachel Cusk	Jacquelyn Mitchard	Mario Vargas Llosa
Therese Fowler	Laura Moriarty	Gerard Woodward

Matt Haig ☺ 1975-

Mark Haddon	Tony Parsons	Will Self
Nick Hornby	Dan Rhodes	Alan Warner

Jennifer Haigh 1968- US

Laurie Graham	Jojo Moyes	Miriam Toews
Alice Hoffman	Ann Patchett	Anne Tyler
Lorna Landvik	Anita Shreve	

Raymond Haigh   Crime: PI

⚲ Samantha Quest • Paul Lomax, PI

Jeff Abbott	Lee Child	Denis Lehane
Sam Bourne	Robert Crais	George P Pelecanos

G
H

Joe Haldeman   1943-   US   Science Fiction: Space opera

also writes as Robert Graham

Brian W Aldiss	Harry Harrison	Lucius Shepard
J G Ballard	Robert A Heinlein	Robert Silverberg
Orson Scott Card	Robert J Sawyer	Dan Simmons
Harlan Ellison	John Scalzi	

James W Hall   1947-   US   Crime: PI

also writes as James Hall

⚐ Thorn ⎤
Alexandra Rafferty, Police photographer ⎦ Florida

Edna Buchanan	Robert Ferrigno	Jonathon King
James Lee Burke	G M Ford	Elmore Leonard
Lee Child	Carl Hiaasen	Darryl Wimberley

M R Hall   Crime: Legal/financial

⚐ Jenny Cooper, Coroner - Severn Vale District

Simon Beckett	Deborah Crombie	Simon Kernick
Stephen Booth	John Harvey	Kathy Reichs

Patricia Hall   1940-   Crime: Police work - UK

is Maureen O'Connor

⚐ DCI Michael Thackeray & Laura Ackroyd
Journalist - 'Bradfield', Yorkshire

David Armstrong	Paul Charles	Lesley Horton
Robert Barnard	John Connor	Adrian Magson
Pauline Bell	Clare Curzon	Stuart Pawson
Ken Bruen	Georgie Hale	Pauline Rowson

Sarah Hall   1974-

🏆 JLR 2006/7

Margaret Atwood	Margaret Forster	Doris Lessing
Melvyn Bragg	Thomas Hardy	Owen Sheers
Neil Cross	D H Lawrence	Gerard Woodward

Tarquin Hall   1969-   Crime: Police work - India

⚐ Vish Puri, PI - Delhi

Agatha Christie	Andrey Kurkov	Farahad Zama
Shamini Flint	Alexander McCall Smith	Anne Zouroudi

Barbara Hambly   1951-   US   Fantasy: Myth

Marion Zimmer Bradley	Amanda Hemingway	Elizabeth Moon
C J Cherryh	Mercedes Lackey	Tim Powers
Louise Cooper	Anne McCaffrey	Melanie Rawn
Michael Jan Friedman	Julian May	Liz Williams

H

Jane Hamilton   1957-   US

Debra Adelaide
Jennifer Donnelly
Catherine Dunne
Barbara Kingsolver

Mary Lawson
Lorrie Moore
Alice Munro

Ann Patchett
Sarah Rayner
Jane Smiley

Laurell K Hamilton   1963-   US   Paranormal

is Laurell Kaye Klein

♣ Anita Blake, Vampire hunter & crime investigator
Merry Gentry, PI in supernatural crime

Kelley Armstrong
Jacqueline Carey
Karen Chance
Charlaine Harris

Kim Harrison
Barb & J C Hendee
Tanya Huff
Jeanne Kalogridis

Holly Lisle
Kim Newman
Anne Rice
Michelle Rowen

Peter F Hamilton   1960-   Science Fiction: Space opera

Kevin J Anderson
Neal Asher
Tony Ballantyne
Iain M Banks

Greg Bear
Lois McMaster Bujold
C J Cherryh
Jaine Fenn

Gary Gibson
Colin Greenland
Robert Reed
Charles Stross

Ruth Hamilton   Saga

Liverpool & Lancashire

Lyn Andrews
Rita Bradshaw
Alexandra Connor

Josephine Cox
Katie Flynn
Meg Henderson

Maureen Lee
Freda Lightfoot

Steve Hamilton   1961-   US   Crime: PI

♛ CWA 2011

♣ Alex McKnight - 'Paradise', Michigan

C J Box
Loren D Estleman
G M Ford
Sue Grafton

Jonathon King
Elmore Leonard
Michael McGarrity
Walter Mosley

Peter Spiegelman
Dana Stabenow
Robert K Tanenbaum
Jess Walter

H

James Hamilton-Paterson   1941-

♛ Whitbread 1989

♣ Gerald Samper - Tuscany

John Banville
Muriel Barbery
Joseph Conrad

Louis de Bernières
Jane Gardam
Alex Garland

Timothy Mo
Nicholas Shakespeare

Dashiell Hammett   1894-1961   US   Crime: PI

also wrote as Peter Collinson

♣ The Continental Op ⎫
   Sam Spade   ⎬ San Francisco

Megan Abbott
Lawrence Block
James Hadley Chase
Loren D Estleman

Kinky Friedman
Stuart M Kaminsky
Ross Macdonald
Michael Malone

Walter Mosley
Leonardo Padura
Don Winslow
Edward Wright

Gerald Hammond 1926- Sco Crime: Amateur sleuth

also writes as **Arthur Douglas**, ⚐ Keith Calder, Gunsmith ⎫ Scottish Borders
Dalby Holden John Cunningham, Kennel owner ⎭

M C Beaton Joyce Holms Peter Turnbull
Dick Francis Catriona McPherson Margaret Yorke
Jonathan Gash

June Hampson Crime: Hardboiled

⚐ Daisy Lane - Gosport, Hampshire

Kimberley Chambers Mandasue Heller Lynda La Plante
Martina Cole Jessie Keane Kevin Lewis
Heather Graham Roberta Kray Sheila Quigley

Lori Handeland 1961- US Paranormal

Werewolves - Wisconsin

Kelley Armstrong Mary Janice Davidson Katie MacAlister
Patricia Briggs Christine Feehan Sara Reinke
Jim Butcher Charlaine Harris Michelle Rowen
Justin Cronin Sherrilyn Kenyon J R Ward

Kristin Hannah 1960- US

Camilla Läckberg Nicholas Sparks Adriana Trigiani
Deborah Lawrenson Danielle Steel Robert James Waller

Sophie Hannah 1971- Chick Lit

Louise Candlish Sam Hayes Laura Moriarty
Alison Penton Harper Lori Lansens Olivia Ryan
Karen Harper

Crime: Psychological

⚐ Charlie Zailer & Simon Waterhouse - CID
S J Bolton Nicci French Frances Hegarty
Mary Higgins Clark Lesley Glaister Val McDermid
Joy Fielding Karen Harper Barbara Vine
Clare Francis Sam Hayes Minette Walters

Maeve Haran 1950- Mature Chick Lit

Charlotte Bingham Claudia Carroll Sinead Moriarty
Claire Calman Sarah Harrison Kathleen Gilles Seidel

Duncan Harding 1926-2007 Sea: Modern

was **Charles Whiting**
Brian Callison Nicholas Monsarrat Justin Scott
James H Cobb Dudley Pope Terence Strong
Alexander Fullerton Patrick Robinson Peter Tonkin

H

Georgina Harding
Historical

Tracy Chevalier	Sue Gee	Per Petterson
Giles Foden	Jojo Moyes	Salley Vickers

Jules Hardy 1958-

Nicholas Evans	Siri Hustvedt	Julie Myerson
Nicci Gerrard	Kazuo Ishiguro	Sarah Rayner

Beverley Harper 1967-2002 Aus
Saga

Frank Coates	Di Morrissey	Wilbur Smith
Bryce Courtenay	Judy Nunn	Rachael Treasure
Tamara McKinley	Katherine Scholes	

Karen Harper 1945- US
Adventure/Thriller: Psychological

Mary Higgins Clark	Clare Francis	Sophie Hannah
Joy Fielding	Nicci French	Frances Hegarty

Tom Harper
Adventure/Thriller

is Edwin Thomas

Will Adams	David Gibbins	Kate Mosse
James Becker	Tom Grace	Paul Sussman
Paul Christopher	A J Hartley	Robyn Young
Richard Doetsch	Greg Loomis	

Historical: Medieval

🏃 Demetrios Askiates - C11th-14th, The Crusades

Bernard Cornwell	Jack Ludlow	Pip Vaughan-Hughes
Simon Levack	Tim Severin	Jack Whyte

C S Harris US
Crime: Historical - C18th & C19th

is Candice Proctor   🏃 Sebastian St Cyr, PI

David Dickinson	Alanna Knight	Elizabeth Peters
Susanna Gregory	S J Parris	C J Sansom

Charlaine Harris 1951- US
Paranormal

is Charlaine Harris Schulz   🏃 Sookie Stackhouse, Vampire • Harper Connelly, Telepath

Kelley Armstrong	Laurell K Hamilton	Tanya Huff
P C & Kristin Cast	Lori Handeland	Sherrilyn Kenyon
Heather Graham	Kim Harrison	Stephenie Meyer
Kerry Greenwood	Barb & J C Hendee	Darren Shan

Jane Harris Ire
Historical

Vanora Bennett	Kim Edwards	Kate Morton
Tracy Chevalier	Liz Jensen	Sarah Waters
Kiran Desai	Katharine McMahon	

Joanne Harris ⌒ ☺ 1964-

Anthony Capella	Sarah Jackman	Lily Prior
Emma Donoghue	Sue Monk Kidd	Michèle Roberts
Sarah Dunant	Sarah Kate Lynch	Barbara Trapido
Helen Fielding	Jojo Moyes	Barbara Wood

Robert Harris ⌒ 1957- Adventure/Thriller

♟ TGR 1993

Paul Adam	Brendan Dubois	Glenn Meade
Ronan Bennett	Gavin Esler	Rebecca Pawel
Murray Davies	Joseph Kanon	Guy Walters
Michael Dobbs	Robert Littell	James Webb

⌒ Historical: Ancient

ᠰ Cicero

Robert Graves	Steven Pressfield	Steven Saylor
Conn Iggulden	Mary Renault	Barry Unsworth
Douglas Jackson		

Rosle Harris Wales Saga

Wales and Liverpool

Anne Baker	Dilly Court	Meg Hutchinson
Anne Bennett	Katie Flynn	Kitty Neale
Amella Carr	Jess Foley	Margaret Thornton
Catrin Collier	Iris Gower	Valerie Wood

Thomas Harris ⌒ 1940- US Adventure/Thriller: Psychological

ᠰ Dr Hannibal Lecter, Serial Killer • Clarice Starling - FBI

Chelsea Cain	Andrew Klavan	Thomas Perry
Thomas H Cook	Cody McFadyen	Scott Sigler
Michael Crichton	Michael Marshall	Boston Teran
John Katzenbach	Jonathan Nasaw	Tim Willocks

Colin Harrison 1960- US Adventure/Thriller

Jeffrey Archer	Phillip Margolin	Scott Turow
Michael Kimball	David Morrell	Tom Wolfe
Natsuo Kirino	John Sandford	

Cora Harrison ☺ Crime: Historical - C16th

ᠰ Judge Mara - Burren, Ireland

Simon Acland	Margaret Frazer	Ellis Peters
Alys Clare	Bernard Knight	Alexander McCall Smith
Ariana Franklin	Simon Levack	Peter Tremayne

☺ also writes children's books

H

Harry Harrison   1925-2012   US   Science Fiction: Humour

also wrote as Felix Boyd, Frank Dempsey

Christie Golden	Joe Haldeman	Larry Niven
Rob Grant	Robert A Heinlein	Robert Rankin
Colin Greenland	Tom Holt	Martin Scott

Kate Harrison   Mature Chick Lit

Lynne Barrett-Lee	Sinead Moriarty	Tina Reilly
Harriet Evans	Elizabeth Noble	Kirsty Scott
Julia Holden	Adele Parks	Julia Williams
Debby Holt		

Kathryn Harrison   1961-   US

Chimamanda Ngozi Adichie	Kate Furnivall	Amy Tan
Monica Ali	Shena Mackay	Mario Vargas Llosa
	David Park	Salley Vickers

Kim Harrison   US   Paranormal

is Dawn Cook   ⚐ Rachel Morgan

Patricia Briggs	Douglas Clegg	Barb & J C Hendee
Jim Butcher	Heather Graham	Suzanne McLeod
Rachel Caine	Laurell K Hamilton	Lilith Saintcrow
Karen Chance	Charlaine Harris	Kim Wilkins

Noëlle Harrison

Lyn Andrews	Leah Fleming	Sharon Owens
Maeve Binchy	Catherine King	D M Purcell
Jane Fallon		

Sarah Harrison   1946-   Aga Saga

Charlotte Bingham	Maeve Haran	Wendy Perriam
Rose Boucheron	Susan Howatch	Rosie Thomas
Winston Graham	Imogen Parker	Grace Wynne-Jones

Stuart Harrison   Adventure/Thriller

Alice Blanchard	Alan Judd	David Morrell
Nicholas Evans	Jonathan Kellerman	Stuart Woods
Greg Iles	Cormac McCarthy	

H

Go to back for lists of
Pseudonyms • Authors by Genre • Characters and Series • Environments
Prize Winners • Classic Authors • Crossover Authors • Further Reading • Websites

Cynthia Harrod-Eagles   1948-

also writes as Elizabeth Bennett, Emma Woodhouse

Gwendoline Butler
Deborah Crombie
Caro Fraser

Gregory Hall
Graham Ison

Crime: Police work - UK

⚱ DI Bill Slider - London

Barry Maitland
Andrew Taylor

Historical

⚱ Morland Dynasty

🏆 Romantic 1993
Katharine Davies
Sandra Gulland
Joanna Hines

Victoria Holt
Rosalind Laker
Fiona Mountain

Reay Tannahill
E V Thompson

Lilian Harry   1939-

also writes as Donna Baker,
Nicola West

⚱ Lyons Corner House Series ⎫
April Grove Series ⎭ Portsmouth

Saga

'Burracombe' village, Devon

Elizabeth Daish
Margaret Dickinson
Audrey Howard

Beryl Matthews
Margaret Mayhew
Victor Pemberton

Mary Jane Staples
Rowena Summers
June Tate

Donald Harstad   1945-   US

Crime: Police work - US

⚱ Dep Sheriff Carl Houseman - Nation County, Iowa

Giles Blunt
C J Box
W E B Griffin
Tony Hillerman

J A Jance
Ed McBain
Michael McGarrity
Archer Mayor

Deon Meyer
Ridley Pearson
Louise Penny

Erin Hart   US

Crime: Police work - Ireland

⚱ Nora Gavin, Pathologist - Ireland

Elizabeth George
Robert Goddard

Susan Hill
P D James

Sharyn McCrumb
Peter Robinson

John Hart   1965-   US

Crime: Legal/financial

🏆 CWA 2009
William Bernhardt
Stephen L Carter
Linda Castillo
David Ellis

James Ellroy
John Grisham
Steve Martini
Brad Meltzer

George P Pelecanos
Patrick Quinlan
Scott Turow
Don Winslow

H

Kent Haruf   1943-   US

Amy Bloom
Leif Enger
Haven Kimmel

Mary Lawson
Alice McDermott
Marilynne Robinson

Carol Shields
Rose Tremain

Caroline Harvey   1943-   Historical

is Joanna Trollope

| Philippa Gregory | Elizabeth Jeffrey | Robin Maxwell |
| Victoria Holt | Judith Lennox | Diana Norman |

Jack Harvey   1960- Sco   Adventure/Thriller

is Ian Rankin

| Dale Brown | Graham Hurley | David L Robbins |
| Jack Higgins | David Martin | Terence Strong |

John Harvey   1938-   Crime: Police work - UK

also writes as Terry Lennox, James Mann   ☆ DI Charlie Resnick - Nottingham
♈ Higham 1979   CWA 2004 & 2007   DC Frank Elder, Retired policeman
                                    DI Will Grayson & DS Helen Walker - Cambridgeshire

Robert Barnard	M R Hall	Chris Paling
Chris Collett	Declan Hughes	Pauline Rowson
Clare Francis	Gene Kerrigan	Sally Spencer
Bartholomew Gill	Iain McDowall	Camilla Way

Michael Harvey   US   Crime: PI

                                            ☆ Michael Kelly - Chicago

Alex Dryden	Richard Montanari	Marcus Sakey
J A Kerley	Reggie Nadelson	Ronald Tierney
Cody McFadyen	Thomas Perry	

John Harwood   1946- Aus   Crime: Historical - C19th

F G Cottam	Claude Izner	Barrie Roberts
Daphne Du Maurier	Joan Lock	Manda Scott
Carol Goodman	Karen Maitland	Sarah Waters
Susan Hill		

H | Louise Harwood   Chick Lit

Trisha Ashley	Julia Holden	Kate Long
Jenny Colgan	Belinda Jones	Sarah Mason
Harriet Evans	Julia Llewellyn	

Milton Hatoum   1952- Braz

| A S Byatt | Gabriel Garcia Márquez | Tomas Eloy Martinez |
| Carlos Fuentes | Luiz Alfredo Garcia-Roza | Mario Vargas Llosa |

John Twelve Hawks   Adventure/Thriller

| Sam Bourne | William Gibson | George Orwell |
| Paul Christopher | Raymond Khoury | Philip Pullman |

Donna Hay
Chick Lit

Elizabeth Bailey
Zoë Barnes
Melissa Hill

Christina Jones
Dorothy Koomson
Sarah Mason

Jane Elizabeth Varley
Sarah Webb

Mo Hayder
Crime: Psychological

TGR 2002   CWA 2011

DI Jack Caffery - London

Ingrid Black
Chelsea Cain
John Connolly
Daniel Hecht

Jilliane Hoffman
Jesse Kellerman
Peter Leonard
Jeff Lindsay

John Macken
Richard Montanari
Steve Mosby
Michael Palmer

Sam Hayes
Adventure/Thriller: Psychological

Mary Higgins Clark
Harlan Coben
Martina Cole
Joy Fielding

Nicci French
Lesley Glaister
Sophie Hannah
Frances Hegarty

Susan Lewis
Tina Reilly
Claire Seeber

Sparkle Hayter
1958-   Can
Crime: Humour

Robin Hudson, TV journalist - New York

Edna Buchanan
Nancy Cohen
Stella Duffy

Liz Evans
Kinky Friedman
Lauren Henderson

Pauline McLynn
Sarah Strohmeyer
Valerie Wilson Wesley

Shirley Hazzard
1931-   US

Miles Franklin 2004

Suzanne Berne
Jill Dawson
Nicci Gerrard

Lesley Glaister
Siri Hustvedt
Thomas Keneally

Anita Shreve
Gillian White

Daniel Hecht
US
Crime: Psychological

Lucrezia 'Cree' Black, Parapsychologist

Carla Banks
Mo Hayder
Christiane Heggan
Alex Kava

Jonathan Kellerman
Sharyn McCrumb
Val McDermid
Jonathan Nasaw

Meg O'Brien
Erica Spindler
Stephen White
Derek Wilson

H

Frances Hegarty
1949-
Crime: Psychological

also writes as Frances Fyfield

Jenny Diski
Nicci French
Gregory Hall
Sophie Hannah

Karen Harper
Sam Hayes
Judith Kelman

Hilary Norman
Sally Spedding
Barbara Vine

Lynne Heitman
US   Crime: PI

🏃 Alex Shanahan - Aviation

Vince Flynn	Peter James	John J Nance
Ken Follett	Gordon Kent	Stella Rimington

Veronica Heley
1933-   Crime: Amateur sleuth

🏃 Ellie Quicke • Bea Abbot - Abbot Agency

Simon Brett	Anthea Fraser	Ann Purser
Kate Charles	Lis Howell	Betty Rowlands
Clare Curzon	Alexander McCall Smith	Rebecca Tope
Ruth Dudley Edwards	Marianne Macdonald	Jill Paton Walsh

Mandasue Heller
Crime: Hardboiled

Manchester

Massimo Carlotto	Roberta Kray	Sheila Quigley
Martina Cole	Lynda La Plante	John Rickards
June Hampson	Kevin Lewis	Lee Weeks
Jessie Keane	Val McDermid	

Zoë Heller
1965-

Jill Dawson	Mary Lawson	Clare Morrall
Anne Fine	Joan Lingard	Julie Myerson
Helen Garner	Valerie Martin	Ann Packer
Nikki Gemmell		

Hellström
see **Roslund**

Barb & J C Hendee
US   Paranormal

🏃 Noble Dead Series

Kelley Armstrong	Cassandra Clare	Stephenie Meyer
Patricia Briggs	Laurell K Hamilton	Lilith Saintcrow
Jim Butcher	Charlaine Harris	J R R Tolkien
Karen Chance	Kim Harrison	

Lauren Henderson
1966-   Crime: Amateur sleuth

🏃 Sam Jones, Sculptress - London

Linda Barnes	Sparkle Hayter	Gillian Slovo
Lindy Cameron	Pauline McLynn	Stella Whitelaw
Stella Duffy	Zoë Sharp	

Meg Henderson
1948-   Sco   Saga

Maggie Craig	Evelyn Hood	Gilda O'Neill
Margaret Thomson Davis	Meg Hutchinson	Frances Paige
Ruth Hamilton		

H

Veronica Henry
Mature Chick Lit

Judy Astley
Elizabeth Bailey
Nina Bell
Jilly Cooper

Rachel Johnson
Marian Keyes
Jill Mansell
Sarah May

Sinead Moriarty
Tasmina Perry
Melanie Rose
Fiona Walker

Philip Hensher   1965-

♈ S Maugham 1997

Jeffrey Archer
William Boyd
Michael Dobbs

John Lanchester
Richard Mason
James Robertson

Tom Sharpe
Talitha Stevenson
Evelyn Waugh

Brian Herbert   1947-   US
Science Fiction: Space opera

also writes jointly with Kevin J Anderson   ⚲ Dune Saga

Brian W Aldiss
Kevin J Anderson
David Brin
Colin Greenland

Frank Herbert
Glenda Larke
Christopher Paolini

Terry Pratchett
Kristine Kathryn Rusch
Charles Stross

Frank Herbert   ⌒   1920-86   US
Science Fiction: Space opera

⚲ Dune Saga

Brian W Aldiss
Kevin J Anderson
David Brin
Brian Herbert

Glenda Larke
Ursula K Le Guin
Larry Niven

Christopher Paolini
Adam Roberts
Sheri S Tepper

James Herbert   1943-
Horror

Richard Bachman
John Connolly
Stephen Gallagher
Peter James

Stephen King
Dean R Koontz
Stephen Laws

Bentley Little
David Moody
Phil Rickman

Richard Herman   1939-   US
Adventure/Thriller

Dale Brown
James H Cobb
Stephen Coonts

Graham Hurley
Greg Iles
Michael Kimball

David Morrell
Bill Napier
Justin Scott

Anne Herries
Historical

is Linda Sole

Elizabeth Bailey
Elizabeth Chadwick
Fiona Mountain

Diana Norman
Jean Plaidy
Reay Tannahill

E V Thompson
Alison Weir

H

⌒ may be suitable for young adults

David Hewson 1953-   Crime: Police work - Italy

🚶 Det Nic Costa & Gianni Peroni - Rome

Andrea Camilleri	Christobel Kent	Martin O'Brien
Michael Dibdin	Donna Leon	Daniel Silva
Elizabeth George	Magdalen Nabb	Fred Vargas
Michele Giuttari	Barbara Nadel	Jenny White

Georgette Heyer 1902-74   Historical Romance: C19th

Elizabeth Aston	Anne Barbour	Fenella-Jane Miller
Jane Austen	Elizabeth Chadwick	Diana Norman
Elizabeth Bailey	Emily Hendrickson	Amanda Quick
Mary Balogh	Stephanie Laurens	Julia Quinn

Carl Hiaasen   ☺ 1953- US   Crime: Humour

🏆 CWA 1992   Florida

Robert G Barrett	Tim Dorsey	Shane Maloney
Christopher Brookmyre	Peter Guttridge	Zane Radcliffe
Nancy Cohen	Peter Leonard	Donald Westlake
Peter Corris	Douglas Lindsay	

Christine Dwyer Hickey   Ire

Julian Barnes	Amanda Craig	Jennifer Johnston
Sebastian Barry	Roopa Farooki	Andrea Levy

Katie Hickman 1960-   Historical

Suzannah Dunn	Diana Gabaldon	Philippa Gregory
Kate Furnivall	Jason Goodwin	Orhan Pamuk

Keigo Higashino 1958- Ja   Adventure/Thriller: Police work - Japan

🚶 Det Galileo

Chelsea Cain	Jeffrey Deaver	Natsuo Kirino
Tom Clancy	Jonathan Kellerman	James Patterson

H

Jack Higgins ☺ 1929-   Adventure/Thriller

also writes as Martin Fallon, James Graham,   🚶 Sean Dillon
Hugh Marlowe; is Harry Patterson

Brett Battles	Daniel Easterman	Stephen Leather
Ted Bell	Colin Forbes	Craig Thomas
Harold Coyle	W E B Griffin	Brad Thor
David Downing	Graham Hurley	Eric Van Lustbader

Julie Highmore   Mature Chick Lit

Raffaella Barker	Rachel Johnson	Bernadette Strachan
Susie Boyt	Chris Manby	Rosie Thomas
Sarah Challis	Elizabeth Noble	Marcia Willett
Rebecca Gregson	Robin Pilcher	Isabel Wolff

Patricia Highsmith ⌒ 1921-95 US Crime: Psychological

also wrote as Claire Morgan ⚲ Tom Ripley - London

Karin Alvtegen	Claire Kilroy	Patrick Quinlan
Gianrico Carofiglio	Jeff Lindsay	Neil White
David Ellis	Gabrielle Lord	Stuart Woods
Douglas Kennedy	Jennifer McMahon	

Lynn Hightower 1956- US Crime: Police work - US

also writes as Lynn S Hightower ⚲ Det Sonora Blair - Cincinnati • Lena Padgett, PI

Patricia D Cornwell	Thomas Laird	Theresa Monsour
Nicci French	Colleen McCullough	Kathy Reichs
Meg Gardiner	Michael Malone	Jess Walter
Tami Hoag	P D Martin	

Charles Higson ⌒ ☺ 1958- Humour

Joseph Connolly	Colin Forbes	Barry Pilton
Ben Elton	Stephen Fry	Alexei Sayle
James Follett	James Hawes	

Jane Hill US Crime: Psychological

Nicci French	Sarah Rayne	Camilla Way
Tess Gerritsen	Danuta Reah	Gillian White
Val McDermid	Minette Walters	Laura Wilson

Lawrence Hill Can

🏆 Commonwealth 2008

Gil Adamson	Andrea Levy	James Robertson
David Guterson	Toni Morrison	Jonathan Tropper
Sue Monk Kidd	Caryl Phillips	

Melissa Hill Ire Chick Lit

Clare Dowling	Cathy Kelly	Geraldine O'Neill
Imogen Edwards-Jones	Monica McInerney	Morag Prunty
Donna Hay	Carole Matthews	Melanie Rose
Alison Jameson	Anita Notaro	Sue Welfare

Reginald Hill ⌒ 1936-2012 Crime: Police work - UK

also wrote as Dick Morland, Patrick Ruell, Charles Underhill ⚲ Joe Sixsmith, PI - Luton
🏆 CWA 1990   Theakston's 2010 DS Pascoe & DI Dalziel - Yorkshire

Glenn Chandler	Lesley Horton	Iain McDowall
Geraldine Evans	Graham Hurley	Brian McGilloway
Georgie Hale	Bill James	Louise Penny
Susan Hill	Ken McCoy	Caro Ramsay

H

Susan Hill ⌒ 1942-

🏆 JLR 1972   Whitbread 1972

Jo Baker	John Harwood	Kate Morton
Sara Donati	Jennifer Johnston	Adam Nevill
Daphne Du Maurier	Elizabeth Kostova	Ann Patchett
Jane Gardam	Penelope Lively	Rebecca Stott

⌒ Crime: Police work - UK

🚶 DCI Simon Serrailler - 'Lafferton'

Kate Charles	Elizabeth George	P D James
Deborah Crombie	Erin Hart	Sarah Rayne
Judith Cutler	Reginald Hill	

Suzette Hill

Crime: Humour

🚶 Rev Francis Oughterard - St Botolphs 'Molehill'

M C Beaton	Catriona McPherson	Charles Todd
Pauline McLynn	Zane Radcliffe	Rebecca Tope

Tony Hillerman 1925-2008   US   Crime: Police work - US

🚶 Jim Chee & Joe Leaphorn - Navajo Reservation, Arizona

Nevada Barr	Robert Ferrigno	Michael McGarrity
C J Box	Donald Harstad	Michael Malone
James Lee Burke	J A Jance	Deon Meyer
Mark de Castrique	Sharyn McCrumb	Eliot Pattison

Matt Hilton 1968-   Adventure/Thriller

🚶 Joe Hunter, Vigilante - US

Jeff Abbott	Brett Battles	Stephen Leather
Adam Baron	Lee Child	Andy McNab

Joanna Hines 1949-   Adventure/Thriller: Psychological

Vena Cork	Lesley Glaister	Adam Nevill
Nicci French	Carol Goodman	Hilary Norman
Frances Fyfield	Stieg Larsson	Minette Walters
Katy Gardner	Rose Melikan	Gillian White

Historical

Daphne Du Maurier	Philippa Gregory	Susanna Kearsley
Winston Graham	Cynthia Harrod-Eagles	Alison Weir

Victoria Hislop ⌒

Margaret Cezair-Thompson	John Fowles	Ann Patchett
Louis de Bernières	Julia Gregson	Alice Sebold
Kim Edwards	Lori Lansens	Sara Sheridan
	Valerie Martin	Gail Tsukiyama

H

Tami Hoag　1959-　US　　　　　　　　Crime: Psychological

🏃 Elena Estes, ex-Cop now horse trainer
Det Sam Kovac & Tinks Liska - Minneapolis Police Dept

Carla Banks	Iris Johansen	Karen Robards
Chelsea Cain	Colleen McCullough	Karen Rose
Heather Graham	Maile Meloy	Jenny Siler
Lynn Hightower	Meg O'Brien	Stephen White

Robin Hobb　🌈　1952-　US　　　　　　Fantasy: Epic

also writes as Megan Lindholm; is Margaret Ogden

Joe Abercrombie	Stephen Deas	Todd McCaffrey
Sarah Ash	Jude Fisher	Fiona McIntosh
Jacqueline Carey	Lian Hearn	Karen Miller
Cecilia Dart-Thornton	Russell Kirkpatrick	Brent Weeks

Peter Hobbs

John Burnside	Jane Harris	Ali Smith
Anne Enright	A L Kennedy	Louisa Young

Peter Hoeg　🌈　1967-　Den

🏆 CWA 1994

Karin Fossum	Henning Mankell	Jane Smiley
Jostein Gaarder	Per Petterson	Jane Urquhart
David Guterson	Annie Proulx	Jan Costin Wagner
Stuart M Kaminsky		

Alice Hoffman　🌈　1952-　US

Sarah Addison Allen	Janette Turner Hospital	Jacquelyn Mitchard
Michael Collins	Sue Monk Kidd	Bella Pollen
Katharine Davies	William Kowalski	Kate Pullinger
Jennifer Haigh	Alice McDermott	Anna Quindlen

Jilliane Hoffman　US　　　　　　　Crime: Legal/financial

🏃 C J Townsend, State Attorney - Miami

Alafair Burke	John Grisham	J A Kerley
Chelsea Cain	Mo Hayder	Richard Montanari
Stella Cameron	Alex Kava	P J Tracy
Tess Gerritsen	Jesse Kellerman	Scott Turow

Paul Hoffman　　　　　　　　　　　Fantasy: Epic

James Barclay	Raymond E Feist	David Gemmell
Steven Erikson	Neil Gaiman	Adrian Tchaikovsky

Chuck Hogan　US　　　　　　　　Adventure/Thriller

Robert Crais	John Hart	Scott Sigler
Joseph Finder	Dennis Lehane	Don Winslow

H

Craig Holden   US   Crime: Legal/financial

David Baldacci   E L Doctorow   Lisa Scottoline
Stephen L Carter   F Scott Fitzgerald   Scott Turow
Linda Davies   John Grisham

Julia Holden   Mature Chick Lit

Kate Harrison   Rachel Johnson   Tina Reilly
Louise Harwood   Sophie Kinsella   Robyn Sisman
Debby Holt   Carmen Reid   Sarah Tucker

Wendy Holden   ⌒   1965-   Mature Chick Lit

also writes as Taylor Holden

Melissa Bank   Gemma Townley   Cathy Woodman
Lucy Diamond   Daisy Waugh   Deborah Wright
Bella Pollen   Isabel Wolff   Liz Young
Carmen Reid

James Holland   1970-   War: Modern

                                              ⚐ Sgt Jack Tanner - WW2
Frank Barnard   James Delingpole   Iain Gale
Elizabeth Darrell   David Fiddimore   Robert Radcliffe

Alan Hollinghurst   1954-

⚑ S Maugham 1989   Black 1994   Man Booker 2004
Gilbert Adair   Armistead Maupin   Christos Tsiolkas
Michael Cunningham   Alex Miller   Edmund White
Patrick Gale   Edward St Aubyn

Joyce Holms   Sco   Crime: Amateur sleuth

            ⚐ Fizz Fitzgerald & Tam Buchanan, Legal student & lawyer - Edinburgh
David Ashton   Gerald Hammond   Betty Rowlands
M C Beaton   Hazel Holt   Rebecca Tope
Natasha Cooper   Quintin Jardine   Jill Paton Walsh
Liz Evans   M R D Meek   Stella Whitelaw

Anne Holt   1958-   Nor   Crime: Police work - Norway

                        ⚐ Supt Yngvar Stubo & Johanna Vik - Oslo
Karin Alvtegen   Kjell Eriksson   Jo Nesbo
K O Dahl   Mari Jungstedt   Roslund and Hellström
Ake Edwardson   Henning Mankell   Maj Sjöwall & Per Wahlöö

Debby Holt   Mature Chick Lit

Katie Fforde   Sophie King   Jill Mansell
Kate Harrison   Debbie Macomber   Robyn Sisman
Julia Holden

H

Tom Holt 🔊 1961- Fantasy: Humour

Douglas Adams
Robert Asprin
George Macdonald Fraser
Craig Shaw Gardner

Rob Grant
Harry Harrison
Walter Moers
Christopher Moore

Robert Rankin
Martin Scott
Andy Secombe
Chris Wooding

🔊 Humour

Jasper Fforde
Garrison Keillor
David Nobbs

Tom Sharpe
Sue Townsend

Nigel Williams
P G Wodehouse

A M Homes 1961- US

Don DeLillo
Kim Edwards
Jonathan Franzen
Alice Hoffman

Catherine Ryan Hyde
Lori Lansens
Mary Lawson
Sam Lipsyte

Hilary Mantel
Jonathan Trigell
Jonathan Tropper
Brady Udall

Ann Hood US Aga Saga

Elizabeth Berg
Mavis Cheek
Rebecca Dean

Patricia Gaffney
Gail Godwin
Catherine Ryan Hyde

Kate Jacobs
Sue Miller
Elizabeth Noble

Evelyn Hood 1936- Sco Saga

also writes as Eve Houston   🚶 Prior's Ford Series • Scotland

Maggie Bennett
Maggie Craig
Meg Henderson

Gwen Kirkwood
Betty McInnes
Linda Sole

Mary Withall
Valerie Wood

Christopher Hope 1944- SA

🏆 Higham 1981   Whitbread 1984

William Boyd
André Brink
Justin Cartwright

J M Coetzee
Damon Galgut
Nadine Gordimer

Pamela Jooste
Amos Oz
Richard Powers

Rachel Hore Aga Saga

Amelia Carr
Margaret
  Cezair-Thompson
Annabel Dilke
Elizabeth Edmondson

Lissa Evans
Sarah Jackman
Prue Leith
Margaret Leroy

Kate Long
Sara MacDonald
Chris Manby
Robin Pilcher

Shifra Horn Isr

Isabel Allende
Laura Esquivel

Doris Lessing
Rohinton Mistry

Salman Rushdie
Célestine Hitiura Vaite

H

Nick Hornby ☺ 1957-   Lad Lit

Guy Bellamy	Glen Duncan	Mick Jackson
Chris Binchy	Matt Dunn	Mil Millington
Chris Cleave	Lissa Evans	John O'Farrell
James Delingpole	Matt Haig	Jonathan Tulloch

Una Horne   Saga

NE England

Rita Bradshaw	Catherine Cookson	Wendy Robertson
Irene Carr	Elizabeth Gill	Janet MacLeod Trotter
Jean Chapman	Alexandra Raife	

Lesley Horton   Crime: Police work - UK

                                     🏃 DI Handford & DS Khalid Ali - Bradford, Yorkshire

Ann Cleeves	Patricia Hall	David Lawrence
John Connor	Reginald Hill	Iain McDowall
Georgie Hale	Graham Hurley	Nick Oldham

Janette Turner Hospital   1942-   Aus

Margaret Atwood	Thomas Keneally	Toni Morrison
Robert Drewe	David Malouf	Michèle Roberts
Alice Hoffman	Alex Miller	Salman Rushdie

Khaled Hosseini   1965-   Afg

Leila Aboulela	Niccolo Ammaniti	Daniel Mason
Chinua Achebe	Nadeem Aslam	Rohinton Mistry
Chimamanda	Abdulrazak Gurnah	Elif Shafak
Ngozi Adichie	Ruth Prawer Jhabvala	Carlos Ruiz Zafón
Thalassa Ali		

Eve Houston   Aga Saga

H

is Evelyn Hood   🏃 Prior's Ford Series - Scotland

Jan Karon	Ann Purser	Rebecca Shaw
Joan Medlicott	Miss Read	Jack Sheffield

Audrey Howard   1929-   Saga

🏆 Romantic 1988   Liverpool & Lancashire

Anne Baker	Adèle Geras	Lilian Harry
Katie Flynn	Elizabeth Gill	Sue Sully
Jess Foley	Rosie Goodwin	Valerie Wood

Elizabeth Jane Howard   1923-

Rachel Billington	Eileen Goudge	Charlotte Moore
Rose Boucheron	Sandra Howard	Rosamunde Pilcher
Victoria Clayton	Angela Huth	Anna Quindlen
Annabel Dilke		

Jonathan L Howard

Fantasy: Humour

⚐ Johannes Cabal

Ben Aaronovitch	Jasper Fforde	Tom Holt
Jim Butcher	Mark Gatiss	Terry Pratchett

Linda Howard   1950-   US

Crime: Romantic suspense

is Linda S Howington

Beverly Barton	Lisa Jackson	J D Robb
Allison Brennan	Judith McNaught	Nora Roberts
Julie Garwood	Karen Robards	Sharon Sala
Heather Graham		

Sandra Howard   1941-

Aga Saga

Diana Appleyard	Elizabeth Jane Howard	Rosy Thornton
Michael Dobbs	Eve Makis	Joanna Trollope
Adèle Geras	Elizabeth Noble	

Lis Howell

Crime: Amateur sleuth

⚐ Suzy Spencer & Robert Clark - Norbridge Chronicles

M C Beaton	Ann Granger	Katherine John
Kate Charles	Janis Harrison	Louise Penny
Ruth Dudley Edwards	Veronica Heley	Ann Purser
Caroline Graham	Hazel Holt	Patricia Wentworth

Harriet Hudson   1938-

Saga

is Amy Myers

Elizabeth Daish	Lesley Pearse	Audrey Willsher
Victoria Holt	Margaret Pemberton	T R Wilson
Sara Hylton	Marcia Willett	Sally Worboyes

Tanya Huff   1957-   Can

Horror

⚐ Henry Fitzroy & Vicki Nelson, PI

Kelley Armstrong	Christine Feehan	Richard Matheson
Keri Arthur	Laurell K Hamilton	Michelle Rowen
Poppy Z Brite	Charlaine Harris	Darren Shan
Mary Janice Davidson	Jeanne Kalogridis	J R Ward

Declan Hughes   1963-   Ire

Crime: PI

⚐ Ed Loy - Dublin

Ken Bruen	John Harvey	Michael Koryta
Raymond Chandler	Arnaldur Indridason	Stuart MacBride
Lee Child	Faye Kellerman	Brian McGilloway
Elizabeth George	Gene Kerrigan	Peter Robinson

H

Go to back for lists of
Pseudonyms • Authors by Genre • Characters and Series • Environments
Prize Winners • Classic Authors • Crossover Authors • Further Reading • Websites

M K Hume　　Aus　　Historical: C7th

is Marilyn K Hume　　♀ King Arthur

Sam Barone	Conn Iggulden	Peter Tremayne
Bernard Cornwell	Robert Low	Jack Whyte

C C Humphreys　　Can　　Historical

♀ Jack Absolute - C18th • Jean Rombaud, Executioner - C16th England

Bernard Cornwell	John Pilkington	Peter Tonkin
Patricia Finney	C J Sansom	John Wilcox
Philip Gooden	Martin Stephen	

Stephen Hunt　　Fantasy: Myth

Alma Alexander	Helen Hollick	Scarlett Thomas
Susanna Clarke	Stephen R Lawhead	Gene Wolfe
G W Dahlquist	Philip Pullman	

Seth Hunter　　Sea: Historical

is Paul Bryers　　♀ Nathan Peake, Naval officer - C18th/19th

C S Forester	Jonathan Lunn	Peter Smalley
Alexander Kent	Patrick O'Brian	Julian Stockwin

Stephen Hunter　　1946-　US　　Adventure/Thriller

Tom Gabbay	Chris Ryan	Paullina Simons
Gwen Hunter	John Sandford	James Webb

Graham Hurley　　1946-　　Adventure/Thriller

Geoffrey Archer	Jack Harvey	Christopher Nicole
Dale Brown	Richard Herman	Chris Ryan
W E B Griffin	Jack Higgins	

Crime: Police work - UK

♀ DI Joe Faraday & DC Paul Winter - Portsmouth

Paul Charles	Lesley Horton	Charlie Owen
Robert Edric	Peter James	Peter Robinson
Georgie Hale	Quintin Jardine	Pauline Rowson
Reginald Hill	Iain McDowall	Peter Temple

Gregg Hurwitz　　1973-　US　　Adventure/Thriller

David Baldacci	Brian Freeman	Patrick Lennon
Linwood Barclay	Scott Frost	Michael Robotham
Harlan Coben	Mark Gimenez	

Siri Hustvedt　　1955-　US

Jeffrey Eugenides	Jhumpa Lahiri	Anita Shreve
Nicci Gerrard	Salman Rushdie	Zadie Smith
Shirley Hazzard	Kamila Shamsie	Tim Winton

H

Meg Hutchinson   1933-2011   Saga

also wrote as Margaret Astbury   Birmingham

Maggie Bennett	Catherine King	Annie Murray
Rita Bradshaw	Gwen Kirkwood	Jessica Stirling
Sara Fraser	Elisabeth McNeill	Rowena Summers
Rosie Harris	Gwen Madoc	Audrey Willsher

Angela Huth   1938-

Elizabeth Buchan	Shena Mackay	Alan Titchmarsh
Katharine Davies	Margaret Mayhew	Louise Tondeur
Elizabeth Jane Howard	Deborah Moggach	Mary Wesley

Shaun Hutson   1958-   Horror

Simon Clark	David Moody	John Saul
James Herbert	Mark Morris	Whitley Strieber
Richard Laymon	Christopher Pike	Koji Suzuki
Bentley Little	Phil Rickman	

Catherine Ryan Hyde   US

Mitch Albom	Elisabeth Hyde	Jodi Picoult
A M Homes	Lori Lansens	Anita Shreve
Ann Hood	Kate Morton	

M J Hyland   1968-   Aus

♛ Encore 2007   Hawthornden 2007

Chimamanda Ngozi Adichie	Matt Haig	Ann Patchett
Mark Haddon	Hilary Mantel	Alice Sebold

Sara Hylton   Saga

Victoria Holt	Claire Lorrimer	Mary Jane Staples
Harriet Hudson	Margaret Pemberton	Danielle Steel
Elizabeth Lord	Judith Saxton	

Conn Iggulden   1971-   Historical: Ancient

☂ Julius Caesar • Genghis Khan

Sam Barone	Douglas Jackson	Scott Oden
Stephen Baxter	Giles Kristian	Alex Rutherford
Robert Harris	Robert Low	Tim Severin
M K Hume	William Napier	Jules Watson

David Ignatius   1950-   US   Adventure/Thriller

Alex Berenson	David Hagberg	James Rollins
Charles Cumming	Glenn Meade	Jon Stock
Alan Furst		

Greg Iles
1960- US Adventure/Thriller

Linwood Barclay	Alan Judd	Christopher Nicole
John Gilstrap	Robert Ludlum	Matthew Reilly
Stuart Harrison	Glenn Meade	Robert Ryan
Richard Herman	Kyle Mills	Theresa Schwegel

Glyn Iliffe
Historical: Ancient

♁ Odysseus - Ancient Greece

Sam Barone	Ben Kane	Scott Oden
Richard Blake	Robert Low	Simon Scarrow
Christian Cameron	Valerio Massimo Manfredi	Harry Sidebottom
Conn Iggulden		

Arnaldur Indridason
1961- Ice   Crime: Police work - Iceland

♛ CWA 2005   ♁ Insp Erlendur Sveinsson & Sigurdur Oli - Reykjavik

Karin Alvtegen	Karin Fossum	Per Petterson
David Ashton	Matti Joensuu	Yrsa Sigurdardottir
Ake Edwardson	Mari Jungstedt	Maj Sjöwall & Per Wahlöö
Kjell Eriksson	Camilla Läckberg	Johan Theorin

Michael Innes
1906-94   Sco   Crime: Police work - UK

was John Innes Mackintosh Stewart   ♁ DI John Appleby - London

Edmund Crispin	Jill Paton Walsh	Neil White
Dorothy L Sayers	Patricia Wentworth	Jacqueline Winspear

Ian Irvine
1950-   Aus   Fantasy: Epic

Stephen Donaldson	Jude Fisher	Juliet E McKenna
David A Drake	Terry Goodkind	Freda Warrington
David Eddings	Robert Jordan	

John Irving
1942-   US

Jonathan Coe	Jim Lynch	Brady Udall
William Kowalski	Larry McMurtry	John Updike
Jonathan Lethem	Tim O'Brien	Tom Wolfe
Sam Lipsyte	Thomas Pynchon	Tobias Wolff

I

Kazuo Ishiguro
1954-   Ja

♛ Holtby 1982   Whitbread 1986   Booker 1989

Michelle de Kretser	Jules Hardy	Michael Ondaatje
Ronald Frame	Elisabeth Hyde	Alice Thompson
Arthur Golden	Patrick McGrath	Adam Thorpe
Andrew Sean Greer	Timothy Mo	Gail Tsukiyama

may be suitable for young adults

Graham Ison
Crime: Police work - UK

🚶 DCI Harry Brock & DS Poole - London • DI Hardcastle & DS Charles Marriott - WWI, London

Paul Charles	Cynthia Harrod-Eagles	Michael Pearce
Barbara Cleverly	Maureen O'Brien	Anne Perry
Martha Grimes	Robin Paige	Charles Todd

Claude Izner   Fr
Crime: Amateur sleuth

is Liliane Korb & Laurence Lefèvre   🚶 Victor Legris, Bookseller - C19th Paris

Agatha Christie	James McGee	Jean François Parot
John Harwood	Catriona McPherson	Iain Pears
Alanna Knight	Pierre Magnan	Dorothy L Sayers
Peter Lovesey		

Sarah Jackman
Aga Saga

Claire Calman	Jessica Duchen	Sara MacDonald
Clare Chambers	Joanne Harris	Elizabeth Wrenn
Lucy Clare	Rachel Hore	

Douglas Jackson   Sco
Historical: Ancient

Ancient Rome

Richard Blake	Conn Iggulden	Tim Severin
Bernard Cornwell	Steven Pressfield	John Stack
Robert Harris	Simon Scarrow	Robyn Young

James H Jackson
Historical

Stephen Baxter	Matthew Kneale	Tim Severin
Robert Edric	Julian Rathbone	Barry Unsworth

Lee Jackson
Crime: Historical - C19th

🚶 Insp Decimus Webb - London

James McCreet	Andrew Martin	Anne Perry
James McGee	Fidelis Morgan	Deanna Raybourn
Edward Marston	Iain Pears	Brian Thompson

Lisa Jackson   US
Crime: Romantic suspense

Is Susan Lynn Crose   🚶 Det Rick Bentz & Det Reuben Montoya - New Orleans

Sam Baker	Sandra Brown	J D Robb
Beverly Barton	Heather Graham	Sharon Sala
Allison Brennan	Linda Howard	Karin Slaughter

Mick Jackson   1960-

🏆 Authors 1998

Neil Cross	Tony Parsons	David Szalay
Mike Gayle	Graham Swift	Betsy Tobin
Nick Hornby		

I
J

Anna Jacobs   1941-   Aus

Saga

also writes as Sherry-Anne Jacobs, Shannah Jay

♀ Annie Gibson - Lancashire
Kershaw Sisters

Julia Bryant	Katharine Davies	Maureen Lee
Catrin Collier	Elizabeth Elgin	Tamara McKinley
Alexandra Connor	Katie Flynn	Elizabeth Murphy
Dilly Court	Catherine King	Annie Murray

Howard Jacobson   1942-

🏆 Bollinger 2000   Wingate 2000 & 2007   Man Booker 2010

Malcolm Bradbury	Allegra Goodman	Piers Paul Read
Michael Chabon	David Grossman	Tom Sharpe
Edward Docx	Amos Oz	Adam Thirlwell
Michael Frayn	Frederic Raphael	

Christian Jacq   1947-   Fr

Historical: Ancient

also writes as J B Livingstone   ♀ Queen of Freedom Trilogy • Stone of Light Trilogy • Ramses
Judge of Egypt • Mysteries of Osiris • Vengeance of the Gods

Jean M Auel	Robert Low	Steven Pressfield
Sam Barone	Colleen McCullough	Manda Scott
Christian Cameron	Valerio Massimo Manfredi	Robyn Young
Margaret George	Michelle Moran	

Ryan David Jahn   US

Crime: Police work - US

🏆 CWA 2010

Linda Castillo	Jennifer Haigh	Jefferson Parker
John Gilstrap	Jon McGregor	Michael Robotham

Bill James   1929-   Wales

Crime: Hardboiled

also writes as David Craig, Judith James;
is James Tucker

♀ Simon Abelard, Intelligence Officer
DCI Colin Harpur & ACC Desmond Iles - Wales

Jeffrey Ashford	Reginald Hill	David Peace
Ken Bruen	Simon Kernick	Mark Timlin
Martin Edwards		

Eloisa James   1964-   US

Historical Romance: C18th

is Mary Bly Vettori

Mary Balogh	Stephanie Laurens	Julia Quinn
Marion Chesney	Fenella-Jane Miller	Anne Rivers Siddons

J Erica James   1960-

🏆 Romantic 2006

Amanda Brookfield	Jojo Moyes	Rebecca Shaw
Lucy Clare	Melissa Nathan	Rosy Thornton
Jan Karon	Ann Purser	Rachael Treasure
Cathy Kelly	Jennie Rooney	

Margaret James — Saga

is Pamela Bennetts

Pamela Bennetts	Barbara Erskine	Anna Jacobs
Rita Bradshaw	Annie Groves	Susanna Kearsley
Christine Courtnay	Lilian Harry	Deborah Lawrenson

P D James 1920- — Crime: Police work - UK

is Phyllis Dorothy James
🏆 CWA 1971, 1975 & 1986
   Theakston's 2011

🏃 Supt Adam Dalgliesh, DI Kate Miskin &
        Sgt Francis Benton-Smith ⎱ London
        Cordelia Gray, PI ⎰

Jane Adams	Vena Cork	Susan Hill
Vivien Armstrong	Ake Edwardson	Morag Joss
Kate Charles	Kate Ellls	Guillermo Martinez
Jodi Compton	Erin Hart	M R D Meek

Peter James 1948- — Crime: Police work - UK

🏃 DS Roy Grace - Brighton

Rennie Airth	Tom Cain	Martin O'Brien
Mark Billingham	Lynne Heitman	Peter Robinson
Benjamin Black	David Lawrence	Pauline Rowson
W J Burley	Iain McDowall	Neil White

Horror

Jonathan Aycliffe	John Farris	Stephen King
Richard Bachman	Stephen Gallagher	Paul Magrs
Jeremy Dyson	James Herbert	Peter Straub

J A Jance 1944- US — Crime: Police work - US

is Judith Ann Jance 🏃 Det J P Beaumont - Seattle • Sheriff Joanna Brady - Bisbee ⎱ Arizona
                        Alison Reynolds, ex-TV Journalist ⎰

Mary Higgins Clark	J A Kerley	Richard Montanari
G M Ford	Ed McBain	Robert B Parker
Donald Harstad	Michael McGarrity	Dana Stabenow
Tony Hillerman	Claire McNab	Ayelet Waldman

Quintin Jardine 1945- Sco — Crime: Police work - UK

also writes as Matthew Reid

🏃 DS Bob Skinner - Edinburgh
Oz Blackstone & Primavera Phillips

Glenn Chandler	Allan Guthrie	Frederic Lindsay
Michael Dobbs	Joyce Holms	Stuart MacBride
Gillian Galbraith	Graham Hurley	Brian McGilloway
Alex Gray	Paul Johnston	Craig Russell

J

Go to back for lists of
Pseudonyms • Authors by Genre • Characters and Series • Environments
Prize Winners • Classic Authors • Crossover Authors • Further Reading • Websites

Michael Jecks   1960-   Crime: Historical - Medieval

also writes as The Medieval Murderers   ⚐ Sir Baldwin Furnshill & Simon Puttock, Bailiff
(with Philip Gooden, Susanne Gregory,   C14th Devon
Bernard Knight, Karen Maitland, Ian Morson, C J Sansom)

Simon Beaufort	Margaret Frazer	S J Parris
Cassandra Clark	Susanna Gregory	Ellis Peters
Paul Doherty	Bernard Knight	Kate Sedley
Ariana Franklin	Pat McIntosh	Peter Tonkin

Elizabeth Jeffrey   Saga

is Olive Whaley

Margaret Dickinson	Jeannie Johnson	Beryl Kingston
Caroline Harvey	Penny Jordan	Mary Mackie
Elizabeth Ann Hill	Margaret Kaine	Robin Maxwell

Roderic Jeffries   1926-   Crime: Police work - Spain

also writes as Peter Alding, Jeffrey Ashford,   ⚐ DI Enrique Alvarez - Mallorca
Roderic Graeme, Graham Hastings

Catherine Aird	Manuel	Rebecca Pawel
José Latour	Vázquez Montalbán	Michael Pearce
Donna Leon	Magdalen Nabb	

Janette Jenkins   1965-

Kate Atkinson	Helen Dunmore	Sadie Jones
Margaret Atwood	Margaret Forster	Kate Muir

Robin Jenkins   1912-2005   Sco

Michael Cannon	Andrew Greig	James Robertson
Ronald Frame	Marion Husband	Alan Spence
Maurice Gee	Andrew O'Hagan	

Maureen Jennings   Can   Crime: Historical - C19th

⚐ Det William Murdoch - Toronto • DI Tom Tyler • Christine Morris

David Ashton	Edward Marston	Anne Perry
Peter Lovesey	Andrew Martin	Jed Rubenfeld
James McGee	Matthew Pearl	Sara Sheridan

Pam Jenoff   US

Steven Carroll	Hilary Green	Marcia Preston
Sue Gee	Irene Nemirovsky	Rachel Seiffert

Lisa Jewell   ⌂   1968-   Mature Chick Lit

🏆 Nathan 2008

Katie Agnew	Jane Costello	Sarah May
Maggie Alderson	Belinda Jones	Clare Naylor
Susannah Bates	Julia Llewellyn	Daisy Waugh
Rebecca Campbell	Josie Lloyd & Emlyn Rees	Laura Zigman

Ruth Prawer Jhabvala 1927- Ger

🏆 Booker 1975

Anita Desai	Abdulrazak Gurnah	Paul Scott
E M Forster	Khaled Hosseini	Kamilia Shamsie
Amitav Ghosh	V S Naipaul	Carolyn Slaughter

Ha Jin 1956- China

Alma Alexander	Anchee Min	Lisa See
Roopa Farooki	Qiu Xiaolong	Amy Tan
Xiaolu Guo	Richard Russo	Mario Vargas Llosa
Yiyun Li		

Matti Joensuu 1948-2011 Fin Crime: Police work - Finland

🚶 Sgt Timo Harjunpaa - Helsinki

Ann Cleeves	Arnaldur Indridason	Jo Nesbo
Ake Edwardson	Mari Jungstedt	Yrsa Sigurdardottir
Kjell Eriksson	Henning Mankell	

Iris Johansen 1938- US Crime: Forensic

🚶 Eve Duncan, Forensic sculptor • Sarah Patrick & Monty, Search & rescue worker & dog

Max Allan Collins	Carol Goodman	Keith McCarthy
Patricia D Cornwell	Tami Hoag	Karen Robards
Lisa Gardner	Judith Kelman	Erica Spindler

Denis Johnson 1949- US

Paul Auster	Don DeLillo	Thomas Pynchon
Trezza Azzopardi	Glen Duncan	Philip Roth
Gordon Burn	Nathan Englander	Jonathan Trigell
Michael Chabon	Graham Greene	Brady Udall

Jane Johnson ☺ Historical Romance

also writes as Jude Fisher, Gabriel King

Barbara Erskine	Kate Mosse	Bella Pollen
Philippa Gregory	Fiona Mountain	Reay Tannahill

Jeannie Johnson Saga

Elizabeth Bailey	Elizabeth Jeffrey	Freda Lightfoot
Margaret Dickinson	Joan Jonker	Carol Rivers
June Francis	Maureen Lee	Mary Jane Staples

Milly Johnson 1964- Chick Lit

Sherry Ashworth	Jane Costello	Carole Matthews
Jo Carnegie	Jane Green	Sheila O'Flanagan
Lucy Cavendish	Kate Lawson	Kirsty Scott
Rowan Coleman	Jill Mansell	Kathleen Gilles Seidel

J

Jennifer Johnston   1930-   Ire

🏆 Authors 1973   Whitbread 1979

Rose Doyle	Nell Leyshon	Valerie Martin
Anne Enright	Joan Lingard	Edna O'Brien
Susan Hill	Shena Mackay	Colm Toibin
Claire Kilroy	Deirdre Madden	Niall Williams

Paul Johnston   1957-   Sco   Crime: PI

🏆 CWA 1997   🏃 Quintilian Dalrymple - C21st Edinburgh • Alex Mavros, PI - Greece
                                                        Matt Wells, Author - London

Eric Brown	Jonathan Kellerman	Paul J McAuley
Chelsea Cain	Douglas Lindsay	J D Robb
Quintin Jardine		

Doug Johnstone   Sco   Crime: Psychological

Tony Black	Peter May	Irvine Welsh
Christopher Brookmyre	Caro Ramsay	

Belinda Jones   1967-   Chick Lit

Linda Green	Carole Matthews	Tess Stimson
Louise Harwood	Melissa Nathan	Paige Toon
Lisa Jewell	Morag Prunty	Daisy Waugh
Lindsey Kelk	Victoria Routledge	Lauren Weisberger

Christina Jones   1948-   Chick Lit

Louise Bagshawe	Anne Dunlop	Sheila Norton
Claire Calman	Donna Hay	Anita Notaro
Jilly Cooper	Kathy Lette	Plum Sykes

Lloyd Jones   1955-   NZ

🏆 Commonwealth 2007   McKitterick 2005

Nathacha Appanah	Greg Day	Matthew Kneale
Murray Bail	Patrick Gale	Christopher Koch
Nicola Barker	Kate Grenville	Gerard Woodward
Peter Carey	Barbara Kingsolver	

Sadie Jones   1967-

🏆 Costa 2008

Melvyn Bragg	Sebastian Faulks	Kate Morton
Anna Davis	Andrea Levy	Fiona Shaw
Kim Edwards	Ian McEwan	

Susanna Jones   1967-   Crime: Psychological

🏆 CWA 2001   JLR 2001

Benjamin Black	Sophie Hannah	Laura Lippman
Nikki French	Matthew Klein	Minette Walters

J

Joan Jonker   1923-2007   Saga
Liverpool

Lyn Andrews	Elizabeth Daish	Penny Jordan
Benita Brown	Margaret Dickinson	Maureen Lee
Alexandra Connor	Jeannie Johnson	Sharon Owens

Pamela Jooste   1946-   SA

Justin Cartwright	Damon Galgut	Doris Lessing
J M Coetzee	Nadine Gordimer	Paul Scott
Giles Foden	Christopher Hope	

Penny Jordan   1946-2011   Saga
also wrote as Caroline Courtney, Annie Groves, Lydia Hitchcock, Melinda Wright;
was Penelope Jones Halsall

Barbara Delinsky	Joan Jonker	Judith McNaught
Anna Jacobs	Margaret Kaine	Una-Mary Parker
Elizabeth Jeffrey	Jayne Ann Krentz	

Robert Jordan   1948-2007   US   Fantasy: Epic
also wrote as Chang Lung, Regan O'Neal, Jackson O'Reilly, Regan O'Reilly;
also wrote with Brandon Sanderson; was James Oliver Rigney, Jr

Ashok K Banker	Andrew McGahan	Sean Russell
Louise Cooper	John Marco	J R R Tolkien
David Farland	Robert Newcomb	Jane Welch
Ian Irvine	Stan Nicholls	Janny Wurts

Alison Joseph   1958-   Crime: Amateur sleuth
♀ Sister Agnes Bourdillon, Nun

Marian Babson	Jonathan Gash	Hazel Holt
William Brodrick	Elizabeth George	Morag Joss
Elizabeth Ferrars	Andrew M Greeley	Marianne Macdonald

Morag Joss   Crime: Psychological
♀ CWA 2003
♀ Sara Selkirk, Cellist - Bath

Hilary Bonner	Alison Joseph	Fiona Mountain
Gregory Hall	Marianne Macdonald	Sarah Rayne
P D James	Guillermo Martinez	Ruth Rendell

Graham Joyce   1954-   Fantasy: Dark
also writes as William Heaney
♀ British Fantasy 1993, 1996, 1997, 2000 & 2009

J

Jonathan Carroll	Liz Jensen	Scott Nicholson
Christopher Fowler	David Martin	Phil Rickman
Robert Holdstock	Mark Morris	

> ⌂ may be suitable for young adults

Alan Judd 1946- Adventure/Thriller

🏆 Guardian 1991   Holtby 1992   🏃 Charles Thoroughgood

John Fullerton	Humphrey Hawksley	Andy McNab
Joseph Garber	Greg Iles	Daniel Silva
Stuart Harrison	John Le Carré	

Mari Jungstedt 1962- Swe   Crime: Police work - Sweden

🏃 CI Anders Knutas - Gotland, Sweden • Det Karin Jacobsson

Karin Alvtegen	Anne Holt	Jo Nesbo
Ake Edwardson	Matti Joensuu	Häkan Nesser
Kjell Erlksson	Camilla Läckberg	Maj Sjöwall & Per Wahlöö
Karin Fossum	Åsa Larsson	Johan Theorin

Ismail Kadare 1936- Alb

🏆 Man Booker Int 2005

John Banville	George Orwell	Bernhard Schlink
Gabriel Garcia Márquez	Orhan Pamuk	Rachel Seiffert
James Meek		

Margaret Kaine Saga

🏆 Sagittarius 2003   1950s Staffordshire potteries

Benita Brown	Freda Lightfoot	Elizabeth Murphy
Elizabeth Jeffrey	Claire Lorrimer	Sharon Owens
Penny Jordan	Gwen Madoc	Lesley Pearse

Jeanne Kalogridis 1954- US Historical

also writes as J M Dillard

Suzannah Dunn	Tanya Huff	Karen Maitland
C W Gortner	Michelle Lovric	Anne Rice
Posie Graeme-Evans	Katharine McMahon	Dan Simmons
Laurell K Hamilton		

Stuart M Kaminsky 1934-2009 US   Crime: Historical - C20th

🏃 Toby Peters - 1940s Hollywood • Insp Porfiry Rostnikov, Police - Moscow
Abe Lieberman, Police - Chicago

Raymond Chandler	David Guterson	Philip Kerr
James Hadley Chase	Dashiell Hammett	Rosemary Martin
James Ellroy	Peter Hoeg	P J Parrish
Michael Gregorio		

J K

Ben Kane 1970- Ire   Historical: Ancient

Ancient Rome

Lindsey Davis	Alex Rutherford	Harry Sidebottom
Paul Doherty	Steven Saylor	John Stack
Glyn Iliffe	Simon Scarrow	David Wishart
Jack Ludlow		

Joseph Kanon　1946-　US　Adventure/Thriller

Ronan Bennett	John Lawton	Robert Ryan
Dan Fesperman	John Le Carré	Alex Scarrow
Robert Harris	Henry Porter	Robert Wilson

Panos Karnezis　1967-　Gre

Roberto Bolano	Helen Dunmore	Orhan Pamuk
Louis de Bernières	James Meek	Carlos Ruiz Zafón

Jan Karon　1937-　US

is Janice Meredith Wilson　　　　　　　　　　　🏃 Mitford Series - USA

Maeve Binchy	Garrison Keillor	Rebecca Shaw
Fannie Flagg	Joan Medlicott	Jack Sheffield
Eve Houston	Ann Purser	Adriana Trigiani
Erica James	Miss Read	

John Katzenbach　1950-　US　Adventure/Thriller

Russell Andrews	Thomas Harris	Theresa Schwegel
Michael Connelly	Dean R Koontz	Stephen White
Jeffery Deaver		

Alex Kava　US　Crime: Psychological

🏃 Maggie O'Dell, FBI Agent

Robert Gregory Browne	J A Kerley	Susan R Sloan
Daniel Hecht	Jonathan Nasaw	Erica Spindler
Jilliane Hoffman	Meg O'Brien	Lisa Tucker
Jonathan Kellerman	Jenny Siler	Stephen White

Guy Gavriel Kay　1954-　Can　Fantasy: Epic

R Scott Bakker	Amanda Hemingway	Greg Keyes
Mark Chadbourn	Robert Holdstock	J R R Tolkien
Charles de Lint	Katharine Kerr	Jane Welch

Jackie Kay　1961-　Sco

🏆 Guardian 1998

John Burnside	Andrew O'Hagan	Alan Spence
Janice Galloway	Marge Piercy	Alice Thompson
A L Kennedy	Ali Smith	Alan Warner

Jessie Keane　Crime: Hardboiled

🏃 Annie Carter, PI - East End, London

Kimberley Chambers	Mandasue Heller	Sheila Quigley
Martina Cole	Roberta Kray	Denise Ryan
June Hampson	Kevin Lewis	

K

Paul Kearney 1967- Ire — Fantasy: Epic

Stephen Donaldson
Kate Elliott
Raymond E Feist

Maggie Furey
David Gemmell

Stephen R Lawhead
Harry Turtledove

Susanna Kearsley 1966- Can

also writes as Emma Cole

Daphne Du Maurier
Robert Goddard
Joanna Hines

Susan Howatch
James Long

Nora Roberts
Mary Stewart

Barbara & Stephanie Keating

are Barbara O'Hanlon & Stephanie Berke — Kenya

Chinua Achebe
Justin Cartwright

Chris Cleave
Nadine Gordimer

Doris Lessing

H R F Keating 1926-2011 — Crime: Police work - UK

also wrote as Evelyn Hervey;
was Henry Raymond Fitzwalter Keating
♈ CWA 1980

🏃 Insp Ghote - Bombay • DS Harriet Martens
'Greater Birchester'

Jason Goodwin
Priscilla Masters

Magdalen Nabb
Michael Pearce

Georges Simenon
Janwillem van de Wetering

Daniel Kehlmann 1975- Ger — Historical

Andrea Barrett
Michael Chabon

Suzannah Dunn
Jonathan Franzen

Patrick Suskind
Colson Whitehead

Garrison Keillor 1942- US — Humour

is Gary Edward Keillor

Richard Ford
Elizabeth Gaskell
Tom Holt

Jan Karon
Lorna Landvik
Armistead Maupin

Richard Russo
Miriam Toews

Lindsey Kelk — Chick Lit

Jane Costello
Lucy Dillon

Emily Giffin
Belinda Jones

Carmen Reid
Lauren Weisberger

Faye Kellerman 1952- US — Crime: Police work - US

🏃 Lt Pete Decker, Officer Cindy Decker & Rina Lazarus - Los Angeles
DS Romulus Poe - Las Vegas

Alafair Burke
Jan Burke
Joy Fielding

Declan Hughes
Ed McBain
P D Martin

Carol O'Connell
Jefferson Parker
Ridley Pearson

K

134

Jesse Kellerman   1978-   US   Crime: Police work - US

Karin Alvtegen   Mo Hayder   Jeff Lindsay
Mark de Castrique   Jilliane Hoffman   Phillip Margolin
Tess Gerritsen

Jonathan Kellerman   1949-   US   Crime: Police work - US
Det Milo Sturgis & Alex Delaware, Psychologist - Los Angeles
Det Petra O'Connor - Hollywood

Jefferson Bass   Stuart Harrison   Jefferson Parker
Alafair Burke   Daniel Hecht   Ridley Pearson
John Connolly   Paul Johnston   Erica Spindler
Robert Ellis   Alex Kava   Stephen White

Cathy Kelly   Ire   Mature Chick Lit
Romantic 2001
Catherine Alliott   Melissa Hill   Patricia Scanlan
Judy Astley   Erica James   Kirsty Scott
Tilly Bagshawe   Josie Lloyd & Emlyn Rees Kate Thompson
Clare Dowling   Geraldine O'Neill   Gemma Townley

Jim Kelly   1957-   Crime: Amateur sleuth
CWA 2006   Philip Dryden, Journalist - Ely, Cambridgeshire
DI Peter Shaw & DS George Valentine - Norfolk

Jo Dereske   G M Ford   Peter Robinson
Martin Edwards   Ed O'Connor   Chris Simms
R J Ellory   Ruth Rendell   Michelle Spring

Sheelagh Kelly   1948-   Saga
Feeney Family - Yorkshire • Prince Family

Helen Cannam   Maureen Lee   Liz Ryan
Beryl Kingston   D M Purcell   Patricia Shaw
Mary A Larkin   Elvi Rhodes

Susan B Kelly   1955-   Crime: Police work - UK
also writes as Susan Kelly   DCI Nick Trevellyan & Alison Hope
Supt Gregory Summers - Thames Valley

Vivien Armstrong   Natasha Cooper   Veronica Stallwood
Paul Charles   Colin Dexter   Charles Todd

James Kelman   1946-   Sco
Black 1989   Booker 1994   Saltire 2008
John Aberdein   Michel Faber   Caryl Phillips
Louise Dean   Alasdair Gray   Alan Warner
Des Dillon   A L Kennedy   Irvine Welsh

may be suitable for young adults

K

Judith Kelman 1945- US Adventure/Thriller

Virginia Andrews	Frances Hegarty	Fiona Mountain
Joy Fielding	Iris Johansen	Hilary Norman
Carol Goodman		

Linda Kelsey Mature Chick Lit

Diana Appleyard	Jane Fallon	Julia Llewellyn
Marita Conlon-McKenna	Cathy Kelly	Annie Sanders

Thomas Keneally   1935- Aus

also writes as William Coyle ♈ Booker 1982

Peter Carey	Maurice Gee	Brian Moore
E L Doctorow	Shirley Hazzard	Julian Rathbone
Robert Drewe	Janette Turner Hospital	Adam Thorpe
Charles Frazier	Andrew McGahan	Tim Winton

A L Kennedy 1965- Sco

is Alison Louise Kennedy
♈ S Maugham 1994   Encore 1996   Costa 2007   Saltire 2007

John Burnside	Michel Faber	Alasdair Gray
Ron Butlin	Ronald Frame	Jackie Kay
Amanda Craig	Janice Galloway	James Kelman
Glen Duncan		

Bernardine Kennedy

Rachel Billington	Lesley Pearse	Anna Quindlen
Susie Boyt	Libby Purves	Anne Tyler
Anne Fine		

Douglas Kennedy 1955- US Adventure/Thriller

♈ TGR 1998

Ann Brashares	Richard North Patterson	Michael Taylor
Nicholas Coleridge	Andrew Rosenheim	Paul Watkins
Patricia Highsmith	Lionel Shriver	Stuart Woods
Andrew Klavan		

Thomas E Kennedy 1944- US

Isabel Allende	Jeffrey Eugenides	David Malouf
Roberto Bolano	Jonathan Franzen	José Saramago

Alexander Kent 1924- Sea: Historical

is Douglas Reeman   ♟ Richard Bolitho • Adam Bolitho

Tom Connery	Seth Hunter	Patrick Rambaud
David Donachie	Jonathan Lunn	Peter Smalley
C S Forester	Philip McCutchan	Julian Stockwin
Alexander Fullerton		

K

Christobel Kent 1962- Crime: Romantic suspense

⚲ Sandro Cellini, PI - Florence

Andrea Camilleri	Lucretia Grindle	Donna Leon
Michael Dibdin	David Hewson	Sara MacDonald
Elizabeth Edmondson		

Gordon Kent US Adventure/Thriller

is Ken & Christian Cameron ⚲ Alan Craik - US Naval Intelligence • Mike Dukas

James Barrington	W E B Griffin	Charles McCarry
Dale Brown	David Hagberg	John J Nance
Tom Clancy	Lynne Heitman	Brad Thor

Sherrilyn Kenyon 1965- US Paranormal

also writes as Kinley MacGregor

Kelley Armstrong	Charlaine Harris	Sara Reinke
Mary Janice Davidson	Holly Lisle	Susan Sizemore
Christine Feehan	Katie MacAlister	J R Ward
Lori Handeland		

J A Kerley US Crime: Police work - US

also writes as Jack Kerley; is John Albert Kerley ⚲ Det Carson Ryder - Southern States

Alex Barclay	J A Jance	Richard Montanari
James Lee Burke	Alex Kava	Steve Mosby
Michael Harvey	Cody McFadyen	Craig Russell
Jilliane Hoffman	P D Martin	Lee Weeks

Simon Kernick 1966- Crime: Hardboiled

⚲ DI John Gallan & DS Tina Boyd - London

Jeff Abbott	Robert Edric	Barry Maitland
Tony Black	Joseph Finder	David Peace
Anna Blundy	M R Hall	Marcus Sakey
Ken Bruen	Bill James	Mark Timlin

Jack Kerouac 1922-69 US

Alex Garland	Larry McMurtry	Thomas Pynchon
Jay McInerney	Ben Okri	John Steinbeck

Katharine Kerr 1944- US Fantasy: Myth

is Nancy Brahtin

Mark Chadbourn	Guy Gavriel Kay	Anne McCaffrey
Cecilia Dart-Thornton	Greg Keyes	Gregory Maguire
Kate Elliott	Stephen R Lawhead	Judith Tarr

Go to back for lists of
Pseudonyms • Authors by Genre • Characters and Series • Environments
Prize Winners • Classic Authors • Crossover Authors • Further Reading • Websites

K

Philip Kerr
1956- Sco   Adventure/Thriller

♛ CWA 2009   ☥ Bernard Gunther - Germany

Geoffrey Archer	David Downing	Stuart M Kaminsky
Ronan Bennett	Robert Edric	John Lawton
Simon Conway	Alan Furst	Tom Rob Smith
Michael Cordy	Michele Giuttari	Nigel West

Gene Kerrigan
Ire   Adventure/Thriller

Dublin

Benjamin Black	John Harvey	Brian McGilloway
Tana French	Declan Hughes	Joseph O'Connor

Kate Kerrigan

is Morag Prunty

Maeve Binchy	Jonathan Safran Foer	Richard Russo
Marika Cobbold	Elizabeth Noble	Carol Shields

Greg Keyes
1963- US   Fantasy: Epic

R Scott Bakker	Stephen R Lawhead	Patrick Rothfuss
James Barclay	Tim Lebbon	Brian Ruckley
Guy Gavriel Kay	Ian R MacLeod	Sean Russell
Katharine Kerr	George R R Martin	Tad Williams

Marian Keyes
1963- Ire   Mature Chick Lit

♛ Nathan 2007

Katie Agnew	Clare Dowling	Louise Kean
Melissa Bank	Niamh Greene	Pauline McLynn
Claudia Carroll	Veronica Henry	Karen Quinn
Rowan Coleman	Milly Johnson	Grace Wynne-Jones

Raymond Khoury
1960- Leb   Adventure/Thriller: Historical

Sam Bourne	Michael Cordy	Chris Kuzneski
Dan Brown	William Dietrich	Arturo Pérez-Reverte
John Case	John Twelve Hawks	Matthew Reilly
Glenn Cooper	Nada Awar Jarrar	Paul Sussman

Sue Monk Kidd
1948- US

Sarah Addison Allen	Lawrence Hill	Jacquelyn Mitchard
Connie May Fowler	Alice Hoffman	Ann Packer
Laurie Graham	Barbara Kingsolver	Nicholas Sparks
Joanne Harris	Lorna Landvik	Miriam Toews

Claire Kilroy
1973- Ire

Sebastian Barry	Patricia Highsmith	Rose Tremain
Roddy Doyle	Jennifer Johnston	William Trevor

K

Garry Kilworth   1941- War: Historical - C19th

also writes as Garry Douglas
🏃 Sgt 'Fancy' Jack Crossman - Crimea War

Roger Carpenter	Iain Gale	Simon Scarrow
Bernard Cornwell	Allan Mallinson	John Wilcox
George Macdonald Fraser		

Michael Kimball 1949- US Adventure/Thriller

David Guterson	Stephen King	Robert Ryan
Colin Harrison	David Morrell	John Sandford
Richard Herman	Christopher Nicole	Alex Scarrow

Haven Kimmel US

Amy Bloom	Fannie Flagg	Adriana Trigiani
Jennifer Donnelly	Kent Haruf	Anne Tyler
Leif Enger	Mary Lawson	

Catherine King Saga

Barbara Taylor Bradford	Iris Gower	Anna Jacobs
Dilly Court	Noëlle Harrison	Rachael Treasure
Katie Flynn	Meg Hutchinson	Valerie Wood

Jonathon King US Crime: Amateur sleuth

🏃 Max Freeman, Retired policeman - Florida

James Lee Burke	Steve Hamilton	John Rickards
Robert Ferrigno	Michael Malone	Martin Walker
James W Hall		

Laurie R King 1952- US Crime: Historical - C20th

also writes as Laurie King
🏃 Sherlock Holmes & Mary Russell - C20th London
Det Kate Martinelli & Det A Hawkin - San Fransisco • Anne Waverley

Jan Burke	Arthur Conan Doyle	Claire McNab
Kenneth Cameron	John Dunning	Robin Paige
Lindy Cameron	Meg Gardiner	Charles Todd
Barbara Cleverly	Paula Gosling	

Stephen King 1947- US Horror

also writes as Richard Bachman
🏃 The Dark Tower Series
🏆 British Fantasy 1999 & 2005

Justin Cronin	Michael Kimball	Adam Nevill
John Farris	Michael Koryta	John Saul
James Herbert	Tim Lebbon	Dan Simmons
Peter James	Gregory Maguire	T M Wright

☺ also writes children's books

K

Barbara Kingsolver 1955- US

♈ Orange 2010

Gail Anderson-Dargatz	Jane Hamilton	Chang-rae Lee
Louise Erdrich	Lloyd Jones	Margaret Leroy
Janet Fitch	Sue Monk Kidd	Jacquelyn Mitchard
Patricia Gaffney	Nicole Krauss	Amy Tan

Beryl Kingston 1931- Saga

🏃 Easter Empire - London

Philip Boast	Elizabeth Jeffrey	Gilda O'Neill
Rose Boucheron	Sheelagh Kelly	Carol Rivers
Hilary Green	Sheila Newberry	June Tate

Sophie Kinsella ⌒ 1969- Chick Lit

is Madeleine Wickham 🏃 Becky Bloomwood • Shopaholic Series

Melissa Bank	Julia Holden	Karen Quinn
Maria Beaumont	Pauline McLynn	Annie Sanders
Claudia Carroll	Holly McQueen	Kathleen Tessaro
Niamh Greene	Eve Makis	Gemma Townley

Russell Kirkpatrick 1961- NZ Fantasy: Epic

Raymond E Feist	Tom Lloyd	Christopher Paolini
Terry Goodkind	Fiona McIntosh	Steph Swainston
Robin Hobb	John Marco	

Gwen Kirkwood Saga

🏃 'Fiarlyden' Series - Scotland

Doris Davidson	Meg Hutchinson	Eileen Ramsay
Christine Marion Fraser	Elisabeth McNeill	Mary Withall
Evelyn Hood		

Andrew Klavan 1954- US Adventure/Thriller: Psychological

also writes as Keith Peterson 🏃 Scott Weiss & Jim Bishop, PI - San Francisco
♈ TGR 1996

Chaz Brenchley	Douglas Kennedy	Tim Willocks
George Dawes Green	Sharyn McCrumb	Stuart Woods
Thomas Harris	Scott Smith	

Matthew Kneale 1960- Historical

♈ S Maugham 1988   JLR 1992   Whitbread 2000

Andrea Barrett	Margaret Elphinstone	Julian Rathbone
William Boyd	James Fleming	James Robertson
Will Davenport	James H Jackson	Jennie Rooney
Robert Drewe	Lloyd Jones	Jane Stevenson

K

Alanna Knight
1923- Sco   Crime: Historical

also writes as Margaret Hope   ☩ DI Jeremy Faro - C19th Edinburgh
Rose McQuinn - C19th Edinburgh • Tam Eildor
Jacobean Scotland

David Ashton	C S Harris	Catriona McPherson
Louis Bayard	Claude Izner	Amy Myers
Carrie Bebris	Joan Lock	Norman Russell
Arthur Conan Doyle	Peter Lovesey	Catherine Shaw

Bernard Knight
1931- Wales   Crime: Historical - Medieval

also writes as The Medieval Murderers   ☩ Sir John de Wolfe, 'Crowner John' - C12th Devon
(with Philip Gooden, Susanne Gregory,
Michael Jecks, Karen Maitland, Ian Morson, C J Sansom)

Alys Clare	Cora Harrison	Ian Morson
Paul Doherty	Michael Jecks	Sharan Newman
Susanna Gregory	Pat McIntosh	Kate Sedley

India Knight
1965-   Mature Chick Lit

Raffaella Barker	Anna Maxted	Kirsty Scott
Emily Barr	Clare Naylor	Daisy Waugh
Lucy Dawson	William Nicholson	Isabel Wolff
Gil McNeil	Adele Parks	

Malcolm Knox
1966- Aus

Richard Bausch	Michael Chabon	Simon Mawer
William Boyd	F Scott Fitzgerald	Tim Winton

Tom Knox
1963-   Adventure/Thriller

is Sean Thomas

Will Adams	Dan Brown	Andy McDermott
Steve Berry	Glenn Cooper	Scott Mariani

Dorothy Koomson
Mature Chick Lit

Trisha Ashley	Margaret Leroy	Alexandra Potter
Suzanne Bugler	Gil McNeil	Carmen Reid
Louise Candlish	Anna McPartlin	Kate Thompson
Donna Hay	Melissa Nathan	Grace Wynne-Jones

Dean R Koontz
☎ 1945- US   Adventure/Thriller

also writes as Brian Coffey, Deanne Dwyer,   ☩ Odd Thomas, Cook
K R Dwyer, Leigh Nicols, Owen West, Aaron Wolfe

Richard Bachman	John Katzenbach	Rick Mofina
Robert Gregory Browne	Richard Laymon	John Saul
Stephen Gallagher	Robert McCammon	Koji Suzuki
James Herbert	Gregory Maguire	Tim Willocks

K

Michael Koryta   US   Horror

Chelsea Cain	Stephen King	Andrew Pyper
Declan Hughes	Archer Mayor	Peter Straub

Elizabeth Kostova   1964-   US

Daphne Du Maurier	Susan Hill	Kate Morton
Arabella Edge	Yann Martel	Audrey Niffenegger
Robert Goddard	Mark Mills	

William Kowalski   1973-   US

Karen Joy Fowler	Alice Hoffman	Jonathan Tropper
David Guterson	John Irving	Anne Tyler

Marek Krajewski   1966-   Pol   Crime

⚐ Captain Eberhard Mock

Michele Giuttari	Roberta Kray	Liza Marklund
Philip Kerr	Lynda La Plante	Henry Porter

Nicole Krauss   1974-   US

Muriel Barbery	Jonathan Franzen	David Szalay
Hester Browne	Barbara Kingsolver	Emma Tennant
Kim Edwards	Claire Messud	Barbara Trapido
Jonathan Safran Foer	Eva Rice	

Roberta Kray   1959-   Crime: Hardboiled

Massimo Carlotto	Mandasue Heller	Kevin Lewis
Martina Cole	Lynda La Plante	Sheila Quigley
June Hampson		

Jayne Ann Krentz   1948-   US   Glitz & Glamour

also writes as Jayne Castle, Stephanie James, Amanda Quick

Sandra Brown	Judith Gould	Judith McNaught
Candace Bushnell	Penny Jordan	Madge Swindells
Janet Dailey		

Giles Kristian   1975-   US   Historical: C8-10th

⚐ Raven Series - Vikings

Bernard Cornwell	Douglas Jackson	Manda Scott
Conn Iggulden	Robert Low	Tim Severin

Richard Kunzmann   1976-   SA   Crime: Police work - South Africa

⚐ Det Harry Mason - Johannesburg • Jacob Tshabalala

Chelsea Cain	Stuart MacBride	Jo Nesbo
Michael Connelly	Deon Meyer	Qiu Xiaolong

K

Hari Kunzru 1969-

🏆 Betty Trask 2002   S Maugham 2003

Peter Carey	Loren D Estleman	Zadie Smith
E L Doctorow	Janice Galloway	Meera Syal

Hanif Kureishi 〈⌒〉 1954-

🏆 Whitbread 1990

Monica Ali	Caryl Phillips	Jonathan Tulloch
Xiaolu Guo	Zadie Smith	Louisa Young
Armistead Maupin	Meera Syal	

Andrey Kurkov 1961- Rus   Crime: Humour

🏃 Lieut Viktor Slutsky - Russia & Ukraine

Boris Akunin	Christopher Fowler	Douglas Lindsay
Tom Bradby	Michael Gregorio	R N Morris
Sam Eastland	Peter Guttridge	

Chris Kuzneski 1969- US   Adventure/Thriller

🏃 Jonathon Payne & D J Jones - MANIAC Special Forces

Will Adams	John Case	Raymond Khoury
James Becker	Michael Cordy	Scott Mariani
Steve Berry	Juan Gómez-Jurado	James Rollins
Sam Bourne	Tom Grace	Paul Sussman

Lynda La Plante 〈⌒〉 1946-   Crime: Police work

🏃 DCI Jane Tennison • Supt Mike Walker • Det Anna Travis & DCI James Langton - London
Lorraine Page, PI - Los Angeles

Martina Cole	Mandasue Heller	Sheila Quigley
John Connor	Roberta Kray	Denise Ryan
June Hampson	Sara Paretsky	Medora Sale

Camilla Läckberg 1971- Swe   Crime: Police work - Sweden

🏃 Det Patrik Hedstrom - Fjällbacka, Sweden

Karin Alvtegen	Mari Jungstedt	Jo Nesbo
Karin Fossum	Stieg Larsson	Håkan Nesser
Tana French	Henning Mankell	Yrsa Sigurdardottir
Arnaldur Indridason		

Mercedes Lackey 1950- US   Fantasy: Epic

Carol Berg	Holly Lisle	Elizabeth Moon
David Farland	Anne McCaffrey	Melanie Rawn
Barbara Hambly	Todd McCaffrey	Mickey Zucker Reichert
Tanith Lee	L E Modesitt Jr	R A Salvatore

〈⌒〉 may be suitable for young adults

K
L

Jhumpa Lahiri 1967- US

🏆 Pulitzer 2000

Chitra Banerjee Divakaruni	Andrew Sean Greer	Anita Nair
Edward Docx	Rani Manicka	Dan Rhodes
Jennifer Egan	Benjamin Markovits	Kamila Shamsie
Roopa Farooki	Claire Messud	Thrity Umrigar

Nick Laird 1975- Ire

🏆 Betty Trask 2006

Kingsley Amis	William Boyd	David Lodge
Kate Atkinson	Ronald Frame	Zadie Smith

Deryn Lake 1937- Crime: Historical - C18th

is Dinah Lampitt 🏃 John Rawlings, Apothecary - C18th London

Gwendoline Butler	Rose Melikan	Imogen Robertson
Janet Gleeson	Matthew Pearl	Catherine Shaw
David Liss	Andrew Pepper	Rosemary Stevens
James McGee		

Cathy Lamb US

Sarah Addison Allen	Fannie Flagg	Debbie Macomber
Rowan Coleman	Ann Hood	Nora Roberts
Kiran Desai		

Shaena Lambert Can

Margaret Atwood	Joyce Carol Oates	Rose Tremain
Alice Munro	Carol Shields	Jane Urquhart

John Lanchester 1962-

🏆 Betty Trask 1996   Hawthornden 1997   Whitbread 1996

Alan Bennett	David Nicholls	Henry Sutton
Jonathan Coe	Talitha Stevenson	Nigel Williams
Philip Hensher		

William Landay US Crime: Police work - US

🏆 CWA 2003 Boston

Michael Connelly	Michael Koryta	Richard Montanari
Robert Crais	David Lawrence	Don Winslow

Lorna Landvik 1954- US

Sarah Addison Allen	Laurie Graham	Jojo Moyes
Elizabeth Berg	Jennifer Haigh	Richard Russo
Lucy Dillon	Sue Monk Kidd	Adriana Trigiani
Fannie Flagg	Maile Meloy	Farahad Zama

Lee Langley   Ind

Tracy Chevalier	Ian McEwan	Arundhati Roy
Patrick Gale	Andrew Miller	Salman Rushdie

Joe R Lansdale   1951- US   Crime: Humour

*Hap Collins & Leonard Pine - Texas • Constable Sunset Jones - 1930s Texas

Poppy Z Brite	Tim Dorsey	Danny King
Robert Crais	Loren D Estleman	Zane Radcliffe

Lori Lansens   Can

Kim Edwards	Catherine Ryan Hyde	Kate Morton
Victoria Hislop	Mary Lawson	Christos Tsiolkas
A M Homes	Toni Morrison	

Glenda Larke   Aus   Fantasy: Epic

Colin Greenland	Frank Herbert	Karen Miller
Brian Herbert	Fiona McIntosh	Christopher Paolini

Mary A Larkin   1935- Ire   Saga

is Mary A McNulty   Northern Ireland

Lyn Andrews	Sheelagh Kelly	Victor Pemberton
Frank Delaney	Geraldine O'Neill	Miss Read
Rose Doyle	Sharon Owens	Denise Robertson

Åsa Larsson   1966- Swe   Crime: Police work - Sweden

*Rebecka Martinsson, Lawyer

K O Dahl	Mari Jungstedt	Maj Sjöwall & Per Wahlöö
Ake Edwardson	Stieg Larsson	Minette Walters
Kjell Eriksson	Jo Nesbo	

Stieg Larsson   1954-2004 Swe   Crime: Amateur sleuth

*Mikael Blomkvist & Lisbeth Salander, Journalist & Computer hacker • Millenium Trilogy

Karin Alvtegen	Åsa Larsson	Maj Sjöwall & Per Wahlöö
Ake Edwardson	Dominique Manotti	Johan Theorin
Tana French	Per Petterson	Linn Ullmann
Camilla Läckberg	Roslund and Hellström	Jan Costin Wagner

José Latour   1940- Cuba   Crime: Police work - Cuba

*Capt Trujillo - Havana

Luiz Alfredo Garcia-Roza	Leonardo Padura	Donald Westlake
Roderic Jeffries	Martin Cruz Smith	Don Winslow
Elmore Leonard		

Go to back for lists of
Pseudonyms • Authors by Genre • Characters and Series • Environments
Prize Winners • Classic Authors • Crossover Authors • Further Reading • Websites

Stephanie Laurens   Aus   Historical Romance: C19th

🏃 The Hon Barnaby Adair • Bastion Club - British Secret Service

Mary Balogh	Emily Hendrickson	Fenella-Jane Miller
Anne Barbour	Georgette Heyer	Julia Quinn
Marion Chesney	Eloisa James	

Stephen R Lawhead   ☏   1950-   US   Fantasy: Myth

C J Cherryh	Katharine Kerr	Caiseal Mor
Helen Hollick	Greg Keyes	Jack Vance
Stephen Hunt	Morgan Llywelyn	Jane Welch
Paul Kearney		

David Lawrence   Crime: Psychological

is David Harsent   🏃 DS Stella Mooney - London

Vivien Armstrong	John Connor	Peter James
Lindsay Ashford	Lesley Horton	Stuart MacBride
Mark Billingham		

Deborah Lawrenson

Caitlin Davies	Douglas Kennedy	Ann Patchett
Kristin Hannah	Judith Lennox	Emma Tennant

Kate Lawson   Mature Chick Lit

also writes as Gemma Fox, Sue Welfare

Jane Fallon	Kate Long	Sarah Tucker
Fiona Gibson	Monica McInerney	Sue Welfare
Milly Johnson	Carole Matthews	

Mary Lawson   1946-   Can

🏆 McKitterick 2003

Raffaella Barker	Jane Hamilton	Alice McDermott
Amy Bloom	Kent Haruf	Lorrie Moore
Joy Chambers	Haven Kimmel	Marilynne Robinson
Julia Gregson	Lori Lansens	Carol Shields

Mike Lawson   US   Adventure/Thriller

🏃 Joe DeMarco

David Baldacci	Barry Eisler	Robert Ryan
Steve Berry	Vince Flynn	Daniel Silva
Sam Bourne		

John Lawton   1949-   Crime: Police work - UK

🏃 CDS Frederick Troy - London

Ted Allbeury	Len Deighton	Joseph Kanon
Stephen J Cannell	Ken Follett	Philip Kerr
Jon Cleary	Alan Furst	Alex Scarrow

Richard Laymon   1947-2001   US   Horror

also wrote as Richard Kelly, Carol Laymon

Clive Barker	Bentley Little	Christopher Pike
John Farris	David Moody	Koji Suzuki
Shaun Hutson	Scott Nicholson	T M Wright
Dean R Koontz		

John Le Carré   ⌒   1931-   Adventure/Thriller

is David John Moore Cornwell   � George Smiley, Spy
♈ CWA 1977 & 2005

Ronan Bennett	David Downing	Joseph Kanon
William Bernhardt	Brian Freemantle	Kyle Mills
John Burdett	Nada Awar Jarrar	Matt Rees
Simon Conway	Alan Judd	Jon Stock

Ursula K Le Guin   ⌒   ☺   1929-   US   Fantasy: Epic

Trudi Canavan	Frank Herbert	Sheri S Tepper
Mike Carey	Christopher Paolini	Karen Traviss
Isobelle Carmody	Geoff Ryman	Gene Wolfe
Mary Gentle	Steph Swainston	Sarah Zettel

Stephen Leather   ⌒   Adventure/Thriller

☖ Dan 'Spider' Shepherd, Undercover cop • Jack Nightingale, PI - London

Geoffrey Archer	Harold Coyle	James Long
Tom Bradby	Jack Higgins	Tim Sebastian
Nick Brownlee	Matt Hilton	Gerald Seymour

Caroline Leavitt   US

Diane Chamberlain	Sue Miller	Anna Quindlen
Margaret Leroy	Jane Moore	Sarah Rayner

David Leavitt   1961-   US

Peter Carey	Michael Chabon	Graham Swift
Justin Cartwright	Patrick McGrath	Edmund White

Tim Lebbon   1969-   Fantasy: Dark

♈ British Fantasy 2007

Storm Constantine	Stephen King	Scott Lynch
Greg Keyes	Brian Lumley	Patrick Rothfuss

Chang-rae Lee   1965-   Kor

Louise Erdrich	Toni Morrison	Amy Tan
David Grossman	Philip Roth	John Updike
Barbara Kingsolver		

Maureen Lee · Saga

♈ Romantic 2000 · 🚶 Pearl Street - Liverpool

Lyn Andrews	Anna Jacobs	Sheelagh Kelly
Anne Baker	Jeannie Johnson	Margaret Mayhew
Annie Groves	Joan Jonker	Elizabeth Murphy
Ruth Hamilton		

Tanith Lee ☎ ☺ 1947- · Fantasy: Dark

also writes as Esther Garber;
is Tanith Lee Kaiine · Venus (Venice)

Dan Abnett	Ben Counter	Holly Lisle
Marion Zimmer Bradley	Cecilia Dart-Thornton	Freda Warrington
C J Cherryh	Mercedes Lackey	Liz Williams

Dennis Lehane 1965- US · Crime: Police work - US

🚶 Patrick Kenzie & Angie Gennaro - Boston, Mass

Megan Abbott	G M Ford	Thomas Perry
Adam Baron	Chuck Hogan	John Sandford
Gordon Burn	Magdalen Nabb	John Shannon
John Connolly	Reggie Nadelson	Boston Teran

Marti Leimbach US

Mark Haddon	Jodi Picoult	Lionel Shriver
Clare Morrall	Alice Sebold	Jonathan Tropper

Prue Leith 1940- · Aga Saga

Rachel Cusk	Katie Fforde	Elizabeth Noble
Elizabeth Edmondson	Rachel Hore	Patricia Scanlan
Kim Edwards		

Simon Lelic 1976- · Crime: Psychological

Belinda Bauer	Tana French	Steve Hamilton
Tom Franklin	Alan Glynn	Sophie Hannah

Judith Lennox 1953- · Saga

Amelia Carr	Rosalind Laker	Rosamunde Pilcher
Rebecca Dean	Tamara McKinley	Mary Stewart
Rosie Goodwin	Imogen Parker	Margaret Thornton
Caroline Harvey		

Donna Leon 1942- US · Crime: Police work - Italy

♈ CWA 2000 · 🚶 Commissario Guido Brunetti - Venice

Andrea Camilleri	David Hewson	Magdalen Nabb
Gianrico Carofiglio	Christobel Kent	Qiu Xiaolong
Michael Dibdin	Giulio Leoni	Ronald Tierney
Michele Giuttari	Carlo Lucarelli	Fred Vargas

Elmore Leonard ⌒ 1925- US Crime: Hardboiled

🏆 CWA 2006

Lawrence Block	Steve Hamilton	Thomas Perry
Tim Dorsey	José Latour	Mario Puzo
Kinky Friedman	Peter Leonard	Donald Westlake
James W Hall	Shane Maloney	Darryl Wimberley

Peter Leonard US Crime: Hardboiled

Michael Connelly	Elmore Leonard	Scott Turow
Mo Hayder	Phillip Margolin	Don Winslow
Carl Hiaasen		

Giulio Leoni It Crime: Historical - C14th

🚶 Dante Alighieri, Amateur sleuth - Florence

Lindsey Davis	Carlo Lucarelli	Caroline Roe
Susanna Gregory	Magdalen Nabb	Carlos Ruiz Zafón
Donna Leon		

Margaret Leroy

Diane Chamberlain	Barbara Kingsolver	Marcia Preston
Giselle Green	Dorothy Koomson	Alice Sebold
Rachel Hore	Jodi Picoult	

John T Lescroart 1948- US Crime: Legal/financial

🚶 Dismas Hardy, Attorney - San Francisco • Abe Glitsky, Policeman

William Bernhardt	Linda Fairstein	Steve Martini
Harry Bingham	James Grippando	Nancy Taylor Rosenberg
Stephen L Carter	David Hosp	Lisa Scottoline

Doris Lessing ⌒ 1919-

also writes as Jane Somers; is Doris Tayler

J M Coetzee	Pamela Jooste	Iris Murdoch
Maggie Gee	Barbara &	Helen Simpson
Nadine Gordimer	Stephanie Keating	Gillian Slovo
Sarah Hall	Anne Michaels	Muriel Spark
Shifra Horn		

Jonathan Lethem 1964- US

🏆 CWA 2000

Michael Chabon	Larry McMurtry	Tom Wolfe
John Irving	Rick Moody	Tobias Wolff
Jim Lynch	John Updike	

☺ also writes children's books

Kathy Lette   1958-   Aus   Chick Lit

Sherry Ashworth	Christina Jones	Alexandra Potter
Meg Cabot	Josie Lloyd & Emlyn Rees	Sara Shepard
Fiona Gibson	Fiona Neill	Laura Zigman
Alison Penton Harper		

Simon Levack   1965-   Crime: Historical - C16th

🏆 CWA 2000   🏃 Yaotl, Slave youth - Mexico

Michael Clynes	Cora Harrison	Peter Tonkin
Paul Doherty	William Napier	Paul Watkins
Tom Harper		

David Levien   US   Crime: Hardboiled

🏃 Frank Behr, ex-Cop now PI

Harlan Coben	John Hart	Christopher Reich
Robert Crais	Michael Harvey	Jim Thompson
Dashiell Hammett		

Andrea Levy   ⌒   1956-

🏆 Orange 2004   Whitbread 2004   Commonwealth 2005

Monica Ali	Sadie Jones	Caryl Phillips
Margaret	Marina Lewycka	Monique Roffey
Cezair-Thompson	Pauline Melville	Zadie Smith
Lawrence Hill		

Kevin Lewis   1970-   Crime: Hardboiled

🏃 DI Stacey Collins - Metropolitan Police

Helen Black	Mandasue Heller	Charlie Owen
Martina Cole	Jessie Keane	Patrick Quinlan
G M Ford	Roberta Kray	Richard Stark
June Hampson		

Roy Lewis   1933-   Wales   Crime: Amateur sleuth

also writes as J R Lewis, David Springfield   🏃 Arnold Landon, Archaeologist - Newcastle
Eric Ward, Solicitor - Tyneside
DI John Crow - Northumberland police

Paul Adam	John Malcolm	Catherine Sampson
Jeffrey Ashford	M R D Meek	Derek Wilson
Kate Ellis		

Susan Lewis   Mature Chick Lit

Louise Bagshawe	Sam Hayes	Imogen Parker
Sally Beauman	Freya North	Danielle Steel
Judith Gould	Fiona O'Brien	

Marina Lewycka ⌒ 1946- Humour

🏆 Bollinger 2005   Saga for Wit 2005

Mavis Cheek	Laura Marney	Dan Rhodes
Mark Haddon	Armistead Maupin	Alexei Sayle
Andrea Levy	Magnus Mills	Paul Torday

Nell Leyshon

Helen Dunmore	Penelope Lively	Adele Parks
Jennifer Johnston	Clare Morrall	William Trevor

Yiyun Li   1972-   China

Xiaolu Guo	Anchee Min	Lisa See
Ha Jin	Qiu Xiaolong	Xinran

Katia Lief   US   Crime: Police work - US

is Kate Pepper   ⚡ Det Karin Schaeffer - Brooklyn

Beverly Barton	Lisa Gardner	J A Kerley
Allison Brennan	Tami Hoag	Karen Rose

Freda Lightfoot   Saga

also writes as Marion Carr   Manchester

Rita Bradshaw	Elizabeth Gill	Jeannie Johnson
Alexandra Connor	Ruth Hamilton	Margaret Kaine
Glenice Crossland	Billy Hopkins	Claire Lorrimer

Catherine Lim   1942-   Sing

Colin Cotterill	Anchee Min	Lisa See
Arthur Golden	Timothy Mo	Amy Tan

John Ajvide Lindqvist   1968-   Swe   Horror

Adam Baker	Chuck Hogan	Anne Rice
Clive Barker	Stephen King	Dan Simmons
Justin Evans	Haruki Murakami	Whitley Strieber
Neil Gaiman	Häkan Nesser	

Douglas Lindsay   1964-   Sco   Crime: Humour

⚡ Barney Thomson, Barber - Scotland

Colin Bateman	Carl Hiaasen	Danny King
Christopher Brookmyre	Paul Johnston	Andrey Kurkov
Tim Dorsey		

Frederic Lindsay   1933-   Sco   Crime: Police work - UK

⚡ DI Jim Meldrum - Scotland

Karen Campbell	Quintin Jardine	Peter Turnbull
Gillian Galbraith	Denise Mina	Louise Welsh
Alex Gray	Ian Rankin	

Jeff Lindsay 1952- US Crime: Psychological

♟ Dexter Morgan, Policeman & serial killer

Karin Alvtegen
R J Ellory
Mo Hayder

Patricia Highsmith
Jesse Kellerman
Cody McFadyen

Chris Mooney
P J Tracy
Laura Wilson

Joan Lingard ☺ 1932- Sco

Anne Fine
Jane Gardam
Sue Gee
Eileen Goudge

Zoë Heller
Jennifer Johnston
Bernard MacLaverty

Deborah Moggach
Meg Rosoff
Fiona Shaw

Elinor Lipman 1950- US

Karen Joy Fowler
Laurie Graham
Carol Shields

Curtis Sittenfeld
Adriana Trigiani

Rebecca Wells
Mary Wesley

Laura Lippman 1959- US Crime: PI

♟ Tess Monaghan - Baltimore

Kate Atkinson
Benjamin Black
Jan Burke
Carol Higgins Clark

Jodi Compton
Richard Flanagan
Tana French
Michael Gruber

Jennifer McMahon
Theresa Monsour
P J Parrish
Susan R Sloan

Sam Lipsyte 1968- US

Michael Cunningham
A M Homes

John Irving
Tom Robbins

Jonathan Tropper
Tom Wolfe

David Liss 1966- US Crime: Historical - C18th

♟ Benjamin Weaver, ex Pugilist

Gwendoline Butler
Janet Gleeson
Michael Gregorio

Deryn Lake
Fidelis Morgan

Imogen Robertson
Derek Wilson

Toby Litt ⌒ 1968-

Jake Arnott
Colin Bateman
David Flusfeder

Ian McEwan
Alistair MacLeod
Hilary Mantel

Haruki Murakami
Tim Parks

Robert Littell 1935- US Adventure/Thriller

♛ CWA 1973

Stephen J Cannell
Nelson DeMille
Ken Follett

Alan Furst
Robert Harris

Charles McCarry
Glenn Meade

Bentley Little   1960-   US   Horror
also writes as Phillip Emmons

Clive Barker	Shaun Hutson	Scott Nicholson
Simon Clark	Richard Laymon	Dan Simmons
James Herbert	Mark Morris	

Penelope Lively   ☺   1933-
♥ Booker 1987

Nina Bawden	Susan Hill	Lorrie Moore
Rachel Billington	Nell Leyshon	Louise Voss
Penelope Fitzgerald	Deirdre Madden	Meg Wolitzer
Sue Gee	Charlotte Mendelson	

Julia Llewellyn   Mature Chick Lit

Cecelia Ahern	Lisa Jewell	Jill Mansell
Lucy Dawson	Rachel Johnson	Melissa Nathan
Jane Fallon	Louise Kean	Carmen Reid
Louise Harwood	Linda Kelsey	Olivia Ryan

Sam Llewellyn   ☺   1948-   Adventure/Thriller

Eoin Colfer	Philip McCutchan	Justin Scott
Bernard Cornwell	Dudley Pope	Peter Tonkin

Josie Lloyd & Emlyn Rees   Chick Lit

Rebecca Campbell	Kathy Lette	Sue Margolis
Lisa Jewell	Serena Mackesy	Isabel Wolff
Cathy Kelly	Chris Manby	Cathy Woodman
Sophie Kinsella	Jill Mansell	

Morgan Llywelyn   1937-   Ire   Historical
also writes as Shannon Lewis

Marion Zimmer Bradley	Diana Norman	Judith Tarr
Charles de Lint	Edith Pargeter	Jack Vance
Stephen R Lawhead	Sharon Penman	Jules Watson
Robert Low		

Joan Lock   Crime: Historical - C19th
⚐ DI Ernest Best - Victorian London

John Harwood	Caro Peacock	Norman Russell
Alanna Knight	Anne Perry	Brian Thompson
Peter Lovesey	Deanna Raybourn	M J Trow
James McCreet		

Go to back for lists of
Pseudonyms • Authors by Genre • Characters and Series • Environments
Prize Winners • Classic Authors • Crossover Authors • Further Reading • Websites

David Lodge ⌒ 1935-

🏆 Hawthornden 1975   Whitbread 1980

Kingsley Amis	Nick Laird	Leslie Thomas
Malcolm Bradbury	Jeffrey Moore	Paul Torday
Chris Cleave	John Mortimer	Keith Waterhouse
Michael Frayn	Alan Sillitoe	Evelyn Waugh

Lesley Lokko 1964- Sco   Glitz & Glamour

Louise Bagshawe	Rebecca Dean	Fiona O'Brien
Tilly Bagshawe	Johanna Lindsey	Tasmina Perry
Sally Beauman	Fern Michaels	Penny Vincenzi
Jackie Collins		

Kate Long   Chick Lit

Louise Candlish	Milly Johnson	Carole Matthews
Lucy Dillon	Kate Lawson	Tasmina Perry
Fiona Gibson	Jill Mansell	Sarah Tucker

Elizabeth Lord   Saga
London

Harry Bowling	Sara Hylton	Elizabeth Waite
Pamela Evans	Mary Jane Staples	Jeanne Whitmee

Gabrielle Lord 1946- Aus   Crime: PI

🚶 PI Gemma Lincoln - Sydney

Peter Corris	Karin Slaughter	Peter Temple
Patricia Highsmith	Carol Smith	Lisa Unger
S J Rozan	Michelle Spring	Minette Walters

Tim Lott ☺ 1956-

🏆 Whitbread 1999

Matt Beaumont	Alex Garland	Kevin Sampson
Neil Cross	John Harding	William Sutcliffe
Stephen Fry	Tobias Hill	

James Lovegrove 1965-   Science Fiction: Near future

J G Ballard	John Meaney	Neal Stephenson
John Birmingham	Michael Marshall Smith	John Wyndham
Eric Brown		

Peter Lovesey 1936-   Crime: Historical - C19th & Police - UK

also writes as Peter Lear   🚶 Sgt Cribb & PC Thackeray - C19th England
🏆 CWA 1978, 1982, 1995, 1996 & 2000   Peter Diamond, Police - C20th Bath

Gyles Brandreth	Alanna Knight	Amy Myers
Sara Fraser	Joan Lock	Andrew Pepper
John Maclachlan Gray	James McCreet	Norman Russell
Claude Izner	Andrew Martin	Catherine Shaw

Michelle Lovric — Historical

also writes as M R Lovric

Tracy Chevalier	Jeanne Kalogridis	Patrick Suskind
Sarah Dunant	Sharon Penman	Barry Unsworth

Robert Low — Sco — Historical: Ancient

♣ Oathsworn Series - Vikings

Sam Barone	Conn Iggulden	Scott Oden
Richard Blake	Glyn Iliffe	Tim Severin
Bernard Cornwell	Giles Kristian	Jack Whyte
M K Hume	Morgan Llywelyn	Robyn Young

Shari Low — 1967- — Sco — Chick Lit

Rebecca Campbell	Kate O'Riordan	Paige Toon
Clare Dowling	Andrea Semple	Sarah Webb
Sabine Durrant	Linda Taylor	

Carlo Lucarelli — 1960- — It — Crime: Police work - Italy

♣ Insp Grazia Negro - Fascist period, Bologna • Comm De Luca - Milan

Andrea Camilleri	Camilla Lackberg	Dominique Manotti
Michael Dibdin	Donna Leon	Magdalen Nabb
Michele Giuttari	Giulio Leoni	Jo Nesbo
Philip Kerr		

Jack Ludlow — 1944- — Historical

is David Donachie

♣ Conquest Trilogy Series - C11th Europe
Republic Series - Ancient Rome

Bernard Cornwell	Ben Kane	Simon Scarrow
Tom Harper	Robert Low	Tim Severin

Robert Ludlum — 1927-2001 — US — Adventure/Thriller

also wrote as Jonathan Ryder, Michael Shepherd

♣ Covert-One Series • Jason Bourne

Brett Battles	Brendan Dubois	Kyle Mills
Ted Bell	Joseph Finder	Douglas Preston
Tom Bradby	Frederick Forsyth	Jon Stock
Tom Cain	Greg Iles	Eric Van Lustbader

Brian Lumley — 1937- — Horror

♣ Harry Keogh

Poppy Z Brite	Mark Morris	Whitley Strieber
Tim Lebbon	Kim Newman	T M Wright
Gregory Maguire	Anne Rice	

☺ also writes children's books

Jonathan Lunn
Sea: Historical

is Daniel Hall

※ Kit Killigrew - C19th

G S Beard	Alexander Kent	Dudley Pope
David Donachie	Philip McCutchan	Peter Smalley
C S Forester	James L Nelson	Julian Stockwin
Seth Hunter	Patrick O'Brian	

Jim Lynch   US

Richard Ford	Jonathan Lethem	Richard Russo
David Guterson	Larry McMurtry	Brady Udall
John Irving	Tom Robbins	

Sarah Kate Lynch   1962- NZ

Anthony Capella	Nicky Pellegrino	Barbara Trapido
Emma Donoghue	Lily Prior	Barbara Wood
Joanne Harris	Michèle Roberts	

Scott Lynch   1978- US
Fantasy: Epic

※ Locke Lamora

Joe Abercrombie	Raymond E Feist	Karen Miller
Chaz Brenchley	Jaine Fenn	Brandon Sanderson
Stephen Donaldson	Tim Lebbon	Steph Swainston
Ian C Esslemont	George R R Martin	Jack Vance

Matt Lynn
War

is Matthew Lynn

James Barrington	David L Robbins	Justin Scott
Andy McNab	Chris Ryan	Eric Van Lustbader

Amin Maalouf   1949- Leb
Adventure/Thriller

James Clavell	Umberto Eco	Julian Rathbone
Bryce Courtenay	Orhan Pamuk	Alan Savage
Daniel Easterman	Arturo Pérez-Reverte	Colin Thubron

Katie MacAlister   1964- US
Paranormal

Patricia Briggs	Sherrilyn Kenyon	Stephenie Meyer
Lori Handeland	Holly Lisle	Anne Rice

Paul J McAuley   1955-
Science Fiction: Technical

also writes as Paul McAuley   ♛ Arthur C Clarke 1996

Gregory Benford	Jack McDevitt	John Meaney
Gary Gibson	Ian McDonald	Linda Nagata
Paul Johnston	Ian R MacLeod	Richard Powers

Roisin McAuley   Ire

Maeve Binchy
Sarah Challis
Rachel Hore

Sinead Moriarty
Rosamunde Pilcher

Alexandra Raife
Rosy Thornton

Ed McBain   1926-2005   US

Crime: Police work - US

also wrote as Curt Cannon, Hunt Collins,
Evan Hunter, Richard Marsten;
was Salvatore Lombino

⁂ Det Steve Carella - 87th Precinct,
'Isola' Police Department

Robert Ellis
Kjell Eriksson
W E B Griffin
Donald Harstad

J A Jance
Faye Kellerman
Michael Malone
Deon Meyer

Carol O'Connell
Robert B Parker
J D Robb
Joseph Wambaugh

Stuart MacBride   Sco

Crime: Police work - UK

also writes as Stuart B MacBride
🏆 CWA 2007

⁂ DS Logan McRae - Aberdeen

Campbell Armstrong
Mark Billingham
Gordon Brown
Karen Campbell

Margaret Duffy
Alex Gray
Allan Guthrie
Declan Hughes

Quintin Jardine
Richard Kunzmann
David Lawrence
Steve Mosby

Patrick McCabe   1955-   Ire

Chris Binchy
Dermot Bolger
Roddy Doyle
Colum McCann

John McGahern
Patrick McGrath
Eoin McNamee

Joseph O'Connor
Andrew O'Hagan
Glenn Patterson

Anne McCaffrey   1926-2011   US   Science Fiction: Space and time

also wrote jointly with Eizabeth Ann Scarborough, Todd McCaffrey

Sarah Ash
Lois McMaster Bujold
James Clemens
Stephen Deas

Barbara Hambly
Katharine Kerr
Mercedes Lackey
Todd McCaffrey

Julian May
Robert Newcomb
Naomi Novik
Christopher Paolini

Todd McCaffrey   1956   US   Science Fiction: Space and time

Terry Brooks
Philip K Dick
Terry Goodkind
Robin Hobb

Mercedes Lackey
Anne McCaffrey
Christopher Priest

Elizabeth Ann
   Scarborough
Connie Willis

may be suitable for young adults

M

157

Alexander McCall Smith ⌒ ☺ 1948- Sco Crime: PI

🏆 Saga for Wit 2003

🚶 Isabel Dalhousie ⎱
44 Scotland Street Series ⎰ Edinburgh
Sunday Philosophy Club Series ⎰

Precious Ramotswe ⎱ Botswana
The No. 1 Ladies' Detective Agency Series ⎰

Corduroy Mansions Series - Pimlico, London
Prof Dr Moritz-Maria von Igelfeld - Regensburg, Germany

Carrie Bebris	Cora Harrison	Ian Sansom
Colin Cotterill	Veronica Heley	Célestine Hitiura Vaite
Nicholas Drayson	Tony Hillerman	Nury Vittachi
Shamini Flint	Catriona McPherson	Farahad Zama

Robert McCammon 1952- US Horror

John Farris	Adam Nevill	Peter Straub
Dean R Koontz	Anne Rice	Whitley Strieber
Graham Masterton	John Saul	T M Wright

Colum McCann 1965- Ire

🏆 IMPAC 2011

Dermot Bolger	Brian Moore	Michael Ondaatje
Patrick McCabe	Joseph O'Connor	Colm Toibin

Ava McCarthy Ire Adventure/Thriller: Legal/financial

is Aiveen McCarthy 🚶 Henrietta (Harry) Martinez, Security consultant - Dublin

Lee Child	Jilliane Hoffman	Mark Pearson
Harlan Coben	David Hosp	P J Tracy
John Grisham	James Patterson	Lee Weeks

Cormac McCarthy 1933- US

🏆 Black 2006   Pulitzer 2007   South-west USA

Russell Banks	Linda Holeman	Marcel Theroux
Pete Dexter	Jeffrey Moore	Willy Vlautin
Richard Flanagan	Stewart O'Nan	Daniel Woodrell
Stuart Harrison	José Saramago	Edward Wright

Keith McCarthy 1960- Crime: Forensic

also writes as Lance Elliot 🚶 Helena Flemming, Solicitor, & John Eisenmenger, Pathologist

Jefferson Bass	Patricia D Cornwell	Kathy Reichs
Simon Beckett	Iris Johansen	Karin Slaughter
Max Allan Collins	Nigel McCrery	

Ken McClure 1942- Sco Crime: Medical

also writes as Ken Begg 🚶 Steven Dunbar

Paul Adam	Robin Cook	Tess Gerritsen
Paul Carson	Michael Crichton	Michael Palmer

M

Ken McCoy 1940- Crime: PI

♜ Sam 'Mad' Carew, ex-Policeman

Jake Arnott	Martin Edwards	Sheila Quigley
Stephen Booth	Reginald Hill	Cath Staincliffe
Martina Cole	Iain McDowall	Martyn Waites
Alan Dunn	Stuart Pawson	R D Wingfield

Saga

North-east England

Catherine Cookson	Denise Robertson	Michael Taylor
Jess Foley	Wendy Robertson	Janet MacLeod Trotter
Kitty Neale	Jean Saunders	Annie Wilkinson
Elvi Rhodes		

James McCreet Crime: Historical - C19th

♜ DI Albert Newsome, Sgt George Williamson & Noah Dyson - Victorian London

Louis Bayard	Peter Lovesey	Andrew Pepper
Lee Jackson	James McGee	Imogen Robertson
Joan Lock		

Nigel McCrery 1953- Crime: Forensic

♜ Sam Ryan, Pathologist - Cambridge • DCI Mark Lapsie

Lin Anderson	Patricia D Cornwell	Val McDermid
Simon Beckett	Aaron Elkins	Kathy Reichs
Benjamin Black	Kathryn Fox	Karin Slaughter
Max Allan Collins	Keith McCarthy	Aline Templeton

Sharyn McCrumb 1948- US Crime: Psychological

♜ Elizabeth McPherson, Anthropologist - Appalachians, East Tennessee
Sheriff Spenser Arrowood

Douglas Adams	Erin Hart	Andrew Klavan
Nevada Barr	Daniel Hecht	Margaret Maron
Janis Harrison	Tony Hillerman	Carol O'Connell
Carolyn G Hart		

Carson McCullers 1917-1967 US

Southern USA

William Faulkner	Sue Monk Kidd	Curtis Sittenfeld
F Scott Fitzgerald	J D Salinger	Willy Vlautin
Connie May Fowler	Anne Rivers Siddons	Alice Walker

Go to back for lists of
Pseudonyms • Authors by Genre • Characters and Series • Environments
Prize Winners • Classic Authors • Crossover Authors • Further Reading • Websites

Colleen McCullough　1937-　Aus　　Crime: Police work - US

is Colleen McCullough-Robinson　　　🏃 Captain Carmine Delmonico - Connecticut

Chelsea Cain	Lynn Hightower	Tami Hoag
Elizabeth George	Susan Hill	Meg O'Brien

Historical

🏃 Masters of Rome Series - Ancient

Margaret George	Mary Renault	Simon Scarrow
Robert Graves	Rosemary Rowe	Patricia Shaw
Christian Jacq	Edward Rutherfurd	Wilbur Smith

Philip McCutchan　1920-1996　　Sea: Historical & Modern

also wrote as Duncan MacNeil

🏃 Donald Cameron ⎱ Royal Navy
St Vincent Halfhyde ⎰

Commodore Kemp, Merchant Marine • Tom Chatto - Merchant Navy
Capt James Ogilvie - Queen's Own Royal Strathspeys

Brian Callison	Alexander Kent	Dudley Pope
Alexander Fullerton	Sam Llewellyn	Patrick Robinson
Richard Howard	Jonathan Lunn	Peter Tonkin

Val McDermid　⌒　1955-　Sco　　Crime: Psychological

🏆 CWA 1995 & 2010　Theakston's 2006　🏃 DCI Carol Jordan & Dr Tony Hill, Psychologist
Kate Brannigan, PI - Manchester
Lindsay Gordon, Journalist - Glasgow
Fiona Cameron, Academic psychologist

S J Bolton	Sophie Hannah	Mark Pearson
Elizabeth Corley	Mandasue Heller	Patrick Redmond
Garry Disher	Jane Hill	Manda Scott
Tana French	Nigel McCrery	Zoë Sharp

Alice McDermott　1953-　US

Kent Haruf	Anne Michaels	Anita Shreve
Alice Hoffman	Carol Shields	Adriana Trigiani
Mary Lawson		

Andy McDermott　1974-　　Adventure/Thriller

🏃 Nina Wilde, Archaeologist, & Eddie Chase, ex-SAS

Lincoln Child	Tom Knox	Matthew Reilly
Harold Coyle	Douglas Preston	James Rollins
Clive Cussler		

Jack McDevitt　1935-　US　　Science Fiction: Space and time

🏃 Alex Benedict

Poul Anderson	Paul J McAuley	Alastair Reynolds
Stephen Baxter	Ken MacLeod	Kurt Vonnegut
Arthur C Clarke	Larry Niven	

Ian McDonald 1960- Science Fiction: Space and time

BSFA 2004, 2007 & 2010

Stephen Baxter	Gwyneth Jones	Linda Nagata
Greg Egan	Paul J McAuley	Brian Stableford
Jon Courtenay Grimwood	Ian R MacLeod	Connie Willis

Marianne MacDonald 1934- Can Crime: Amateur sleuth

Dido Hoare, Antiquarian bookseller - London

John Dunning	Hazel Holt	Fiona Mountain
Carolyn G Hart	Alison Joseph	Ann Purser
Veronica Heley	Morag Joss	Veronica Stallwood

Ross Macdonald 1915-83 US Crime: PI

also wrote as John Macdonald, John Ross Macdonald; was Kenneth Millar

Lew Archer - California

Megan Abbott	James Crumley	James Sallis
Lawrence Block	Dashiell Hammett	Peter Spiegelman
Raymond Chandler	George P Pelecanos	Edward Wright
James Hadley Chase		

Sara MacDonald Aga Saga

Sally Beauman	Adèle Geras	Charlotte Moore
Sarah Challis	Rachel Hore	Robin Pilcher
Annabel Dilke	Sarah Jackman	Rosamunde Pilcher
Elizabeth Edmondson	Christobel Kent	Marcia Willett

Nick McDonell 1984- US

Charles Cumming	John Fowles	Jay McInerney
Jonathan Safran Foer	Graham Greene	Olen Steinhauer

Sophia McDougall 1981- Historical

Stephen Baxter	Steven Saylor	Harry Turtledove
Conn Iggulden	Simon Scarrow	David Wishart
Allan Massie	Robert Silverberg	

Iain McDowall Sco Crime: Police work - UK

DCI Jacobson & DS Kerr - 'Crowby', Midlands

Hilary Bonner	John Harvey	Peter James
Stephen Booth	Reginald Hill	Ken McCoy
Joseph Connolly	Lesley Horton	Pauline Rowson
Colin Dexter	Graham Hurley	Aline Templeton

M

Ian McEwan ☎ ☺ 1948-

🏆 Whitbread 1987   Booker 1998   WHSmith 2002   Black 2005   Bollinger 2010

Gilbert Adair	Peter Ho Davies	Richard Mason
Iain Banks	Sadie Jones	Claire Messud
Anita Brookner	Toby Litt	Blake Morrison
Chris Cleave	Patrick McGrath	Linn Ullmann

Cody McFadyen 1968- US   Crime: Psychological

🏃 Smoky Barrett, FBI Special Agent

Gregory Hall	J A Kerley	Boris Starling
Thomas Harris	Jeff Lindsay	P J Tracy
Michael Harvey	Richard Montanari	Lisa Unger
David Hosp	Chris Mooney	

Andrew McGahan 1966- Aus   Adventure/Thriller

🏆 Miles Franklin 2005

Murray Bail	Robert Jordan	Graham Masterton
Kate Grenville	Thomas Keneally	Tim Winton

John McGahern 1934-2006 Ire

John Banville	Patrick McCabe	Edna O'Brien
Sebastian Barry	Eoin McNamee	David Park
James Joyce	Brian Moore	William Wall

Michael McGarrity 1939- US   Crime: Police work - US

🏃 Kevin Kerney - New Mexico

Nevada Barr	Steve Hamilton	J A Jance
C J Box	Donald Harstad	Archer Mayor
Robert Ferrigno	Tony Hillerman	

James McGee 1950-   Crime: Historical - C19th

is Glen Moy   🏃 Matthew Hawkwood, Bow Street runner

David Ashton	Lee Jackson	Andrew Pepper
Louis Bayard	Deryn Lake	Anne Perry
Iain Gale	James McCreet	C J Sansom
Claude Izner	Edward Marston	Brian Thompson

Brian McGilloway 1974- Ire   Crime: Police work - UK

🏃 Insp Benedict Devlin - Londonderry

Mark Billingham	Reginald Hill	Eoin McNamee
Benjamin Black	Declan Hughes	Andrew Nugent
Kenneth Cameron	Quintin Jardine	Ian Rankin
Bartholomew Gill	Gene Kerrigan	Matt Rees

Patrick McGrath   1950-

Michel Faber
Kazuo Ishiguro
David Leavitt

Patrick McCabe
Ian McEwan

Graham Swift
Tobias Wolff

Elizabeth McGregor   Crime: Psychological

also writes as Holly Fox

Kate Atkinson
Nicci French
J Wallis Martin

Meg O'Brien
Louis Sanders
Carol Smith

Barbara Vine
Sue Walker
Gillian White

Jon McGregor   1976-

♈ Betty Trask 2003   IMPAC 2012

Chris Cleave
Jonathan Coe

David Lodge
Helen Simpson

Paul Torday
Jonathan Trigell

Jay McInerney   1955-   US

Charles Bukowski
Bret Easton Ellis
F Scott Fitzgerald
Michael Jan Friedman

Jack Kerouac
Nick McDonell
Armistead Maupin

Chuck Palahnuik
J D Salinger
Matt Thorne

Monica McInerney   1965-   Aus   Mature Chick Lit

Liz Byrski
Colette Caddle
Clare Dowling
Anne Dunlop

Melissa Hill
Cathy Kelly
Kate Lawson
Anna McPartlin

Jojo Moyes
Morag Prunty
Tina Reilly
Jane Wenham-Jones

Betty McInnes   Sco   Saga

Scotland

Maggie Craig
Doris Davidson

Evelyn Hood
Anna Jacobs

Elisabeth McNeill
Pamela Oldfield

Fiona McIntosh   1960-   Aus   Fantasy: Epic

also writes as Lauren Crow

David Eddings
Jennifer Fallon
Pamela Freeman
Elizabeth Haydon

Amanda Hemingway
Robin Hobb
Russell Kirkpatrick
Glenda Larke

Karen Miller
Elizabeth Moon
Melanie Rawn
Margaret Weis

Pat McIntosh   Sco   Crime: Historical - Medieval

⚘ Gil Cunningham, Notary in training - Glasgow

Simon Acland
Simon Beaufort
Alys Clare
Susanna Gregory

Michael Jecks
Bernard Knight
Shirley McKay
The Medieval Murderers

Candace Robb
Kate Sedley
Peter Tremayne

Hope McIntyre 1946-   Crime: Amateur sleuth

is Caroline Upcher   ⚘ Lee Bartholomew, Ghost writer - London

Judith Cutler	Shane Maloney	Veronica Stallwood
Anthea Fraser	Gwen Moffat	Rebecca Tope

M Shena Mackay 1944- Sco

Kate Atkinson	Angela Huth	Marge Piercy
Anita Burgh	Jennifer Johnston	Gwendoline Riley
Mavis Cheek	Valerie Martin	Muriel Spark
Kathryn Harrison	Kate Muir	

Shirley McKay   Crime: Historical - C16th

⚘ Hew Cullan, Lawyer - St Andrews

Simon Beaufort	Patricia Finney	Pat McIntosh
P F Chisholm	Philip Gooden	C J Sansom
Michael Clynes		

John Macken   Crime: Psychological

⚘ Reuben Maitland - Forensic scientist

Mark Billingham	Mo Hayder	Stuart MacBride
Stephen Booth	Peter James	Val McDermid
Robin Cook	J A Kerley	Mark Pearson
Alex Gray		

Juliet E McKenna 1965-   Fantasy: Epic

Joe Abercrombie	Jude Fisher	George R R Martin
James Barclay	Elizabeth Haydon	K J Parker
David Farland	Ian Irvine	Freda Warrington

Grant McKenzie   Sco   Adventure/Thriller

Lee Child	Michael Connelly	Richard Montanari
Harlan Coben	Jeffery Deaver	Paullina Simons

Serena Mackesy   Chick Lit

Jessica Adams	Louise Kean	Sue Margolis
Zoë Barnes	Cathy Kelly	Melissa Nathan
Helen Fielding	Josie Lloyd & Emlyn Rees	Kate O'Riordan
Jane Green	Chris Manby	

Mary Mackie   Saga

also writes as Alex Andrews, Caroline Charles,   Lincolnshire
Cathy Christopher, Mary Christopher, Susan Stevens   Norfolk

Margaret Dickinson	Elizabeth Murphy	Sue Sully
Elizabeth Jeffrey	Judith Saxton	T R Wilson
Connie Monk		

Tamara McKinley 1948- Aus Saga

🏃 Oceania Series

Frank Coates	Di Morrissey	Patricia Shaw
Domenica de Rosa	Kate Morton	Rachael Treasure
Beverley Harper	Judy Nunn	Peter Watt
Judith Lennox	Katherine Scholes	

Adrian McKinty 1968- Ire Crime: Hardboiled

🏃 Michael Forsythe, US Mercenary

Jake Arnott	Lorenzo Carcaterra	Denise Ryan
Alex Berenson	Andy McNab	Jim Thompson
Benjamin Black		

Bernard MacLaverty 1942- Ire

Seamus Deane	Allan Massie	Julian Rathbone
Ronald Frame	Joseph O'Connor	Adam Thorpe
Joan Lingard	David Park	Niall Williams
Deirdre Madden		

Alistair MacLean ⌒ 1922-87 Sco Adventure/Thriller

also wrote as Ian Stuart

Brett Battles	Andy McNab	Nevil Shute
David Downing	Nicholas Monsarrat	Terence Strong
James Follett	Alan Savage	Peter Tonkin
Hammond Innes		

Ian R MacLeod 1956- Science Fiction: Space and time

🏆 Arthur C Clarke 2009

Greg Keyes	Ian McDonald	Alastair Reynolds
Paul J McAuley	China Miéville	Charles Stross

Ken MacLeod 1954- Sco Science Fiction: Space and time

🏆 BSFA 1999 & 2008

Steve Aylett	Jack McDevitt	Richard Morgan
Iain M Banks	John Meaney	Adam Roberts
Ray Bradbury	China Miéville	Robert J Sawyer
Greg Egan		

Suzanne McLeod Paranormal

Kelley Armstrong	Karen Chance	Kim Harrison
Patricia Briggs	Lori Handeland	Richelle Mead

⌒ may be suitable for young adults

Pauline McLynn   1962-   Ire   Crime: Humour

† Leo Street, PI - Dublin

Janet Evanovich	Lauren Henderson	Zane Radcliffe
Liz Evans	Suzette Hill	Sarah Strohmeyer
Sparkle Hayter		

Mature Chick Lit

Cecelia Ahern	Jane Green	Gil McNeil
Susie Boyt	Marian Keyes	Libby Purves
Harriet Evans	Sophie Kinsella	Polly Williams

Jennifer McMahon   1968-   US   Crime: Romantic suspense

Beverly Barton	Patricia Highsmith	Karen Robards
Christiane Heggan	Laura Lippman	Sharon Sala

Katharine McMahon   Historical

Margaret Cezair-Thompson	Philippa Gregory	Robin Maxwell
Suzannah Dunn	Julia Gregson	Edith Pargeter
Patrick Gale	Jane Harris	Patricia Shaw
	Jeanne Kalogridis	

Terry McMillan   1951-   US

Candace Bushnell	Sue Monk Kidd	Rebecca Wells
Eric Jerome Dickey	Toni Morrison	Valerie Wilson Wesley
Esther Freud	Alice Walker	Meg Wolitzer
John Irving		

Kristina McMorris

Kristin Hannah	Sinead Moriarty	Robert James Waller
Maeve Haran	Adriana Trigiani	Julia Williams

Larry McMurtry   ⌒   1936-   US

♔ Pulitzer 1986

Pat Conroy	John Irving	James A Michener
Thomas Eidson	Jack Kerouac	Richard Russo
Nicholas Evans	Jonathan Lethem	Willy Vlautin
Charles Frazier	Jim Lynch	

Andy McNab   ⌒   ☺   1960-   War: Modern

† Nick Stone - SIS • War Torn Series - Afghanistan

Patrick Bishop	John Fullerton	Matt Lynn
Murray Davies	Joseph Garber	Adrian McKinty
Barry Eisler	Matt Hilton	Scott Mariani
Duncan Falconer	Alan Judd	Chris Ryan

M

Claire McNab   1940-   Aus   Crime: Police work - Australia

also writes as Claire Carmichael   ☨ Denise Cleever, Intelligence agent - Australia
                                DI Carol Ashton - Sydney • Kylie Kendall, PI - Los Angeles

Jan Burke	Peter Guttridge	Chris Niles
Jon Cleary	J A Jance	Carol O'Connell
Stella Duffy	Laurie R King	Medora Sale

Judith McNaught   1944-   US

Catherine Coulter	Linda Howard	Amanda Quick
Barbara Delinsky	Penny Jordan	LaVyrle Spencer
Judith Gould	Jayne Ann Krentz	Danielle Steel

Debbie Macomber   1948-   US   Mature Chick Lit

Lucy Dawson	Tina Reilly	Kathleen Gilles Seidel
Katie Fforde	Patricia Scanlan	Sarah Tucker
Debby Holt		

Anna McPartlln   1972-   Ire   Chick Lit

Rowan Coleman	Dorothy Koomson	Gil McNeil
Emily Giffin	Monica McInerney	Alexandra Potter

Catriona McPherson   1965-   Sco   Crime: Amateur sleuth

also writes as Catriona McCloud   ☨ Dandy Gilver - 1920s Scotland

Carrle Bebris	Carola Dunn	Suzette Hill
David Stuart Davies	Joanne Fluke	Claude Izner
Arthur Conan Doyle	Dolores Gordon-Smith	Alanna Knight
Nicholas Drayson	Gerald Hammond	Alexander McCall Smith

Holly McQueen   Chick Lit

Trisha Ashley	Katie Fforde	Jill Mansell
Jane Costello	Sophie Kinsella	Alexandra Potter

Deirdre Madden   1960-   Ire

♈ S Maugham 1989

Sebastian Barry	Penelope Lively	Edna O'Brien
Jennifer Johnston	Bernard MacLaverty	William Trevor

Gwen Madoc   Wales   Saga

                                                   Swansea

June Francis	Beryl Matthews	Mary Jane Staples
Meg Hutchinson	Gilda O'Neill	Janet Tanner
Margaret Kaine	Sharon Owens	Dee Williams

Pierre Magnan
1922-2012 Fr Crime: Police work - France

🚶 Commissaire Laviolette - Provence

Colin Cotterill
Stephen Done
Caroline Graham

Claude Izner
Barry Maitland
Guillermo Martinez

Jean François Parot
Fred Vargas

M Paul Magrs ☺ 1969- Horror

🚶 Brenda & Effie - Whitby

Jeremy Dyson
Jasper Fforde

Peter James
Eve Makis

Magnus Mills
Haruki Murakami

Adrian Magson
Crime: Police work - Europe

🚶 Riley Gavin, Journalist & Frank Palmer, ex-Military Investigator
Insp Lucas Rocco - 1960s France • Harry Tate, MI5 Officer

Jo Bannister
Christopher Brookmyre
Caroline Carver

Margaret Duffy
Patricia Hall

Katherine John
Denise Mina

Gregory Maguire 1954- US Fantasy: Myth

Simon Clark
Katharine Kerr
Stephen King

Dean R Koontz
Brian Lumley

Tim Powers
Philip Pullman

Barry Maitland 1941- Sco Crime: Police work - UK

🚶 DCI David Brock & DS Kathy Kolla - London

Jo Bannister
Mark Billingham
Victoria Blake
Stephen Booth

Anthea Fraser
Cynthia Harrod-Eagles
Simon Kernick

Pierre Magnan
Ed O'Connor
Peter Temple

Karen Maitland Historical

also writes as The Medieval Murderers (with Philip Gooden, Susanna Gregory,
Michael Jeck, Bernard Knight, Ian Morson, C J Sansom)

Ariana Franklin
Sussana Gregory

John Harwood
Jeanne Kalogridis

Iain Pears
Barry Unsworth

Andrei Makine 1957- Fr

🏆 IMPAC 2008

Chris Cleave
Helen Dunmore
Clare Morrall

David Peace
Philip Roth
Colm Toibin

John McGahern
David Mitchell
Irene Nemirovsky

Go to back for lists of
Pseudonyms • Authors by Genre • Characters and Series • Environments
Prize Winners • Classic Authors • Crossover Authors • Further Reading • Websites

Allan Mallinson

War: Historical

🏃 Matthew Hervey, Captain - C19th Light Dragoons

G S Beard
Roger Carpenter
Tom Connery
Bernard Cornwell

Alexander Fullerton
Iain Gale
Richard Howard
Garry Kilworth

Christopher Nicole
Patrick O'Brian
Patrick Rambaud
John Wilcox

M

Martin Malone   Ire

John Banville
Sebastian Barry

F G Cottam
John McGahern

Brian Moore
Joseph O'Connor

Michael Malone   1942- US

Crime: Police work - US

🏃 Chief Cuddy Mangum & Det Justin Savile - 'Hillston', North Carolina

James Lee Burke
Thomas H Cook
Mark de Castrique
Dashiell Hammett

Lynn Hightower
Tony Hillerman
Jonathon King
Ed McBain

Jefferson Parker
P J Parrish
Stuart Woods

Shane Maloney   1953- Aus

Crime: Amateur sleuth

🏃 Murray Whelan, Political adviser - Melbourne

Robert G Barrett
Christopher Brookmyre
Jon Cleary

Garry Disher
Carl Hiaasen
Elmore Leonard

Hope McIntyre
Don Winslow

David Malouf   1934- Aus

🏆 Commonwealth 1991   IMPAC 1996   Miles Franklin 1991

Murray Bail
Peter Carey
Steven Carroll
James Clavell

Robert Drewe
Richard Flanagan
Maurice Gee

Janette Turner Hospital
Ben Okri
Morris West

Chris Manby   1972-

Chick Lit

also writes as Stephanie Ash, Lizzie Jordan, Chrissie Manby

Jessica Adams
Meg Cabot
Julie Highmore
Rachel Hore

Josie Lloyd & Emlyn Rees
Serena Mackesy
Sue Margolis
Sinead Moriarty

Fiona Neill
Linda Taylor
Kate Thompson
Gemma Townley

Valerio Massimo Manfredi   1943- It

Historical

🏃 Alexander the Great

Almudena Grandes
Robert Graves
Glyn Iliffe
Christian Jacq

Allan Massie
Steven Pressfield
Mary Renault

Manda Scott
Wilbur Smith
Robyn Young

Rani Manicka   Malay

Jim Crace	Chitra Banerjee Divakaruni	Jhumpa Lahiri
Jill Dawson	Nadine Gordimer	David Mitchell

Henning Mankell   ⌒   ☺   1948-   Swe   Crime: Police work - Sweden

♥ CWA 2001   ☂ Insp Kurt Wallander - Ystad

Ake Edwardson	Camilla Läckberg	Yrsa Sigurdardottir
Kjell Eriksson	Llza Marklund	Johan Theorin
Anne Holt	Häkan Nesser	Linn Ullmann
Matti Joensuu	Roslund and Hellström	Janwillem van de Wetering

Dominique Manotti   Fr   Crime: Police work - France

♥ CWA 2008   ☂ Supt Theo Daquin - Paris

Mari Jungstedt	Carlo Lucarelli	Johan Theorin
Stieg Larsson	Häkan Nesser	Fred Vargas

Jill Mansell   ⌒   1957-   Mature Chick Lit

Tilly Bagshawe	Debby Holt	Gemma Townley
Nina Bell	Milly Johnson	Julia Williams
Meg Cabot	Holly McQueen	Polly Williams
Jane Costello	Bernadette Strachan	Cathy Woodman

Hilary Mantel   ⌒   1952-

♥ Holtby 1990   Hawthornden 1996   Man Booker 2009 & 2012

Candida Crewe	Toby Litt	Piers Paul Read
Rachel Cusk	Paul Magrs	Alice Sebold
A M Homes	Julie Myerson	Henry Sutton
M J Hyland		

John Marco   US   Fantasy: Epic

James Barclay	David Farland	Robert Jordan
Peter V Brett	Raymond E Feist	Russell Kirkpatrick
Terry Brooks	Robin Hobb	Brent Weeks
Steven Erikson		

Phillip Margolin   1944-   US   Crime: Legal/financial

also writes as Phillip M Margolin   ☂ Amanda Jaffe, Defence Attorney

William Bernhardt	Steve Martini	Nancy Taylor Rosenberg
Colin Harrison	Barbara Parker	John Sandford
Jesse Kellerman	Richard North Patterson	Lisa Scottoline
Peter Leonard		

Sue Margolis   Chick Lit

Cecelia Ahern	Serena Mackesy	Sheila O'Flanagan
Catherine Alliott	Chris Manby	Isabel Wolff
Josie Lloyd & Emlyn Rees	Jane Moore	

Scott Mariani
Sco — Adventure/Thriller

⚘ Ben Hope, ex SAS

Sam Bourne	Paul Christopher	Tom Knox
Dan Brown	Glenn Cooper	Chris Kuzneski
John Case	Tom Grace	Andy McNab
Lee Child	A J Hartley	E V Seymour

M

Javier Marias
1951- Spain — Adventure/Thriller: Psychological

🏆 IMPAC 1997 ⚘ Jacques Deza, Intelligence agent

Roberto Bolano	Manuel Vázquez	Arturo Pérez-Reverte
Gabriel Garcia Márquez	Montalbán	José Saramago
Luiz Alfredo Garcia-Roza		

Juliet Marillier
1948- NZ — Fantasy: Myth

Sarah Ash	Trudi Canavan	Charles de Lint
Jean M Auel	Storm Constantine	Caiseal Mor
Ashok K Banker	Cecilia Dart-Thornton	Jules Watson

Liza Marklund
1962- Swe — Crime: Amateur sleuth

⚘ Annika Bengtzon, Journalist - Stockholm

James Brownley	Karin Fossum	Jo Nesbo
Edna Buchanan	Denise Hamilton	Hakan Nesser
Jan Burke	Camilla Lackberg	Maj Sjöwall & Per Wahlöö
G M Ford	Henning Mankell	

Benjamin Markovits
US

Peter Ackroyd	T C Boyle	Jhumpa Lahiri
Martin Amis	A S Byatt	Edna O'Brien
Sebastian Barry		

Laura Marney
Sco — Humour

Des Dillon	Fiona Gibson	Zoë Strachan
Anne Donovan	Marina Lewycka	Lynne Truss

Margaret Maron
1959- US — Crime: Amateur sleuth

⚘ Deborah Knott, Judge - North Carolina • Sigrid Harald - New York Police

Nevada Barr	Mark de Castrique	Carolyn G Hart
Lilian Jackson Braun	Joanne Fluke	Sharyn McCrumb
Jan Burke	W E B Griffin	Martin Walker
Carol Higgins Clark	Janis Harrison	

Michael Marshall
1965- — Adventure/Thriller

is Michael Marshall Smith ⚘ Ward Hopkins, ex-CIA

Alex Barclay	Thomas Harris	Jason Pinter
Chelsea Cain	Richard Morgan	John Rickards
Jeffery Deaver	Steve Mosby	Nick Stone
Joseph Finder	James Patterson	James Twining

Edward Marston 1940- Wales Crime: Historical

also writes as Conrad Allen, Martin Inigo, ⚲ Nicholas Bracewell - Theatre - C16th ⎫
A E Marston, Christopher Mountjoy; Ralph Delchard & Gervase Bret - C11th ⎬ England
is Keith Miles Christopher Redmayne & Jonathan Bale - C17th ⎭
Insp Robert Colbeck - C19th London
Captain Daniel Rawson - C17th & C18th France • C19th railways of England

David Ashton	Iain Gale	James McGee
Christie Dickason	Philip Gooden	Andrew Martin
Stephen Done	Dolores Gordon-Smith	Andrew Pepper
Patricia Finney	Lee Jackson	Martin Stephen

Yann Martel 1963- Spain

🏆 Man Booker 2002

Murray Bail	Louis de Bernières	David Mitchell
Iain Banks	Mark Haddon	V S Naipaul
Susanna Clarke	Elizabeth Kostova	D B C Pierre
Jim Crace	Alistair MacLeod	Arundhati Roy

Andrew Martin 1952- Crime: Historical - C19th

🏆 CWA 2011 ⚲ DS Jim Stringer, Railway detective

John Maclachlan Gray	Edward Marston	Deanna Raybourn
Lee Jackson	Anne Perry	Frank Tallis
Peter Lovesey		

David Martin 1946- US Horror

is David Lozell Martin

Chaz Brenchley	Graham Masterton	Whitley Strieber
Jack Harvey	Richard Matheson	Koji Suzuki
Graham Joyce	Kim Newman	

George R R Martin 1948- US Fantasy: Epic

James Barclay	Greg Keyes	Brandon Sanderson
Isobelle Carmody	Scott Lynch	Harry Turtledove
C J Cherryh	Juliet E McKenna	Jack Vance
Maggie Furey	Patrick Rothfuss	Brent Weeks

P D Martin Aus Adventure/Thriller

is Phillipa Deane Martin ⚲ Sophie Anderson, FBI agent - US Southern States

Allison Brennan	Lynn Hightower	J D Robb
Robert Ellis	Faye Kellerman	Karen Rose
Janet Evanovich	J A Kerley	

Valerie Martin 1948- US

🏆 Orange 2003

Margaret Atwood	Zoë Heller	Clare Morrall
Pat Barker	Victoria Hislop	Toni Morrison
Kim Edwards	Jennifer Johnston	Julie Myerson
Helen Garner	Shena Mackay	Ann Patchett

M

Guillermo Martinez   1962-   Arg   Crime: Psychological

Colin Dexter	Morag Joss	Fred Vargas
Michele Giuttari	Pierre Magnan	Carlos Ruiz Zafón
P D James	Matthew Pearl	

Steve Martini   1946-   US   Crime: Legal/financial

⚘ Paul Madriani, Lawyer - San Diego

Harry Bingham	Mark Gimenez	John T Lescroart
Alafair Burke	James Grippando	Phillip Margolin
Julie Compton	Andrew Gross	Brad Meltzer
Linda Fairstein	John Hart	Robert K Tanenbaum

Daniel Mason   1976-   US

Michelle de Kretser	Khaled Hosseini	Mark Slouka
Sebastian Faulks	George Orwell	Alan Spence
Amitav Ghosh	Lionel Shriver	Colin Thubron

Richard Mason   1978-   SA

Muriel Barbery	Philip Hensher	Andrew Miller
Vanora Bennett	Ian McEwan	Rose Tremain
Sebastian Faulks		

Sarah Mason   Chick Lit

🏆 Romantic 2003

Trisha Ashley	Louise Harwood	Olivia Ryan
Claire Calman	Donna Hay	Jennifer Weiner
Anne Dunlop	Melissa Nathan	Arabella Weir

Allan Massie   1938-   Sco

Michael Dobbs	Ronald Frame	Frederic Raphael
Sebastian Faulks	Bernard MacLaverty	Alan Spence

Historical: Ancient

Christian Cameron	Robert Nye	Marilyn Todd
R S Downie	Rosemary Rowe	Paul Waters
Sophia McDougall	Steven Saylor	Jules Watson
Valerio Massimo Manfredi	Harry Sidebottom	David Wishart

Priscilla Masters   1952-   Crime: Police work - UK

⚘ DI Joanna Piercy & DS Mike Korpanski - 'Moorlands', Staffordshire
Martha Gunn, Coroner - Shrewsbury

Jo Bannister	John Connor	Margaret Duffy
Stephen Booth	Deborah Crombie	Marjorie Eccles
Glenn Chandler	Judith Cutler	H R F Keating

M

Graham Masterton   1946-   Sco   Horror

also writes as Alan Blackwood, Thomas Luke   ⚑ Harry Erskine, Mystic • Jim Rook

Bret Easton Ellis	Stephen Gallagher	David Martin
John Farris	Robert McCammon	Kim Newman
Christopher Fowler	Andrew McGahan	Whitley Strieber

M

Richard Matheson   1926-   US   Horror

also writes as Logan Swanson

Tanya Huff	David Martin	Peter Straub
Dean R Koontz	Brian Stableford	Koji Suzuki
Stephen Laws		

Beryl Matthews   Saga

⚑ Webster Family

Benita Brown	Gwen Madoc	Mary Jane Staples
Elizabeth Elgin	Judith Saxton	June Tate
Lilian Harry		

Carole Matthews   Mature Chick Lit

Jessica Adams	Claudia Carroll	Belinda Jones
Catherine Alliott	Jane Costello	Kate Lawson
Tilly Bagshawe	Isla Dewar	Kate Long
Zoë Barnes	Milly Johnson	Olivia Ryan

Armistead Maupin   ⌒   1944-   US

⚑ Tales of the City

Michael Arditti	Garrison Keillor	Jay McInerney
Robert G Barrett	Hanif Kureishi	Tomas Eloy Martinez
Patrick Gale	Marina Lewycka	Christos Tsiolkas
Alan Hollinghurst	John D MacDonald	Edmund White

Simon Mawer   1948-

🏆 McKitterick 1990

Beryl Bainbridge	Sebastian Faulks	Iris Murdoch
Richard Bausch	Michael Frayn	Andrew O'Hagan
William Boyd	Andrew Greig	Niall Williams

Anna Maxted   ☺   1969-   Chick Lit

⚑ Tom and Matt Series

Catherine Alliott	Sabine Durrant	India Knight
Sam Baker	Lisa Jewel	Kate Long
Elizabeth Buchan	Louise Kean	Jane Moore
Martina Devlin	Sophie Kinsella	Adele Parks

☺ also writes children's books

Robin Maxwell 1948- US   Historical

Suzannah Dunn	Sandra Gulland	Katharine McMahon
Melanie Gifford	Caroline Harvey	Edith Pargeter
Philippa Gregory	Elizabeth Jeffrey	Maureen Peters

Peter May 1951- Sco   Crime: Police work - China

𝕜 Det Li Yan & Margaret Campbell, Pathologist

Ann Cleeves	Andy Oakes	Lisa See
Patricia D Cornwell	Qiu Xiaolong	Martin Cruz Smith
Colin Cotterill	Kathy Reichs	Michael Walters

Sarah May 1972-   Mature Chick Lit

Sarah Duncan	Veronica Henry	Carmen Reid
Maeve Haran	Lisa Jewell	Isabel Wolff

Eric Mayer   see **Mary Reed**

Margaret Mayhew   Saga

Anne Baker	Hilary Green	Anna Jacobs
Lily Baxter	Annie Groves	Maureen Lee
Anne Bennett	Lilian Harry	Victor Pemberton
Elizabeth Elgin	Angela Huth	Rachael Treasure

Archer Mayor 1950- US   Crime: Police work - US

𝕜 Lt Joe Gunther - Brattleboro, Vermont

Giles Blunt	Michael Koryta	Theresa Monsour
Paula Gosling	Michael McGarrity	Robert B Parker
Donald Harstad	Henning Mankell	

Richelle Mead 1976- US   Paranormal

Kelley Armstrong	Rachel Caine	Kim Newman
Ann Brashares	P C & Kristin Cast	Sara Reinke
Patricia Briggs	Suzanne McLeod	Lilith Saintcrow

Glenn Meade 1957- Ire   Adventure/Thriller

Campbell Armstrong	Frederick Forsyth	Greg Iles
Alex Barclay	Robert Harris	Robert Littell
Tom Clancy	David Ignatius	Daniel Silva

Go to back for lists of
Pseudonyms • Authors by Genre • Characters and Series • Environments
Prize Winners • Classic Authors • Crossover Authors • Further Reading • Websites

The Medieval Murderers

Crime: Historical - Medieval

also write individually as Philip Gooden, Susanna Gregory, Michael Jecks, Bernard Knight, Karen Maitland, Ian Morson, C J Sansom

Simon Beaufort	Ariana Franklin	Ellis Peters
Alys Clare	Margaret Frazer	Candace Robb
Paul Doherty	Pat McIntosh	Peter Tremayne

James Meek 1962- Sco

🏆 Ondaatje 2006

Peter Ackroyd	Ismail Kadare	Orhan Pamuk
Louis de Bernières	Panos Karnezis	Edward St Aubyn
Helen Dunmore	Michael Moorcock	Barry Unsworth
Will Ferguson		

Rose Melikan US

Crime: Amateur sleuth

🏃 Mary Finch - C18th

Judith Cutler	Janet Gleeson	Deryn Lake
Daphne Du Maurier	Joanna Hines	Iain Pears

Maile Meloy 1972- US

Tami Hoag	Judy Nunn	Lesley Pearse
Rachel Johnson	Tea Obreht	Bella Pollen
Lorna Landvik	Ann Packer	Anita Shreve

Brad Meltzer 1970- US

Adventure/Thriller: Legal/financial

David Baldacci	Linda Davies	Steve Martini
Stephen L Carter	John Hart	Christopher Reich
Julie Compton	John McLaren	Michael Ridpath
Michael Connelly		

Pauline Melville 1948- Guy

🏆 Guardian 1990   Whitbread 1997   Commonwealth 1991

Patricia Duncker	Andrea Levy	Bernice Rubens
Graham Greene	Sharon Maas	Evelyn Waugh

Charlotte Mendelson 1972-

🏆 JLR 2003   S Maugham 2004

Kate Atkinson	Stevie Davies	Sue Gee
Anita Brookner	Susan Fletcher	Penelope Lively
Sylvia Brownrigg	Margaret Forster	Maggie O'Farrell

Joe Meno 1974- US

Chris Cleave	Jeffrey Eugenides	David Nicholls
Don DeLillo	David Mitchell	Lionel Shriver

Patrick Mercer   1956-   War: Historical - C19th

☺ Antony Morgan - Indian Mutiny

Bernard Cornwell	Richard Howard	Allan Mallinson
Iain Gale	Garry Kilworth	John Wilcox
Adrian Goldsworthy		

Jed Mercurio

Pat Conroy	David Nicholls	Curtis Sittenfeld
Cormac McCarthy	Stewart O'Nan	Martin Cruz Smith

Claire Messud   1966-   US

♟ Encore 2000

Michael Chabon	Ian McEwan	Edith Wharton
Jennifer Egan	Irene Nemirovsky	Colson Whitehead
Nicole Krauss	Anne Tyler	Tim Winton
Jhumpa Lahiri		

Deon Meyer   1958-   SA   Crime

♟ Zatopek 'Zet' van Heerden, Retired policeman - South Africa • Det Bernie Griessel

Lee Child	Tony Hillerman	Ed McBain
Michael Connelly	Arnaldur Indridason	Michael Stanley
Donald Harstad	Richard Kunzmann	Joseph Wambaugh

Stephenie Meyer   1973-   US   Paranormal

♟ Twilight Saga

Rachel Caine	Cassandra Clare	Anne McCaffrey
Isobelle Carmody	Charlaine Harris	Anne Rice
P C & Kristin Cast	Barb & J C Hendee	Darren Shan
Karen Chance	Katie MacAlister	Chris Wooding

Anne Michaels   1958-   Can

♟ Guardian 1997   Orange 1997 & 2010   Wingate 1997

Louis Begley	Caryl Phillips	Rachel Seiffert
Doris Lessing	Michèle Roberts	Miriam Toews
Alice McDermott	Bernhard Schlink	Jane Urquhart
Alistair MacLeod		

Fern Michaels   1933-   US   Glitz & Glamour

is Mary Ruth Kuczkir   ♟ Sisterhood Series

Jackie Collins	Johanna Lindsey	LaVyrle Spencer
Jude Deveraux	Lesley Lokko	Danielle Steel
Eileen Goudge	Debbie Macomber	

☺ also writes children's books

China Miéville ☺ 1972-   Fantasy

🏆 Arthur C Clarke 2001, 2005 & 2010   British Fantasy 2001 & 2003   BSFA 2009

Stephen Baxter	Ian R MacLeod	Kim Stanley Robinson
Mike Carey	Ken MacLeod	Michael Marshall Smith
Jaine Fenn	Philip Pullman	Jeff Vandermeer
Mary Gentle	Alastair Reynolds	David Zindell

M

Alex Miller 1936- Aus

🏆 Commonwealth 1993   Miles Franklin 1993 & 2003

Murray Bail	David Malouf	Craig Silvey
Peter Carey	Hisham Matar	Peter Temple
J M Coetzee	Tea Obreht	Tim Winton
Andrew McGahan	Julie Orringer	

Andrew Miller 1960-

🏆 Black 1997   IMPAC 1999   Costa 2011

A S Byatt	Hilary Mantel	Colin Thubron
Tracy Chevalier	Richard Mason	Rose Tremain
Alan Hollinghurst	Julian Rathbone	Barry Unsworth
Ian McEwan	Jane Stevenson	Peter Watt

Fenella-Jane Miller   Historical Romance

Mary Balogh	Emily Hendrickson	Stephanie Laurens
Anne Barbour	Georgette Heyer	Amanda Quick
Marion Chesney	Eloisa James	

Karen Miller Aus   Fantasy: Epic

is K E Mills

Joe Abercrombie	Pamela Freeman	Scott Lynch
David Bilsborough	Robin Hobb	Fiona McIntosh
Stephen Donaldson	Glenda Larke	Brandon Sanderson
Raymond E Feist	Tom Lloyd	Karen Traviss

Sue Miller 1943- US

Russell Banks	Patricia Gaffney	Marge Piercy
Elizabeth Berg	Nikki Gemmell	Luanne Rice
Holly Chamberlin	Linda Gillard	Lynne Sharon Schwartz
Connie May Fowler	Ann Hood	Christina Schwarz

Kyle Mills 1966- US   Adventure/Thriller

🏃 Mark Beamon - FBI

David Baldacci	Vince Flynn	John Le Carré
Dale Brown	Frederick Forsyth	Robert Ludlum
Tom Clancy	Greg Iles	John Sandford
Brendan Dubois	Paul Johnston	

Magnus Mills 1954-   Humour

🏆 McKitterick 1999

Alan Bennett	Andrew Holmes	James Robertson
Jonathan Coe	Marina Lewycka	Graham Swift
Roddy Doyle	Paul Magrs	Keith Waterhouse
Nicholas Drayson	Dan Rhodes	Mark Watson

Mark Mills

🏆 CWA 2004

Paul Adam	Linda Davies	Elizabeth Kostova
Joy Chambers	Daphne Du Maurier	Bella Pollen
Chris Cleave	Robert Goddard	Catherine Shaw
Matthew D'Ancona	Babs Horton	Paul Torday

Anchee Min 1957- China   Historical

🏃 Empress Orchid Series

Kate Furnivall	Yiyun Li	Su Tong
Arthur Golden	Catherine Lim	Amy Tan
Xiaolu Guo	Shan Sa	Xinran
Ha Jin	Sara Sheridan	

Denise Mina 1966- Sco   Crime: Amateur sleuth

🏆 CWA 1998   🏃 Maureen O'Donnell - Glasgow and London
Paddy Meehan, Journalist - Glasgow • DC Alex Morrow - Glasgow police

Tony Black	Gillian Galbraith	Adrian Magson
Gordon Brown	Alex Gray	Manda Scott
Kenneth Cameron	Allan Guthrie	Aline Templeton
Tana French	Frederic Lindsay	Louise Welsh

Rohinton Mistry 1952- Can

🏆 Commonwealth 1992 & 1996   Holtby 1996

Chimamanda Ngozi Adichie	Amit Chaudhuri	Shifra Horn
Aravind Adiga	Amitav Ghosh	Khaled Hosseini
Thalassa Ali	Abdulrazak Gurnah	R K Narayan
Vikram Chandra	Helon Habila	M G Vassanji

Jacquelyn Mitchard 1955- US

Jill Barnett	Tessa Hadley	Mary Alice Monroe
Elizabeth Berg	Alice Hoffman	Jodi Picoult
Elizabeth Flock	Sue Monk Kidd	Marcia Preston
Therese Fowler	Barbara Kingsolver	Lisa Tucker

David Mitchell   1969-

♟ JLR 1999   Faber 2005

Karl Alexander	Louis de Bernières	Jack O'Connell
Susanna Clarke	Joolz Denby	Gail Tsukiyama
Jonathan Coe	Yann Martel	Jane Urquhart
Jim Crace	Haruki Murakami	Banana Yoshimoto

M

Timothy Mo   1953-

♟ Faber 1979   Hawthornden 1982   Black 1999

Michelle de Kretser	James Hamilton-Paterson	Catherine Lim
Alex Garland	Kazuo Ishiguro	Caryl Phillips
Arthur Golden	Christopher Koch	Amy Tan

L E Modesitt Jr   1943-   US   Fantasy: Epic

Erde

C J Cherryh	Simon Green	R A Salvatore
Louise Cooper	Mercedes Lackey	Janny Wurts
David A Drake	Mickey Zucker Reichert	

Walter Moers   1957-   Ger   Fantasy: Humour

Neil Gaiman	Christopher Moore	Terry Pratchett
Tom Holt	Larry Niven	Connie Willis

G J Moffat   Sco   Adventure/Thriller

🕴 Alex Cahill & Logan Finch, Security advisors - Glasgow

Karen Campbell	John Grisham	Stuart MacBride
Deborah Crombie	John Hart	Caro Ramsay

Rick Mofina   Can   Adventure/Thriller

🕴 Jason Wade, Crime reporter - Seattle

Linwood Barclay	Michael Crichton	James Patterson
Michael Connelly	Dean R Koontz	Ridley Pearson

Deborah Moggach   1948-

also writes as Deborah Hough

Carol Birch	Esther Freud	Eve Makis
Candida Crewe	Sue Gee	Susan Vreeland
Jill Dawson	Angela Huth	Gillian White
Barbara Ewing	Joan Lingard	

Connie Monk   Saga

West Country

Pip Granger	Mary Mackie	Dee Williams
Elizabeth Ann Hill	Janet Tanner	Janet Woods
Claire Lorrimer	Margaret Thornton	

Aly Monroe · Adventure/Thriller

🏆 CWA 2012 · 🏃 Peter Cotton, Spy

Charles Cumming	Joseph Kanon	Martin Cruz Smith
Graham Greene	John Le Carré	Robert Wilson

Grace Monroe · Adventure/Thriller

is Linda Watson-Brown & Maria Thomson · 🏃 Brodie MacLennan, Lawyer - Edinburgh

Victoria Blake	Steve Mosby	Claire Seeber
Alice Blanchard	Karen Rose	Paullina Simons
Elizabeth Corley		

Mary Alice Monroe · US

Mary Kay Andrews	Therese Fowler	Marcia Preston
Jill Barnett	Nicci Gerrard	Anne Rivers Siddons
Elizabeth Flock	Jacquelyn Mitchard	

Richard Montanari · 1952- · US · Adventure/Thriller

🏃 Jessica Balzano & Kevin Byrne - Cleveland, USA • Jack Paris - Cleveland, USA

Chelsea Cain	Jilliane Hoffman	Steve Mosby
Kathryn Fox	J A Jance	Jason Pinter
Michael Harvey	J A Kerley	P J Tracy
Mo Hayder	Cody McFadyen	Lee Weeks

Santa Montefiore · 1970-

Cecilia Ahern	Marika Cobbold	Kate Morton
Judy Astley	Domenica de Rosa	Susan Sallis
Amanda Brookfield	Jessica Duchen	Penny Vincenzi
Sarah Challis	Tamara McKinley	Marcia Willett

David Moody · Horror

Clive Barker	Richard Laymon	Alex Scarrow
James Herbert	Phil Rickman	Scott Sigler
Shaun Hutson		

Rick Moody · 1961- · US

Jeffrey Eugenides	John Irving	Philip Roth
Jonathan Safran Foer	Jonathan Lethem	John Updike
Mark Haddon	Tom McCarthy	

Susan Moody · 1940- · Crime: Amateur sleuth

also writes as Susannah James, Susan Madison, Susan Elizabeth Donaldson · 🏃 Penny Wanawake, Photographer · 🏃 Cassie Swann, Professional bridge player

Elizabeth George	Erin Hart	Sharyn McCrumb
Robert Goddard	Susan Hill	Peter Robinson

Elizabeth Moon 1945- US   Fantasy: Epic

is Susan Moon

Terry Brooks	Barbara Hambly	Andy Remic
Lois McMaster Bujold	Mercedes Lackey	R A Salvatore
Kate Elliott	Fiona McIntosh	Freda Warrington
Pamela Freeman	Mickey Zucker Reichert	Margaret Weis

Chris Mooney US   Adventure/Thriller

🏃 CSI Darby McCormick

Alex Barclay	Brian Freeman	Jason Pinter
Chelsea Cain	Jeff Lindsay	Karen Rose
Thomas H Cook	Cody McFadyen	Craig Russell
Kathryn Fox	Mark Pearson	Lee Weeks

Michael Moorcock 🔗 1939-   Fantasy: Epic

also writes as Edward P Bradbury, James Colvin, Bill Barclay
🏆 Guardian 1977

Jonathan Carroll	Mary Gentle	James Meek
Storm Constantine	Katherine Kurtz	Linda Nagata
Louise Cooper	Wil McCarthy	Christopher Priest
Philip K Dick	Julian May	Kristine Kathryn Rusch

Brian Moore 1921-1999 Can

Dermot Bolger	Colum McCann	Joseph O'Connor
Graham Greene	John McGahern	Colm Toibin
Thomas Keneally	Martin Malone	Tim Winton

Charlotte Moore 1959-   Aga Saga

also writes as Charlotte McKay

Judy Astley	Elizabeth Jane Howard	Robin Pilcher
Elizabeth Buchan	Penelope Lively	Kate Saunders
Patricia Fawcett	Sara MacDonald	Mary Wesley

Christopher Moore 1946- US   Fantasy: Humour

Robert Asprin	Tom Holt	Robert Rankin
Tim Dorsey	Walter Moers	Tom Robbins
Neil Gaiman	Chuck Palahniuk	Andy Secombe
Craig Shaw Gardner	Terry Pratchett	

Jane Moore 1962-   Mature Chick Lit

Lucy Diamond	Anna Maxted	Patricia Scanlan
Olivia Goldsmith	Sheila O'Flanagan	Plum Sykes
Sue Margolis	Adele Parks	

M

Jeffrey Moore   Can

Kingsley Amis	David Lodge	Michael Ondaatje
Michael Frayn	Cormac McCarthy	Alan Sillitoe

Lorrie Moore   1957-   US

🏆 Irish Times 1999

Sebastian Faulks	Penelope Lively	Mark Slouka
Jane Hamilton	Alice Munro	Anne Tyler
Mary Lawson		

Caiseal Mor   Aus   Fantasy: Myth

Ashok K Banker	Cecilia Dart-Thornton	Juliet Marillier
James Barclay	Charles de Lint	Judith Tarr
Marion Zimmer Bradley	Stephen R Lawhead	Sarah Zettel

Michelle Moran   1980-   US   Historical

🏃 Nefertiti - Egypt

Christian Cameron	Christian Jacq	Wilbur Smith
Margaret George	Colleen McCullough	Judith Tarr

Fidelis Morgan   1952-   Crime: Historical - C17th

also writes as Morgan Benedict   🏃 Countess Ashby-de-la-Zouche and Alpiew, Maid
C17th London

Gwendoline Butler	Janet Gleeson	David Liss
P F Chisholm	Philip Gooden	Iain Pears
Christie Dickason	Lee Jackson	Laura Joh Rowland

Jude Morgan   1962-   Historical

also writes as T R Wilson; is Tim Wilson

Vanora Bennett	Clare Clark	Philippa Gregory
Tracy Chevalier	Suzannah Dunn	Susan Vreeland

Sinead Moriarty   Ire   Mature Chick Lit

🏃 Emma Hamilton

Cecelia Ahern	Maeve Haran	Chris Manby
Judy Astley	Kate Harrison	Sheila O'Flanagan
Colette Caddle	Veronica Henry	Allison Pearson

Clare Morrall   1952-

Margaret Atwood	Marti Leimbach	Alice Sebold
Holly Chamberlin	Andrei Makine	Salley Vickers
Chris Cleave	Valerie Martin	Amanda Eyre Ward
Zoë Heller	Julie Myerson	Giles Waterfield

David Morrell 1943- Can · Adventure/Thriller

☂ Rambo • Frank Balenger

Campbell Armstrong	Stuart Harrison	Michael Kimball
David Baldacci	Humphrey Hawksley	Alan Savage
Julie Compton	Richard Herman	Eric Van Lustbader
Colin Harrison		

R N Morris · Crime: Police work - Russia

is Roger N Morris ☂ Det Porfiry Petrovich - C19th St Petersburg

Boris Akunin	Jason Goodwin	Michael Pearce
John Burdett	Clio Gray	William Ryan
Kenneth Cameron	Michael Gregorio	Frank Tallis
Sam Eastland	Andrey Kurkov	Laura Wilson

Blake Morrison 1950-

Peter Ackroyd	Julian Barnes	Patrick Gale
Martin Amis	Sebastian Barry	Ian McEwan
Paul Auster	Margaret Drabble	Graham Swift

Toni Morrison 1931- US

is Chloe Anthony Wofford ☂ Pulitzer 1988

Matthew D'Ancona	Lori Lansens	Kate Pullinger
Allegra Goodman	Chang-rae Lee	Marilynne Robinson
Lawrence Hill	Terry McMillan	Amy Tan
Janette Turner Hospital	Valerie Martin	Alice Walker

Di Morrissey 1948- Aus · Saga

☂ Lily Barton

Joy Chambers	Tamara McKinley	Nicholas Sparks
Frank Coates	Judy Nunn	Rosie Thomas
Beverley Harper	Katherine Scholes	Rachael Treasure

Ian Morson 1947- · Crime: Historical - C13th

also writes as The Medievel Murderers ☂ William Falconer, Regent Master
(with Philip Gooden, Susanna Gregory, Oxford University
Michael Jecks, Bernard Knight, ☂ Nick Zuliani, Adventurer
Karen Maitland, C J Sansom) Mongolia

Alys Clare	Ellis Peters	Kate Sedley
Michael Jecks	Candace Robb	Peter Tremayne
Bernard Knight	Caroline Roe	

John Mortimer 1923-2009 · Humour

☂ Horace Rumpole, Barrister - London • Leslie Titmus - 'Rapstone Valley'

Malcolm Bradbury	David Lodge	Keith Waterhouse
Caro Fraser	Frederic Raphael	P G Wodehouse

Kate Morton   1976-   Aus

Jo Baker	Robert Goddard	Elizabeth Kostova
Joy Chambers	Julia Gregson	Lori Lansens
Jennifer Donnelly	Susan Hill	Bella Pollen
Kim Edwards	Sadie Jones	Talitha Stevenson

M

Steve Mosby   Crime: Psychological

🏆 CWA 2012   🚶 DI Andrew Hicks

Mo Hayder	Michael Marshall	Meg O'Brien
J A Kerley	Grace Monroe	Thomas Perry
Stuart MacBride	Richard Montanari	Karin Slaughter

Walter Mosley   1952-   US   Crime: Hardboiled

🏆 CWA 1991   🚶 Easy Rawlins • Socrates Fortlow
          Fearless Jones & Paris Minton - Los Angeles • Leonid McGill - New York

Stephen Donaldson	Dashiell Hammett	James Sallis
Gordon Ferris	Leonardo Padura	Cath Staincliffe
Steve Hamilton	Chuck Palahniuk	Jason Starr

Kate Mosse   ⌒   1961-   Historical

Jo Baker	Michael Gruber	Chris Kuzneski
Paul Christopher	Tom Harper	Arturo Pérez-Reverte
Sara Donati	Jane Johnson	Manda Scott
Barbara Erskine	Raymond Khoury	Rebecca Stott

Fiona Mountain   Crime: Amateur sleuth

                                         🚶 Natasha Blake, Genealogist

Mary Higgins Clark	Judith Kelman	Betty Rowlands
Carol Goodman	Marianne MacDonald	Patricia Sprinkle
Morag Joss	Gwen Moffat	

| Historical

Vanora Bennett	Barbara Erskine	Anne Herries
Clare Clark	Cynthia Harrod-Eagles	Rosalind Laker

Jojo Moyes   1969-

🏆 Romantic 2004 & 2011

Maeve Binchy	Fannie Flagg	Joanne Harris
Sarah Challis	Adèle Geras	Erica James
Nicholas Coleridge	Laurie Graham	Lorna Landvik
Jennifer Donnelly	Jennifer Haigh	Monica McInerney

Kate Muir   Sco

Kate Atkinson	Isla Dewar	Shena Mackay
Joan Barfoot	Linda Gillard	Maggie O'Farrell

Thomas Mullen   US   Historical

Geraldine Brooks	Charles Frazier	Tim O'Brien
Justin Cronin	China Miéville	Colson Whitehead

Marcia Muller   1944-   US   Crime: PI

🏃 Sharon McCone - San Francisco • Jeanna Stark

Nicola Barker	Stella Duffy	P J Parrish
Linda Barnes	Meg Gardiner	Rick Riordan
Cara Black	Sara Paretsky	John Shannon
Carol Higgins Clark		

Alice Munro   1931-   Can

🏆 WHSmith 1995   Man Booker Int 2009

Richard Bausch	Shaena Lambert	Muriel Spark
Sylvia Brownrigg	Alistair MacLeod	Amy Tan
Richard Ford	Lorrie Moore	Miriam Toews
Jane Hamilton	Lynne Sharon Schwartz	William Trevor

Haruki Murakami   1949-   Ja

Roberto Bolano	Bret Easton Ellis	Paul Magrs
James Clavell	Peter Hoeg	David Mitchell
Michelle de Kretser	Natsuo Kirino	Linn Ullmann
Jeremy Dyson	Toby Litt	

Iris Murdoch   ⌒   1919-1999

🏆 Whitbread 1974   Booker 1978

Jostein Gaarder	Simon Mawer	A N Wilson
Doris Lessing	Emma Tennant	

Gerald Murnane   1939-   Aus

🏆 Patrick White 1999

Hugo Claus	Hans Fallada	W G Sebald
Teju Cole	V S Naipaul	Rachel Seiffert

Elizabeth Murphy   Saga

🏃 Ward Family

Anne Baker	Anna Jacobs	Mary Mackie
Benita Brown	Margaret Kaine	Margaret Thornton
Katie Flynn	Maureen Lee	

Margaret Murphy   1959-   Crime: Psychological

🏃 DIs Rickman and Foster - Liverpool

Ingrid Black	Babs Horton	Sarah Rayne
Joy Fielding	J Wallis Martin	Chris Simms
Frances Fyfield	Ridley Pearson	Laura Wilson

Annie Murray 1960- Saga

Birmingham

Rita Bradshaw
Amelia Carr
Jean Chapman
Alexandra Connor

Dilly Court
Sara Fraser
Hilary Green
Meg Hutchinson

Anna Jacobs
Sheila Newberry
Rowena Summers
June Tate

M
N

Amy Myers 1938- Crime: Historical

also writes as Laura Daniels,
Harriet Hudson

⚡ Auguste Didier, Chef - C19th Europe
Peter & Georgia Marsh,
Marsh & Daughter Series - C20th England

David Ashton
Sara Fraser
Peter J Heck

Alanna Knight
Peter Lovesey
Elizabeth Peters

Catherine Shaw
M J Trow

Julie Myerson 1960-

Susan Fletcher
Nicci Gerrard
Jules Hardy

Zoë Heller
Hilary Mantel
Valerie Martin

Clare Morrall
Ann Patchett
Sarah Rayner

Magdalen Nabb ☺ 1947-2007 Crime: Police work - Italy

⚡ Marshal Guarnaccia - Florence

Michael Dibdin
Michele Giuttari
David Hewson
Roderic Jeffries

H R F Keating
Dennis Lehane
Donna Leon

Giulio Leoni
Carlo Lucarelli
Georges Simenon

Barbara Nadel Crime: Police work - Turkey

🏆 CWA 2005   ⚡ Cetin Ikmen - Istanbul • Francis Hancock, Undertaker - London, East End

Michael Dibdin
Luiz Alfredo Garcia-Roza
Jason Goodwin
David Hewson

Manuel Vázquez
Montalbán
Orhan Pamuk
Eliot Pattison

Michael Pearce
Qiu Xiaolong
Elif Shafak
Jenny White

Reggie Nadelson US Crime: PI

⚡ Artie Cohen - New York

Lawrence Block
Raymond Chandler
Michael Connelly
Robert Crais

Loren D Estleman
Michael Harvey
Camilla Lackberg

Dennis Lehane
Jo Nesbo
S J Rozan

Linda Nagata 1960- US Science Fiction: Technical

is Linda Webb

Iain M Banks
Paul J McAuley
Wil McCarthy

Ian McDonald
Michael Moorcock
Kim Stanley Robinson

Brian Stableford
Robert Charles Wilson

V S Naipaul   1932-   Trin

🏆 Booker 1971

Chimamanda
  Ngozi Adichie
Nathacha Appanah
Vikram Chandra
Joseph Conrad

Kiran Desai
Chitra Banerjee
  Divakaruni
Abdulrazak Gurnah
Helon Habila

Ruth Prawer Jhabvala
Orhan Pamuk
Monique Roffey
M G Vassanji

Anita Nair   Ind

Rupa Bajwa
Kavita Daswani
Kiran Desai
Roopa Farooki

Amitav Ghosh
Manju Kapur
Jhumpa Lahiri

Amulya Malladi
Arundhati Roy
Thrity Umrigar

William Napier   1965-   Historical: Ancient

is Christopher Hart   🏃 Attila the Hun - C5th

Sam Barone
Stephen Baxter
Bernard Cornwell
Michael Curtis Ford

Iain Gale
Conn Iggulden
Simon Levack
Scott Oden

Steven Pressfield
Anthony Riches
Alex Rutherford

R K Narayan   1906-2001   Ind

was Rasipuram Krishnaswamy Narayan

Vikram Chandra
Amit Chaudhuri

Anita Desai
Rohinton Mistry

Arundhatl Roy
Vikram Seth

Clare Naylor   Chick Lit

Lucy Dawson
Martina Devlin
Lisa Jewell

India Knight
Sheila Norton
Anita Notaro

Robyn Sisman
Plum Sykes
Lauren Weisberger

Kitty Neale   Saga

is Brenda Warren   South London

Harry Bowling
Dilly Court
Josephine Cox
Leah Fleming

Katie Flynn
Jess Foley
Ruth Hamilton
Rosie Harris

Ken McCoy
Mary Jane Staples
Dee Williams
Sally Worboyes

Fiona Neill   Mature Chick Lit

Jenny Colgan
Kathy Lette

Chris Manby
Adele Parks

Alexandra Potter
Fiona Walker

Go to back for lists of
Pseudonyms • Authors by Genre • Characters and Series • Environments
Prize Winners • Classic Authors • Crossover Authors • Further Reading • Websites

James L Nelson 1962- US Sea: Historical

⚲ Thomas Marlowe, ex Pirate - USA • Brethren of the Coast Trilogy
Revolution at Sea Saga • Samuel Bowater - American Civil War • Captain Isaac Biddlecomb

David Donachie
C S Forester
Alexander Kent
Dewey Lambdin
Jonathan Lunn
Patrick O'Brian
Peter Smalley
Julian Stockwin
Richard Woodman

Irene Nemirovsky 1903-1942 Ukr

Pat Barker
Louis Begley
John Boyne
Sebastian Faulks
Pam Jenoff
Claire Messud
Elliot Perlman
Bernhard Schlink
Rachel Seiffert

N

Jo Nesbo 1959- Nor Crime: Police work - Norway

⚲ DI Harry Hole - Oslo

Ake Edwardson
Karin Fossum
Anne Holt
Matti Joensuu
Richard Kunzmann
Camilla Läckberg
Åsa Larsson
Häkan Nesser
Yrsa Sigurdardottlr
Frank Tallis
Johan Theorin
Jan Costin Wagner

Häkan Nesser 1950- Swe Crime: Police work - Sweden

⚲ Insp Van Veeteren

Karin Alvtegen
Kate Atkinson
Colin Dexter
Ake Edwardson
Kjell Eriksson
Karin Fossum
Mari Jungstedt
Camilla Läckberg
Henning Mankell
Dominique Manotti
Jo Nesbo
Roslund and Hellström

Adam Nevill 1969- Horror

also writes as Lindsay Gordon

F G Cottam
Daphne Du Maurier
Neil Gaiman
Susan Hill
Joanna Hines
Stephen King
Robert McCammon
Dan Simmons

Stuart Neville 1972- Ire Adventure/Thriller

⚲ Gerry Fegan - Belfast

Ken Bruen
James Ellroy
John Hart
Declan Hughes
Brian McGilloway
Eoin McNamee

Sheila Newberry Saga

WW2

Catherine Cookson
June Francis
Elizabeth Ann Hill
Beryl Kingston
Beryl Matthews
Annie Murray
Gilda O'Neill
June Tate
Dee Williams

Robert Newcomb US Fantasy: Epic

Sarah Ash
James Barclay
Carol Berg
James Clemens
Stephen Donaldson
Raymond E Feist
Terry Goodkind
Robert Jordan
Anne McCaffrey

Kim Newman   1959-   Paranormal

also writes as Jack Yeovil   Anno Dracula Series • Diogenes Club Series

Poppy Z Brite	Mark Hodder	Graham Masterton
Christopher Fowler	Brian Lumley	Richelle Mead
Laurell K Hamilton	David Martin	Alan Moore

David Nicholls   1966-

Guy Bellamy	Nicholas Coleridge	Jed Mercurio
Chris Binchy	Sam Holden	Geoff Nicholson
Ann Brashares	John Lanchester	Francine Prose
Jonathan Coe	Joe Meno	Matt Thorne

William Nicholson   1948-

Chris Cleave	Jon McGregor	John Updike
India Knight	Tim O'Brien	Gerard Woodward

Christopher Nicole   1930-   Adventure/Thriller

also writes as Caroline Gray, Mac Marlow, Alan Savage, Andrew York

James Clavell	Greg Iles	Allan Mallinson
James H Cobb	Michael Kimball	Eric Van Lustbader
Graham Hurley		

Audrey Niffenegger   1963-   US   Fantasy: Contemporary

Karl Alexander	Barbara Erskine	Elizabeth Kostova
Ann Brashares	Diana Gabaldon	Eva Rice
Paulo Coelho	Nada Awar Jarrar	Alice Sebold
Harlan Ellison	Raymond Khoury	Carlos Ruiz Zafón

Larry Niven   1938-   US   Science Fiction: Space and time

also writes jointly with Jerry Pournelle

Kevin J Anderson	Ben Bova	Jack McDevitt
Neal Asher	Christie Golden	Walter Moers
Isaac Asimov	Harry Harrison	Kim Stanley Robinson
Greg Bear	Frank Herbert	

Garth Nix   1963-   Aus   Fantasy: Myth

Trudi Canavan	William Nicholson	Judith Tarr
Isobelle Carmody	Tim Powers	Brent Weeks
Lian Hearn	Philip Pullman	Chris Wooding

David Nobbs   1935-   Humour

 Reginald Perrin

Roddy Doyle	Marina Lewycka	Paul Torday
Andrew Holmes	Leslie Thomas	Nigel Williams
Tom Holt	Alan Titchmarsh	P G Wodehouse

Elizabeth Noble 1968-   Mature Chick Lit

Zoë Barnes   Julie Highmore   Prue Leith
Marika Cobbold   Ann Hood   Kate Saunders
Fiona Gibson   Sandra Howard   Bernadette Strachan
Kate Harrison   Kate Kerrigan   Madeleine Wickham

Diana Norman 1935-2011   Historical

also wrote as Arianna Franklin
Barbara Ewing   Georgette Heyer   Jean Plaidy
Caroline Harvey   Morgan Llywelyn   Connie Willis
Anne Herries   Maureen Peters

Hilary Norman

also writes as Alexandra Henry
Sally Beauman   Susan Lewis   Lesley Pearse
Celia Brayfield   Lesley Lokko   Victoria Routledge

Adventure/Thriller

🏃 Det Sam Becket

Mary Higgins Clark   Lesley Glaister   Judith Kelman
Martina Cole   Sophie Hannah   Karen Rose
Clare Francis

Freya North 🎧 1968-   Chick Lit

🏆 Romantic 2008
Maggie Alderson   Sheila Norton   Daisy Waugh
Alison Jameson   Bella Pollen   Deborah Wright
Susan Lewis   Karen Quinn   Laura Zigman
Melissa Nathan

Sheila Norton   Chick Lit

Lynne Barrett-Lee   Gil McNeil   Freya North
Claire Calman   Clare Naylor   Liz Young
Christina Jones

Naomi Novik 1973- US   Fantasy: Epic

🏃 Capt William Laurence & Temeraire - C19th Dragon Air Force
Joe Abercrombie   Neil Gaiman   Christopher Paolini
Patricia Briggs   Simon Green   Philip Pullman
Trudi Canavan   Anne McCaffrey   Andrzej Sapkowski
Jennifer Fallon

Andrew Nugent Ire   Crime: Police work - Ireland

🏃 Insp Denis Lennon & Sgt Molly Power - Dublin
Benjamin Black   Tana French   Brian McGilloway
William Brodrick   Andrew M Greeley   Andrew Taylor

Judy Nunn   1945-   Aus   Saga

Frank Coates	Di Morrissey	Wilbur Smith
Beverley Harper	Imogen Parker	Rachael Treasure
Tamara McKinley	Lesley Pearse	Polly Williams
Maile Meloy	Alexandra Raife	Elizabeth Wrenn

Malla Nunn   Aus   Crime: Police work - South Africa

ᔆ Det Emmanuel Cooper - 1950s South Africa

Tana French	Pamela Jooste	Michael Stanley
Nadine Gordimer	Gillian Slovo	Andrew Taylor
Reginald Hill		

N O

Robert Nye   1939-

ᵠ Guardian 1976   Hawthornden 1976

Peter Ackroyd	Julian Rathbone	Rose Tremain
John Fowles	Iain Sinclair	Barry Unsworth
Allan Massie	Jane Stevenson	

Patrick O'Brian   ⌒   1914-2000   Sea: Historical

was Richard Patrick Russ   ᔆ Jack Aubrey & Stephen Maturin - C18th/19th

G S Beard	Richard Howard	Allan Mallinson
Tom Connery	Seth Hunter	James L Nelson
David Donachie	Jonathan Lunn	Peter Smalley
C S Forester		

Edna O'Brien   ⌒   1932-   Ire

Ronan Bennett	Jennifer Johnston	Alice Munro
Dermot Bolger	John McGahern	Joyce Carol Oates
Clare Boylan	Deirdre Madden	Fay Weldon
Anne Enright	Benjamin Markovits	Niall Williams

Fiona O'Brien   Ire   Glitz & Glamour

Tilly Bagshawe	Susan Lewis	Carmen Reid
Jackie Collins	Lesley Lokko	Patricia Scanlan
Louise Kean	Anita Notaro	

Martin O'Brien   Crime: Police work - France

also writes as Jack Drummond   ᔆ CI Daniel Jacquot - Marseilles

Andrea Camilleri	Peter James	Georges Simenon
Agatha Christie	Jean François Parot	Fred Vargas
David Hewson		

Tim O'Brien   1946-   US

Michael Collins	Charles Frazier	William Nicholson
Michael Cunningham	John Irving	Jayne Anne Phillips
Richard Ford		

Carol O'Connell 1947- US

Crime: Police work - US

🅺 Sgt Kathleen Mallory - New York

Linda Davies	Thomas Laird	Claire McNab
Meg Gardiner	Ed McBain	Theresa Monsour
Faye Kellerman	Sharyn McCrumb	Kathy Reichs

Jack O'Connell 1959- US

Fantasy: Contemporary

🅺 Quinsigamond Series

J G Ballard	Neil Gaiman	David Mitchell
Susanna Clarke	William Gibson	Philip Pullman

Joseph O'Connor 1963- Ire

Sebastian Barry	Gene Kerrigan	Martin Malone
Dermot Bolger	Patrick McCabe	Brian Moore
Roddy Doyle	Colum McCann	William Trevor
Charles Frazier	Bernard MacLaverty	Niall Williams

O

John O'Farrell 1962-

Lad Lit: Humour

Guy Bellamy	John Harding	Tony Parsons
James Delingpole	Nick Hornby	Mark Watson
Lissa Evans		

Maggie O'Farrell 1972- Ire

🏆 Costa 2010 S Maugham 2005

Manette Ansay	Linda Gillard	Elliot Perlman
Louise Candlish	Tessa Hadley	Sarah Rayner
Susan Fletcher	Charlotte Mendelson	Helen Simpson
Patricia Gaffney	Kate Muir	Roma Tearne

Sheila O'Flanagan 1962- Ire

Chick Lit

Rowan Coleman	Milly Johnson	Geraldine O'Neill
Martina Devlin	Sue Margolis	Lesley Pearse
Clare Dowling	Jane Moore	Plum Sykes

Andrew O'Hagan 1968- Sco

🏆 Holtby 1999 Black 2003

Ronan Bennett	Janice Galloway	Owen Sheers
Michael Cannon	Robin Jenkins	Alan Spence
Glen Duncan	Patrick McCabe	Edward St Aubyn
Giles Foden	Simon Mawer	Giles Waterfield

Stewart O'Nan 1961- US

Thomas Eidson	Charles Frazier	Cormac McCarthy
Louise Erdrich	David Guterson	Richard Russo

Geraldine O'Neill   Ire   Saga

Maeve Binchy
Marita Conlon-McKenna
Melissa Hill

Cathy Kelly
Mary A Larkin
Sheila O'Flanagan

Joan O'Neill
D M Purcell
Liz Ryan

Gilda O'Neill   1951-2010   Saga

East End of London

Pip Granger
Meg Henderson
Beryl Kingston

Gwen Madoc
Sheila Newberry
Pamela Oldfield

Carol Rivers
June Tate
Jeanne Whitmee

Joan O'Neill ⌒ ☺ Ire   Saga

Ireland

Marita Conlon-McKenna
Josephine Cox
Frank Delaney

Rose Doyle
Catherine Dunne
Iris Gower

Geraldine O'Neill
Liz Ryan
Nicola Thorne

Perri O'Shaughnessy   US   Crime: Legal/financial

is Pamela & Mary O'Shaughnessy   ☦ Nina Reilly, Attorney - Lake Tahoe, California

Alafair Burke
Linda Davies
Linda Fairstein

Nancy Taylor Rosenberg
Lisa Scottoline

Susan R Sloan
Robert K Tanenbaum

Joyce Carol Oates ⌒ ☺ 1938- US

also writes as Lauren Kelly, Rosamond Smith

Katharine Davies
Jenny Diski
William Faulkner
Connie May Fowler

Gail Godwin
Sue Monk Kidd
Shaena Lambert
Edna O'Brien

Cynthia Ozick
Francine Prose
Marilynne Robinson
Edith Wharton

Scott Oden   1967-   US   Historical: Ancient

Sam Barone
Bernard Cornwell
Michael Curtis Ford

Conn Iggulden
Glyn Iliffe
Robert Low

William Napier
Steven Pressfield
Wilbur Smith

Ben Okri   1959-   Nigeria

🏆 Booker 1991

Chinua Achebe
Roopa Farooki
Gabriel Garcia Márquez

Helon Habila
Jack Kerouac
David Malouf

Helen Oyeyemi
Caryl Phillips

Pamela Oldfield ☺ 1931-   Saga

☦ Heron Saga - Kent • Foxearth Trilogy

Tessa Barclay
Christine Marion Fraser
Betty McInnes

Gilda O'Neill
Victor Pemberton
Carol Rivers

Jeanne Whitmee
Janet Woods

Nick Oldham   1956-   Crime: Police work - UK

♣ DCI Henry Christie - Blackpool

Judith Cutler   Nicholas Rhea   Mark Timlin
Lesley Horton   Sally Spencer   R D Wingfield
Stuart Pawson   Leslie Thomas

Michael Ondaatje   ⌒   1943-   Sri Lan

🏆 Irish Times 2001   Booker 1992
Anthony Capella   Colum McCann   Jennie Rooney
Michelle de Kretser   Alistair MacLeod   Mark Slouka
Romesh Gunesekera   Jeffrey Moore   Miriam Toews
Kazuo Ishiguro   Francine Prose   M G Vassanji

Charlie Owen   Crime: Police work - UK

♣ DCI Harrison - 'Handstead New Town', Manchester

Allan Guthrie   Kevin Lewis   Louise Welsh
Graham Hurley   Joseph Wambaugh   John Williams

Sharon Owens   1968-   Ire   Saga

Margaret Dickinson   Margaret Kaine   Annie Sanders
Katie Fforde   Mary A Larkin   Kate Thompson
Noëlle Harrison   Gwen Madoc   Paige Toon
Joan Jonker

Helen Oyeyemi   1984-

Chimamanda   Kiran Desai   Ben Okri
  Ngozi Adichie   Sebastian Faulks   Ali Smith
Nathacha Appanah   Helon Habila

Amos Oz   1939-   Isr

Saul Bellow   William Faulkner   Christopher Hope
Michael Chabon   David Grossman   Howard Jacobson

Cynthia Ozick   1928-   US

Lisa Appignanesi   Joyce Carol Oates   Philip Roth
Vladimir Nabokov   Marilynne Robinson   John Updike

Ann Packer   1959-   US

Helen Garner   Laura Moriarty   Anita Shreve
Zoë Heller   Nicky Pellegrino   Lionel Shriver
Sue Monk Kidd   Ann Purser   Anne Tyler
Maile Meloy   Alice Sebold

☺ also writes children's books

O P

Leonardo Padura   1955-   Cuba   Crime: Police work - Cuba

is Loenardo Padura Fuehtes   ⚐ Insp Mario Conde - Havana

James Lee Burke	Raymond Chandler	José Latour
Andrea Camilleri	Dashiell Hammett	Walter Mosley

Lynda Page   1950-   Saga

Leicester

Lyn Andrews	Sara Fraser	Margaret Thornton
Rita Bradshaw	Hilary Green	Audrey Willsher
Katie Flynn	Billy Hopkins	

Robin Paige   US   Crime: Historical - C19th

is Susan Wittig Albert and Bill Albert   ⚐ Sir Charles Sheridan, Peer & Kate Ardleigh, Writer
1900 England

Catherine Aird	Graham Ison	David Roberts
David Dickinson	Laurie R King	Charles Todd
Carola Dunn	Deanna Raybourn	Jacqueline Winspear

P Chuck Palahniuk   1961-   US

Lorenzo Carcaterra	Stephen Donaldson	Walter Mosley
Douglas Coupland	Bret Easton Ellis	Scott Sigler
Don DeLillo	James Ellroy	

Liza Palmer   US   Chick Lit

Meg Cabot	Tess Stimson	Jennifer Weiner
Emily Giffin	Kathleen Tessaro	Polly Williams

Michael Palmer   1942-   US   Adventure/Thriller: Medical

Jefferson Bass	Michael Crichton	Mo Hayder
Paul Carson	Tess Gerritsen	Ken McClure
Robin Cook	Leonard Goldberg	

Philip Palmer   Science Fiction: Space opera

Dan Abnett	Iain M Banks	Kristine Kathryn Rusch
Neal Asher	Alastair Reynolds	Sean Williams

C M Palov   Adventure/Thriller

also writes as and is Chloe Palov

Will Adams	David Gibbins	Tom Knox
Glenn Cooper	Tom Harper	Chris Kuzneski

Go to back for lists of
Pseudonyms • Authors by Genre • Characters and Series • Environments
Prize Winners • Classic Authors • Crossover Authors • Further Reading • Websites

Orhan Pamuk   1952-   Tur   Crime: Historical

🏆 IMPAC 2003   Istanbul

Louis de Bernières   Katie Hickman   Barbara Nadel
Umberto Eco   Ismail Kadare   Elif Shafak
Maureen Freely   Amin Maalouf   Jenny White
Jason Goodwin   James Meek   Carlos Ruiz Zafón

Sara Paretsky   1947-   US   Crime: PI

🏆 CWA 1988, 2002 & 2004   🏃 V I Warshawski - Chicago

Cara Black   Reg Gadney   John Shannon
Anna Blundy   Lynda La Plante   Zoë Sharp
Lindy Cameron   Stieg Larsson   Gillian Slovo
Carol Higgins Clark   Marcus Sakey   Dana Stabenow

Edith Pargeter   1913-95   Historical

also wrote as Ellis Peters

Margaret George   Katharine McMahon   Jean Plaidy
Rosalind Laker   Robin Maxwell   Nigel Tranter
Morgan Llywelyn   Sharon Penman

Imogen Parker   1958-   Mature Chick Lit

Maeve Binchy   Kate Grenville   Susan Lewis
Victoria Clayton   Sarah Harrison   Judy Nunn
Sarah Duncan   Judith Lennox   Kathleen Gilles Seidel

Jefferson Parker   1953-   US   Crime: Police work - US

also writes as T Jefferson Parker   California

John Connolly   Faye Kellerman   Ridley Pearson
Barry Eisler   Jonathan Kellerman   John Shannon
John Gilstrap   Michael Malone   Joseph Wambaugh

Robert B Parker   1932-2010   US   Crime: PI

                                    🏃 Spenser, PI ⎱
                                 Sunny Randall, PI ⎰ Boston, Mass
                            Chief Jesse Stone - 'Paradise', Mass

Lawrence Block   Dick Francis   Thomas Perry
Harlan Coben   Kinky Friedman   John Shannon
Robert Crais   J A Jance   Richard Stark
Eric Jerome Dickey   Ed McBain   Donald Westlake

Adele Parks   1969-   Mature Chick Lit

Katie Agnew   Lucy Dawson   Anna Maxted
Trisha Ashley   Niamh Greene   Jane Moore
Emily Barr   Kate Harrison   Fiona Neill
Jane Costello   India Knight   Tess Stimson

P

197

Tim Parks   1954-

🏆 JLR 1986   S Maugham 1986   Betty Trask 1986

Julian Barnes	Bret Easton Ellis	Piers Paul Read
William Boyd	Toby Litt	Barbara Trapido
Domenica de Rosa	Amanda Prantera	

Jean François Parot   1946-   Fr   Crime: Historical - C18th

🏃 Nicolas Le Floch - C18th Paris

Boris Akunin	Claude Izner	Martin O'Brien
Jeffery Deaver	Pierre Magnan	Georges Simenon

S J Parris   1974-   Crime: Historical - C16th

is Stephanie Merritt   🏃 Giordano Bruno, Spy

Rory Clements	Susanna Gregory	Michael Jecks
Michael Clynes	C S Harris	C J Sansom
Philip Gooden		

P J Parrish   US   Crime: Police work - US

is Kristy & Kelly Montee   🏃 Det Louis Kincaid & Det Joe Frye - Miami, Florida

Linda Barnes	Stuart M Kaminsky	Michael Malone
Patricia D Cornwell	Laura Lippman	Marcia Muller

Julie Parsons   1951-   Ire   Adventure/Thriller: Psychological

Mary Higgins Clark	Lucretia Grindle	Louis Sanders
Vena Cork	Ruth Rendell	Barbara Vine
Neil Cross	Liz Rigbey	Margaret Yorke
Sarah Diamond		

Tony Parsons   🌉   1953-   Lad Lit

🏃 Harry Silver

Chris Binchy	Mike Gayle	Mick Jackson
Paul Burke	Matt Haig	John O'Farrell
Neil Cross	John Harding	Ben Richards
Matt Dunn	Sam Holden	Matt Whyman

Ann Patchett   1963-   US

🏆 Orange 2002

Trezza Azzopardi	Helen Garner	M J Hyland
Andrea Barrett	Jennifer Haigh	Valerie Martin
Louise Dean	Jane Hamilton	Jane Urquhart
Margaret Drabble	Victoria Hislop	Susan Vreeland

Louise Patten   1954-   Mature Chick Lit

Louise Bagshawe	Veronica Henry	Lesley Lokko
Fiona Gibson	Belinda Jones	Patricia Scanlan
Maeve Haran	Marian Keyes	

James Patterson 1947- US Crime: Psychological

also writes jointly with Gabrielle Charbonnet, Peter De Jonge, Andrew Gross, Michael Ledwidge, Lisa Marklund, Maxine Paetro, Howard Roughan

Det Alex Cross - Washington DC
'Women's Murder Club' - San Francisco
Hugh de Lac - Medieval France
Det Michael Bennett, NYPD • Maximum Ride

Chelsea Cain
Jeffery Deaver
Robert Ellis
Brian Freemantle
Heather Graham
Jonathan Kellerman
Dennis Lehane
Michael Marshall
Rick Mofina
Chris Mooney
Lisa Unger
Lee Weeks

Richard North Patterson 1947- US Crime: Legal/financial

Christopher Paget, Attorney - San Francisco

Janet Fitch
James Grippando
David Hosp
Douglas Kennedy
Phillip Margolin
Michael Ridpath
Nancy Taylor Rosenberg

James Pattinson 1915-2009 Adventure/Thriller

Brian Callison
James H Cobb
Clive Cussler
Alexander Fullerton
Hammond Innes
Douglas Reeman

P

Stuart Pawson 1940- Crime: Police work - UK

DI Charlie Priest - Yorkshire

Robert Barnard
Pauline Bell
Chris Collett
Georgie Hale
Patricia Hall
Ken McCoy
Nick Oldham
Nicholas Rhea
Peter Turnbull

David Peace 1967- Crime: Hardboiled

Black 2004

Red Riding Quartet - Yorkshire • Det Minami - Tokyo • Tokyo Trilogy

Jake Arnott
Ken Bruen
Gordon Burn
Lorenzo Carcaterra
Bill James
Simon Kernick
Eoin McNamee
Andrei Makine
Ian Rankin
Danuta Reah

Caro Peacock Crime: Historical - C19th

is Gillian Linscott

Liberty Lane - Amateur sleuth

Carola Dunn
Sara Fraser
John Maclachlan Gray
Joan Lock
Anne Perry
Deanna Raybourn
Norman Russell
Sarah Waters

Michael Pearce 1933- Crime: Historical - C20th

CWA 1993

The Mamur Zapt (Gareth Owen), Secret police - early C20th Egypt
Dmitri Kameron, Lawyer - Tsarist Russia • Seymour, Special Branch

Boris Akunin
Suzanne Arruda
Barbara Cleverly
Jason Goodwin
Michael Gregorio
Graham Ison
Roderic Jeffries
H R F Keating
R N Morris
Barbara Nadel
Elizabeth Peters
Laura Joh Rowland

Matthew Pearl   1975-   US   Crime: Historical

Lee Child	Deryn Lake	Richard Powers
Ildefonso Falcones	Guillermo Martinez	Jed Rubenfeld
Jonathan Franzen	Christopher Paolini	Frank Tallis

Iain Pears   1955-   Crime: Amateur sleuth

♁ Jonathan Argyll, Art historian

Gwendoline Butler	John Maclachlan Gray	Rose Melikan
John Dunning	Claude Izner	Keith Miles
Earlene Fowler	Lee Jackson	Arturo Pérez-Reverte
Philip Gooden	Karen Maitland	Derek Wilson

Tim Pears   1956-

♇ Hawthornden 1994

Kate Atkinson	Glen Duncan	Andrew O'Hagan
Tim Binding	Robert Edric	J B Priestley
Jonathan Coe	William Faulkner	Giles Waterfield

P Lesley Pearse   1945-   Saga

Zoë Barnes	Harriet Hudson	Judy Nunn
Emma Blair	Margaret Kaine	Sheila O'Flanagan
Jilly Cooper	Bernardine Kennedy	Michael Taylor
Leah Fleming	Hilary Norman	Polly Williams

Mark Pearson   Crime: Police work - UK

♁ DI Jack Delaney - London

Mark Billingham	Val McDermid	Peter Robinson
Elena Forbes	John Macken	Lee Weeks
Alex Gray	Chris Mooney	

Ridley Pearson   1953-   US   Crime: Police work - US

also writes as Wendell McCall, Joyce Reardon   ♁ Sgt Lou Boldt & Daphne Matthews,
Forensic psychologist - Seattle

Giles Blunt	Faye Kellerman	Jefferson Parker
Jeffery Deaver	Jonathan Kellerman	John Sandford
W E B Griffin	Rick Mofina	P J Tracy
Donald Harstad	Margaret Murphy	Jess Walter

George P Pelecanos   1957-   US   Crime: Hardboiled

also writes as George Pelecanos   ♁ Nick Stefanos
Derek Strange & Terry Quinn } Washington DC

Jeff Abbott	R J Ellory	Patrick Quinlan
Edward Bunker	John Hart	Marcus Sakey
James Lee Burke	Thomas Laird	Jim Thompson
James Crumley	Ross Macdonald	Edward Wright

Nicky Pellegrino 1964- It

Trisha Ashley	Domenica de Rosa	Ann Packer
Amanda Craig	Sarah Kate Lynch	Frances Paige

Margaret Pemberton 1943- Historical

also writes as Maggie Hudson, Rebecca Dean ⚹ London Sequence

Harry Bowling	Harriet Hudson	Patricia Shaw
Dorothy Dunnett	Sara Hylton	Nicola Thorne
Margaret Elphinstone	Judith Saxton	

Victor Pemberton Saga

London

Philip Boast	Billy Hopkins	Pamela Oldfield
Harry Bowling	Mary A Larkin	Carol Rivers
Pamela Evans	Claire Lorrimer	Mary Jane Staples
Lilian Harry	Margaret Mayhew	Sally Worboyes

Sharon Penman 1945- US Historical

⚹ Justin de Quincey - C12th France • Henry II & Eleanor of Acquitaine - C12th England

Elizabeth Chadwick	Helen Hollick	Edith Pargeter
Will Davenport	Morgan Llywelyn	Mary Stewart
Dorothy Dunnett	Michelle Lovric	Nigel Tranter

Louise Penny 1958- Can Crime: Police work - Canada

🏆 CWA 2006 ⚹ CI Armand Gamache - Quebec

David Armstrong	Ann Cleeves	Donald Harstad
Simon Beckett	Barbara Cleverly	Reginald Hill
Giles Blunt	Christopher Fowler	Lis Howell
Stephen Booth	Elly Griffiths	Jeffrey Siger

Andrew Pepper Crime: Historical - C19th

⚹ Pyke, Bow Street runner

Louis Bayard	James McCreet	Barrie Roberts
John Maclachlan Gray	James McGee	Rosemary Stevens
Deryn Lake	Edward Marston	Jenny White
Peter Lovesey	Anne Perry	

Arturo Pérez-Reverte 1951- Spain Adventure/Thriller: Historical

⚹ Captain Alatriste - C17th Spain

Andrea Camilleri	Amin Maalouf	Kate Mosse
Umberto Eco	Javier Marias	Rebecca Pawel
Ildefonso Falcones	Manuel Vázquez	Iain Pears
Almudena Grandes	Montalbán	
Raymond Khoury		

Elliot Perlman   1964-   Aus

🏆 Betty Trask 1999

Peter Corris	Irene Nemirovsky	Peter Temple
Robert Drewe	Maggie O'Farrell	Markus Zusak
Jonathan Franzen	Philip Roth	

Wendy Perriam   1940-

Kingsley Amis	Sarah Harrison	Emma Tennant
Clare Boylan	Gwendoline Riley	Fay Weldon

Tom Perrotta   1961-   US

Justin Cartwright	Richard Russo	Jonathan Tropper
Anne Enright	Curtis Sittenfeld	John Updike

Anne Perry   1938-   NZ   Crime: Historical - C19th/20th

🚶 Insp Thomas Pitt & Charlotte Pitt ⎫ C19th England
Insp William Monk & Hester Monk ⎭
World War 1 Series - C20th England

Suzanne Arruda	Kerry Greenwood	James McGee
David Ashton	Graham Ison	Andrew Martin
David Dickinson	Lee Jackson	Caro Peacock
Sara Fraser	Joan Lock	Andrew Pepper

Thomas Perry   1947-   US   Adventure/Thriller: Psychological

🚶 Jane Whitefield, Native American

Lawrence Block	Thomas Harris	Elmore Leonard
James Lee Burke	Michael Harvey	Steve Mosby
Michael Connelly	Dennis Lehane	Robert B Parker
Robert Ellis		

Leif G W Persson   1945-   Swe   Crime: Police work - Sweden

is Leif Gustav Willy Persson

Kjell Eriksson	Åsa Larsson	Håkan Nesser
Camilla Läckberg	Stieg Larsson	Olen Steinhauer

Elizabeth Peters   ⌒   1927-   US   Crime: Historical & Modern

also writes as Barbara Michaels;   🚶 Amelia Peabody - Egyptologist
is Barbara Mertz   Vicky Bliss - Art Historian

Barbara Cleverly	Sara Fraser	Michael Pearce
Clare Curzon	C S Harris	Lynda S Robinson
David Dickinson	Amy Myers	

⌒ may be suitable for young adults

Ellis Peters ⌒ 1913-95   Crime: Historical - Medieval

was Edith Pargeter
🏆 CWA 1980

🕴 Brother Cadfael - C13th Shropshire
CI George Felse, Police - UK

Simon Beaufort	Margaret Frazer	Michael Jecks
Cassandra Clark	Andrew M Greeley	The Medieval Murderers
Paul Doherty	Susanna Gregory	Ian Morson
Ariana Franklin	Cora Harrison	Mary Reed and Eric Mayer

Maureen Peters   1935-2008   Wales   Historical

also wrote as Veronica Black, Catherine Darby, Elizabeth Law

Tracy Chevalier	Diana Norman	Kate Tremayne
Rosalind Laker	Jean Plaidy	Barbara Wood
Robin Maxwell	Reay Tannahill	

Alice Peterson   Mature Chick Lit

Louise Candlish	Erica James	Victoria Routledge
Lucy Diamond	Imogen Parker	Paige Toon

Per Petterson   1952-   Nor

🏆 IMPAC 2007   Independent Foreign Fiction 2006

Roberto Bolano	Stieg Larsson	Marcel Theroux
Peter Hoeg	Toni Morrison	Jill Paton Walsh
Arnaldur Indridason	Mark Slouka	

Caryl Phillips   1958-   St Kitts

🏆 Sunday Times 1992   Black 1993   Commonwealth 2004

Nadeem Aslam	Hanif Kureishi	Timothy Mo
Xiaolu Guo	Andrea Levy	Ben Okri
Lawrence Hill	Anne Michaels	Monique Roffey
James Kelman		

Jayne Anne Phillips   1952-   US

Paul Auster	Tim O'Brien	Marilynne Robinson
Don DeLillo	Thomas Pynchon	Marcel Theroux
Louise Erdrich		

Jodi Picoult ⌒ 1967-   US

Manette Ansay	Karen Joy Fowler	Marti Leimbach
Suzanne Bugler	Patricia Gaffney	Margaret Leroy
Diane Chamberlain	Giselle Green	Jacquelyn Mitchard
Connie May Fowler	Elisabeth Hyde	Curtis Sittenfeld

Marge Piercy   1936-   US

🏆 Arthur C Clarke 1993

Louise Doughty	Sue Miller	Robert James Waller
Jackie Kay	Jane Smiley	Louisa Young
Shena Mackay		

P

D B C Pierre   1961-   US

is Peter Findlay   🏆 Bollinger 2003   Man Booker 2003   Whitbread 2003

Martin Amis	Marina Lewycka	Lionel Shriver
Paul Auster	Yann Martel	Jonathan Trigell

Christopher Pike   🎧 ☺   1954-   US   Horror

is Kevin Christopher McFadden

Shaun Hutson	Scott Nicholson	John Saul
Stephen Laws	Phil Rickman	Peter Straub
Richard Laymon		

Robin Pilcher   1950-   Sco   Aga Saga

Amanda Brookfield	Julie Highmore	Charlotte Moore
Marika Cobbold	Rachel Hore	Rosamunde Pilcher
Elizabeth Edmondson	Kate Long	Alexandra Raife
Sarah Grazebrook	Sara MacDonald	Jean Saunders

Rosamunde Pilcher   1924-   Aga Saga

also writes as Jane Fraser   🏆 Romantic 1996

Sarah Challis	Adèle Geras	Robin Pilcher
Lucy Clare	Elizabeth Jane Howard	Sally Stewart
Victoria Clayton	Judith Lennox	Alan Titchmarsh
Annabel Dilke	Sara MacDonald	Marcia Willett

Barry Pilton   Wales   Humour

Michael Frayn	James Hawes	John O'Farrell
Stephen Fry	Charles Higson	Keith Waterhouse

Jason Pinter   1979-   US   Adventure/Thriller

🕴 Henry Parker, Journalist - New York

Colin Bateman	Tess Gerritsen	Richard Montanari
Christopher Brookmyre	J A Kerley	Chris Mooney
Jeffery Deaver	Michael Marshall	

Jean Plaidy   1906-93   Historical

also wrote as Philippa Carr, Victoria Holt; was Eleanor Alice Burford Hibbert

Christie Dickason	Sandra Gulland	Edith Pargeter
Dorothy Dunnett	Anne Herries	Maureen Peters
Margaret George	Diana Norman	Alison Weir
C W Gortner		

Belva Plain   1919-2010   US   Saga

🕴 Werner Family - USA

Janet Dailey	Joan Medlicott	Sue Sully
Barbara Delinsky	Anne Rivers Siddons	Rosie Thomas
Jude Deveraux	LaVyrle Spencer	

P

Bella Pollen

Melissa Bank	Jane Johnson	Kate Morton
Alice Hoffman	Maile Meloy	Freya North
Wendy Holden	Mark Mills	Anita Notaro

Dudley Pope   1925-1997   Sea: Historical & Modern

G S Beard	C S Forester	Jonathan Lunn
Tom Connery	Duncan Harding	Philip McCutchan
David Donachie	Sam Llewellyn	

Henry Porter   1953-   Adventure/Thriller

🏆 CWA 2005   ☆ Robert Harland

Ronan Bennett	Jon Evans	Joseph Kanon
Alex Berenson	David Fiddimore	Stella Rimington
Charles Cumming	John Fullerton	E V Seymour
David Downing	Jean-Christophe Grangé	Robert Wilson

Alexandra Potter   1970-   Chick Lit

Jessica Adams	Kathy Lette	Bernadette Strachan
Megan Crane	Anna McPartlin	Paige Toon
Helen Fielding	Holly McQueen	Sarah Tucker
Dorothy Koomson	Fiona Neill	Fiona Walker

Richard Powers   1957-   US

William Boyd	Richard Ford	Thomas Pynchon
Don DeLillo	Christopher Hope	Colson Whitehead
Jonathan Safran Foer	Matthew Pearl	

Science Fiction: Near future

🏆 WHSmith 2004

Neal Asher	Paul J McAuley	Neal Stephenson
John Birmingham	Lucius Shepard	Tobias Wolff
Jeffrey Eugenides		

Tim Powers   1952-   US   Fantasy: Contemporary

also writes as William Ashbless (with James P Blaylock)

Charles de Lint	Gary Gibson	Garth Nix
Philip K Dick	Barbara Hambly	K J Parker
Neil Gaiman	Robert Holdstock	Connie Willis
Mary Gentle	Gregory Maguire	Gene Wolfe

Terry Pratchett   ⌂ ☺ 1948-   Fantasy: Humour

also writes jointly with Stephen Baxter, Vadim Jean, Jacqueline Simpson   ☆ Discworld

🏆 BSFA 1989   Bollinger 2012

Robert Asprin	Simon Green	Robert Rankin
Jasper Fforde	Brian Herbert	Andy Secombe
Craig Shaw Gardner	Walter Moers	Kim Wilkins
Rob Grant	Christopher Moore	Chris Wooding

Steven Pressfield   1943- US   Historical

Ancient Greece

Stephen Baxter	Robert Harris	William Napier
Bernard Cornwell	Douglas Jackson	Scott Oden
Michael Curtis Ford	Christian Jacq	Tim Severin
Robert Graves	Valerio Massimo Manfredi	Jack Whyte

Douglas Preston   1956- US   Adventure/Thriller

also writes jointly with Lincoln Child   ☥ Aloysius Pendergast, FBI Special agent - New York

Dan Brown	Michael Crichton	Robert Ludlum
Lincoln Child	Richard Doetsch	Andy McDermott
Michael Cordy	David Gibbins	Bill Napier
Harold Coyle	Brian Haig	James Rollins

Katie Price   1978-   Glitz & Glamour

is Katrina Alexandra Infield (Jordan)

Celia Brayfield	Jackie Collins	Johanna Lindsey
Candace Bushnell	Olivia Goldsmith	Harold Robbins

P Christopher Priest   1943-   Science Fiction: Space and time

🏆 Black 1995   BSFA 1974, 1998, 2002 & 2011   Arthur C Clarke 2003

J G Ballard	Michael Moorcock	Connie Willis
Philip K Dick	Robert Silverberg	Robert Charles Wilson
Todd McCaffrey	H G Wells	David Zindell

Lily Prior   Humour

Anthony Capella	Laura Esquivel	Sarah Kate Lynch
Mavis Cheek	Joanne Harris	Ian Sansom
Chitra Banerjee Divakaruni		

Francine Prose   1947- US

A S Byatt	David Nicholls	Michael Ondaatje
J M Coetzee	Joyce Carol Oates	Jane Smiley

Annie Proulx   1935- US

also wrote previously as E Annie Proulx   🏆 Irish Times 1993   Pulitzer 1994

Suzanne Berne	Louise Erdrich	Peter Hoeg
Kiran Desai	Fannie Flagg	Marilynne Robinson
Robb Forman Dew	Jonathan Franzen	Donna Tartt
Thomas Eidson		

Morag Prunty   1964- Ire   Chick Lit

also writes as Kate Kerrigan

Cecelia Ahern	Melissa Hill	Tess Stimson
Hester Browne	Belinda Jones	Jennifer Weiner
Colette Caddle	Monica McInerney	Laura Zigman
Claudia Carroll		

Malcolm Pryce   1960-   Wales   Crime: Humour

⚇ Louie Knight, PI - Aberystwyth

Linwood Barclay	Jasper Fforde	Robert Lewis
Colin Bateman	Christopher Fowler	Ian Sansom
Christopher Brookmyre	Mark Gatiss	L C Tyler
Tim Dorsey	Danny King	

Kate Pullinger   Can

A S Byatt	Alice Hoffman	John Updike
J M Coetzee	Toni Morrison	Jeanette Winterson

Philip Pullman   ☏ ☺ 1946-   Fantasy

🏆 Whitbread 2001

Eoin Colfer	Stephen Hunt	Garth Nix
G W Dahlquist	Sergei Lukyanenko	Naomi Novik
Elizabeth Garner	Gregory Maguire	Jack O'Connell
Mary Gentle	China Miéville	Christopher Paolini

D M Purcell   1945-   Ire   Saga P

also wrote previously as Deirdre Purcell   Ireland

Frank Delaney	Geraldine O'Neill	Patricia Scanlan
Rose Doyle	Liz Ryan	Kate Thompson
Noëlle Harrison	Susan Sallis	Sally Worboyes
Sheelagh Kelly		

Ann Purser   Crime: Amateur sleuth

⚇ Lois Meade, Cleaner - 'Long Farnden'

Caroline Graham	Veronica Heley	Marianne MacDonald
Ann Granger	Hazel Holt	Betty Rowlands
Patricia Harwin	Lis Howell	

Ann Purser

'Round Ringford'

Marika Cobbold	Nora Naish	Rebecca Shaw
Eve Houston	Ann Packer	Jack Sheffield
Erica James	Miss Read	Célestine Hitiura Vaite
Jan Karon	Jean Saunders	

Libby Purves   1950-

Candida Clark	Pauline McLynn	Louise Voss
Anne Fine	Elizabeth Palmer	Louise Wener
Patricia Gaffney	Allison Pearson	Ann Widdecombe
Bernardine Kennedy	Joanna Trollope	

☺ also writes children's books

Mario Puzo 1920-1999 US

⚞ The Godfather

Lorenzo Carcaterra	Harold Robbins	Joseph Wambaugh
Elmore Leonard	Boston Teran	Donald Westlake

Thomas Pynchon 1937- US

Paul Auster	Joseph Heller	Jayne Anne Phillips
Roberto Bolano	John Irving	Richard Powers
Don Delillo	Denis Johnson	Tom Robbins
Nathan Englander	Norman Mailer	Colson Whitehead

Andrew Pyper 1968- Can Crime: Psychological

Stephen Booth	Dennis Lehane	Erica Spindler
Nicci French	John Saul	Peter Straub
Michael Koryta	Chris Simms	Stephen White

Qiu Xiaolong 1953- China Crime: Police work - China

⚞ Insp Chen - Shanghai

Luiz Alfredo Garcia-Roza	Donna Leon	Frank Tallis
Xiaolu Guo	Yiyun Li	Nury Vittachi
Ha Jin	Peter May	Michael Walters
Richard Kunzmann	Barbara Nadel	Xinran

Amanda Quick 1948- US Historical Romance

also writes as Jayne Castle; is Jayne Ann Krentz

Elizabeth Bailey	Julie Garwood	Fenella-Jane Miller
Catherine Coulter	Georgette Heyer	Julia Quinn
Elizabeth Darrell	Judith McNaught	Patricia Shaw

Sheila Quigley 1947- Crime: Hardboiled

⚞ DI Lorraine Hunt - Sunderland

Lindsay Ashford	Mandasue Heller	Lynda La Plante
Martina Cole	Jessie Keane	Ken McCoy
June Hampson	Roberta Kray	

Anna Quindlen 1953- US

Elizabeth Berg	Alice Hoffman	Miriam Toews
Robb Forman Dew	Elizabeth Jane Howard	Ann Tyler
Margaret Forster	Bernardine Kennedy	Michael White
Linda Grant	Jane Smiley	

Julia Quinn 1970- US Historical Romance

is Julie Cotler Pottinger

Elizabeth Bailey	Marion Chesney	Stephanie Laurens
Mary Balogh	Georgette Heyer	Amanda Quick
Anne Barbour	Eloisa James	

P
Q

Karen Quinn   US   Mature Chick Lit

Jane Green	Gil McNeil	Paige Toon
Marian Keyes	Freya North	Lauren Weisberger
Sophie Kinsella	Victoria Routledge	Sue Welfare

Robert Radcliffe   War: Modern

is Robert Mawson

Frank Barnard	James Holland	Derek Robinson
David Fiddimore	Marion Husband	Paul Watkins
Andrew Greig		

R T Raichev   Crime: Amateur sleuth

                             🏃 Antonia Darcy & Hugh Payne

Carola Dunn	Veronica Stallwood	Jill Paton Walsh
David Roberts	Charles Todd	Jacqueline Winspear

Alexandra Raife   Saga

                                      Scotland

Margaret Thomson Davis	Elvi Rhodes	Mary Stewart
Judy Nunn	Denise Robertson	Janet Tanner
Robin Pilcher	Liz Ryan	Adriana Trigiani
Miss Read	Linda Sole	T R Wilson

Caro Ramsay   Sco   Crime: Hardboiled

                                       Glasgow

Lin Anderson	Gordon Brown	Alex Gray
Ray Banks	Elena Forbes	Reginald Hill
Mark Billingham	Gillian Galbraith	Ian Rankin

Eileen Ramsay   Sco   Saga

                                      Scotland

Emma Blair	Doris Davidson	Miss Read
Jessica Blair	Adèle Geras	Denise Robertson
Maggie Craig	Gwen Kirkwood	Mary Withall

Ian Rankin   ⌒   1960-   Sco   Crime: Police work - UK

also writes as Jack Harvey   🏃 DI John Rebus & DC Siobhan Clarke - Edinburgh
🏆 CWA 1997 & 2005   Malcolm Fox - Complaints Department

Lin Anderson	Gillian Galbraith	Frederic Lindsay
Ray Banks	Alex Gray	Brian McGilloway
Robert G Barrett	Allan Guthrie	David Peace
Tony Black	Tobias Hill	Caro Ramsay

Robert Rankin   ⌒   1949-   Science Fiction: Humour

Douglas Adams	Harry Harrison	Terry Pratchett
Karl Alexander	Tom Holt	Martin Scott
Jasper Fforde	Christopher Moore	Andy Secombe
Rob Grant		

Q R

Frederic Raphael 1931- US

Saul Bellow	Howard Jacobson	John Mortimer
Margaret Drabble	Allan Massie	Edward St Aubyn

Ron Rash 1953- US

Chris Cleave	Charles Frazier	Marilynne Robinson
Tom Franklin	Sara Gran	Daniel Woodrell

Julian Rathbone 1935-2008 Adventure/Thriller

🏃 Comm Jan Argand

Campbell Armstrong	James Follett	Julian Jay Savarin
Suzanne Berne	Christopher Nicole	Craig Thomas

Historical

John Boyne	Thomas Keneally	Robert Nye
Melvyn Bragg	Matthew Kneale	James Robertson
James H Jackson	Andrew Miller	Barry Unsworth

Melanie Rawn 1954- US Fantasy: Epic

also writes as Ellen Randolph

Sarah Ash	Louise Cooper	Mercedes Lackey
Carol Berg	Barbara Hambly	Fiona McIntosh
Marion Zimmer Bradley	Katherine Kurtz	Margaret Weis

R

Deanna Raybourn 1968- US Crime: Historical - C19th

🏃 Lady Julia Grey & PI Nicholas Brisbane, Amateur sleuth - Yorkshire Moors

Suzanne Arruda	Joan Lock	Robin Paige
David Ashton	Andrew Martin	Caro Peacock
Lee Jackson		

Sarah Rayne Crime: Psychological

also writes as Frances Gordon, Bridget Wood; is Bridget Wood

Carla Banks	Sarah Diamond	Morag Joss
Hilary Bonner	Jane Hill	Margaret Murphy
Caroline Carver	Susan Hill	Patrick Redmond
Vena Cork	Babs Horton	Sally Spedding

Sarah Rayner

Nicci Gerrard	Jules Hardy	Maggie O'Farrell
Jane Hamilton	Julie Myerson	Gillian White

Miss Read 1913- Saga

is Mrs Dora Saint 🏃 Fairacre • Thrush Green

Eve Houston	Ann Purser	Ann B Ross
Jan Karon	Alexandra Raife	Rebecca Shaw
Mary A Larkin	Eileen Ramsay	Jack Sheffield
Claire Lorrimer		

Piers Paul Read 1941-

🏆 Black 1988   Hawthornden 1970

Kingsley Amis	Howard Jacobson	Tim Parks
Malcolm Bradbury	Hilary Mantel	Nicholas Shakespeare

John Rector   US   Adventure/Thriller: Psychological

Linwood Barclay	Harlan Coben	Tom Franklin
James Lee Burke	Barry Eisler	Andrew Klavan

Patrick Redmond   1966-   Crime: Psychological

Nicci French	Sarah Rayne	Tony Strong
Robert Goddard	Boris Starling	Barbara Vine
Val McDermid		

Mary Reed and Eric Mayer   US   Crime: Historical - Ancient

🏃 John the Eunuch, Lord Chamberlain - C6th Constantinople

Alys Clare	Ellis Peters	Lynda S Robinson
Margaret Frazer	John Maddox Roberts	Peter Tremayne
Lauren Haney		

Douglas Reeman   1924-   Sea: Modern

also writes as Alexander Kent   🏃 Mike Blackwood

Brian Callison	Alexander Fullerton	James Pattinson
Roger Carpenter	Hammond Innes	Patrick Robinson
James H Cobb		

R

Emlyn Rees   see Josie Lloyd

Matt Rees   1967-   Wales   Crime: Amateur sleuth

🏆 CWA 2008   🏃 Omar Yussef - Palestine

Elizabeth George	Arnaldur Indridason	Brian McGilloway
Jason Goodwin	John Le Carré	Minette Walters

Christopher Reich   1961-   US   Crime: Legal/financial

Harry Bingham	Brad Meltzer	E V Seymour
John Burdett	Jonathan Nasaw	Robert K Tanenbaum
John Grisham	Michael Ridpath	Scott Turow

Mickey Zucker Reichert   1962-   US   Fantasy: Epic

Terry Brooks	Katherine Kurtz	Elizabeth Moon
David Eddings	Mercedes Lackey	R A Salvatore
Terry Goodkind	L E Modesitt Jr	Janny Wurts

Kathy Reichs ⌒ 1950- US   Crime: Forensic

       ♁ Dr Temperance Brennan, Pathologist - Montreal & North Carolina

Jefferson Bass	Aaron Elkins	Lynn Hightower
Simon Beckett	Linda Fairstein	Keith McCarthy
Beverly Connor	Kathryn Fox	Nigel McCrery
Patricia Cornwell	Leonard Goldberg	Carol O'Connell

Matthew Reilly 1974- Aus   Adventure/Thriller

     ♁ Capt Shane Schofield - US Marine Corps • Jack West Jr, Soldier

Steve Berry	William Dietrich	Greg Iles
Lincoln Child	James Follett	Raymond Khoury
Stephen Coonts	David Gibbins	Andy McDermott
Harold Coyle	W E B Griffin	David L Robbins

Andy Remic   Fantasy: Epic

David A Drake	David Gemmell	Elizabeth Moon
Neil Gaiman	Simon Green	

Ruth Rendell ⌒ 1930-   Crime: Police work - UK

also writes as Barbara Vine   ♁ CI George Wexford - 'Kingsmarkham'
🏆 CWA 1976, 1984 & 1986

W J Burley	J Wallis Martin	Michael Robotham
Ake Edwardson	Maureen O'Brien	Dorothy Simpson
Morag Joss	Julie Parsons	June Thomson
Jim Kelly	Nicholas Rhea	Laura Wilson

Alastair Reynolds 1966- Wales   Science Fiction: Space opera

🏆 BSFA 2001

Kevin J Anderson	Ian R MacLeod	Robert Reed
Neal Asher	John Meaney	Adam Roberts
Jaine Fenn	China Miéville	Kim Stanley Robinson
Jack McDevitt	Philip Palmer	Tricia Sullivan

Nicholas Rhea 1936-   Crime: Police work - UK

also writes as Andrew Arncliffe,   ♁ PC Nick Parish - 'Adensfield', Yorkshire
Christopher Coram, James Ferguson,   DS Mark Pemberton
Tom Ferris; is Peter Norman Walker   DI Montague Pluke

Robert Barnard	Nick Oldham	Jack Sheffield
Caroline Graham	Stuart Pawson	Leslie Thomas
J M Gregson	Ruth Rendell	M J Trow
Katherine John		

Dan Rhodes 1972-

🏆 Authors 2003

Michel Faber	Jhumpa Lahiri	Magnus Mills
Mark Haddon	Marina Lewycka	Evelyn Waugh

Elvi Rhodes   c 1930-   Saga

Yorkshire

Helen Cannam	Ken McCoy	Susan Sallis
Elizabeth Gill	Elisabeth McNeill	Linda Sole
Sheelagh Kelly	Alexandra Raife	

Anne Rice   1941-   US   Paranormal

also writes as Anne Rampling   ☩ Vampire Chronicles

R Scott Bakker	Jeanne Kalogridis	Robert McCammon
Poppy Z Brite	John Ajvide Lindqvist	Stephenie Meyer
Storm Constantine	Brian Lumley	Kim Wilkins
Laurell K Hamilton	Katie MacAlister	

Luanne Rice   1955-   US   Crime: Romantic suspense

Barbara Taylor Bradford	Sue Miller	Sharon Sala
Barbara Delinsky	Nora Roberts	Danielle Steel

Anthony Riches   Historical: Ancient

☩ Marcus Valerius Aquila, Roman soldier - England

Michael Curtis Ford	Robert Low	Simon Scarrow
Conn Iggulden	Allan Massie	Harry Sidebottom
Ben Kane	Scott Oden	John Stack

Phil Rickman   Paranormal

also writes as Will Kingdom, Thom Madley   ☩ Merrily Watkins, Exorcist

Carla Banks	Graham Joyce	Christopher Pike
F G Cottam	Stephen Laws	Sally Spedding
James Herbert	David Moody	Kim Wilkins
Shaun Hutson	Scott Nicholson	

Michael Ridpath   1961-   Adventure/Thriller: Legal/financial

☩ Alex Calder, Bond trader • Det Magnus Jonson - Iceland

Harry Bingham	James Grippando	Richard North Patterson
Linda Davies	John Grisham	Christopher Reich
Reg Gadney	Brad Meltzer	

Gwendoline Riley   1979-

🏆 S Maugham 2008

Anita Brookner	Shena Mackay	Ali Smith
Esther Freud	Wendy Perriam	Emma Tennant

Stella Rimington   1935-   Adventure/Thriller

☩ Liz Carlyle, MI5

Alex Berenson	Jon Evans	Lynne Heitman
Linda Davies	Dan Fesperman	Gayle Lynds
Len Deighton	Ian Fleming	Chris Petit
Gavin Esler	Alan Furst	Henry Porter

R

Mike Ripley   1952-   Crime: Amateur sleuth

🏆 CWA 1989 & 1991   🏃 Fitzroy Maclean Angel, Taxi driver - London

Gilbert Adair	Danny King	Mark Timlin
Colin Bateman	Chris Niles	Patricia Wentworth
Alan Dunn	Leslie Thomas	R D Wingfield
Joanne Fluke		

Carol Rivers   1947-   Saga

Isle of Dogs, London

Elizabeth Adler	Annie Groves	Gilda O'Neill
Anita Burgh	Jeannie Johnson	Victor Pemberton
Pamela Evans	Beryl Kingston	Mary Jane Staples
Pip Granger	Pamela Oldfield	Elizabeth Waite

Karen Robards   1954-   US   Crime: Romantic suspense

Sandra Brown	Linda Howard	J D Robb
Julie Garwood	Iris Johansen	Nora Roberts
Tami Hoag	Jennifer McMahon	

Candace Robb   1950-   Crime: Historical - Medieval

🏃 Owen Archer - C14th York • Margaret Kerr - C13th Scotland

Simon Beaufort	Susanna Gregory	Ian Morson
Alys Clare	Pat McIntosh	Caroline Roe
Cassandra Clark	The Medieval Murderers	Kate Sedley
Ariana Franklin		

R

J D Robb   1950-   US   Crime: Police work - US

also writes as Nora Roberts; is Elly Wilder   🏃 Eve Dallas - Future New York

Beverly Barton	Kerry Greenwood	Ed McBain
Allison Brennan	Linda Howard	P D Martin
Robert Ellis	Lisa Jackson	Karen Robards
Heather Graham	Paul Johnston	Sharon Sala

Harold Robbins   1912-1997   US   Glitz & Glamour

also wrote as Frank Lane; was Harold Rubin

Millenia Black	Jackie Collins	Mario Puzo
Sandra Brown	Katie Price	Sidney Sheldon
Nicholas Coleridge		

Tom Robbins   1936-   US

Joseph Heller	Sam Lipsyte	Thomas Pynchon
John Irving	Jim Lynch	Tobias Wolff

Bethan Roberts

Jennifer Donnelly	Elizabeth Kostova	Kate Morton
Kim Edwards	Judith Lennox	Elliot Perlman

John Maddox Roberts 1947- US　　Crime: Historical - Ancient

also writes as Mark Ramsay　　♟ Decius Caecelius Metellus the Younger
Politics - Ancient Rome

Lindsey Davis	Lynda S Robinson	Marilyn Todd
Lauren Haney	Rosemary Rowe	Paul Waters
Mary Reed and Eric Mayer	Steven Saylor	David Wishart

Michèle Roberts 1949- Fr

🏆 WHSmith 1993

Emma Donoghue	Sarah Kate Lynch	Jeanette Winterson
Joanne Harris	Anne Michaels	Virginia Woolf
Janette Turner Hospital		

Nora Roberts 1950- US　　Crime: Romantic suspense

also writes as J D Robb; is Elly Wilder　　♟ Three Sisters Island Trilogy • Quinn Family

Beverly Barton	Jude Deveraux	Luanne Rice
Sandra Brown	Eileen Goudge	Karen Robards
Candace Bushnell	Linda Howard	Sharon Sala
Janet Dailey	Susanna Kearsley	Célestine Hitiura Vaite

Denise Robertson　　Saga

♟ Beloved People Trilogy - NE England

Irene Carr	Mary A Larkin	Eileen Ramsay
Jean Chapman	Ken McCoy	Janet Tanner
Catherine Cookson	Alexandra Raife	Janet MacLeod Trotter

Imogen Robertson　　Crime: Amateur sleuth

♟ Harriet Westerman & Gabriel Crowther - C18th England

Alan Bradley	Deryn Lake	James McCreet
David Dickinson	David Liss	Jacqueline Winspear
Janet Gleeson		

James Robertson 1958- Sco　　Historical

🏆 Saltire 2010

William Boyd	Robin Jenkins	Robert Louis Stevenson
Margaret Elphinstone	Raymond Khoury	Rebecca Stott
Philip Hensher	Matthew Kneale	Jonathan Tropper
Lawrence Hill	Julian Rathbone	Markus Zusak

Wendy Robertson　　Saga

'Priorton', NE England

Irene Carr	Elizabeth Elgin	Ken McCoy
Jean Chapman	Jess Foley	Janet MacLeod Trotter
Josephine Cox	Una Horne	Valerie Wood

R

Derek Robinson 1932- War: Modern

Frank Barnard	Murray Davies	Robert Radcliffe
Patrick Bishop	David Fiddimore	Guy Walters
Francis Cottam	W E B Griffin	Paul Watkins

Kim Stanley Robinson 1952- US Science Fiction: Near future

♈ BSFA 1992

Greg Bear	China Miéville	Alastair Reynolds
Ben Bova	Linda Nagata	Robert J Sawyer
Michael Crichton	Larry Niven	Brian Stableford
Steven Gould		

Marilynne Robinson 1944-

♈ Orange 2009   Pulitzer 2005

Geraldine Brooks	Kent Haruf	Joyce Carol Oates
Richard Ford	Mary Lawson	Jayne Anne Phillips
David Guterson	Toni Morrison	Annie Proulx

Patrick Robinson 1940- Ire Sea: Modern

🏃 Admiral Arnold Morgan, US National Security Advisor

Dale Brown	Philip McCutchan	Peter Tonkin
James H Cobb	Douglas Reeman	Robin White
Duncan Harding		

Peter Robinson 1950- Crime: Police work - UK

🏃 CI Alan Banks - Yorkshire

Rennie Airth	Erin Hart	Jim Kelly
Kate Atkinson	Declan Hughes	Mark Pearson
Chris Collett	Graham Hurley	Pauline Rowson
Colin Dexter	Peter James	Aline Templeton

Michael Robotham 1960- Aus Crime: Psychological

🏃 Joseph O'Loughlin

David Baldacci	Gregg Hurwitz	Jonathan Nasaw
Linwood Barclay	Patrick Lennon	Ruth Rendell
Mark Gimenez		

Justina Robson Science Fiction: Near future

Eric Brown	Jon Courtenay Grimwood	Andrzej Sapkowski
Hal Duncan	Sergei Lukyanenko	Robert J Sawyer
William Gibson	Richard Morgan	Tricia Sullivan
Steven Gould		

Monique Roffey 1965- Trin

Monica Ali	Roopa Farooki	V S Naipaul
Margaret Cezair-Thompson	Andrea Levy	Caryl Phillips

R

Jane Rogers 1952

🏆 S Maugham 1985   Arthur C Clarke 2012

Margaret Atwood	Jane Gardam	Hilary Mantel
Carol Birch	Kate Grenville	D J Taylor

James Rollins 1961- US   Adventure/Thriller

also writes as James Clemens   🏃 Sigma Force

Will Adams	Michael Byrnes	David Ignatius
James Becker	Glenn Cooper	Andy McDermott
Steve Berry	Michael Cordy	Douglas Preston
S J Bolton	Thomas Greanias	Paul Sussman

Jennie Rooney 1980-

Amanda Brookfield	Erica James	Michael Ondaatje
Michelle de Kretser	Matthew Kneale	Miriam Toews

Karen Rose US   Crime: Psychological

🏃 Daniel Vartanian

Allison Brennan	Tami Hoag	Hilary Norman
Vena Cork	P D Martin	Claire Seeber
Elizabeth Corley	Grace Monroe	P J Tracy
Christiane Heggan	Chris Mooney	Lee Weeks

Melanie Rose   Chick Lit

Cecelia Ahern	Sarah Duncan	Melissa Hill
Lucy Dillon	Veronica Henry	Madeleine Wickham

Nancy Taylor Rosenberg 1946- US   Crime: Legal/financial

🏃 Lily Forrester, DA - California

Alafair Burke	John T Lescroart	Perri O'Shaughnessy
Carol Higgins Clark	John McLaren	Richard North Patterson
Linda Fairstein	Phillip Margolin	Susan R Sloan

Andrew Rosenheim 1955- US   Adventure/Thriller

Sebastian Faulks	Daniel Mason	Chris Paling
Douglas Kennedy	Simon Mawer	Paul Watkins

Roslund and Hellström Swe   Crime: Police work - Sweden

are Anders Roslund & Börge Hellström   🏃 Det Insp Ewert Grens & Det Sven Sunkist
🏆 CWA 2011

Karin Alvtegen	Stieg Larsson	Häkan Nesser
Anne Holt	Henning Mankell	Maj Sjöwall & Per Wahlöö

Go to back for lists of
Pseudonyms • Authors by Genre • Characters and Series • Environments
Prize Winners • Classic Authors • Crossover Authors • Further Reading • Websites

Meg Rosoff 🌈 ☺ US

Debra Adelaide	Joan Lingard	Jeanette Winterson
Jennifer Donnelly	Mary Stanley	Markus Zusak
Anne Fine		

Ann B Ross US Humour

🏃 Miss Julia - Southern States

Janet Evanovich	Laurie Graham	Miss Read
Fannie Flagg	Mary A Larkin	Adriana Trigiani

Philip Roth 1933- US

🏆 Pulitzer 1998
  WHSmith 2001 & 2005
  Man Booker Int 2011

🏃 Nathan Zuckerman, US novelist

Saul Bellow	Dave Eggers	Rick Moody
T C Boyle	David Grossman	Elliot Perlman
Michael Chabon	Denis Johnson	Adam Thirlwell
Edward Docx	Chang-rae Lee	Colson Whitehead

Patrick Rothfuss 1973- US Fantasy: Epic

R Scott Bakker	Amanda Hemingway	J K Rowling
Chaz Brenchley	Greg Keyes	Brian Ruckley
Steven Erikson	Tim Lebbon	Adrian Tchaikovsky
Pamela Freeman	George R R Martin	

Victoria Routledge 1975- Mature Chick Lit

Trisha Ashley	Anita Notaro	Linda Taylor
Celia Brayfield	Karen Quinn	Lauren Weisberger
Belinda Jones	Robyn Sisman	Deborah Wright
Melissa Nathan		

Rosemary Rowe 🌈 1942- Crime: Historical - Ancient

is Rosemary Aitken

🏃 Libertus, Mosaicist - Roman Britain

Philip Boast	Colleen McCullough	Steven Saylor
Lindsey Davis	Allan Massie	Marilyn Todd
Margaret Doody	John Maddox Roberts	David Wishart

Michelle Rowen Can Paranormal

also writes as Michelle Maddox

Patricia Briggs	Lori Handeland	Jeanne Kalogridis
Laurell K Hamilton	Tanya Huff	Kim Newman

🌈 may be suitable for young adults

Betty Rowlands
1923-   Crime: Amateur sleuth

♰ Melissa Craig, Writer - Cotswolds • Sukey Reynolds, Scene of Crime Officer

Natasha Cooper	Veronica Heley	Fiona Mountain
Marjorie Eccles	Joyce Holms	Ann Purser
Ann Granger	Gwen Moffat	Catherine Sampson

J K Rowling   ☺   1965-   Fantasy: Epic

is Joanne Kathleen Rowling   ♰ Harry Potter
♈ WHSmith 2006

Jim Butcher	Lian Hearn	Garth Nix
Isobelle Carmody	Sergei Lukyanenko	Christopher Paolini
P C & Kristin Cast	Stephenie Meyer	Patrick Rothfuss
Eoin Colfer	William Nicholson	

Pauline Rowson
Crime: Police work - UK

♰ DI Andy Horton - Hayling Island

Robert Barnard	Patricia Hall	Iain McDowall
Pauline Bell	John Harvey	Peter Robinson
Ann Cleeves	Graham Hurley	Dorothy Simpson
Colin Dexter	Peter James	Neil White

Arundhati Roy   1961-   Ind

♈ Booker 1997

Aravind Adiga	Kiran Desai	Anita Nair
Monica Ali	Roopa Farooki	R K Narayan
Vikram Chandra	Amitav Ghosh	Vikram Seth
Amit Chaudhuri	Lee Langley	Thrity Umrigar

Jed Rubenfeld   US   Crime: Historical - C18th/19th

Carola Dunn	James McGee	Matthew Pearl
Maureen Jennings	Edward Marston	Andrew Pepper
Alannah Knight	Andrew Martin	Anne Perry

Bernice Rubens   1928-2004

♈ Booker 1970

Beryl Bainbridge	Pauline Melville	A N Wilson
Anita Brookner	Carolyn Slaughter	Jeanette Winterson
Margaret Drabble		

Brian Ruckley   Sco   Fantasy: Epic

R Scott Bakker	Greg Keyes	Patrick Rothfuss
Steven Erikson	Katherine Kurtz	Sean Russell
David Gemmell	Tom Lloyd	

James Runcie
Historical

Tracy Chevalier	Melanie Gifford	Salley Vickers
Barbara Ewing	Jason Goodwin	Susan Vreeland

R

Kristine Kathryn Rusch 1960- US Science Fiction: Space and time

also writes as Kristine Grayson, Kris Nelscott, Sandy Schofield
writes jointly with Dean Wesley Smith

Kevin J Anderson	Michael Moorcock	Robert Silverberg
Christie Golden	Philip Palmer	Robert Charles Wilson
Brian Herbert	R A Salvatore	David Zindell
J V Jones		

Salman Rushdie ⌂ ☺ 1947-

♈ Black 1981   Booker 1981   Whitbread 1988 & 1995   Best of the Booker 2008

Aravind Adiga	Richard Flanagan	Vikram Seth
Amit Chaudhuri	David Grossman	Kamila Shamsie
Michelle de Kretser	Shifra Horn	Vikas Swarup
Anita Desai	Siri Hustvedt	M G Vassanji

Craig Russell 1956- Sco Crime: Hardboiled

♈ CWA 2008   ☇ Det Jan Fabel - Hamburg • Lennox, PI - Glasgow

Tony Black	J A Kerley	John Rickards
Allan Guthrie	Richard Montanari	Boris Starling
Quintin Jardine	Chris Mooney	Jenny White

Norman Russell Crime: Historical - C19th

☇ DI Saul Jackson & Sgt Bottomley - Warwickshire, England

Arthur Conan Doyle	Joan Lock	Rosemary Stevens
Peter J Heck	Peter Lovesey	M J Trow
Alanna Knight	Caro Peacock	

Sean Thomas Russell 1952- Can Sea: Historical

also writes as T F Banks, S Thomas Russell   ☇ Lieut Charles Hayden - Napoleonic Wars
is Sean Russell

G S Beard	Richard Howard	Patrick O'Brian
David Donachie	Seth Hunter	Julian Stockwin

Richard Russo 1949- US

♈ Pulitzer 2002

Andrea Barrett	Garrison Keillor	Larry McMurtry
Ron Butlin	Kate Kerrigan	Stewart O'Nan
Richard Ford	Lorna Landvik	Anne Tyler
Ha Jin	Jim Lynch	Michael White

Alex Rutherford Historical: C16th

is Diana & Michael Preston   ☇ Empire of the Moghul Series - Central Asia

Sam Barone	Conn Iggulden	William Napier
David Gemmell	Ben Kane	Scott Oden

☺ also writes children's books

Edward Rutherfurd ⌒ 1948- Historical

is Francis E Wintle

Jean M Auel	Frank Delaney	Colleen McCullough
Stephen Baxter	Christie Dickason	James A Michener
Clare Clark	Ken Follett	Manda Scott
Bernard Cornwell	Kathleen O'Neal Gear	Leon Uris

Chris Ryan ⌒ ☺ 1961- Adventure/Thriller

Geoffrey Archer	Duncan Falconer	Graham Hurley
Michael Asher	Joseph Garber	Matt Lynn
Patrick Bishop	Stephen Hunter	Andy McNab
Murray Davies		

Denise Ryan Crime: Hardboiled

🏃 Shannon Flinder, Criminal lawyer - Liverpool

Megan Abbott	Martina Cole	Lynda La Plante
Helen Black	Jessie Keane	Adrian McKinty
Kimberley Chambers		

Liz Ryan Saga

Ireland

Maeve Binchy	Sheelagh Kelly	D M Purcell
Marita Conlon-McKenna	Geraldine O'Neill	Alexandra Raife
Frank Delaney	Joan O'Neill	Olivia Ryan

Robert Ryan Adventure/Thriller

also writes as Tom Neale

Barry Eisler	Joseph Kanon	Mike Lawson
Alan Furst	Michael Kimball	Guy Walters
Greg Iles		

Geoff Ryman 1951- Can

Paul Auster	Louise Erdrich	Christopher Koch
Jim Crace	Amitav Ghosh	Adam Thorpe

Science Fiction: Near future

🏆 Arthur C Clarke 1990 & 2006   BSFA 2005

Frank Herbert	Ursula K Le Guin	Gene Wolfe
Gwyneth Jones	Jeff Noon	John Wyndham

Lilith Saintcrow ⌒ 1976- US Paranormal

also writes as Lili St Crow

Rachel Caine	Kim Harrison	Richelle Mead
P C & Kristin Cast	Barb & J C Hendee	Susan Sizemore

⌒ may be suitable for young adults

R
S

Marcus Sakey   US   Adventure/Thriller

Lee Child	Simon Kernick	Sara Paretsky
Michael Harvey	Jo Nesbo	George P Pelecanos

James Sallis   1944-   US   Crime: Hardboiled

⚲ Lew Griffin, Academic - New Orleans • John Turner, ex-Policeman - Tennessee

James Lee Burke	Walter Mosley	Boston Teran
Raymond Chandler	Cath Staincliffe	John Williams
Ross Macdonald	Jason Starr	

Susan Sallis   1929-   Saga

also writes as Susan Meadmore   ⚲ Rising Family - West Country

Rosemary Aitken	Santa Montefiore	Sally Stewart
Gloria Cook	D M Purcell	Rowena Summers
Elizabeth Elgin	Elvi Rhodes	

R A Salvatore   1959-   US   Fantasy: Epic

Sara Douglass	Mercedes Lackey	Mickey Zucker Reichert
David A Drake	L E Modesitt Jr	Kristine Kathryn Rusch
Ian C Esslemont	Elizabeth Moon	Margaret Weis

Annie Sanders   Mature Chick Lit

is Annie Ashworth & Meg Sanders

Judy Astley	Gil McNeil	Lou Wakefield
Harriet Evans	Sharon Owens	Sue Welfare
Linda Kelsey	Sarah Tucker	Isabel Wolff
Sophie Kinsella		

Brandon Sanderson   1975-   US   Fantasy: Epic

also wrote with Robert Jordan

Joe Abercrombie	Jennifer Fallon	George R R Martin
Terry Brooks	Scott Lynch	Brent Weeks

John Sandford   1944-   US   Crime: Police work - US

is John Roswell Camp   ⚲ Lucas Davenport ⎫ Minneapolis
                                              Prey Series ⎭

Kidd & LuEllen, Con artist & computer hacker - Mississippi • Det Virgil Flowers - Minnesota

Ingrid Black	Scott Frost	Dennis Lehane
Alafair Burke	Colin Harrison	Phillip Margolin
Jodi Compton	Stephen Hunter	Ridley Pearson
Thomas H Cook	Michael Kimball	James Siegel

Go to back for lists of
Pseudonyms • Authors by Genre • Characters and Series • Environments
Prize Winners • Classic Authors • Crossover Authors • Further Reading • Websites

C J Sansom 1952-

Crime: Historical - C16th

also writes as The Medieval Murderers (with Philip Gooden, Susanna Gregory, Michael Jecks, Bernard Knight, Karen Maitland, Ian Morson)

♐ CWA 2005

☿ Dr Matthew Shardlake
Henrician London

Simon Acland	Ildefonso Falcones	James McGee
P F Chisholm	Patricia Finney	Shirley McKay
Cassandra Clark	C S Harris	S J Parris
Rory Clements	C C Humphreys	Peter Tonkin

Ian Sansom

Crime: Amateur sleuth

☿ Israel Armstrong, Mobile librarian

Colin Bateman	Peter Guttridge	Lily Prior
Carrie Bebris	Robert Lewis	Malcolm Pryce
Christopher Brookmyre	Alexander McCall Smith	Sue Townsend
Joanne Fluke		

José Saramago 1922-2010 Por

John Banville	William Golding	Javier Marias
Roberto Bolano	Cormac McCarthy	George Orwell

Kate Saunders

Aga Saga

Claire Calman	Charlotte Moore	Robyn Sisman
Lucy Clare	Nora Naish	Mary Wesley
Philippa Gregory	Elizabeth Noble	

Alan Savage 1930-

War: Modern

is Christopher Nicole

Frank Barnard	David Fiddimore	David Morrell
James Clavell	Amin Maalouf	Eric Van Lustbader
Elizabeth Darrell	Alistair MacLean	Guy Walters

Julian Jay Savarin

Adventure/Thriller

Geoffrey Archer	Nick Brownlee	Wilbur Smith
Campbell Armstrong	Stephen Coonts	Craig Thomas
Dale Brown	Clive Cussler	

Robert J Sawyer 1960- Can

Science Fiction: Near future

Joe Haldeman	Kim Stanley Robinson	Nick Sagan
Ken MacLeod	Justina Robson	Tad Williams

Judith Saxton 1936-

Saga

also writes as Katie Flynn, Judy Turner

☿ Neyler Family

Janet Dailey	Beryl Matthews	Janet Tanner
Sara Hylton	Margaret Pemberton	Nicola Thorne
Mary Mackie	Linda Sole	Jeanne Whitmee

S

Dorothy L Sayers 📞 1893-1957 Crime: Amateur sleuth

🚶 Lord Peter Wimsey

James Anderson	Dolores Gordon-Smith	Ngaio Marsh
Alan Bradley	Martha Grimes	L C Tyler
Kenneth Cameron	Hazel Holt	Jill Paton Walsh
Mark Gatiss	Michael Innes	Patricia Wentworth

Alexei Sayle 1952- Humour

Anna Blundy	Charles Higson	Will Self
Paul Burke	Marina Lewycka	Matt Thorne
Will Ferguson	Mil Millington	

Steven Saylor 1956- US Crime: Historical - Ancient

🚶 Gordianus the Finder - Ancient Rome • Pinarius family

Lindsey Davis	Robert Harris	Lynda S Robinson
Margaret Doody	Ben Kane	Rosemary Rowe
R S Downie	Sophia McDougall	Marilyn Todd
Lauren Haney	John Maddox Roberts	David Wishart

John Scalzi 1969- US Science Fiction: Space opera

Orson Scott Card	Joe Haldeman	Neal Stephenson
Cory Doctorow	Robert A Heinlein	Charles Stross
Gary Gibson	Dan Simmons	

Patricia Scanlan 1956- Ire Mature Chick Lit

Catherine Alliott	Prue Leith	Fiona O'Brien
Maria Beaumont	Debbie Macomber	D M Purcell
Claudia Carroll	Jane Moore	Robyn Sisman
Cathy Kelly	Anita Notaro	Jane Elizabeth Varley

Alex Scarrow 📞 ☺ Adventure/Thriller

John Case	Michael Kimball	Gareth O'Callaghan
Frederick Forsyth	John Lawton	Tim Sebastian
Robert Harris	David Moody	Robin White
Joseph Kanon		

Simon Scarrow 📞 ☺ 1962- Historical

🚶 Lucius Cornelius Macro & Quintus Licinus Cato, Centurians - C1st AD, Roman Europe
Duke of Wellington & Napoleon Bonaparte - C18th & C19th Europe

Sam Barone	Iain Gale	Garry Kilworth
Richard Blake	Glyn Iliffe	Jack Ludlow
Roger Carpenter	Douglas Jackson	Sophia McDougall
R S Downie	Ben Kane	Patrick Rambaud

📞 may be suitable for young adults

Bernhard Schlink 1944- Ger

Pat Barker	James Fleming	Irene Nemirovsky
Louis Begley	Ismail Kadare	Rachel Seiffert
John Boyne	Anne Michaels	William Styron
Hans Fallada		

Crime: PI

ᛘ Gerhard Self - Germany

Kate Atkinson	P D James	Craig Russell
Michael Chabon	Henning Mankell	

Katherine Scholes 1959- Aus

Joseph Finder	Tamara McKinley	Gareth O'Callaghan
Beverley Harper	Di Morrissey	Peter Watt

Lynne Sharon Schwartz 1939- US

Jonathan Safran Foer	Sue Miller	Anita Shreve
Nicole Krauss	Alice Munro	Amy Tan

Christina Schwarz US Adventure/Thriller: Psychological

Mary Higgins Clark	Janet Fitch	Sue Miller
Joy Fielding	Clare Francis	Susan R Sloan

Theresa Schwegel US Crime: Police work - US

Chicago

Alex Berenson	Greg Iles	Jess Walter
Robert Crais	John Katzenbach	Joseph Wambaugh
Sue Grafton	Karin Slaughter	

Justin Scott 1944- US Adventure/Thriller

also writes as Paul Garrison

ᛘ Ben Abbott, Real Estate Agent - Connecticut

Brian Callison	Duncan Harding	Matt Lynn
James H Cobb	Richard Herman	Nicholas Monsarrat
Clive Cussler	Sam Llewellyn	Eric Van Lustbader
James Follett		

Kirsty Scott Sco Mature Chick Lit

Alison Penton Harper	Milly Johnson	India Knight
Kate Harrison	Cathy Kelly	Gil McNeil

S

Go to back for lists of
Pseudonyms • Authors by Genre • Characters and Series • Environments
Prize Winners • Classic Authors • Crossover Authors • Further Reading • Websites

Manda Scott Sco — Crime: Psychological

also writes as M C Scott

⃛ Kellen Stewart - Glasgow

Lin Anderson	Val McDermid	Sally Spedding
Alex Gray	J Wallis Martin	Barbara Vine
John Harwood	Denise Mina	Louise Welsh

Historical

⃛ Boudica - Roman Britain

Jean M Auel	Valerio Massimo Manfredi	Harry Sidebottom
Christian Cameron	Kate Mosse	Leon Uris
Christian Jacq	Mary Renault	Paul Waters
Giles Kristian	Edward Rutherfurd	

Lisa Scottoline 1955- US — Crime: Legal/financial

⃛ Rosato & Associates - Philadelphia

William Bernhardt	John T Lescroart	Perri O'Shaughnessy
Linda Fairstein	John McLaren	Susan R Sloan
Craig Holden	Phillip Margolin	Erica Spindler

Alice Sebold 1963- US

Kate Atkinson	Victoria Hislop	Hilary Mantel
Anita Diamant	M J Hyland	Clare Morrall
Mark Haddon	Marti Leimbach	Ann Packer
Zoë Heller	Margaret Leroy	Lionel Shriver

Andy Secombe — Fantasy: Humour

Douglas Adams	Christopher Moore	Robert Rankin
Jasper Fforde	Terry Pratchett	Martin Scott
Tom Holt		

Kate Sedley 1926- — Crime: Historical - Medieval

is Brenda Clarke

⃛ Roger the Chapman - C15th England

Simon Acland	Susanna Gregory	Pat McIntosh
P F Chisholm	Michael Jecks	Ian Morson
Alys Clare	Bernard Knight	Candace Robb
Ariana Franklin		

Kathleen Gilles Seidel US — Mature Chick Lit

Mary Balogh	Alison Penton Harper	Debbie Macomber
Jane Green	Milly Johnson	Imogen Parker
Maeve Haran		

Rachel Seiffert 1971-

Margaret Atwood	Maggie Gee	Anne Michaels
Trezza Azzopardi	Tessa Hadley	Irene Nemirovsky
Julian Barnes	Ismail Kadare	Bernhard Schlink
Louis Begley		

Will Self 1961-

🏆 Bollinger 2008   Faber 1993

J G Ballard	Bret Easton Ellis	Tobias Hill
Iain Banks	Niall Griffiths	Ben Richards
Glen Duncan	Matt Haig	Alexei Sayle

Vikram Seth 1952- Ind

🏆 Commonwealth 1994   WHSmith 1994

Aravind Adiga	Amitav Ghosh	Salman Rushdie
Amit Chaudhuri	R K Narayan	Paul Scott
Kiran Desai	Orhan Pamuk	Vikas Swarup
John Galsworthy	Arundhati Roy	

Tim Severin 1940- Historical

🚶 Thorgils Leiffson, Viking - C11th • Hector Lynch, Seafarer - C17th

Stephen Baxter	Douglas Jackson	Jack Ludlow
Bernard Cornwell	James H Jackson	Steven Pressfield
Tom Harper	Giles Kristian	Wilbur Smith
Conn Iggulden	Robert Low	Robyn Young

E V Seymour Adventure/Thriller

🚶 Paul Tallis, Unofficial MI5 officer

Alex Berenson	Henry Porter	Jon Stock
Charles Cumming	Christopher Reich	James Twining
Scott Mariani		

Gerald Seymour 1941- Adventure/Thriller

Campbell Armstrong	Simon Conway	Stephen Leather
James Barrington	Clive Egleton	Charles McCarry
Tom Bradby	Gavin Esler	James Siegel
John Burdett	Frederick Forsyth	Nigel West

Elif Shafak 1971- Tur

Isabel Allende	Khaled Hosseini	Rose Tremain
Paulo Coelho	Barbara Nadel	Jenny White
Jason Goodwin	Orhan Pamuk	

Nicholas Shakespeare 1957-

🏆 S Maugham 1990

Malcolm Bradbury	Graham Greene	Piers Paul Read
Louis de Bernières	James Hamilton-Paterson	Rose Tremain
Louise Dean	Ann Patchett	Mario Vargas Llosa

Kamila Shamsie 1973- Pak

Nadeem Aslam	Romesh Gunesekera	Jhumpa Lahiri
Kiran Desai	Siri Hustvedt	Salman Rushdie

S

Darren Shan ☎ ☺ 1972-   Paranormal

also writes as D B Shan; is Darren O'Shaughnessy

Kelley Armstrong	Justin Cronin	Tanya Huff
Cassandra Clare	Charlaine Harris	Stephenie Meyer

John Shannon   1943-   US   Crime: PI

🯅 Jack Liffey - Los Angeles

Raymond Chandler	Dennis Lehane	Jefferson Parker
Michael Connelly	Marcia Muller	Robert B Parker
Robert Crais	Sara Paretsky	Rick Riordan

Zoë Sharp   Crime: Amateur sleuth

🯅 Charlie Fox, Self-defence expert

Cara Black	Sue Grafton	Sara Paretsky
Janet Evanovich	Lauren Henderson	Cath Staincliffe
Liz Evans	Val McDermid	

Tom Sharpe ☎ 1928-   Humour

🯅 Henry Wilt

Anna Blundy	George Macdonald Fraser	Tom Holt
Jonathan Coe	James Hawes	Howard Jacobson
Joseph Connolly	Philip Hensher	Geoff Nicholson
Lissa Evans		

Catherine Shaw   Crime: Amateur sleuth

is Leila Schneps

🯅 Vanessa Duncan - C19th Cambridge

Alanna Knight	Mark Mills	Jill Paton Walsh
Deryn Lake	Amy Myers	Patricia Wentworth
Peter Lovesey	Rebecca Tope	

S

Fiona Shaw

Beryl Bainbridge	Penelope Fitzgerald	Sadie Jones
Pat Barker	Jane Gardam	Joan Lingard

Patricia Shaw   1928-   Aus   Historical

Sheelagh Kelly	Katharine McMahon	Amanda Quick
Colleen McCullough	Margaret Pemberton	E V Thompson
Tamara McKinley		

Rebecca Shaw   Saga

🯅 Barleybridge Series • Turnham Malpas Series

Patricia Fawcett	Joan Medlicott	Célestine Hitiura Vaite
Eve Houston	Ann Purser	Ann Widdecombe
Erica James	Miss Read	Annie Wilkinson
Jan Karon	Jack Sheffield	

Owen Sheers   1974-   Wales

Melvyn Bragg	Nicholas Drayson	Sarah Hall
Peter Ho Davies	Andrew Greig	Andrew O'Hagan

Jack Sheffield   1945-   Saga

⋔ Jack Sheffield, Head teacher - Yorkshire

Iris Gower	Joan Medlicott	Nicholas Rhea
Eve Houston	Ann Purser	Rebecca Shaw
Jan Karon	Miss Read	

Sidney Sheldon   1917-2007   US   Adventure/Thriller

Jeffrey Archer	Lorenzo Carcaterra	Wilbur Smith
Millenia Black	Nicholas Coleridge	Danielle Steel
Barbara Taylor Bradford	Harold Robbins	

Sara Sheridan   1968-   Sco   Historical

⋔ Mirabelle Bevan

Margaret Cezair-Thompson	Julia Gregson	Anchee Min
Kate Furnivall	Victoria Hislop	Kate Morton
Robert Goddard	Katharine McMahon	Nicola Upson

Carol Shields   1935-2003   Can

🏆 Pulitzer 1995   Orange 1998

Trezza Azzopardi	Kent Haruf	Alice McDermott
Joan Barfoot	Kate Kerrigan	Lionel Shriver
Sylvia Brownrigg	Mary Lawson	Nicholas Sparks
Patrick Gale	Elinor Lipman	Miriam Toews

Anita Shreve   1946-   US

Elizabeth Berg	Jennifer Haigh	Maile Meloy
Louise Candlish	Shirley Hazzard	Ann Packer
Diane Chamberlain	Siri Hustvedt	Lynne Sharon Schwartz
Helen Garner	Catherine Ryan Hyde	Curtis Sittenfeld

Lionel Shriver   ⌒   1957-   US

🏆 Orange 2005

Neil Cross	Marti Leimbach	D B C Pierre
Susan Fletcher	Daniel Mason	Alice Sebold
Allegra Goodman	Joe Meno	Carol Shields
Douglas Kennedy	Ann Packer	Talitha Stevenson

Nevil Shute   ⌒   1899-1960   Adventure/Thriller

was Nevil Shute Norway

Jon Cleary	Hammond Innes	Nicholas Monsarrat
Ernest Hemingway	Alistair MacLean	Morris West

S

Anne Rivers Siddons   1936-   US   Saga

Manette Ansay   Eloisa James   Rosie Thomas
Pat Conroy   Carson McCullers   Adriana Trigiani
Janet Dailey   Mary Alice Monroe   Joanna Trollope
Karen Joy Fowler   Belva Plain   Rebecca Wells

Harry Sidebottom   Historical: Ancient
                                           Ancient Rome

Christian Cameron   Glyn Iliffe   Manda Scott
Lindsey Davis   Ben Kane   John Stack
Michael Curtis Ford Allan Massie

Jeffrey Siger   US   Crime: Police work - Greece
                                     ⃛ Det Andreas Kaldis

Andrea Camilleri   Paul Johnston   Louise Penny
Michael Dibdin   Donna Leon   Anne Zouroudi

Scott Sigler   US   Horror

Robin Cook   Chuck Hogan   Chuck Palahniuk
Michael Crichton   Stephen King   Dan Simmons
Thomas Harris   David Moody

Yrsa Sigurdardottir   1963-   Ice   Crime: Amateur sleuth
                                 ⃛ Thora Gudmundsdottir, Lawyer

Ake Edwardson   Matti Joensuu   Henning Mankell
Karin Fossum   Mari Jungstedt   Jo Nesbo
Arnaldur Indridason Camilla Läckberg   Jan Costin Wagner

Alan Sillitoe   1928-2010

Kingsley Amis   D H Lawrence   Stanley Middleton
Melvyn Bragg   David Lodge   Graham Swift

Daniel Silva   1960-   US   Adventure/Thriller
      ⃛ Michael Osbourne - CIA • Gabriel Allon - Israeli Secret Service

Brett Battles   Juan Gómez-Jurado   Boris Starling
Ted Bell   David Hewson   Jon Stock
Charles Cumming   Alan Judd   Nick Stone
Richard Flanagan   Mike Lawson   Brad Thor

Amy Silver   Chick Lit

Trisha Ashley   Lindsey Kelk   Carmen Reid
Miranda Dickinson   Carole Matthews   Julia Williams
Lucy Dillon

Robert Silverberg   1935-   US   Science Fiction: Space and time

also writes as Calvin M Knox, David Osborne, Robert Randall

Arthur C Clarke	Sophia McDougall	Kristine Kathryn Rusch
David Eddings	Julian May	Freda Warrington
Joe Haldeman	Christopher Priest	

Roger Silverwood   Crime: Police work - UK

🕴 DI Michael Angel - Bromersley, South Yorkshire

Caroline Graham	Sally Spencer	Camilla Way
Dorothy Simpson	June Thomson	Neil White

Georges Simenon   ⌒   1903-89   Belg   Crime: Police work - France

🕴 Commissaire Jules Maigret - Paris

A C Baantjer	Magdalen Nabb	Janwillem van de Wetering
Andrea Camilleri	Martin O'Brien	Fred Vargas
K O Dahl	Jean François Parot	Anne Zouroudi
H R F Keating		

Dan Simmons   1948-   US   Horror

Richard Bachman	John Ajvide Lindqvist	Scott Smith
Clive Barker	Bentley Little	Whitley Strieber
Jeanne Kalogridis	Adam Nevill	T M Wright
Stephen King		

Science Fiction: Space opera

🏆 British Fantasy 1990   BSFA 1991

Kevin J Anderson	Orson Scott Card	John Scalzi
Poul Anderson	Arthur C Clarke	Lucius Shepard
Neal Asher	Joe Haldeman	Scott Sigler
David Brin	C S Lewis	

Chris Simms   Crime: Psychological

🕴 DI Jon Spicer - Manchester

Mark Billingham	Margaret Murphy	Carol Smith
Jim Kelly	Ed O'Connor	Barbara Vine
Denise Mina	Andrew Pyper	Laura Wilson

Paullina Simons   1963-   US   Adventure/Thriller

is Paullina Handler

Victoria Blake	Jeffery Deaver	Stephen Hunter
Alice Blanchard	Nicholas Evans	Grace Monroe
Pat Conroy	John Gilstrap	Claire Seeber
Elizabeth Corley	Gwen Hunter	Scott Smith

Go to back for lists of
Pseudonyms • Authors by Genre • Characters and Series • Environments
Prize Winners • Classic Authors • Crossover Authors • Further Reading • Websites

S

Helen Simpson 1959-

♟ S Maugham 1991   Sunday Times 1991   Hawthornden 2001

Kate Atkinson	Helen Dunmore	Jon McGregor
Richard Bausch	Doris Lessing	Maggie O'Farrell

Iain Sinclair 1943-

♟ Black 1991   Encore 1992

Peter Ackroyd	Alasdair Gray	Chris Petit
Charles Dickens	Geoff Nicholson	Nicholas Royle
Christopher Fowler	Robert Nye	

Robyn Sisman   US   Mature Chick Lit

Louise Bagshawe	Debby Holt	Kate Saunders
Helen Fielding	Clare Naylor	Patricia Scanlan
Olivia Goldsmith	Victoria Routledge	Sarah Tucker
Julia Holden		

Curtis Sittenfeld 1976- US

Sarah Addison Allen	Carson McCullers	J D Salinger
Melissa Bank	Jed Mercurio	Anita Shreve
Diane Chamberlain	Alice Munro	Betsy Tobin
Elinor Lipman	Jodi Picoult	Tom Wolfe

Susan Sizemore 1951- US   Paranormal

Lara Adrian	Sherrilyn Kenyon	Lilith Saintcrow
Christine Feehan	Sara Reinke	J R Ward

S

Maj Sjöwall & Per Wahlöö   Swe   Crime: Police work - Sweden

🏃 Martin Beck - Stockholm

Karin Alvtegen	Arnaldur Indridason	Stieg Larsson
K O Dahl	Mari Jungstedt	Liza Marklund
Karin Fossum	Åsa Larsson	Roslund and Hellström
Anne Holt		

Carolyn Slaughter

♟ Faber 1977

Thalassa Ali	Ruth Prawer Jhabvala	Sharon Maas
E M Forster	Manju Kapur	Bernice Rubens

Karin Slaughter 1971- US   Crime: Forensic

🏃 Sara Linton, Medical examiner, & Jeffrey Tolliver, Police chief - 'Heartsdale', Georgia
Will Trent, Special agent, Criminal Apprehension Team - Atlanta

Beverly Barton	Joolz Denby	Lisa Jackson
Alafair Burke	Kathryn Fox	Keith McCarthy
Chelsea Cain	Lisa Gardner	Nigel McCrery
Stella Cameron	Andrew Gross	Erica Spindler

Mark Slouka   US

Peter Ho Davies	Lorrie Moore	Per Petterson
Patrick Gale	Michael Ondaatje	Markus Zusak
Daniel Mason		

Gillian Slovo   1952-   SA

J M Coetzee	Lauren Henderson	Sara Paretsky
Martin Edwards	Doris Lessing	Michelle Spring

Peter Smalley   Aus   Sea: Historical - C18th

🏆 JLR 1973   🚶 Capt William Rennie & Lieut James Hayter - C18th/19th

G S Beard	C S Forester	Jonathan Lunn
David Donachie	Seth Hunter	Patrick O'Brian
John Drake	Alexander Kent	Julian Stockwin

Jane Smiley   1949-   US

🏆 Pulitzer 1992

Gil Adamson	Jane Hamilton	Betsy Tobin
Thomas Eidson	Marge Piercy	Robert James Waller
Molly Gloss	Francine Prose	Meg Wolitzer
Kate Grenville	Anna Quindlen	Banana Yoshimoto

Ali Smith   🌈   1962-   Sco

🏆 Encore 2002   Whitbread 2005

John Burnside	Alasdair Gray	Gwendoline Riley
Ron Butlin	Jackie Kay	Zoë Strachan
Janice Galloway	Helen Oyeyemi	Alice Thompson

Anna Smith   Sco   Crime: Amateur sleuth

🚶 Rosie Gilmour, Journalist - Glasgow

Mark Billingham	Nicci French	Matthew Klein
Christopher Brookmyre	Mo Hayder	Lynda La Plante
Martina Cole	Mandasue Heller	Denise Mina

Carol Smith   Crime: Psychological

Anna Blundy	Gabrielle Lord	Tony Strong
Sarah Diamond	Elizabeth McGregor	Laura Wilson
Babs Horton	Chris Simms	

Martin Cruz Smith   🌈   1942-   US   Crime: Police work - Russia

also writes as Martin Quinn, Simon Quinn   🚶 Insp Arkady Renko - USSR
🏆 CWA 1981

Ronan Bennett	Charles Cumming	Jed Mercurio
John Burdett	Garry Disher	Tom Rob Smith
Stephen J Cannell	José Latour	Peter Spiegelman
Thomas H Cook	Charles McCarry	Michael White

S

233

Michael Marshall Smith 1965- Science Fiction: Near future

also writes as Michael Marshall, M M Smith ♛ British Fantasy 1995

Christopher Fowler China Miéville Tad Williams
William Gibson Jeff Noon John Wyndham
James Lovegrove Neal Stephenson

Tom Rob Smith 1979- US Adventure/Thriller

♛ CWA 2008 ⚐ Leo Demidov, KGB officer - 1950s Russia

Ted Allbeury Colin Forbes Martin Cruz Smith
Nelson DeMille Alan Furst David Szalay
Sam Eastland Philip Kerr

Wilbur Smith 1933- Zam Adventure/Thriller

Michael Asher Nelson DeMille Judy Nunn
Nick Brownlee Jean-Christophe Grangé Julian Jay Savarin
Frank Coates Beverley Harper Sidney Sheldon
Bryce Courtenay Paul Henke

Historical: Ancient Egypt

Joy Chambers Valerio Massimo Manfredi Mary Renault
Margaret George Michelle Moran Tim Severin
Christian Jacq Scott Oden Paul Sussman
Colleen McCullough

Zadie Smith ⌒ 1975-

♛ Black 2000 Guardian 2000 Whitbread 2000 Betty Trask 2001
Sunday Times 2001 Wingate 2003 Orange 2006 S Maugham 2006

Leila Aboulela Linda Grant Nick Laird
Monica Ali Siri Hustvedt Andrea Levy
Trezza Azzopardi Hari Kunzru Alex Wheatle
Amit Chaudhuri Hanif Kureishi Louisa Young

Linda Sole Saga

also writes as Lynn Granville, Anne Herries, Emma Quincey ⚐ Rose Saga

Margaret Dickinson Elvi Rhodes Grace Thompson
Evelyn Hood Judith Saxton Kate Tremayne
Alexandra Raife E V Thompson Jeanne Whitmee

Muriel Spark ⌒ 1918-2006 Sco

Paul Bailey Shena Mackay Anne Tyler
Anita Brookner Candida McWilliam Evelyn Waugh
Ronald Firbank Alice Munro

⌒ may be suitable for young adults

Nicholas Sparks   1965-   US

Mitch Albom	Janet Fitch	Jane Urquhart
Ann Brashares	Sue Monk Kidd	Robert James Waller
Holly Chamberlin	Carol Shields	Sarah Willis
Nicholas Evans	Rosie Thomas	

Sally Spedding   Crime: Psychological

Nicci French	Danuta Reah	Manda Scott
Frances Hegarty	Phil Rickman	Barbara Vine
Sarah Rayne	Louis Sanders	Sue Walker

Sally Spencer   Crime: Police work - UK

also writes as James Garcia Woods;
is Alan Rustage

⚉ DCI Charlie Woodend ⎱ Lancashire
DCI Monika Panatowski ⎰
Insp Sam Blackstone - C19th London

David Armstrong	J M Gregson	Roger Silverwood
Caroline Graham	John Harvey	Aline Templeton
Ann Granger	Nick Oldham	June Thomson

Erica Spindler   1957-   US   Crime: Psychological

Ingrid Black	Christiane Heggan	Andrew Pyper
Linda Castillo	Iris Johansen	Lisa Scottoline
Lisa Gardner	Alex Kava	Karin Slaughter
Daniel Hecht	Jonathan Kellerman	Stephen White

Edward St Aubyn   1960-

⚉ Patrick Melrose

S

J G Ballard	James Meek	Evelyn Waugh
Jennifer Egan	Andrew O'Hagan	Edmund White
Patrick Gale	Frederic Raphael	Gerard Woodward
Alan Hollinghurst	John Updike	

Dana Stabenow   1952-   US   Crime: PI

⚉ Kate Shugak • Sgt Liam Campbell
Alaska

Linda Barnes	Meg Gardiner	Theresa Monsour
Giles Blunt	Elly Griffiths	Sara Paretsky
C J Box	Steve Hamilton	S J Rozan
Eric Jerome Dickey	J A Jance	Stephen White

Lyndon Stacey   Crime: Amateur sleuth

Horse racing

Simon Brett	Catriona McPherson	Graeme Roe
Dick Francis	Iain Pears	Don Winslow
John Francome		

John Stack

Sea: Historical

Ancient Roman navy

Sam Barone	Douglas Jackson	Robert Low
Michael Curtis Ford	Ben Kane	Harry Sidebottom

Cath Staincliffe   1956-

Crime: PI

⚕ Sal Kilkenny - Manchester

Cara Black	Ken McCoy	Zoë Sharp
John Connor	Walter Mosley	Valerie Wilson Wesley
Judith Cutler	James Sallis	Stella Whitelaw

Veronica Stallwood

Crime: Amateur sleuth

⚕ Kate Ivory, Writer - Oxford

Natasha Cooper	Hope McIntyre	M J Trow
Susan B Kelly	R T Raichev	Jill Paton Walsh
Marianne Macdonald	Michelle Spring	

Michael Stanley   SA

Crime: Police work - South Africa

is Michael Sears & Stanley Trollip   ⚕ Det David 'Kubu' Bengu - Botswana

Donald Harstad	Richard Kunzmann	Deon Meyer
Tony Hillerman	Alexander McCall Smith	Malla Nunn

Mary Jane Staples   1911-2007

Saga

also wrote as James Sinclair, Reginald Staples   ⚕ Staples Family - London • Adams Family

Benita Brown	Jeannie Johnson	Kitty Neale
Pip Granger	Elizabeth Lord	Victor Pemberton
Lilian Harry	Gwen Madoc	Carol Rivers
Sara Hylton	Beryl Matthews	Audrey Willsher

S

Richard Stark   1933-2008   US

Crime: Hardboiled

was Donald Westlake   ⚕ Parker, Master criminal

Lawrence Block	G M Ford	Robert B Parker
James Lee Burke	Kevin Lewis	Donald Westlake
Robert Crais		

Boris Starling   1969-

Crime: Psychological

🏆 TGR 2000

John Connolly	Gareth O'Callaghan	Daniel Silva
Natsuo Kirino	Patrick Redmond	Tony Strong
Cody McFadyen	Craig Russell	P J Tracy

Danielle Steel   1947-   US

Saga

Barbara Taylor Bradford	Sara Hylton	Luanne Rice
Olivia Darling	Susan Lewis	Sidney Sheldon
Jude Deveraux	Judith McNaught	LaVyrle Spencer
Eileen Goudge	Una-Mary Parker	

John Steinbeck ☎ 1902-68 US

Gail Anderson-Dargatz	Jack Kerouac	Paul Theroux
Will Ferguson	Lori Lansens	Leon Uris
F Scott Fitzgerald	Norman Mailer	Willy Vlautin
Ernest Hemingway	William Styron	

Olen Steinhauer 1970- US Adventure/Thriller

🏃 Milo Weaver, Spy

Ken Bruen	Alex Dryden	Nick McDonell
John Burdett	Barry Eisler	Peter Temple
Andrea Camilleri	Alan Furst	Robert Wilson
Michael Dibdin		

Kay Stephens Saga

🏃 Stonemoor Series - Yorkshire

Aileen Armitage	Alexandra Connor	Kate Tremayne
Anne Bennett	Elizabeth Elgin	Valerie Wood
Helen Cannam		

Neal Stephenson 1959- US Science Fiction: Near future

also writes as Stephen Bury 🏆 Arthur C Clarke 2004

Tony Ballantyne	Jon Courtenay Grimwood	John Scalzi
John Birmingham	James Lovegrove	Michael Marshall Smith
Cory Doctorow	Richard Powers	Jeff Vandermeer
Greg Egan	Nick Sagan	John Wyndham

Talitha Stevenson 1977-

Jonathan Coe	John Lanchester	Lionel Shriver
Philip Hensher	Kate Morton	Evelyn Waugh

Mary Stewart ☎ 1916- Sco

Helen Hollick	Sharon Penman	Sue Sully
Susanna Kearsley	Alexandra Raife	Janet Tanner
Judith Lennox	Sally Stewart	Mary Withall

Sally Stewart Saga

Elizabeth Daish	Rosamunde Pilcher	Mary Stewart
Christine Marion Fraser	Susan Sallis	Mary Withall
Elisabeth McNeill		

Tess Stimson Chick Lit

Claudia Carroll	Linda Green	Morag Prunty
Lucy Dawson	Rachel Johnson	Isabel Wolff
Martina Devlin	Belinda Jones	Laura Zigman
Emily Giffin	Adele Parks	

S

Jessica Stirling 1935- Sco — Saga

also writes as Caroline Crosby; is Hugh C Rae (formerly with Margaret M Coghlan)

Clare Kelso • Nicholson Family • Patterson Family Holly Beckman - Glasgow • Conway Family

Scotland

Emma Blair
Maggie Craig
Doris Davidson
Margaret Thomson Davis
Christine Marion Fraser
Meg Hutchinson
Elisabeth McNeill
Frances Paige

Jon Stock 1966- — Adventure/Thriller

Daniel Marchant, ex MI6 officer

Paul Adam
Tom Cain
David Ignatius
John Le Carré
Robert Ludlum
E V Seymour
Daniel Silva

Julian Stockwin 1944- — Sea: Historical

Thomas Paine Kydd - C18th/19th England

G S Beard
David Donachie
John Drake
C S Forester
Seth Hunter
Alexander Kent
Jonathan Lunn
James L Nelson
Peter Smalley

Nick Stone 1961- — Adventure/Thriller

CWA 2006

PI Max Mingus - Miami

Simon Beckett
Mark Billingham
John Connolly
Robert Ellis
Michael Marshall
Gareth O'Callaghan
Tim Sebastian
Daniel Silva

S

Rebecca Stott 1964- — Historical

Margaret Elphinstone
Barbara Erskine
Susan Hill
Matthew Kneale
Kate Mosse
James Robertson

Bernadette Strachan 1962- — Chick Lit

Lynne Barrett-Lee
Harriet Evans
Julie Highmore
Jill Mansell
Elizabeth Noble
Alexandra Potter
Plum Sykes

Zoë Strachan 1975- Sco

Isla Dewar
Anne Donovan
Janice Galloway
Laura Marney
Kate Muir
Ali Smith

Peter Straub 1943- US — Horror

Richard Bachman
Jonathan Carroll
Bret Easton Ellis
John Farris
Michael Koryta
Stephen Laws
Robert McCammon
Richard Matheson
Christopher Pike
Andrew Pyper
T M Wright

Whitley Strieber 1945- US Horror

Ramsey Campbell	John Ajvide Lindqvist	David Martin
John Farris	Brian Lumley	Graham Masterton
Shaun Hutson	Robert McCammon	Dan Simmons

Sarah Strohmeyer US Crime: Humour

🏃 Bubbles Yablonsky, Journalist - Lehigh, Pennsylvania

Linda Barnes	Joanne Fluke	Rosemary Martin
Nancy Cohen	Sparkle Hayter	Ayelet Waldman
Janet Evanovich	Pauline McLynn	Donald Westlake
Liz Evans		

Terence Strong 1946- War: Modern

Brian Callison	W E B Griffin	Paul Henke
Duncan Falconer	Duncan Harding	Alistair MacLean
David Fiddimore	Jack Harvey	David L Robbins

Charles Stross 1964- Science Fiction: Space opera

Poul Anderson	Orson Scott Card	Brian Herbert
Iain M Banks	Cory Doctorow	Ian R MacLeod
Stephen Baxter	Jaine Fenn	John Scalzi
Lois McMaster Bujold	Peter F Hamilton	Sean Williams

William Styron 1925-2006 US

Pat Conroy	Norman Mailer	John Steinbeck
William Faulkner	Bernhard Schlink	Alice Walker
Ernest Hemingway		

S

Tricia Sullivan 1968- US Science Fiction: Space opera

also writes as Valery Leith 🏆 Arthur C Clarke 1999

Neal Asher	Richard Morgan	Adam Roberts
Iain M Banks	Alastair Reynolds	Justina Robson

Rowena Summers 1932- Saga

also writes as Rachel Moore; is Jean Saunders West Country

Lyn Andrews	Lilian Harry	Susan Sallis
Anne Baker	Meg Hutchinson	Sue Sully
Anita Burgh	Annie Murray	E V Thompson

Patrick Suskind 🕿 1949- Ger

Isabel Allende	Laura Esquivel	Daniel Kehlmann
Alessandro Baricco	Carlos Fuentes	Michelle Lovric
Paulo Coelho	Gabriel Garcia Márquez	

Paul Sussman   1968-2012   Adventure/Thriller

🏃 Insp Khalifa - Luxor, Egypt

Steve Berry	Tom Harper	James Rollins
Dan Brown	Raymond Khoury	Wilbur Smith
David Gibbins	Chris Kuzneski	

Grant Sutherland   Aus   War: Historical

🏃 Alistair Douglas, Spy - C18th • Decipherer's Chronicles

G S Beard	James McGee	Andrew Pepper
Garry Kilworth	Allan Mallinson	Julian Stockwin

Koji Suzuki   1957- Ja   Horror

Simon Clark	Richard Laymon	Richard Matheson
Shaun Hutson	David Martin	T M Wright
Dean R Koontz		

Karen Swan   Glitz & Glamour

Millenia Black	Lucy Dillon	Lulu Taylor
Jo Carnegie	Fiona O'Brien	Sasha Wagstaff
Rebecca Chance		

Vikas Swarup   Ind

Aravind Adiga	Kiran Desai	Vikram Seth
Vikram Chandra	Amitav Ghosh	M G Vassanji
Amit Chaudhuri	Salman Rushdie	

S Graham Swift   1949-

🏆 Faber 1983   Guardian 1983   Holtby 1983   Black 1996   Booker 1996

Julian Barnes	Maggie Gee	Alan Sillitoe
Margaret Drabble	Mick Jackson	Gillian White
Anne Enright	David Leavitt	T R Wilson
John Fowles	Patrick McGrath	Gerard Woodward

Madge Swindells   Crime: Romantic suspense

Jackie Collins	Heather Graham	Johanna Lindsey
Judith Gould	Jayne Ann Krentz	Jean Saunders

David Szalay   1974- Can

🏆 Betty Trask 2008   Faber 2009

Sam Eastland	Linda Grant	Nicole Krauss
Jennifer Egan	Mick Jackson	Tom Rob Smith

Go to back for lists of
Pseudonyms • Authors by Genre • Characters and Series • Environments
Prize Winners • Classic Authors • Crossover Authors • Further Reading • Websites

Frank Tallis
Crime: Historical - C20th

☛ Dr Max Liebermann, Psychoanalyst, & DI Oskar Rheinhardt - early 1900s, Vienna

Boris Akunin	Andrew Martin	Matthew Pearl
Clio Gray	R N Morris	Qiu Xiaolong
Michael Gregorio	Jo Nesbo	Michael Walters
Philip Kerr		

Amy Tan   1952-   US

Anita Desai	Barbara Kingsolver	Timothy Mo
Kate Furnivall	Chang-rae Lee	Toni Morrison
Kathryn Harrison	Catherine Lim	Alice Munro
Ha Jin	Anchee Min	Gail Tsukiyama

Robert K Tanenbaum   US
Crime: Legal/financial

☛ Roger 'Butch' Karp, Asst Chief DA - New York

Linda Fairstein	Steve Hamilton	Christopher Reich
Frances Fyfield	Steve Martini	Peter Spiegelman
James Grippando	Perri O'Shaughnessy	

Reay Tannahill   1929-2007   Sco
Historical

☙ Romantic 1990

Maggie Craig	Diana Gabaldon	Anne Herries
Dorothy Dunnett	Cynthia Harrod-Eagles	Maureen Peters
Barbara Erskine		

Janet Tanner
Saga

also writes as Amelia Carr   ☛ Hillsbridge Family - Somerset

Amelia Carr	Connie Monk	Judith Saxton
Dilly Court	Alexandra Raife	Mary Stewart
Sara Fraser	Denise Robertson	Grace Thompson
Gwen Madoc		

June Tate   1930s-
Saga

WW2

Julia Bryant	Lilian Harry	Annie Murray
Elizabeth Elgin	Beryl Kingston	Sheila Newberry
June Francis	Beryl Matthews	Gilda O'Neill

Andrew Taylor   1951-
Crime: Police work - UK

also writes as Andrew Saville, John Robert Taylor   ☛ Jill Francis & DI Richard Thornhill
☙ CWA 1982, 2001, 2003 & 2009   'Lydmouth', 1950s Welsh Borders
Roth Trilogy - North London

Benjamin Black	Gregory Hall	Sue Walker
William Brodrick	Cynthia Harrod-Eagles	Camilla Way
Ann Cleeves	Andrew Nugent	Laura Wilson
David Stuart Davies	L C Tyler	R D Wingfield

T

D J Taylor 1960-

is David J Taylor

Julian Barnes	Barbara Kingsolver	Blake Morrison
John Fowles	D H Lawrence	Salley Vickers

Lulu Taylor   Glitz & Glamour

Louise Bagshawe	Jackie Collins	Tasmina Perry
Tilly Bagshawe	Olivia Darling	Penny Vincenzi

Michael Taylor   Saga

R F Delderfield	Lesley Pearse	Kate Tremayne
Douglas Kennedy	Sue Sully	Dee Williams
Ken McCoy	E V Thompson	

Adrian Tchaikovsky   Fantasy: Epic

Joe Abercrombie	Pamela Freeman	Patrick Rothfuss
Steven Erikson	Tom Lloyd	Brent Weeks

Roma Tearne   Sri Lan

Chimamanda Ngozi Adichie	Candida Clark	Maggie O'Farrell
Kate Atkinson	Romesh Gunesekera	Rose Tremain

Peter Temple   1946-   Aus   Crime: PI

♛ CWA 2007   Miles Franklin 2010   ⚐ Jack Irish - Melbourne

Benjamin Black	Garry Disher	Gabrielle Lord
Giles Blunt	Susan Hill	Barry Maitland
Caroline Carver	Graham Hurley	Elliot Perlman
Peter Corris	Matthew Klein	Olen Steinhauer

Aline Templeton   Sco   Crime: Police work - UK

⚐ DI Marjory Fleming - Scotland

Hilary Bonner	Alex Gray	Denise Mina
Natasha Cooper	Nigel McCrery	Peter Robinson
Lesley Glaister	Iain McDowall	Sally Spencer

Emma Tennant   1937-   Sco

also writes as Catherine Aydy

Elizabeth Aston	Nicole Krauss	Eva Rice
Penelope Fitzgerald	Iris Murdoch	Gwendoline Riley
Esther Freud	Wendy Perriam	Fay Weldon
Elizabeth Gaskell		

Boston Teran   US   Crime: Hardboiled

🏆 CWA 2000   🧍 Sheriff John Victor Sully - California

Alice Blanchard	James Crumley	Dennis Lehane
Lorenzo Carcaterra	Robert Ferrigno	James Sallis
Massimo Carlotto	Thomas Harris	Jason Starr

Kathleen Tessaro   US   Chick Lit

Susannah Bates	Emily Giffin	Sara Shepard
Anna Davis	Louise Kean	Rosy Thornton
Anne Dunlop	Sophie Kinsella	Lauren Weisberger
Sabine Durrant	Andrea Semple	

Johan Theorin   1963-   Swe   Crime: Psychological

🏆 CWA 2009   Öland, Sweden

Karin Alvtegen	Mari Jungstedt	Dominique Manotti
Karin Fossum	Stieg Larsson	Jo Nesbo
Arnaldur Indridason	Henning Mankell	

Marcel Theroux   1968-   Adventure/Thriller

🏆 S Maugham 2002

Lesley Glaister	Cormac McCarthy	Jayne Anne Phillips
Sophie Hannah	Per Petterson	Barbara Vine

Paul Theroux   ☎   1941-   US

🏆 Whitbread 1978   Black 1981

Candida Clark	Romesh Gunesekera	John Steinbeck
Pat Conroy	Abdulrazak Gurnah	Adam Thorpe
Giles Foden	Gunnar Kopperud	Colin Thubron
Maureen Freely	Yann Martel	

Adam Thirlwell   1978-

Martin Amis	Edward Docx	Philip Roth
Julian Barnes	Howard Jacobson	Graham Swift

T

Craig Thomas   1942-2011   Adventure/Thriller

also wrote as David Grant

Geoffrey Archer	Tom Gabbay	Julian Rathbone
Harold Coyle	Jack Higgins	Julian Jay Savarin
James Follett	John J Nance	

Go to back for lists of
Pseudonyms • Authors by Genre • Characters and Series • Environments
Prize Winners • Classic Authors • Crossover Authors • Further Reading • Websites

Leslie Thomas   1931-   Wales

		Wales
George Macdonald Fraser	Geoff Nicholson	Alan Titchmarsh
Joseph Heller	David Nobbs	Keith Waterhouse
David Lodge		

Crime: Police work - UK

🕴 'Dangerous' Davies

Natasha Cooper	Nicholas Rhea	June Thomson
Katherine John	Mike Ripley	Neil White
Nick Oldham		

Rosie Thomas   1947-   Wales   Saga

also writes as Jancy King   🏆 Romantic 1985 & 2007

Barbara Taylor Bradford	Rowan Coleman	Anne Rivers Siddons
Liz Byrski	Sarah Harrison	Nicholas Sparks
Candida Clark	Belva Plain	Jane Elizabeth Varley

Scarlett Thomas   1972-   Fantasy

Susanna Clarke	G W Dahlquist	Neil Gaiman
Douglas Coupland	Barbara Ewing	Stephen Hunt

Alice Thompson   Sco

🏆 Black 1996

Ron Butlin	Kazuo Ishiguro	Ali Smith
Janice Galloway	Jackie Kay	Louise Welsh

Brian Thompson   1935-   Crime: Historical - C19th

🕴 Bella Wallis, Crime novelist - London

John Maclachlan Gray	Lee Jackson	James McGee
Peter J Heck	Joan Lock	Barrie Roberts

T E V Thompson   1931-2012   Historical

also wrote as James Munro   🕴 Retallick Family

Gloria Cook	Anne Herries	Rowena Summers
R F Delderfield	Elizabeth Ann Hill	Michael Taylor
Winston Graham	Patricia Shaw	Kate Tremayne
Cynthia Harrod-Eagles	Linda Sole	Barbara Wood

Grace Thompson   Wales   Saga

also writes as Kay Christopher   🕴 Valley Series - Wales • Pendragon Island Series

Catrin Collier	Linda Sole	Elizabeth Waite
Catherine Cookson	Janet Tanner	Annie Wilkinson
Iris Gower	Margaret Thornton	Dee Williams

☺ also writes children's books

Jim Thompson 1906-1977   US   Crime: Hardboiled

Megan Abbott   Jack Higgins   Jason Starr
Edward Bunker   Adrian McKinty   John Williams
James Crumley   George P Pelecanos   Don Winslow
James Ellroy

Kate Thompson   ☏ ☺ 1956-   Mature Chick Lit
Ireland

Colette Caddle   Cathy Kelly   Sharon Owens
Martina Devlin   Dorothy Koomson   D M Purcell
Louise Kean   Chris Manby

June Thomson   1930-   Crime: Police work - UK

🏃 DCI Jack Finch - Essex

W J Burley   Anthea Fraser   Sally Spencer
Arthur Conan Doyle   Ruth Rendell   Leslie Thomas
Elizabeth Ferrars   Roger Silverwood

Rupert Thomson   1955-

Douglas Clegg   Jim Crace   John Fowles
Douglas Coupland   Suzannah Dunn   Amanda Prantera

Brad Thor   1970-   US   Adventure/Thriller

🏃 Scot Harvath, Secret Service agent

David Baldacci   Clive Cussler   Jack Higgins
Ted Bell   Vince Flynn   Gordon Kent
Tom Clancy   Brian Haig   Daniel Silva

Matt Thorne   1974-   Lad Lit

🏆 Encore 2000
David Baddiel   David Nicholls   Alexei Sayle
Neil Cross   Nicholas Royle   William Sutcliffe
Jay McInerney   Kevin Sampson

Nicola Thorne   SA   Saga

also writes as Katherine Yorke; is Rosemary Ellerbeck   🏃 Champagne Series
Askham Family

Tessa Barclay   Elizabeth Ann Hill   Judith Saxton
Barbara Taylor Bradford   Joan O'Neill   Barbara Whitnell
Annabel Dilke   Margaret Pemberton   Barbara Wood

Margaret Thornton   1934-   Saga

Blackpool

Jessica Blair   June Francis   Elizabeth Murphy
Julia Bryant   Rosie Harris   Lynda Page
Alexandra Connor   Judith Lennox   Grace Thompson
Glenice Crossland   Connie Monk   Barbara Whitnell

Rosy Thornton

Susannah Bates	Sandra Howard	Alan Titchmarsh
Charlotte Bingham	Erica James	Barbara Trapido
Hester Browne	Kathleen Tessaro	Deborah Wright

Adam Thorpe 1956-

♈ Holtby 1993

Paul Auster	Thomas Keneally	Geoff Ryman
Thomas Hardy	Bernard MacLaverty	Paul Theroux
Kazuo Ishiguro		

Ronald Tierney 1944- US
Crime: PI

♀ Deets Shanahan - Indianapolis

Andrea Camilleri	Ann Granger	Donna Leon
Michael Dibdin	Michael Harvey	Rick Riordan
Loren D Estleman		

Mark Timlin 1950-
Crime: PI

also writes as Johnny Angelo, Jim Ballantyne, Tony Williams ♀ Nick Sharman - London

Jake Arnott	Simon Kernick	Mike Ripley
Ken Bruen	Nick Oldham	Louise Welsh
Bill James		

Alan Titchmarsh 1950-
Humour

Melvyn Bragg	Eve Makis	Leslie Thomas
Katie Fforde	David Nobbs	Rosy Thornton
Angela Huth	Rosamunde Pilcher	Keith Waterhouse

Betsy Tobin 1961- US
Historical

Thomas H Cook	Mick Jackson	Jane Smiley
Emma Donoghue	Curtis Sittenfeld	Jeanette Winterson

Charles Todd US
Crime: Historical - C20th

is Charles & Caroline Todd ♀ Insp Ian Rutledge - 1920s England

Rennie Airth	Elly Griffiths	Laurie R King
David Armstrong	Martha Grimes	Robin Paige
Pat Barker	Suzette Hill	R T Raichev
Mark Gatiss	Susan B Kelly	Nicola Upson

Marilyn Todd 1958-
Crime: Historical - Ancient

♀ Claudia Seferius - Ancient Rome • Iliona, High Priestess - Ancient Greece

Philip Boast	Allan Massie	Steven Saylor
Lindsey Davis	John Maddox Roberts	Peter Tremayne
Margaret Doody	Rosemary Rowe	David Wishart

Miriam Toews   Can

Sarah Addison Allen
Mark Haddon
Jennifer Haigh
Garrison Keillor

Sue Monk Kidd
Anne Michaels
Alice Munro
Michael Ondaatje

Anna Quindlen
Jennie Rooney
J D Salinger
Carol Shields

Colm Toibin   1955-   Ire

🏆 Encore 1993   IMPAC 2006   Costa 2009

Peter Ackroyd
Jennifer Johnston
Colum McCann
Eoin McNamee

Andrei Makine
Brian Moore
David Park
Glenn Patterson

Christos Tsiolkas
William Wall
Niall WIlliams

J R R Tolkien 🎧 ☺ 1892-1973   Fantasy: Epic

was John Ronald Reuel Tolkien

R Scott Bakker
James Barclay
David Bilsborough
Terry Brooks

Cecilia Dart-Thornton
Elizabeth Haydon
Barb & J C Hendee
Robert Jordan

Guy Gavriel Kay
Christopher Paolini
Tad Williams
Sarah Zettel

Peter Tonkin   1950-   Crime: Historical - C16th

🚶 Tom Musgrave, Master of Defence - C16th England

P F Chisholm
Michael Clynes
Patricia Finney

Philip Gooden
Michael Jecks
Simon Levack

John Pilkington
C J Sansom

Sea: Modern

🚶 Mariner Series

Duncan Harding
C C Humphreys
Hammond Innes

Sam Llewellyn
Philip McCutchan
Alistair MacLean

Nicholas Monsarrat
Patrick Robinson

Rebecca Tope   1948-   Crime: Amateur sleuth

🚶 Drew Slocombe, Undertaker - Devon • PC Den Cooper - Devon

Liz Evans
Ann Granger
Veronica Heley
Suzette Hill

Joyce Holms
Hazel Holt
Hope McIntyre

Chris Niles
Catherine Shaw
Stella Whitelaw

Paul Torday   1946-

🏆 Bollinger 2007

Chris Cleave
Kim Edwards
Michael Frayn
Marina Lewycka

David Lodge
Jon McGregor
Mark Mills

David Nobbs
Sue Townsend
Evelyn Waugh

🎧 may be suitable for young adults

T

247

Gemma Townley — Chick Lit

Linda Green
Wendy Holden
Cathy Kelly

Sophie Kinsella
Chris Manby

Jill Mansell
Lauren Weisberger

Sue Townsend ⌢ ☺ 1946- — Humour

🚶 Adrian Mole

Alan Bennett
Clare Boylan
Fiona Gibson

Laurie Graham
Tom Holt
Sue Limb

Ian Sansom
Paul Torday
Lou Wakefield

P J Tracy ⌢ US — Crime: Psychological

is P J & Traci Lambrecht

Russell Andrews
Linda Castillo
John Connolly
Brian Freeman

Jilliane Hoffman
Natsuo Kirino
Jeff Lindsay
Cody McFadyen

Richard Montanari
Ridley Pearson
Karen Rose
Boris Starling

Nigel Tranter 1909-2000 Sco — Historical

also wrote as Nye Tredgold

Dorothy Dunnett
Margaret Elphinstone

Winston Graham
Edith Pargeter

Sharon Penman
Julian Rathbone

Barbara Trapido 1941- SA

Jane Austen
Amanda Craig
Joanne Harris

Nicole Krauss
Sarah Kate Lynch
Tim Parks

Amanda Prantera
Eva Rice
Rosy Thornton

Karen Traviss — Science Fiction: Near future

Greg Bear
Lois McMaster Bujold

Colin Greenland
Ursula K Le Guin

Karen Miller
Sara Zettel

Rachael Treasure Aus — Saga

Beverley Harper
Erica James

Catherine King
Tamara McKinley

Margaret Mayhew
Judy Nunn

Rose Tremain ⌢ 1943-

🏆 Black 1992   Whitbread 1999   Orange 2008

Louise Dean
Sarah Dunant
Arabella Edge
Helen Garner

Maggie Gee
Kent Haruf
Claire Kilroy
Shaena Lambert

Richard Mason
Andrew Miller
Nicholas Shakespeare
Roma Tearne

T

Kate Tremayne

Historical Romance

is Pauline Bentley

🏃 Loveday Series - Cornwall

Winston Graham	Maureen Peters	Michael Taylor
Philippa Gregory	Linda Sole	E V Thompson
Susan Howatch	Kay Stephens	

Peter Tremayne   1943-   Ire

Crime: Historical - Medieval

also writes as Peter MacAlan; is Peter Beresford Ellis

🏃 Sister Fidelma - C7th Ireland

Simon Acland	M K Hume	Sharan Newman
Margaret Frazer	Pat McIntosh	Mary Reed and Eric Mayer
Andrew M Greeley	The Medieval Murderers	Marilyn Todd
Cora Harrison	Ian Morson	

William Trevor   1928-   Ire

🏆 Whitbread 1976, 1983 & 1994

John Banville	Ronald Frame	Nell Leyshon
Sebastian Barry	Andrew Sean Greer	Deirdre Madden
Richard Bausch	Susan Hill	Joseph O'Connor
Frank Delaney	Claire Kilroy	David Park

Jonathan Trigell   1974-

🏆 JLR 2004

Ron Butlin	Denis Johnson	D B C Pierre
Nathan Englander	Jon McGregor	Brady Udall
A M Homes	Vladimir Nabokov	Alan Warner

Adriana Trigiani   1964-   US

Saga

🏃 Big Stone Gap Series - Virginia

Elizabeth Berg	Jan Karon	Alice McDermott
Leif Enger	Haven Kimmel	Alexandra Raife
Fannie Flagg	Lorna Landvik	Ann B Ross
Patricia Gaffney	Elinor Lipman	Anne Rivers Siddons

Joanna Trollope   ☎   1943-

Aga Saga

also writes as Caroline Harvey   🏆 Romantic 1980

Diana Appleyard	Sarah Duncan	Kate Long
Claire Calman	Catherine Dunne	Libby Purves
Anne Doughty	Caro Fraser	Anne Rivers Siddons
Jessica Duchen	Sandra Howard	Jane Elizabeth Varley

Jonathan Tropper   1970-   US

Matt Beaumont	Mark Haddon	Sam Lipsyte
Michael Cunningham	Lawrence Hill	Mil Millington
Frank Delaney	A M Homes	Lisa Tucker
Richard Ford	William Kowalski	Brady Udall

T

Janet MacLeod Trotter 1958-   Saga

NE England

Irene Carr	Una Horne	Wendy Robertson
Catherine Cookson	Ken McCoy	Barbara Whitnell
Elizabeth Gill	Denise Robertson	Annie Wilkinson

M J Trow 1949- Wales   Crime: Amateur sleuth

is Meirion James Trow

☜ Peter Maxwell, Teacher
Det Supt Sholto Lestrade - C19th England

Arthur Conan Doyle	Amy Myers	Norman Russell
Sarah Grazebrook	David Pirie	Veronica Stallwood
Joan Lock	Nicholas Rhea	

Lynne Truss   Humour

Alan Bennett	Isla Dewar	Laura Marney
Susie Boyt	Helen Fielding	Arabella Weir
Mavis Cheek	Jane Green	Louise Wener

Christos Tsiolkas 1965- Aus

🏆 Commonwealth 2009

Vikram Chandra	Armistead Maupin	Jeanette Winterson
Alan Hollinghurst	Colm Toibin	Tim Winton
Lori Lansens	Sarah Waters	

Gail Tsukiyama US

| Victoria Hislop | David Mitchell | Banana Yoshimoto |
| Kazuo Ishiguro | Amy Tan | Carlos Ruiz Zafón |

Sarah Tucker   Mature Chick Lit

Alison Penton Harper	Kate Long	Robyn Sisman
Julia Holden	Debbie Macomber	Polly Williams
Sophie King	Alexandra Potter	Grace Wynne-Jones
Kate Lawson	Annie Sanders	Liz Young

Jonathan Tulloch

🏆 Betty Trask 2000

| Pat Barker | Nick Hornby | David Mitchell |
| Linda Grant | Hanif Kureishi | Bernhard Schlink |

Peter Turnbull 1950-   Crime: Police work - UK

☜ P Division - Glasgow • DCI Hennessy & DS Yellich - York

Jo Bannister	Geraldine Evans	Frederic Lindsay
Robert Barnard	Gerald Hammond	Stuart Pawson
Pauline Bell	Katherine John	

Scott Turow 1949- US — Crime: Legal/financial

🏆 CWA 1987

Stephen L Carter	James Grippando	Craig Holden
Julie Compton	Colin Harrison	Peter Leonard
David Ellis	John Hart	Christopher Reich
Mark Gimenez	Jilliane Hoffman	Tony Strong

Harry Turtledove 1949- US — Fantasy: Epic

also writes as Eric G Iverson, N H Turtletaub

Carol Berg	Mary Gentle	George R R Martin
Sara Douglass	Paul Kearney	William Nicholson
David Farland	Sophia McDougall	Guy Walters

James Twining 1972- — Adventure/Thriller

🏃 Tom Kirk, Art thief

Steve Berry	Juan Gómez-Jurado	E V Seymour
Sam Bourne	Tom Grace	Paul Watkins
Clive Cussler	Thomas Greanias	Nigel West
David Gibbins	Michael Marshall	Tim Willocks

Anne Tyler 🌈 1941- US

🏆 Pulitzer 1989

Manette Ansay	Karen Joy Fowler	Claire Messud
Joan Barfoot	Jennifer Haigh	Lorrie Moore
Candida Crewe	Bernardine Kennedy	Ann Packer
Suzannah Dunn	William Kowalski	Richard Russo

L C Tyler — Crime: Humour

is Len C Tyler   🏃 Elsie Thirkettle & Ethelred Tressider, Literary agent & Crime writer

Boris Akunin	Agatha Christie	Dorothy L Sayers
Alan Bradley	Malcolm Pryce	Andrew Taylor
Simon Brett		

Brady Udall US

Jonathan Franzen	Denis Johnson	Jonathan Trigell
A M Homes	Jim Lynch	Jonathan Tropper
John Irving		

Linn Ullmann 1966- Nor

William Golding	Ian McEwan	Haruki Murakami
Sadie Jones	Claire Messud	Evelyn Waugh

Thrity Umrigar 1961- Ind

Chitra Banerjee Divakaruni	Jhumpa Lahiri	Preethi Nair
	Amulya Malladi	Arundhati Roy
Roopa Farooki	Anita Nair	Meera Syal

T U

Lisa Unger   1970-   US   Crime: Psychological

is Lisa Miscione

Chelsea Cain	Gabrielle Lord	James Patterson
Linda Castillo	Cody McFadyen	Jenny Siler
Kathryn Fox		

Barry Unsworth   ☏   1930-2012   Historical

♛ Booker 1992

John Banville	James H Jackson	Andrew Miller
Robert Edric	Michelle Lovric	Robert Nye
James Fleming	Karen Maitland	Julian Rathbone
Robert Harris	James Meek	Peter Watt

John Updike   1932-2009   US

♛ Pulitzer 1982 & 1991

Saul Bellow	John Irving	Cynthia Ozick
Justin Cartwright	Chang-rae Lee	Kate Pullinger
E L Doctorow	Jonathan Lethem	Edward St Aubyn
Jeffrey Eugenides	Rick Moody	Tobias Wolff

Nicola Upson   Crime: Amateur sleuth

🕈 Josephine Tey - 1930s

Carrie Bebris	Charles Todd	Laura Wilson
Barbara Cleverly	Jill Paton Walsh	Jacqueline Winspear

Leon Uris   1924-2003   US

Frank Delaney	James A Michener	John Steinbeck
Ken Follett	Edward Rutherfurd	Morris West

Jane Urquhart   1949-   Can

Louise Dean	Shaena Lambert	Ann Patchett
Thomas Eidson	Anne Michaels	Nicholas Sparks
David Guterson	David Mitchell	Robert James Waller

Janwillem van de Wetering   1931-2008   Neth   Crime: Police work - Netherlands

🕈 Adjutant Grijpstra & Sgt de Gier - Amsterdam

Karin Alvtegen	H R F Keating	Liza Marklund
A C Baantjer	Henning Mankell	Georges Simenon

Eric Van Lustbader   1946-   US   Crime: PI

also writes as Eric Lustbader   🕈 Nicholas Linnear - Japan • Jason Bourne

James Barrington	Robert Ludlum	Christopher Nicole
Dale Brown	Matt Lynn	Alan Savage
Bryce Courtenay	David Morrell	Justin Scott
Jack Higgins		

Jack Vance   1916-   US   Fantasy: Myth

Iain M Banks	Morgan Llywelyn	Christopher Paolini
Neil Gaiman	Scott Lynch	Adam Roberts
Stephen R Lawhead	George R R Martin	Jeff Vandermeer

Jeff Vandermeer   1968-   US   Science Fiction: Space and time

Ken MacLeod	Neal Stephenson	Gene Wolfe
China Miéville	Jack Vance	David Zindell

Fred Vargas   1957-   Fr   Crime: Police work - France

is Frédérique Audouin-Rouzeau   ⚹ Commissaire Adamsberg - Paris
♛ CWA 2006, 2007 & 2009

S J Bolton	Pierre Magnan	Martin O'Brien
K O Dahl	Dominique Manotti	Georges Simenon
Colin Dexter	Guillermo Martinez	Michael Walters
David Hewson	Manuel Vázquez	
Donna Leon	Montalbán	

Mario Vargas Llosa   1936-   Peru

Isabel Allende	Carlos Fuentes	Ha Jin
Roberto Bolano	Tessa Hadley	Tomas Eloy Martinez
Louis de Bernières	Kathryn Harrison	Nicholas Shakespeare
Maureen Freely	Milton Hatoum	

Jane Elizabeth Varley   Mature Chick Lit

Diana Appleyard	Donna Hay	Joanna Trollope
Louise Bagshawe	Patricia Scanlan	Salley Vickers
Sarah Grazebrook	Rosie Thomas	Penny Vincenzi

M G Vassanji   1950-   Can

is Moyez G Vassanji

J M Coetzee	V S Naipaul	Salman Rushdie
Rohinton Mistry	Michael Ondaatje	Vikas Swarup

Salley Vickers   ◠   1948-

Anita Brookner	Sarah Dunant	Clare Morrall
Sylvia Brownrigg	Patricia Duncker	James Runcie
Jill Dawson	Sue Gee	Jane Elizabeth Varley
Anita Diamant	Kathryn Harrison	Susan Vreeland

Vendela Vida   1972-   US

Jennifer Egan	Allegra Goodman	Edward St Aubyn
Jonathan Franzen	Nicole Krauss	David Szalay
Julia Glass		

V

Penny Vincenzi 1939- Glitz & Glamour

⚷ Lytton Trilogy

Elizabeth Adler	Sandra Brown	Lesley Lokko
Sally Beauman	Jackie Collins	Lulu Taylor
Nina Bell	Rebecca Dean	Jane Elizabeth Varley
Barbara Taylor Bradford	Olivia Goldsmith	Laura Zigman

Barbara Vine 1930- Crime: Psychological

is Ruth Rendell ♔ CWA 1987 & 1991

Carol Anne Davis	Frances Hegarty	Manda Scott
Katy Gardner	Elizabeth McGregor	Jenny Siler
Sophie Hannah	Julie Parsons	Chris Simms
Carolyn G Hart	Patrick Redmond	Sally Spedding

Nury Vittachi 1958- Sri Lan Crime: Amateur sleuth

⚷ C F Wong, Feng Shui consultant - Far East

Barbara Cleverly	Alexander McCall Smith	Qiu Xiaolong
Colin Cotterill	Andy Oakes	Lisa See

Willy Vlautin US

E L Doctorow	Cormac McCarthy	Larry McMurtry
John Irving	Carson McCullers	John Steinbeck

Kurt Vonnegut ⌒ 1922-2007 US Science Fiction: Space and time

Brian W Aldiss	William Gibson	Jack McDevitt
J G Ballard	Alasdair Gray	Jeff Noon
Philip K Dick	Aldous Huxley	Jules Verne

Louise Voss

also writes jointly with Mark Edwards

Candida Clark	Eve Makis	Louise Tondeur
Penelope Lively	Libby Purves	Célestine Hitiura Vaite

Susan Vreeland 1946- US Historical

V
W

Tracy Chevalier	Arabella Edge	Ann Patchett
Will Davenport	Marina Fiorato	James Runcie
Anita Diamant	Deborah Moggach	Salley Vickers
Sarah Dunant	Jude Morgan	

Jan Costin Wagner 1972- Ger Crime: Police work - Finland

⚷ Det Kimmo Joentaa - Finland

Ake Edwardson	Peter Hoeg	Jo Nesbo
Karin Fossum	Stieg Larsson	Yrsa Sigurdardottir

Sasha Wagstaff 1971-   Glitz & Glamour

Rebecca Chance   Veronica Henry   Lulu Taylor
Jilly Cooper   Karen Swan   Fiona Walker
Olivia Darling

Per Wahlöö   see **Maj Sjöwall**

Elizabeth Waite   Saga

London

Philip Boast   Pip Granger   Grace Thompson
Harry Bowling   Elizabeth Lord   Jeanne Whitmee
Pamela Evans   Carol Rivers   Audrey Willsher

Christopher Wakling   1970-

Anna Davis   Esther Freud   James Hamilton-Paterson
Emma Donoghue   Alex Garland   Christos Tsiolkas

Alice Walker   1944-   US

🏆 Pulitzer 1983

Emma Donoghue   Carson McCullers   Toni Morrison
William Faulkner   Terry McMillan   William Styron
Harper Lee

Fiona Walker   1969-   Chick Lit

Jessica Adams   Susie Boyt   Fiona Neill
Catherine Alliott   Jo Carnegie   Alexandra Potter
Louise Bagshawe   Jilly Cooper   Julia Williams
Emily Barr   Veronica Henry   Cathy Woodman

Martin Walker   US   Crime: Police work - France

🚶 Capt Bruno Courrèges - Périgord, France

Anthony Capella   Donna Leon   Martin O'Brien
Caroline Carver   Margaret Maron   Georges Simenon
Jonathon King

Robert James Waller   1939-   US

Nicholas Evans   Marge Piercy   Nicholas Sparks
Richard Ford   Anita Shreve   Jane Urquhart
Molly Gloss   Jane Smiley

W

Helen Walsh   1977-

John Burnside   Niall Griffiths   Sadie Jones
Diane Chamberlain   A M Homes   Ian McEwan

Jill Paton Walsh ☺ 1937-

| Peter Ackroyd | Umberto Eco | Per Petterson |
| A S Byatt | Jane Gardam | Catherine Shaw |

Crime: Amateur sleuth

🕴 Imogen Quy, Nurse - St Agatha's College, Cambridge • Lord Peter Wimsey & Harriet Vane

Suzanne Arruda	Veronica Heley	R T Raichev
Simon Brett	Joyce Holms	Dorothy L Sayers
Colin Dexter	Michael Innes	Veronica Stallwood
Ruth Dudley Edwards	Chris Niles	Nicola Upson

Jess Walter US   **Crime:** Police work - US

🕴 Caroline Maybry - Spokane, Washington State

Giles Blunt	Thomas Laird	Theresa Schwegel
Steve Hamilton	Theresa Monsour	Jenny Siler
Lynn Hightower	Ridley Pearson	

Guy Walters   War

Elizabeth Darrell	Rebecca Pawel	Alan Savage
David Fiddimore	Derek Robinson	Harry Turtledove
Robert Harris	Robert Ryan	

Michael Walters   **Crime:** Police work - Mongolia

🕴 Insp Nergui - Serious crime squad, Ulaan Bataan

Andrea Camilleri	Andy Oakes	Frank Tallis
Peter May	Qiu Xiaolong	Fred Vargas
Jo Nesbo	Lisa See	

Minette Walters ⌒ 1949-   **Crime:** Psychological

🏆 CWA 1992, 1994 & 2003

Lindsay Ashford	Sophie Hannah	Stieg Larsson
Ingrid Black	Jane Hill	Gabrielle Lord
Candida Clark	Joanna Hines	Matt Rees
Carol Anne Davis	Åsa Larsson	Claire Seeber

Joseph Wambaugh 1937- US   **Crime:** Police work - US

LAPD, California

James Ellroy	Theresa Monsour	Theresa Schwegel
W E B Griffin	Charlie Owen	Martin Cruz Smith
Ed McBain	Jefferson Parker	Stuart Woods
Deon Meyer	Mario Puzo	

W

Go to back for lists of
Pseudonyms • Authors by Genre • Characters and Series • Environments
Prize Winners • Classic Authors • Crossover Authors • Further Reading • Websites

J R Ward
US   Paranormal

is Jessica Bird

Lara Adrian	Mary Janice Davidson	Tanya Huff
Kelley Armstrong	Christine Feehan	Sherrilyn Kenyon
Keri Arthur	Lori Handeland	Susan Sizemore
P C & Kristin Cast	Charlaine Harris	

Alan Warner
1964-   Sco

🏆 S Maugham 1996   Encore 1998

John Aberdein	Matt Haig	Jonathan Trigell
Iain Banks	Jackie Kay	Irvine Welsh
Ron Butlin	James Kelman	

Freda Warrington
1956-   Fantasy: Epic

Robert Asprin	Sara Douglass	Juliet E McKenna
James Barclay	Ian Irvine	Elizabeth Moon
Storm Constantine	J V Jones	K J Parker
Ben Counter	Tanith Lee	Robert Silverberg

Giles Waterfield
1949-

🏆 McKitterick 2001

Vanora Bennett	Andrew O'Hagan	Salley Vickers
Patrick Gale	Tim Pears	Evelyn Waugh
Clare Morrall		

Keith Waterhouse
☎   1929-2009   Humour

🚶 Billy Liar

Malcolm Bradbury	Magnus Mills	Leslie Thomas
Ben Elton	John Mortimer	Alan Titchmarsh
Andrew Holmes	Barry Pilton	Mark Watson
David Lodge	Linda Taylor	

Paul Waters
Historical: Ancient

Roman Empire

Christian Cameron	Allan Massie	Manda Scott
R S Downie	Mary Renault	David Wishart
Robert Graves	John Maddox Roberts	

Sarah Waters
1966-   Wales

🏆 Sunday Times 2000   S Maugham 2000   CWA 2002

Leila Aboulela	Emma Donoghue	Caro Peacock
Clare Clark	Posie Graeme-Evans	Jane Stevenson
F G Cottam	Jane Harris	Christos Tsiolkas
Stevie Davies	John Harwood	Colson Whitehead

W

Paul Watkins   1964-   Wales   Adventure/Thriller

♥ Encore 1990   Holtby 1995

Douglas Kennedy	Robert Radcliffe	James Twining
Simon Levack	Derek Robinson	Nigel West
Gareth O'Callaghan	Andrew Rosenheim	

Jules Watson   Aus   Historical: Ancient

🏃 Dalriada Trilogy - Roman and Celtic Britain

Jean M Auel	Morgan Llywelyn	Allan Massie
Conn Iggulden	Juliet Marillier	Jack Whyte

Mark Watson   1980-   Humour

Guy Bellamy	Magnus Mills	Paul Torday
James Delingpole	John O'Farrell	Keith Waterhouse

Peter Watt   Aus   Historical

Bryce Courtenay	Andrew Miller	Katherine Scholes
Robert Drewe	Amanda Prantera	Barry Unsworth
Tamara McKinley		

Daisy Waugh   1967-   Chick Lit

Wendy Holden	Belinda Jones	Freya North
Rachel Hore	India Knight	Tina Reilly
Lisa Jewell	Gil McNeil	Sarah Webb

Evelyn Waugh   ⌒   1903-66

Malcolm Bradbury	Pauline Melville	Talitha Stevenson
Joseph Connolly	Dan Rhodes	Paul Torday
Philip Hensher	Muriel Spark	Linn Ullmann
David Lodge	Edward St Aubyn	Giles Waterfield

Brent Weeks   US   Fantasy: Epic

Joe Abercrombie	Robin Hobb	Garth Nix
Trudi Canavan	Tom Lloyd	Brandon Sanderson
Mark Chadbourn	George R R Martin	Adrian Tchaikovsky
Terry Goodkind		

Lee Weeks   Adventure/Thriller

🏃 Det Johnny Mann

Jeffery Deaver	Richard Montanari	Mark Pearson
Lisa Gardner	Chris Mooney	Karen Rose
Mandasue Heller	James Patterson	Neil White
J A Kerley		

W

⌒ may be suitable for young adults

Jennifer Weiner 1970- US · Chick Lit

Maggie Alderson
Melissa Bank
Emily Barr
Lucy Dawson

Helen Fielding
Janet Fitch
Kate Jacobs
Sarah Mason

Morag Prunty
Carmen Reid
Lisa Tucker

Alison Weir 1951- · Historical: C16th

Vanora Bennett
Christie Dickason
Suzannah Dunn
Marina Fiorato

C W Gortner
Posie Graeme-Evans
Clio Gray
Philippa Gregory

Anne Herries
Jean Plaidy
Deborah Wright
Robyn Young

Arabella Weir 1957- · Mature Chick Lit

Sherry Ashworth
Mavis Cheek
Lucy Diamond

Imogen Edwards-Jones
Laurie Graham
Sue Limb

Sarah Mason
Lynne Truss

Margaret Weis 1948- US · Fantasy: Epic

Terry Brooks
David A Drake
Fiona McIntosh

Elizabeth Moon
William Nicholson

Melanie Rawn
R A Salvatore

Lauren Weisberger 1977- US · Chick Lit

Sam Baker
Claudia Carroll
Anna Davis
Jane Fallon

Belinda Jones
Lindsey Kelk
Clare Naylor
Karen Quinn

Victoria Routledge
Sara Shepard
Kathleen Tessaro
Gemma Townley

Fay Weldon 1933-

Beryl Bainbridge
Elizabeth Buchan
Margaret Forster

Edna O'Brien
Wendy Perriam

Emma Tennant
Jeanette Winterson

Sue Welfare · Mature Chick Lit

also writes as Gemma Fox; is Kate Lawson

Marita Conlon-McKenna
Jane Costello
Kate Fenton

Melissa Hill
Kate Lawson
Karen Quinn

Annie Sanders
Julia Williams

Rebecca Wells 1963- US

Louisiana

Louise Erdrich
Fannie Flagg
Karen Joy Fowler

Elinor Lipman
Terry McMillan

Anne Rivers Siddons
Sarah Willis

W

Irvine Welsh 🕶 1958- Sco

Tony Black	Roddy Doyle	James Kelman
Des Dillon	Niall Griffiths	Alan Warner

Louise Welsh 1968- Sco Crime: Hardboiled

🏆 CWA 2002

Lin Anderson	Frederic Lindsay	Manda Scott
Jake Arnott	Denise Mina	Alice Thompson
Helen Black	Charlie Owen	Mark Timlin
Alex Gray	George P Pelecanos	

Mary Wesley 1912-2002

Clare Chambers	Angela Huth	Jean Saunders
Victoria Clayton	Elinor Lipman	Kate Saunders
Jane Gardam	Charlotte Moore	Lou Wakefield
Adèle Geras	Nora Naish	Amanda Eyre Ward

Donald Westlake 1933-2008 US Crime: Humour

also wrote as Tucker Coe, Allan Marshall,
Richard Stark, Donald E Westlake

🏃 John Dortmunder, Burglar

Nancy Cohen	José Latour	Richard Stark
Tim Dorsey	Elmore Leonard	Sarah Strohmeyer
Carl Hiaasen	Robert B Parker	

Edmund White 1940- US

Patrick Gale	David Leavitt	Armistead Maupin
Alan Hollinghurst	Jay McInerney	Edward St Aubyn

Gillian White

also writes as Georgina Fleming

Helen Dunmore	Shirley Hazzard	Sarah Rayner
Linda Grant	Deborah Moggach	Graham Swift

Adventure/Thriller: Psychological

Sarah Diamond	Lucretia Grindle	Elizabeth McGregor
Lesley Glaister	Jane Hill	Stanley Pottinger
Carol Goodman	Joanna Hines	Claire Seeber

Jenny White US Historical

🏃 Kamil Pasha, Magistrate - C19th Istanbul

Jason Goodwin	Orhan Pamuk	Craig Russell
David Hewson	Andrew Pepper	Elif Shafak
Barbara Nadel		

W

Go to back for lists of
Pseudonyms • Authors by Genre • Characters and Series • Environments
Prize Winners • Classic Authors • Crossover Authors • Further Reading • Websites

Michael White US Historical

Ken Follett	Stewart O'Nan	Richard Russo
Charles Frazier	Anna Quindlen	Martin Cruz Smith

Neil White 1965- Crime: Police work - UK

♁ DC Laura McGanity & Jack Garrett - Lancashire

Beverly Barton	Peter James	Leslie Thomas
Mark Billingham	Pauline Rowson	Camilla Way
Patricia Highsmith	Roger Silverwood	Lee Weeks
Michael Innes		

Stephen White US Crime: Psychological

♁ Alan Gregory, Psychologist - Boulder, Colorado

Jeffery Deaver	John Katzenbach	Meg O'Brien
David Ellis	Alex Kava	Andrew Pyper
Daniel Hecht	Jonathan Kellerman	Erica Spindler
Tami Hoag	Jonathan Nasaw	Dana Stabenow

Colson Whitehead 1970- US

Jonathan Safran Foer	Daniel Kehlmann	Thomas Pynchon
E M Forster	Claire Messud	Philip Roth
Joseph Heller	Richard Powers	Sarah Waters

Jeanne Whitmee Saga

London

Pamela Evans	Gilda O'Neill	Elizabeth Waite
Elizabeth Lord	Judith Saxton	Barbara Whitnell
Pamela Oldfield	Linda Sole	Dee Williams

Barbara Whitnell Saga

Cornwall

Rosemary Aitken	Nicola Thorne	Jeanne Whitmee
Iris Gower	Margaret Thornton	Barbara Wood
Claire Lorrimer	Janet MacLeod Trotter	

Jack Whyte 1940- Sco Historical: C12th

♁ Camulod Series - Europe & Near East • Templar Trilogy

Bernard Cornwell	M K Hume	Mary Renault
Ken Follett	Robert Low	Jules Watson
Tom Harper	Steven Pressfield	Robyn Young

W

Madeleine Wickham 1969- Aga Saga

also writes as Sophie Kinsella

Judy Astley	Melanie Rose	Sarah Willis
Amanda Brookfield	Jean Saunders	Meg Wolitzer
Megan Crane	Lou Wakefield	Grace Wynne-Jones
Elizabeth Noble	Amanda Eyre Ward	

Ann Widdecombe   1947-

| Annabel Dilke | Libby Purves | Amanda Eyre Ward |
| Erica James | Rebecca Shaw | Marcia Willett |

John Wilcox   War: Historical - C19th

♁ Capt Simon Fonthill & Sgt '352' Jenkins - Boer War

Roger Carpenter	Richard Howard	Allan Mallinson
Bernard Cornwell	C C Humphreys	Patrick Rambaud
Iain Gale	Garry Kilworth	

Kim Wilkins   ⌒   1970-   Aus   Fantasy

also writes as Kimberley Freeman

| Kelley Armstrong | Kim Harrison | Anne Rice |
| Poppy Z Brite | Terry Pratchett | Phil Rickman |

Marcia Willett   1945-   Saga

also writes as Willa Marsh   ♁ Chadwick Family

Amelia Carr	Julie Highmore	Santa Montefiore
Elizabeth Edmondson	Harriet Hudson	Rosamunde Pilcher
Adèle Geras	Kate Long	Ann Widdecombe
Rebecca Gregson	Sara MacDonald	Annie Wilkinson

Adam Williams   Historical

| Aravind Adiga | Kate Furnivall | Lisa See |
| Ken Follett | C J Sansom | Sara Sheridan |

Dee Williams   Saga

East End, London

Pip Granger	Connie Monk	Grace Thompson
Annie Groves	Sheila Newberry	Jeanne Whitmee
Gwen Madoc	Michael Taylor	Annie Wilkinson

Julia Williams   Mature Chick Lit

Trisha Ashley	Kate Harrison	Sue Welfare
Lucy Dillon	Jill Mansell	Isabel Wolff
Harriet Evans	Fiona Walker	

Niall Williams   1958-   Ire

Dermot Bolger	Simon Mawer	Edna O'Brien
Jennifer Johnston	Joseph O'Connor	Colm Toibin
Bernard MacLaverty		

W

Polly Williams   Mature Chick Lit

Catherine Alliott	Sophie King	Judy Nunn
Lucy Cavendish	Pauline McLynn	Lesley Pearse
Jane Fallon	Jill Mansell	Sarah Tucker
Jane Green		

Tad Williams ⌒ 1957- US — Fantasy: Epic

David Bilsborough	David Eddings	Sean Russell
Terry Brooks	Greg Keyes	J R R Tolkien
David A Drake	Stan Nicholls	

⌒ — Science Fiction: Near future

Steve Aylett	Robert J Sawyer	Michael Marshall Smith
Jon Courtenay Grimwood	Lucius Shepard	David Zindell
Nick Sagan		

Lauren Willig 1977- US — Historical Romance

Mary Balogh	Georgette Heyer	Julia Quinn
Anne Barbour	Eloisa James	Deanna Raybourn

Tim Willocks 1957- — Adventure/Thriller

Thomas H Cook	John Katzenbach	Dean R Koontz
Thomas Harris	Andrew Klavan	James Twining

Audrey Willsher — Saga

London • Leicestershire

Harriet Hudson	Lynda Page	Annie Wilkinson
Meg Hutchinson	Mary Jane Staples	Sally Worboyes
Joan Medlicott	Elizabeth Waite	

A N Wilson 1950

🏆 JLR 1978 — 🚶 Lampitt Chronicles

Julian Barnes	Edward Docx	Anthony Powell
Malcolm Bradbury	Iris Murdoch	Bernice Rubens

Derek Wilson 1935- — Crime: Historical - C18th

also writes as Jonathan Kane

🚶 George Keene, Spy
Nathaniel Gye, Parapsychologist • Tim Lacy - Art world

Earlene Fowler	Roy Lewis	John Malcolm
Janet Gleeson	David Liss	Iain Pears
Daniel Hecht		

Edward Wilson — Adventure/Thriller

Charles Cumming	Philip Kerr	Stella Rimington
Alan Furst	Henry Porter	Tom Rob Smith
David Ignatius		

W

James Wilson 1948- — Historical

Kate Atkinson	Daphne Du Maurier	David Guterson
Geraldine Brooks	Charles Frazier	Irene Nemirovsky

Laura Wilson 1964- Crime: Psychological

🏆 CWA 2008   🕴 DI Ted Stratton - 1940s London

Carol Anne Davis	Jeff Lindsay	Chris Simms
Sarah Diamond	R N Morris	Carol Smith
Carol Goodman	Margaret Murphy	Andrew Taylor
Jane Hill	Ruth Rendell	Nicola Upson

Robert Wilson 1957- Adventure/Thriller

🏆 CWA 1999   🕴 Bruce Medway - West Africa • Insp Javier Falcon - Portugal

Ronan Bennett	Dan Fesperman	J Wallis Martin
Peter Corris	Alan Furst	Henry Porter
Charles Cumming	Reg Gadney	Olen Steinhauer
David Downing	Joseph Kanon	

Darryl Wimberley 1949- US Crime: Police work - US

🕴 Det Barrett Raines - Florida

Lawrence Block	James W Hall	Robert B Parker
James Lee Burke	Elmore Leonard	John Sandford

R D Wingfield 1928-2007 Crime: Police work - UK

was Rodney David Wingfield   🕴 DI Jack Frost - 'Denton'

Kate Atkinson	Kate Ellis	M R D Meek
Robert Barnard	Andrew Holmes	Nick Oldham
Chris Collett	Katherine John	Mike Ripley
Deborah Crombie	Ken McCoy	Andrew Taylor

David Wingrove 1954- Science Fiction: Near future

Neal Asher	Greg Egan	Peter F Hamilton
Orson Scott Card	Steven Erikson	Philip Pullman

Don Winslow 1953- US Crime: Amateur sleuth

🕴 Neal Carey - Nevada

Edward Bunker	Dashiell Hammett	Peter Leonard
Robert Crais	John Hart	Shane Maloney
Jo Dereske	Chuck Hogan	Patrick Quinlan
Loren D Estleman	José Latour	Edward Wright

Jacqueline Winspear 1955- Crime: PI

🕴 Maisie Dobbs - WW1 & onwards, London & Kent

James Anderson	Ann Granger	R T Raichev
Carrie Bebris	Patricia Harwin	David Roberts
Alan Bradley	Michael Innes	Imogen Robertson
Barbara Cleverly	Robin Paige	Nicola Upson

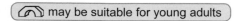

🕭 may be suitable for young adults

Jeanette Winterson ☺ 1959-

🏆 Whitbread 1985   JLR 1987

Isabel Allende	Laura Esquivel	Bernice Rubens
Iain Banks	Kate Pullinger	Betsy Tobin
Emma Donoghue	Michèle Roberts	Christos Tsiolkas
Patricia Duncker	Meg Rosoff	Fay Weldon

Tim Winton 1960- Aus

🏆 Miles Franklin 1992, 2002 & 2009

Murray Bail	Helen Garner	Claire Messud
Peter Carey	Siri Hustvedt	Brian Moore
Steven Carroll	Thomas Keneally	Christos Tsiolkas
Robert Drewe	Andrew McGahan	

David Wishart 1952- Sco   Crime: Historical - Ancient

🏃 Marcus Corvinus - Ancient Rome

Philip Boast	Ben Kane	Rosemary Rowe
Lindsey Davis	Sophia McDougall	Steven Saylor
Margaret Doody	Allan Massie	Marilyn Todd
R S Downie	John Maddox Roberts	Paul Waters

Mary Withall Sco   Saga

🏃 Eisdalsa Island Trilogy - Scotland

Maggie Craig	Gwen Kirkwood	Elleen Ramsay
Christine Marion Fraser	Elisabeth McNeill	Mary Stewart
Evelyn Hood	Frances Paige	Sally Stewart

P G Wodehouse ⌒ 1881-1975   Humour

was Pelham (Plum) Grenville Wodehouse   🏃 Jeeves, Butler • Bertie Wooster

James Anderson	Stephen Fry	John Mortimer
Alan Bennett	Dolores Gordon-Smith	David Nobbs
George Macdonald Fraser	Tom Holt	Nigel Williams

Gene Wolfe 1931- US   Fantasy: Literary

🏆 BSFA 1981

Robert Holdstock	Julian May	Geoff Ryman
Stephen Hunt	Tim Powers	Jeff Vandermeer
Ursula K Le Guin	Adam Roberts	

Tom Wolfe ⌒ 1931- US

Bret Easton Ellis	John Irving	Norman Mailer
F Scott Fitzgerald	Jonathan Lethem	Curtis Sittenfeld
Colin Harrison	Sam Lipsyte	Gore Vidal

W

☺ also writes children's books

Isabel Wolff
Mature Chick Lit

Catherine Alliott	Wendy Holden	Sarah May
Raffaella Barker	India Knight	Annie Sanders
Sarah Duncan	Josie Lloyd & Emlyn Rees	Tess Stimson
Julie Highmore	Sue Margolis	Julia Williams

Tobias Wolff 1945- US

Don DeLillo	John Irving	Richard Powers
F Scott Fitzgerald	Jonathan Lethem	Tom Robbins
Richard Ford	Patrick McGrath	John Updike

Meg Wolitzer 1959- US

Louise Doughty	Alison Lurie	Jane Smiley
Penelope Lively	Terry McMillan	Madeleine Wickham

Barbara Wood 1947-
Historical

Janet Dailey	Sarah Kate Lynch	Nicola Thorne
Iris Gower	Maureen Peters	Barbara Whitnell
Joanne Harris	E V Thompson	

Valerie Wood
Saga

also writes as Val Wood

Jessica Blair	Rosie Goodwin	Catherine King
Irene Carr	Rosie Harris	Wendy Robertson
Jess Foley	Evelyn Hood	Kay Stephens
Jean Fullerton	Audrey Howard	

Chris Wooding ⌒ ☺ 1977-
Fantasy: Humour

Joe Abercrombie	Tom Holt	Garth Nix
Iain M Banks	Stephenie Meyer	Terry Pratchett
Stephen Deas		

Cathy Woodman
Mature Chick Lit

⚑ Harry Bowling 2002   ⚘ Otter House Vets Series - 'Talyton', Devon

Cecelia Ahern	Wendy Holden	Jill Mansell
Louise Bagshawe	Louise Kean	Fiona Walker
Irene Carr	Josie Lloyd & Emlyn Rees	Sally Worboyes

W Daniel Woodrell 1953- US

Ozark Mountains - Missouri

Nicholas Evans	Charles Frazier	Cormac McCarthy
William Faulkner	David Guterson	Willy Vlautin

Janet Woods   Aus   Saga

C19th Dorset

Tessa Barclay   Julia Bryant   Connie Monk
Anne Bennett   Claire Lorrimer   Pamela Oldfield
Rose Boucheron

Stuart Woods   1938- US   Adventure/Thriller

🚶 Stone Barrington, PI - New York • Chief Holly Barker, Police - Florida

John Gilstrap   Patricia Highsmith   Michael Malone
James Grippando   Douglas Kennedy   Joseph Wambaugh
Stuart Harrison   Andrew Klavan

Sally Worboyes   Saga

London • Kent

Elizabeth Daish   Kitty Neale   Audrey Willsher
Pip Granger   Victor Pemberton   Cathy Woodman
Harriet Hudson   D M Purcell

Edward Wright   US   Crime: PI

🏆 CWA 2001, 2006   🚶 John Ray Horn   Los Angeles

James Ellroy   Cormac McCarthy   George P Pelecanos
Dashiell Hammett   Ross Macdonald   Don Winslow

Janny Wurts   1953- US   Fantasy: Epic

Jonathan Carroll   Katherine Kurtz   Mickey Zucker Reichert
Louise Cooper   L E Modesitt Jr   Steph Swainston
Robert Jordan   Elizabeth Moon

John Wyndham   ⌒ 1903-69   Science Fiction: Near future

was John Wyndham Harris

Brian W Aldiss   Robert A Heinlein   Michael Marshall Smith
Isaac Asimov   Geoff Ryman   Neal Stephenson
Philip K Dick

Xinran   ⌒ 1958- China

is Xinran Xve

Alma Alexander   Yiyun Li   Lisa See
Arthur Golden   Anchee Min   Su Tong
Xiaolu Guo   Qiu Xiaolong

W
X
Y

Margaret Yorke   1924-   Crime: Psychological

is Margaret Beda Nicholson   🚶 Patrick Grant
🏆 CWA 1999

Jane Adams   Gerald Hammond   Danuta Reah
Louise Doughty   Julie Parsons   Louis Sanders
Elizabeth Ferrars

Banana Yoshimoto 1964- Ja

| Jim Crace | Natsuo Kirino | Jane Smiley |
| Kate Grenville | David Mitchell | Gail Tsukiyama |

Robyn Young 1975- Historical: Medieval

🏃 Robert the Bruce - Knights Templar • C13th Scotland

Christian Cameron	Douglas Jackson	Sharan Newman
Bernard Cornwell	Christian Jacq	Tim Severin
Tom Harper	Robert Low	Alison Weir
Richard Howard	Valerio Massimo Manfredi	Jack Whyte

Carlos Ruiz Zafón ☺ 1964- Spain Adventure/Thriller

Thalassa Ali	Leif Enger	Giulio Leoni
John Boyne	Ildefonso Falcones	Guillermo Martinez
Paulo Coelho	Khaled Hosseini	Orhan Pamuk
Umberto Eco	Panos Karnezis	Gail Tsukiyama

Farahad Zama Ind

🏆 Nathan 2009

| Kiran Desai | Shamini Flint | Alexander McCall Smith |
| Nicholas Drayson | Lorna Landvik | Célestine Hitiura Vaite |

Sarah Zettel 1966- US Fantasy: Myth

also writes as C L Anderson, Marissa Day

Ashok K Banker	C S Lewis	Judith Tarr
David Eddings	Caiseal Mor	J R R Tolkien
Ursula K Le Guin		

David Zindell 1952- US Science Fiction: Space and time

Iain M Banks	China Miéville	Brian Stableford
Orson Scott Card	Christopher Priest	Jules Verne
Mark Chadbourn	Kristine Kathryn Rusch	Tad Williams
Harlan Ellison	Lucius Shepard	Robert Charles Wilson

Anne Zouroudi 1959- Crime: Police work - Greece

🏃 Det Hermes Diaktoros - Greece

Andrea Camilleri	Shamini Flint	Jeffrey Siger
Agatha Christie	Roderick Jeffries	Georges Simenon
Barbara Cleverly	Donna Leon	

Markus Zusak ☺ Aus

Chinua Achebe	Kathryn Harrison	James Robertson
Thalassa Ali	Irene Nemirovsky	Meg Rosoff
John Boyne	Orhan Pamuk	Mark Slouka
G W Dahlquist	Elliot Perlman	Sarah Waters

Y Z

Pseudonyms

Many writers use pseudonyms, and some write under several different names. This section provides an index to some of the alternative names used by authors included in the main A-Z listing which do not have a separate entry.

A

Susan Wittig Albert and Bill Albert	Robin Paige
Rosemary Aitken	Rosemary Rowe
Peter Alding	Roderic Jeffries
Vanessa Alexander	Paul Doherty
Conrad Allen	Edward Marston
C L Anderson	Marissa Day; Sarah Zettel
V C Andrews	Virginia Andrews (with Andrew Neiderman)
Alex Andrews	Mary Mackie
Johnny Angelo	Mark Timlin
Anna Apostolou	Paul Doherty
Gary Edric Armitage	Robert Edric
Andrew Arncliffe	Nicholas Rhea
Stephanie Ash	Chris Manby
William Ashbless	Tim Powers (with James P Blaylock)
Jeffrey Ashford	Roderic Jeffries
Annie Ashworth (with Meg Sanders)	Annie Sanders
Margaret Astbury	Meg Hutchinson
Elizabeth Aston	Elizabeth Edmondson
Frédérique Audouin-Rouzeau	Fred Vargas
Jonathan Aycliffe	Daniel Easterman
Catherine Aydy	Emma Tennant

B

Richard Bachman	Stephen King
Donna Baker	Lilian Harry
Alex Baldwin	W E B Griffin
Jim Ballantyne	Mark Timlin
T F Banks	Sean Thomas Russell
Bill Barclay	Michael Moorcock
Bernard Bastable	Robert Barnard
Simon Beaufort	Susanna Gregory
Ken Begg	Ken McClure
Morgan Benedict	Fidelis Morgan
Elizabeth Bennett	Cynthia Harrod-Eagles
Pamela Bennetts	Margaret James
Pauline Bentley	Kate Tremayne
Stephanie Berke (with Barbara O'Hanlon)	Barbara & Stephanie Keating
Jessica Bird	J R Ward
Cleo Birdwell	Don DeLillo
Campbell Black	Campbell Armstrong
Veronica Black	Maureen Peters
Grant Blackwood	Clive Cussler
Alan Blackwood	Graham Masterton
Iain Blair	Emma Blair
Sterling Blake	Gregory Benford
Patrick Blake	Clive Egleton

Sharon J Bolton	S J Bolton
Judith Bordill	Marjorie Eccles
Jean Bowden	Tessa Barclay
Felix Boyd	Harry Harrison
Edward P Bradbury	Michael Moorcock
Sally Bradford	Barbara Taylor Bradford
Nancy Brahtin	Katharine Kerr
Jane Brindle	Josephine Cox
Helen Brooks	Rita Bradshaw
Danielle Brown	Dan Brown
Jack Du Brul	Clive Cussler
Francis Bryan	Frank Delaney
Paul Bryers	Seth Hunter
Marie Buchanan	Clare Curzon
Stephen Bury	Neal Stephenson
Richard Butler	Ted Allbeury
William E Butterworth III	W E B Griffin

C

Patricia Cabot	Meg Cabot
John Roswell Camp	John Sandford
Nancy Cane	Nancy Cohen
Jack Cannon	Nelson DeMille
Curt Cannon	Ed McBain
Claire Carmichael	Claire McNab
Marion Carr	Freda Lightfoot
Philippa Carr	Jean Plaidy
Jenny Carroll	Meg Cabot
Jayne Castle	Jayne Ann Krentz; Amanda Quick
Grace Cavendish	Patricia Finney
Caroline Charles	Mary Mackie
Carol A Chase	Kate Charles
Grigory Chkhartishvillihas	Boris Akunin
Cathy Christopher	Mary Mackie
Mary Christopher	Mary Mackie
Kay Christopher	Grace Thompson
Erin St Claire	Sandra Brown
Brenda Clarke	Kate Sedley
James Clemens	James Rollins
Michael Clynes	Paul Doherty
Tucker Coe	Donald Westlake
Brian Coffey	Dean R Koontz
Emma Cole	Susanna Kearsley
Hunt Collins	Ed McBain
Peter Collinson	Dashiell Hammett
James Colvin	Michael Moorcock
Roxanne Longstreet Conrad	Rachel Caine
Dawn Cook	Kim Harrison
Christopher Coram	Nicholas Rhea
David John Moore Cornwell	John Le Carré
Caroline Courtney	Penny Jordan
William Coyle	Thomas Keneally
David Craig	Bill James
Caroline Crosby	Jessica Stirling

D

Susan Lynn Crose	Lisa Jackson
Lauren Crow	Fiona McIntosh
Lili St Crow	Lilith Saintcrow
Dirk Cussler	Clive Cussler
Laura Daniels	Amy Myers
Catherine Darby	Maureen Peters
Iris Davies	Iris Gower
Marissa Day	C L Anderson; Sarah Zettel
Frank Dempsey	Harry Harrison
J M Dillard	Jeanne Kalogridis
Craig Dirgo	Clive Cussler
James L Docherty	James Hadley Chase
Susan Elizabeth Donaldson	Susan Moody
Arthur Douglas	Gerald Hammond
Garry Douglas	Garry Kilworth
Billy Douglass	Barbara Delinsky
Bonnie Drake	Barbara Delinsky
Shannon Drake	Heather Graham
Emma Drummond	Elizabeth Darrell
Jack Drummond	Martin O'Brien
Ann Dukthas	Paul Doherty
Deanne Dwyer	Dean R Koontz
K R Dwyer	Dean R Koontz

E

James Eliot	John Case
Rosemary Ellerbeck	Nicola Thorne
Lance Elliot	Keith McCarthy
Peter Beresford Ellis	Peter Tremayne
Phillip Emmons	Bentley Little
Jonathan Evans	Brian Freemantle

F

Ruth Fablan	Aileen Armitage
Martin Fallon	Jack Higgins
James Ferguson	Nicholas Rhea
Tom Ferris	Nicholas Rhea
Peter Findlay	D B C Pierre
Jude Fisher	Jane Johnson
Georgina Fleming	Gillian White
Gemma Fox	Kate Lawson; Sue Welfare
Holly Fox	Elizabeth McGregor
Jane Fraser	Rosamunde Pilcher
Gail Frazer	Margaret Frazer
Jonathan Freedland	Sam Bourne
Kimberley Freeman	Kim Wilkins
Sean French (with Nicci Gerrard)	Nicci French
Loenardo Padura Fuehtes	Leonardo Padura

G

Katie Gallagher	Sarah Addison Allen
W R Gallaher	Judith Gould
Esther Garber	Tanith Lee
Jose Irazu Garmendia	Bernardo Atxaga
Peter Garrison	Craig Shaw Gardner
Paul Garrison	Justin Scott
Frances Gordon	Sarah Rayne
Lindsay Gordon	Adam Nevill

C L Grace	Paul Doherty
Roderic Graeme	Roderic Jeffries
Vanessa Graham	Anthea Fraser
Robert Graham	Joe Haldeman
James Graham	Jack Higgins
Jim Grant	Lee Child
Jonathan Grant	Jonathan Gash
David Grant	Craig Thomas
Lynn Granville	Linda Sole
Caroline Gray	Christopher Nicole
Kristine Grayson	Kristine Kathryn Rusch
Patricia Grey	Liz Evans

H

Steffie Hall	Janet Evanovich
Daniel Hall	Jonathan Lunn
Dorothy Halliday	Dorothy Dunnett
Penelope Jones Halsall	Penny Jordan
Paullina Handler	Paullina Simons
Elizabeth Hankin	Elizabeth Gill
Paul Harding	Paul Doherty
Ross Harding	David Gemmell
Elizabeth Harris	Alys Clare
John Wyndham Harris	John Wyndham
David Harrison	Tom Bale
Chip Harrison	Lawrence Block
David Harsent	David Lawrence
Christopher Hart	William Napier
Geraldine Hartnett	Geraldine Evans
Graham Hastings	Roderic Jeffries
Kate Hatfield	Natasha Cooper
William Heaney	Graham Joyce
Alexandra Henry	Hilary Norman
Nancy Herndon	Elizabeth Chadwick
Evelyn Hervey	H R F Keating
Eleanor Alice Burford Hibbert	Jean Plaidy
Lydia Hitchcock	Penny Jordan
Dalby Holden	Gerald Hammond
Taylor Holden	Wendy Holden
Victoria Holt	Jean Plaidy
Margaret Hope	Alanna Knight
Barbara Hope-Lewis	Barbara Erskine
Jim & Carolyn Hougan	John Case
Deborah Hough	Deborah Moggach
Linda S Howington	Linda Howard
Jeffrey Hudson	Michael Crichton
Maggie Hudson	Margaret Pemberton
Ann Hulme	Ann Granger
Evan Hunter	Ed McBain
Christopher Hyde	Paul Christopher
Jennifer Hyde	Marjorie Eccles

I
J

Martin Inigo	Edward Marston
Eric G Iverson	Harry Turtledove
Everatt Jackson	Margaret Dickinson

Sherry-Anne Jacobs	Anna Jacobs
Vanessa James	Sally Beauman
Judith James	Bill James
Stephanie James	Jayne Ann Krentz
Susannah James	Susan Moody
Shannah Jay	Anna Jacobs
Jon Jefferson (with Dr Bill Bass)	Jefferson Bass
Katherine John	Catrin Collier
Jordan	Katie Price
Laura Jordan	Sandra Brown
Lizzie Jordan	Chris Manby

K

Tanith Lee Kaiine	Tanith Lee
Jonathan Kane	Derek Wilson
Dan Kavanagh	Julian Barnes
Paul Kavanagh	Lawrence Block
Susannah Kells	Bernard Cornwell
Patrick Kelly	Ted Allbeury
Richard Kelly	Richard Laymon
Lauren Kelly	Joyce Carol Oates
Paul Kemprecos	Clive Cussler
Samuel M Key	Charles de Lint
Gabriel King	Jane Johnson
Jancy King	Rosie Thomas
Will Kingdom	Phil Rickman
Laurell Kaye Klein	Laurell K Hamilton
Calvin M Knox	Robert Silverberg
Liliane Korb (with Laurence Lefèvre)	Claude Izner
Mary Ruth Kuczkir	Fern Michaels

L

Kurt Ladner	Nelson DeMille
P J & Traci Lambrecht	P J Tracy
Dinah Lampitt	Deryn Lake
Frank Lane	Harold Robbins
John Lange	Michael Crichton
Elizabeth Law	Maureen Peters
Carol Laymon	Richard Laymon
Clare Layton	Natasha Cooper
Peter Lear	Peter Lovesey
Laurence Lefèvre (with Liliane Korb)	Claude Izner
Annie Leith	Anita Burgh
Valery Leith	Tricia Sullivan
Terry Lennox	John Harvey
Isabelle Lewis	Kerry Greenwood
J R Lewis	Roy Lewis
Shannon Lewis	Morgan Llywelyn
Megan Lindholm	Robin Hobb
Gillian Linscott	Caro Peacock
Rosina Lippi	Sara Donati
J B Livingstone	Christian Jacq
Salvatore Lombino	Ed McBain
Thomas Luke	Graham Masterton
Steve Rune Lundin	Steven Erikson
Chang Lung	Robert Jordan

M

Eric Lustbader	Eric Van Lustbader
Peter MacAlan	Peter Tremayne
Wendell McCall	Ridley Pearson
Catriona McCloud	Catriona McPherson
John Macdonald	Ross Macdonald
Denis McEoin	Daniel Easterman
Kevin Christopher McFadden	Christopher Pike
Kinley MacGregor	Sherrilyn Kenyon
Kinn Hamilton McIntosh	Catherine Aird
Charlotte McKay	Charlotte Moore
Duncan MacNeil	Philip McCutchan
Mary A McNulty	Mary A Larkin
Michelle Maddox	Michelle Rowen
Susan Madison	Susan Moody
Thom Madley	Phil Rickman
James Mann	John Harvey
Catherine Marchant	Catherine Cookson
Ambrose Gran Raymond Marll	James Hadley Chase
Mac Marlow	Christopher Nicole
Hugh Marlowe	Jack Higgins
Willa Marsh	Marcia Willett
Allan Marshall	Donald Westlake
Richard Marsten	Ed McBain
Brad Matthews	Nelson DeMille
Robert Mawson	Robert Radcliffe
John Maxwell	Brian Freemantle
Susan Meadmore	Susan Sallis
Stephanie Merritt	S J Parris
Barbara Mertz	Elizabeth Peters
Barbara Michaels	Elizabeth Peters
T J Middleton	Tim Binding
Keith Miles	Edward Marston
Kenneth Millar	Ross Macdonald
K E Mills	Karen Miller
Lisa Miscione	Lisa Unger
Sue Mongredien	Lucy Diamond
Kristy & Kelly Montee	P J Parrish
Susan Moon	Elizabeth Moon
Rachel Moore	Rowena Summers
Philippa Morgan	Philip Gooden
Claire Morgan	Patricia Highsmith
Dick Morland	Reginald Hill
Christopher Mountjoy	Edward Marston
Glen Moy	James McGee
James Munro	E V Thompson
Simon Myles	Ken Follett

N

Grant Naylor	Rob Grant (with Doug Naylor)
Patricia Neal	Fannie Flagg
Tom Neale	Robert Ryan
Kris Nelscott	Kristine Kathryn Rusch
Leigh Nicols	Dean R Koontz

O

E G O'Brien	Arthur C Clarke

	Maureen O'Connor	Patricia Hall
	Barbara O'Hanlon (with Stephanie Berke)	Barbara & Stephanie Keating
	Regan O'Neal	Robert Jordan
	Jackson O'Reilly	Robert Jordan
	Regan O'Reilly	Robert Jordan
	Darren O'Shaughnessy	Darren Shan
	Margaret Ogden	Robin Hobb
	David Osborne	Robert Silverberg
P	Chloe Palovis	C M Palov
	Harry Patterson	Jack Higgins
	Kate Pepper	Katia Lief
	Will Peterson	Mark Billingham
	Keith Peterson	Andrew Klavan
	Rhona Petrie	Clare Curzon
	Elizabeth Pewsey	Elizabeth Edmondson
	Julie Cotler Pottinger	Julia Quinn
	Heather Graham Pozzessere	Heather Graham
	Diana & Michael Preston	Alex Rutherford
	Candice Proctor	C S Harris
	Mary Monica Pulver	Margaret Frazer
Q	Aileen Quigley	Aileen Armitage
	Emma Quincey	Linda Sole
	Martin Quinn	Martin Cruz Smith
	Simon Quinn	Martin Cruz Smith
R	Robert Radcliffe	Robert Mawson
	Hugh C Rae	Jessica Stirling
	Richard Raine	Colin Forbes
	Anne Rampling	Anne Rice
	Mark Ramsay	John Maddox Roberts
	Robert Randall	Robert Silverberg
	Ellen Randolph	Melanie Rawn
	Alis A Rasmussen	Kate Elliott
	René Brabazon Raymond	James Hadley Chase
	Joyce Reardon	Ridley Pearson
	Matthew Reid	Quintin Jardine
	James Oliver Rigney, Jr	Robert Jordan
	Harold Rubin	Harold Robbins
	Patrick Ruell	Reginald Hill
	Richard Patrick Russ	Patrick O'Brian
	Amanda Russell	Ellen Feldman
	Alan Rustage	Sally Spencer
	Jonathan Ryder	Robert Ludlum
	Rachel Ryn	Sandra Brown
S	Mrs Dora Saint	Miss Read
	Meg Sanders (with Annie Ashworth)	Annie Sanders
	Jean Saunders	Rowena Summers
	Andrew Saville	Andrew Taylor
	Raymond Sawkins	Colin Forbes
	Leila Schneps	Catherine Shaw
	Sandy Schofield	Kristine Kathryn Rusch
	Charlaine Harris Schulz	Charlaine Harris
	Ariana Scott	Elizabeth Adler

Alicia Scott	Lisa Gardner
Michael Sears (with Stanley Trollip)	Michael Stanley
Michael Shepherd	Robert Ludlum
James Sinclair	Mary Jane Staples
Ainslie Skinner	Paula Gosling
Rosamond Smith	Joyce Carol Oates
Jane Somers	Doris Lessing
Bill Spence	Jessica Blair
David Springfield	Roy Lewis
Reginald Staples	Mary Jane Staples
Ruth Stenstreem	Marian Babson
Reed Stephens	Stephen Donaldson
Susan Stevens	Mary Mackie
John Innes Mackintosh Stewart	Michael Innes
Ian Stuart	Alistair MacLean
Logan Swanson	Richard Matheson
John Tarrant	Clive Egleton
Doris Tayler	Doris Lessing
Bernard Taylor	Jess Foley
John Robert Taylor	Andrew Taylor
David Thomas	Tom Cain
Edwin Thomas	Tom Harper
Sean Thomas	Tom Knox
Maria Thomson (with Linda Watson-Brown)	Grace Monroe
Nye Tredgold	Nigel Tranter
Stanley Trollip (with Michael Sears)	Michael Stanley
James Tucker	Bill James
Judy Turner	Katie Flynn; Judith Saxton
N H Turtletaub	Harry Turtledove
Charles Underhill	Reginald Hill
Caroline Upcher	Hope McIntyre
Mary Bly Vettori	Eloisa James
Elizabeth Villars	Ellen Feldman
Martyn and Linda Waites	Tania Carver
Peter Norman Walker	Nicholas Rhea
Brenda Warren	Kitty Neale
Diana Jean Gabaldon Watkins	Diana Gabaldon
Linda Watson-Brown (with Maria Thomson)	Grace Monroe
Linda Webb	Linda Nagata
Nicola West	Lilian Harry
Owen West	Dean R Koontz
Mary Westmacott	Agatha Christie
Olive Whaley	Elizabeth Jeffrey
Charles Whiting	Duncan Harding
Elly Wilder	J D Robb
Tony Williams	Mark Timlin
Charles Willis	Arthur C Clarke
Janice Meredith Wilson	Jan Karon
T R Wilson	Jude Morgan
Jack Winchester	Brian Freemantle
Tom Winship	John Connor
Francis E Wintle	Edward Rutherfurd

T

U
V
W

Chloe Anthony Wofford	Toni Morrison
Aaron Wolfe	Dean R Koontz
Jane Wolstenholme	Jane Costello
Dave Wolverton	David Farland
Bridget Wood	Sarah Rayne
Emma Woodhouse	Cynthia Harrod-Eagles
James Garcia Woods	Sally Spencer
Daphne Wright	Natasha Cooper
Melinda Wright	Penny Jordan
Xinran Xve	Xinran
Jack Yeovil	Kim Newman
Andrew York	Christopher Nicole
Katherine Yorke	Nicola Thorne

Authors listed by Genre

It is almost impossible to identify accurately individual authors with one particular section of genre fiction; often there is no 'cut-off' point between, for instance, **War** and **Adventure**; between **Fantasy**, **Science Fiction** and **Horror**; or between **Historical** and **Saga**. So, although in the main sequence this Guide indicates under the names of each author the genre in which they usually write, and these names are repeated again in the lists that follow, it is suggested that readers also refer to linking genres — and in particular to the main list — to discover new names that could become firm favourites.

Some categories — **Adventure/Thriller**, **Crime**, **Fantasy**, **Science Fiction**, **Sea Stories** and **War** — have been sub-divided to help readers find writers they will enjoy. Do remember that some authors use a different name when they write in another genre, while others will produce an occasional book which is quite different in character to their usual style. Always look at the book jacket and the introduction before you borrow or purchase.

Adventure/Thriller

Stories with fast-moving plots, exotic settings, usually larger-than-life main characters, and with the action full of thrilling and daring feats. Many of these authors specialised in stories set in the period of the cold war but, increasingly, now they have a political, financial, industrial espionage or terrorist background.

Paul Adam
Will Adams
Ted Allbeury
Geoffrey Archer
Jeffrey Archer
Campbell Armstrong
David Baldacci
Alex Barclay
Linwood Barclay
Brett Battles
James Becker
Ted Bell
Ronan Bennett
Alex Berenson
Steve Berry
Tim Binding
Sean Black
Anna Blundy
Sam Bourne
Tom Bradby
Dale Brown
Dan Brown
Nick Brownlee
Mary Burton

Michael Byrnes
Tom Cain
Stella Cameron
Stephen J Cannell
Lorenzo Carcaterra
John Case
Lee Child
Lincoln Child
Paul Christopher
Tom Clancy
Frank Coates
Simon Conway
Stephen Coonts
Glenn Cooper
Michael Cordy
Jack Coughlin
Bryce Courtenay
Harold Coyle
Charles Cumming
Clive Cussler
Len Deighton
Nelson DeMille
Eric Jerome Dickey
Alex Dryden

Brendan Dubois
Daniel Easterman
Tom Egeland
Clive Egleton
Barry Eisler
David Ellis
Gavin Esler
Duncan Falconer
Dan Fesperman
Joseph Finder
Ian Fleming
Vince Flynn
James Follett
Ken Follett
Colin Forbes
Frederick Forsyth
Tom Franklin
Brian Freemantle
Scott Frost
Alexander Fullerton
Alan Furst
Lisa Gardner
David Gibbins
Matthew Glass

Alan Glynn
Robert Goddard
Tom Grace
Sara Gran
Jean-Christophe Grangé
Thomas Greanias
Andrew Gross
Tom Harper
Robert Harris
Colin Harrison
Stuart Harrison
Jack Harvey
John Twelve Hawks
Richard Herman
Jack Higgins
Matt Hilton
Chuck Hogan
Stephen Hunter
Graham Hurley
Gregg Hurwitz
David Ignatius
Greg Iles
Alan Judd
Joseph Kanon
John Katzenbach
Judith Kelman
Douglas Kennedy
Gordon Kent
Philip Kerr
Gene Kerrigan
Michael Kimball
Tom Knox
Dean R Koontz
Chris Kuzneski
Mike Lawson
John Le Carré
Stephen Leather
Robert Littell
Sam Llewellyn
Robert Ludlum
Amin Maalouf
Andy McDermott
Andrew McGahan
Grant McKenzie
Alistair MacLean
Scott Mariani
Michael Marshall
P D Martin

Glenn Meade
Kyle Mills
G J Moffat
Rick Mofina
Aly Monroe
Grace Monroe
Richard Montanari
Chris Mooney
David Morrell
Stuart Neville
Christopher Nicole
Hilary Norman
C M Palov
James Pattinson
Jason Pinter
Henry Porter
Douglas Preston
Julian Rathbone
Matthew Reilly
Stella Rimington
James Rollins
Andrew Rosenheim
Chris Ryan
Robert Ryan
Marcus Sakey
Julian Jay Savarin
Alex Scarrow
Justin Scott
E V Seymour
Gerald Seymour
Sidney Sheldon
Nevil Shute
Daniel Silva
Paullina Simons
Tom Rob Smith
Wilbur Smith
Oien Steinhauer
Jon Stock
Nick Stone
Paul Sussman
Marcel Theroux
Craig Thomas
Brad Thor
James Twining
Paul Watkins
Lee Weeks
Tim Willocks

Edward Wilson
Robert Wilson
Stuart Woods
Carlos Ruiz Zafón

Historical
Stephen Baxter
Armand Cabasson
David Downing
Raymond Khoury
Arturo Pérez-Reverte

Legal/financial
Jeff Abbott
Harry Bingham
John Burdett
Alafair Burke
Linda Davies
Ava McCarthy
Brad Meltzer
Michael Ridpath

Medical
Robin Cook
Michael Palmer

PI
Gordon Ferris

Police work - Japan
Keigo Higashino

Psychological
Mary Higgins Clark
Vena Cork
Gillian Flynn
Clare Francis
Nicci French
Katy Gardner
Lesley Glaister
Lucretia Grindle
Karen Harper
Thomas Harris
Sam Hayes
Joanna Hines
Andrew Klavan
Javier Marias
Julie Parsons
Thomas Perry
John Rector
Christina Schwarz
Gillian White

Aga Saga

A phrase that came into being in the early 1990s, the Aga Sagas are novels based upon the middle-class surroundings of the type of person who typically owns an Aga cooker, but who is not immune to the emotional dilemmas that can confront all classes of society.

Trisha Ashley
Judy Astley
Maeve Binchy
Charlotte Bingham
Amanda Brookfield
Elizabeth Buchan
Sarah Challis
Clare Chambers
Lucy Clare
Victoria Clayton
Marika Cobbold
Amanda Craig

Domenica de Rosa
Barbara Delinsky
Annabel Dilke
Rose Doyle
Jessica Duchen
Elizabeth Edmondson
Patricia Fawcett
Kate Fenton
Patricia Gaffney
Adèle Geras
Sarah Harrison
Ann Hood

Rachel Hore
Eve Houston
Sandra Howard
Sarah Jackman
Prue Leith
Sara MacDonald
Charlotte Moore
Robin Pilcher
Rosamunde Pilcher
Kate Saunders
Joanna Trollope
Madeleine Wickham

Chick Lit

Stories written by young women for other young women, usually with a central plot of boyfriend mishaps and the problems of staying in shape.

Jessica Adams
Katie Agnew
Cecelia Ahern
Catherine Alliott
Sherry Ashworth
Louise Bagshawe
Zoë Barnes
Emily Barr
Nina Bell
Meg Cabot
Colette Caddle
Rebecca Campbell
Louise Candlish
Claudia Carroll
Lucy Cavendish
Holly Chamberlin
Elise Chidley
Julie Cohen
Rowan Coleman
Jenny Colgan
Marita Conlon-McKenna
Victoria Connelly
Jane Costello
Megan Crane
Lucy Dawson
Lucy Diamond

Miranda Dickinson
Lucy Dillon
Clare Dowling
Sarah Duncan
Anne Dunlop
Imogen Edwards-Jones
Harriet Evans
Jane Fallon
Katie Fforde
Helen Fielding
Ciara Geraghty
Fiona Gibson
Emily Giffin
Jane Green
Linda Green
Niamh Greene
Sophie Hannah
Maeve Haran
Kate Harrison
Louise Harwood
Donna Hay
Veronica Henry
Julie Highmore
Melissa Hill
Julia Holden
Wendy Holden

Debby Holt
Lisa Jewell
Milly Johnson
Belinda Jones
Christina Jones
Lindsey Kelk
Cathy Kelly
Linda Kelsey
Marian Keyes
Sophie Kinsella
India Knight
Dorothy Koomson
Kate Lawson
Kathy Lette
Susan Lewis
Julia Llewellyn
Josie Lloyd & Emlyn Rees
Kate Long
Shari Low
Monica McInerney
Serena Mackesy
Pauline McLynn
Debbie Macomber
Anna McPartlin
Holly McQueen
Chris Manby

Jill Mansell
Sue Margolis
Sarah Mason
Carole Matthews
Anna Maxted
Sarah May
Jane Moore
Sinead Moriarty
Clare Naylor
Fiona Neill
Elizabeth Noble
Freya North
Sheila Norton
Sheila O'Flanagan
Liza Palmer
Imogen Parker

Adele Parks
Louise Patten
Alice Peterson
Alexandra Potter
Morag Prunty
Karen Quinn
Melanie Rose
Victoria Routledge
Annie Sanders
Patricia Scanlan
Kirsty Scott
Kathleen Gilles Seidel
Amy Silver
Robyn Sisman
Tess Stimson
Bernadette Strachan

Kathleen Tessaro
Kate Thompson
Rosy Thornton
Gemma Townley
Sarah Tucker
Jane Elizabeth Varley
Fiona Walker
Daisy Waugh
Jennifer Weiner
Arabella Weir
Lauren Weisberger
Sue Welfare
Julia Williams
Polly Williams
Isabel Wolff
Cathy Woodman

Crime

This type of novel is usually characterised by the clues which gradually lead the reader to the final solution, often within an atmosphere of rising tension or danger. Although there are basically two types of detective - the private investigator **(PI)** and the official policeman - there are an increasing number of subgenres within these two broad headings. The style of crime writing has been divided, in the majority of cases, into separate headings, and under each is shown the list of authors who usually, but not always, write in that vein.

James Benn
Zoë Ferraris

George Dawes Green
Marek Krajewski

Deon Meyer

Amateur sleuth

Gilbert Adair
Suzanne Arruda
Marian Babson
Robert G Barrett
Carrie Bebris
C J Box
Alan Bradley
Gyles Brandreth
Simon Brett
William Brodrick
Frances Brody
James Brownley
Jan Burke
Caroline Carver
Kate Charles
Agatha Christie
Harlan Coben
Lesley Cookman
Natasha Cooper

Mark de Castrique
Jo Dereske
Martin Edwards
Ruth Dudley Edwards
Joanne Fluke
Dick Francis
John Francome
Frances Fyfield
Jonathan Gash
Mark Gatiss
Dolores Gordon-Smith
Andrew M Greeley
Gerald Hammond
Veronica Heley
Lauren Henderson
Joyce Holms
Lis Howell
Claude Izner
Alison Joseph

Jim Kelly
Jonathon King
Stieg Larsson
Roy Lewis
Marianne MacDonald
Hope McIntyre
Catriona McPherson
Shane Maloney
Liza Marklund
Margaret Maron
Rose Melikan
Denise Mina
Susan Moody
Fiona Mountain
Iain Pears
Ann Purser
R T Raichev
Matt Rees
Mike Ripley

Crime

Amateur Sleuth (continued)

Imogen Robertson
Betty Rowlands
Ian Sansom
Dorothy L Sayers
Zoë Sharp
Catherine Shaw

Yrsa Sigurdardottir
Anna Smith
Lyndon Stacey
Veronica Stallwood
Rebecca Tope

M J Trow
Nicola Upson
Nury Vittachi
Jill Paton Walsh
Don Winslow

Forensic

Lin Anderson
Jefferson Bass
Simon Beckett
Beverly Connor
Patricia D Cornwell

Colin Cotterill
Jeffery Deaver
Kathryn Fox
Iris Johansen

Keith McCarthy
Nigel McCrery
Kathy Reichs
Karin Slaughter

Hardboiled

Megan Abbott
Jake Arnott
Adam Baron
Helen Black
Lawrence Block
Gordon Brown
Ken Bruen
James Lee Burke
Kimberley Chambers
James Hadley Chase
Martina Cole
Alan Dunn
James Ellroy
Robert Ferrigno

G M Ford
Heather Graham
Allan Guthrie
June Hampson
Mandasue Heller
Bill James
Jessie Keane
Simon Kernick
Roberta Kray
Elmore Leonard
Peter Leonard
David Levien
Kevin Lewis

Adrian McKinty
Walter Mosley
David Peace
George P Pelecanos
Sheila Quigley
Caro Ramsay
Craig Russell
Denise Ryan
James Sallis
Richard Stark
Boston Teran
Jim Thompson
Louise Welsh

Historical

Louis Bayard
Paul Doherty
Susanna Gregory
Alanna Knight
Edward Marston
Amy Myers
Orhan Pamuk
Matthew Pearl
Lindsey Davis Ancient
R S Downie Ancient
Nick Drake Ancient
Mary Reed and Eric Mayer
                    Ancient
John Maddox Roberts Ancient
Rosemary Rowe Ancient
Steven Saylor Ancient
Marilyn Todd Ancient
David Wishart Ancient
Ian Morson C13th

Michael Pearce C13th
Cassandra Clark C14th
Giulio Leoni C14th
Patricia Finney C16th
Philip Gooden C16th
Cora Harrison C16th
Simon Levack C16th
Shirley McKay C16th
S J Parris C16th
C J Sansom C16th
Frank Tallis C16th
Charles Todd C16th
Peter Tonkin C16th
Fidelis Morgan C17th
Deryn Lake C18th
David Liss C18th
Jean François Parot C18th
Derek Wilson C18th
C S Harris C18th/C19th

Jed Rubenfeld C18th/C19th
Boris Akunin C19th
David Ashton C19th
Jason Goodwin C19th
Clio Gray C19th
Michael Gregorio C19th
John Harwood C19th
Lee Jackson C19th
Maureen Jennings C19th
Joan Lock C19th
Peter Lovesey C19th
James McCreet C19th
James McGee C19th
Andrew Martin C19th
Robin Paige C19th
Caro Peacock C19th
Andrew Pepper C19th
Deanna Raybourn C19th
Norman Russell C19th

Historical (continued)

Brian Thompson C19th
Anne Perry C19th/C20th
Kenneth Cameron C20th
Barbara Cleverly C20th
David Dickinson C20th
Stephen Done C20th
Carola Dunn C20th
Stuart M Kaminsky C20th

Laurie R King C20th
P F Chisholm Medieval
Alys Clare Medieval
Ariana Franklin Medieval
Margaret Frazer Medieval
Michael Jecks Medieval
Bernard Knight Medieval

Pat McIntosh Medieval
The Medieval Murderers
Medieval
Ellis Peters Medieval
Candace Robb Medieval
Kate Sedley Medieval
Peter Tremayne Medieval

Historical & Modern

Elizabeth Peters

Humour

Linwood Barclay
Bateman
Christopher Brookmyre
Nancy Cohen
Tim Dorsey
Janet Evanovich
Jasper Fforde

Christopher Fowler
Kinky Friedman
Sparkle Hayter
Carl Hiaasen
Suzette Hill
Andrey Kurkov
Joe R Lansdale

Douglas Lindsay
Pauline McLynn
Malcolm Pryce
Sarah Strohmeyer
L C Tyler
Donald Westlake

Legal/financial

William Bernhardt
Julie Compton
Linda Fairstein
Mark Gimenez
James Grippando
John Grisham
M R Hall

John Hart
Jilliane Hoffman
Craig Holden
John T Lescroart
Phillip Margolin
Steve Martini
Perri O'Shaughnessy

Richard North Patterson
Christopher Reich
Nancy Taylor Rosenberg
Lisa Scottoline
Robert K Tanenbaum
Scott Turow

Medical

Tess Gerritsen

Ken McClure

PI

Kate Atkinson
Ray Banks
Linda Barnes
Cara Black
Tony Black
Lindy Cameron
Raymond Chandler
Carol Higgins Clark
Peter Corris
Robert Crais
James Crumley
Stephen Donaldson
Arthur Conan Doyle
Stella Duffy
Robert Edric
Loren D Estleman

Liz Evans
Meg Gardiner
Juan Gómez-Jurado
Sue Grafton
Kerry Greenwood
Raymond Haigh
James W Hall
Steve Hamilton
Dashiell Hammett
Michael Harvey
Lynne Heitman
Declan Hughes
Paul Johnston
Laura Lippman
Gabrielle Lord
Alexander McCall Smith

Ken McCoy
Ross Macdonald
Marcia Muller
Reggie Nadelson
Sara Paretsky
Robert B Parker
Bernhard Schlink
John Shannon
Dana Stabenow
Cath Staincliffe
Peter Temple
Ronald Tierney
Mark Timlin
Eric Van Lustbader
Jacqueline Winspear
Edward Wright

Genre

Genre

Police work - UK

Catherine Aird
Rennie Airth
David Armstrong
Vivien Armstrong
Tom Bale
Jo Bannister
Robert Barnard
M C Beaton
Mark Billingham
Alison Bruce
W J Burley
Karen Campbell
Paul Charles
Ann Cleeves
Chris Collett
John Connor
Elizabeth Corley
Adam Creed
Deborah Crombie
Clare Curzon
Judith Cutler
Colin Dexter
Margaret Duffy
Marjorie Eccles
Kate Ellis
Geraldine Evans

Elena Forbes
Anthea Fraser
Gillian Galbraith
Elizabeth George
Caroline Graham
Ann Granger
Alex Gray
J M Gregson
Elly Griffiths
Martha Grimes
Patricia Hall
Cynthia Harrod-Eagles
John Harvey
Reginald Hill
Susan Hill
Lesley Horton
Graham Hurley
Michael Innes
Graham Ison
P D James
Peter James
Quintin Jardine
H R F Keating
Susan B Kelly
John Lawton

Frederic Lindsay
Peter Lovesey
Stuart MacBride
Iain McDowall
Brian McGilloway
Barry Maitland
Priscilla Masters
Nick Oldham
Charlie Owen
Stuart Pawson
Mark Pearson
Ian Rankin
Ruth Rendell
Nicholas Rhea
Peter Robinson
Pauline Rowson
Roger Silverwood
Sally Spencer
Andrew Taylor
Aline Templeton
Leslie Thomas
June Thomson
Peter Turnbull
Neil White
R D Wingfield

Police work - US

Alafair Burke
Chelsea Cain
Chris Carter
Linda Castillo
Jodi Compton
Michael Connelly
Robert Ellis
Brian Freeman
Paula Gosling
W E B Griffin
Donald Harstad
Lynn Hightower
Tony Hillerman

Ryan David Jahn
J A Jance
Faye Kellerman
Jesse Kellerman
Jonathan Kellerman
J A Kerley
Lynda La Plante
William Landay
Dennis Lehane
Katia Lief
Ed McBain
Colleen McCullough
Michael McGarrity

Michael Malone
Archer Mayor
Carol O'Connell
Jefferson Parker
P J Parrish
Ridley Pearson
J D Robb
John Sandford
Theresa Schwegel
Jess Walter
Joseph Wambaugh
Darryl Wimberley

Police work - other foreign

Shamini Flint Asia
Garry Disher Australia
Claire McNab Australia
Giles Blunt Canada
Louise Penny Canada
Peter May China

Qiu Xiaolong China
José Latour Cuba
Leonardo Padura Cuba
Jussi Adler-Olsen Denmark
Adrian Magson Europe
Matti Joensuu Finland

Jan Costin Wagner Finland
Xavier-Marie Bonnot France
Pierre Magnan France
Dominique Manotti France
Martin O'Brien France
Georges Simenon France

Police work - other foreign (continued)

Fred Vargas France
Martin Walker France
Jeffrey Siger Greece
Anne Zouroudi Greece
Arnaldur Indridason Iceland
Tarquin Hall India
Benjamin Black Ireland
Erin Hart Ireland
Andrew Nugent Ireland
Andrea Camilleri Italy
Michael Dibdin Italy
Conor Fitzgerald Italy
Michele Giuttari Italy
David Hewson Italy
Donna Leon Italy

Carlo Lucarelli Italy
Magdalen Nabb Italy
Michael Walters Mongolia
Janwillem van de Wetering
Netherlands
Karin Fossum Norway
Anne Holt Norway
Jo Nesbo Norway
Sam Eastland Russia
R N Morris Russia
Martin Cruz Smith Russia
Richard Kunzmann South
Africa
Malla Nunn South Africa
Michael Stanley South Africa

Roderic Jeffries Spain
Ake Edwardson Sweden
Kjell Eriksson Sweden
Mari Jungstedt Sweden
Camilla Läckberg Sweden
Åsa Larsson Sweden
Henning Mankell Sweden
Häkan Nesser Sweden
Leif G W Persson Sweden
Roslund and Hellström
Sweden
Maj Sjöwall & Per Wahlöö
Sweden
Barbara Nadel Turkey

Psychological

Jane Adams
Karin Alvtegen
Belinda Bauer
S J Bolton
Stephen Booth
Gianrico Carofiglio
Tania Carver
Jane Casey
John Connolly
Thomas H Cook
F G Cottam
Sarah Diamond
R J Ellory
Joy Fielding
Helen Fitzgerald
Tana French
Sophie Hannah
Mo Hayder
Daniel Hecht
Frances Hegarty

Patricia Highsmith
Jane Hill
Tami Hoag
Doug Johnstone
Susanna Jones
Morag Joss
Alex Kava
David Lawrence
Simon Lelic
Jeff Lindsay
Sharyn McCrumb
Val McDermid
Cody McFadyen
Elizabeth McGregor
John Macken
Guillermo Martinez
Steve Mosby
Margaret Murphy
James Patterson

Andrew Pyper
Sarah Rayne
Patrick Redmond
Michael Robotham
Karen Rose
Manda Scott
Chris Simms
Carol Smith
Sally Spedding
Erica Spindler
Boris Starling
Johan Theorin
P J Tracy
Lisa Unger
Barbara Vine
Minette Walters
Stephen White
Laura Wilson
Margaret Yorke

Romantic suspense

Elizabeth Adler
Sam Baker
Beverly Barton
Allison Brennan
Sandra Brown

Heather Graham
Linda Howard
Lisa Jackson
Christobel Kent
Jennifer McMahon

Luanne Rice
Karen Robards
Nora Roberts
Madge Swindells

Fantasy

Fantasy novels – as distinct from Science Fiction – deal with the impossible, being based on magic or the supernatural. They follow no scientific 'rules', only the whim of the author. While there are many sub-divisions in the world of Fantasy, we have used six sub-genres to help readers find the kind of book they most enjoy: **Contemporary** – the intrusion of the fantastic into modern life; **Dark** – Fantasy which incorporates a sense of horror; **Epic** – books in which heroes and heroines wage epic combat with forces of evil; **Myth** – authors who place their stories in worlds of myth, saga and legend; **Humour** – not all fantasy is dark, and these authors write light and humorous stories, often including elements of familiar folk tales; **Literary** – the characters of fiction and literature in general take on reality in a fantasy world rich in literary allusion.

Susanna Clarke
China Miéville

Philip Pullman
Scarlett Thomas

Kim Wilkins

Contemporary
Mark Chadbourn
Charles de Lint

Neil Gaiman
Audrey Niffenegger

Jack O'Connell
Tim Powers

Dark
Jonathan Carroll
Storm Constantine

Simon Green
Graham Joyce

Tim Lebbon
Tanith Lee

Epic
Joe Abercrombie
James Barclay
Marion Zimmer Bradley
Chaz Brenchley
Terry Brooks
Trudi Canavan
Jacqueline Carey
Isobelle Carmody
Cinda Williams Chima
Eoin Colfer
Louise Cooper
Stephen Deas
Stephen Donaldson
Sara Douglass
David Eddings
Kate Elliott
Steven Erikson
Ian C Esslemont
Chris Evans
Jennifer Fallon
David Farland
Raymond E Feist

Pamela Freeman
C S Friedman
Maggie Furey
David Gemmell
Mary Gentle
Terry Goodkind
Robin Hobb
Paul Hoffman
Ian Irvine
Robert Jordan
Guy Gavriel Kay
Paul Kearney
Greg Keyes
Russell Kirkpatrick
Mercedes Lackey
Glenda Larke
Ursula K Le Guin
Scott Lynch
Fiona McIntosh
Juliet E McKenna
John Marco
George R R Martin

Karen Miller
L E Modesitt Jr
Elizabeth Moon
Michael Moorcock
Robert Newcomb
Naomi Novik
Melanie Rawn
Mickey Zucker Reichert
Andy Remic
Patrick Rothfuss
J K Rowling
Brian Ruckley
R A Salvatore
Brandon Sanderson
Adrian Tchaikovsky
J R R Tolkien
Harry Turtledove
Freda Warrington
Brent Weeks
Margaret Weis
Tad Williams
Janny Wurts

Humour
Craig Shaw Gardner
Tom Holt
Jonathan L Howard

Walter Moers
Christopher Moore
Terry Pratchett

Andy Secombe
Chris Wooding

Literary
Gene Wolfe

Myth

C J Cherryh	Katharine Kerr	Caiseal Mor
Cecilia Dart-Thornton	Stephen R Lawhead	Garth Nix
Barbara Hambly	Gregory Maguire	Jack Vance
Stephen Hunt	Juliet Marillier	Sarah Zettel

Glitz and Glamour

This genre features the modern world of big business and entertainment, with generous helpings of sex, violence and avarice.

Tilly Bagshawe	Olivia Darling	Fiona O'Brien
Sally Beauman	Jude Deveraux	Katie Price
Celia Brayfield	Eileen Goudge	Harold Robbins
Candace Bushnell	Judith Gould	Karen Swan
Jo Carnegie	Jayne Ann Krentz	Lulu Taylor
Rebecca Chance	Lesley Lokko	Penny Vincenzi
Jackie Collins	Fern Michaels	Sasha Wagstaff
Jilly Cooper		

Historical

Another very popular category, where fictional characters are set against an actual historical perspective, with close and realistic links between fiction and fact. Some are based on real people and events, while others are purely imaginary.

Thalassa Ali	James Fleming	Jeanne Kalogridis
Jean M Auel	Ken Follett	Daniel Kehlmann
Vanora Bennett	Kate Furnivall	Matthew Kneale
John Boyne	Diana Gabaldon	Morgan Llywelyn
Geraldine Brooks	Elizabeth Garner	Michelle Lovric
Marion Chesney	Kathleen O'Neal Gear	Jack Ludlow
Tracy Chevalier	Margaret George	Colleen McCullough
Gloria Cook	Amitav Ghosh	Sophia McDougall
Bernard Cornwell	Melanie Gifford	Katharine McMahon
Elizabeth Darrell	C W Gortner	Karen Maitland
Martin Davies	Posie Graeme-Evans	Valerio Massimo Manfredi
Rebecca Dean	Winston Graham	Robin Maxwell
Sara Donati	Philippa Gregory	Fenella-Jane Miller
Jennifer Donnelly	Georgina Harding	Anchee Min
Sarah Dunant	Jane Harris	Michelle Moran
Dorothy Dunnett	Cynthia Harrod-Eagles	Jude Morgan
Arabella Edge	Caroline Harvey	Kate Mosse
Robert Edric	Anne Herries	Fiona Mountain
Margaret Elphinstone	Katie Hickman	Thomas Mullen
Barbara Erskine	Joanna Hines	Diana Norman
Barbara Ewing	C C Humphreys	Edith Pargeter
Ildefonso Falcones	James H Jackson	Margaret Pemberton
Marina Fiorato	Jane Johnson	Sharon Penman

Historical (continued)

Maureen Peters
Jean Plaidy
Steven Pressfield
Amanda Quick
Julia Quinn
Julian Rathbone
James Robertson
James Runcie
Edward Rutherfurd
Simon Scarrow
Manda Scott
Tim Severin
Patricia Shaw
Sara Sheridan
Rebecca Stott
Reay Tannahill
E V Thompson
Betsy Tobin
Nigel Tranter
Kate Tremayne
Barry Unsworth
Susan Vreeland
Peter Watt

Jenny White
Michael White
Adam Williams
Lauren Willig
James Wilson
Barbara Wood
Sam Barone Ancient
A L Berridge Ancient
Richard Blake Ancient
Christian Cameron Ancient
Robert Harris Ancient
Conn Iggulden Ancient
Glyn Iliffe Ancient
Douglas Jackson Ancient
Christian Jacq Ancient
Ben Kane Ancient
Robert Low Ancient
Allan Massie Ancient
William Napier Ancient
Scott Oden Ancient
Anthony Riches Ancient
Harry Sidebottom Ancient

Wilbur Smith Ancient
Paul Waters Ancient
Jules Watson Ancient
M K Hume C7th
Giles Kristian C8-10th
Simon Acland C11th
Jack Whyte C12th
Angus Donald C13th
Rory Clements C16th
Suzannah Dunn C16th
Alex Rutherford C16th
Alison Weir C16th
Christie Dickason C17th
William Dietrich C18th
Eloisa James C18th
Clare Clark C18th & 19th
Emma Darwin C18th & 19th
Georgette Heyer C19th
Stephanie Laurens C19th
Elizabeth Chadwick Medieval
Tom Harper Medieval
Robyn Young Medieval

Historical Romance

These novels have a history-dependent plot, with the authors frequently setting their stories during periods of change and general unrest. Settings are usually based in historical reality while characters may be real or imaginary. Romance plays a strong role in the story line.

Marion Chesney
Elizabeth Darrell
Jane Johnson
Fenella-Jane Miller

Amanda Quick
Julia Quinn
Kate Tremayne
Lauren Willig

Eloisa James C18th
Georgette Heyer C19th
Stephanie Laurens C19th

Horror

This section includes authors who frequently write suspense and horror, where the storyline involves pursuit and eventual escape – often from the supernatural, demonic or the occult.

Clive Barker
Poppy Z Brite
Ramsey Campbell
Simon Clark
Christopher Fowler
James Herbert
Tanya Huff
Shaun Hutson
Peter James
Stephen King

Michael Koryta
Richard Laymon
John Ajvide Lindqvist
Bentley Little
Brian Lumley
Robert McCammon
Paul Magrs
David Martin
Graham Masterton

Richard Matheson
David Moody
Adam Nevill
Christopher Pike
Scott Sigler
Dan Simmons
Peter Straub
Whitley Strieber
Koji Suzuki

Genre

A select group of authors whose novels are mainly written to amuse.

Alan Bennett
Mavis Cheek
Jonathan Coe
Joseph Connolly
Roddy Doyle
Michael Frayn
Stephen Fry
Charles Higson
Tom Holt

Garrison Keillor
Marina Lewycka
Laura Marney
Magnus Mills
John Mortimer
David Nobbs
Barry Pilton
Lily Prior
Ann B Ross

Alexei Sayle
Tom Sharpe
Alan Titchmarsh
Sue Townsend
Lynne Truss
Keith Waterhouse
Mark Watson
P G Wodehouse

Lad Lit

Nick Hornby and Tony Parsons began the male equivalent to Chick Lit. Written about men in the same age range who have trouble expressing their emotions.

Matt Beaumont
Matt Dunn

Mike Gayle
Nick Hornby

Tony Parsons
Matt Thorne

Humour

James Delingpole

John O'Farrell

Mature Chick Lit

The books portray a world where slightly older women juggle the demands of career and relationships in new and non-traditional ways, and the stories have an emphasis on friendship but not necessarily on romance.

Catherine Alliott
Emily Barr
Nina Bell
Louise Candlish
Lucy Cavendish
Holly Chamberlin
Rowan Coleman
Marita Conlon-McKenna
Sarah Duncan
Jane Fallon
Katie Fforde
Fiona Gibson
Jane Green
Maeve Haran
Kate Harrison
Veronica Henry
Julie Highmore
Julia Holden
Wendy Holden
Debby Holt

Lisa Jewell
Cathy Kelly
Linda Kelsey
Marian Keyes
India Knight
Dorothy Koomson
Kate Lawson
Susan Lewis
Julia Llewellyn
Monica McInerney
Pauline McLynn
Debbie Macomber
Jill Mansell
Carole Matthews
Sarah May
Jane Moore
Sinead Moriarty
Fiona Neill
Elizabeth Noble
Imogen Parker

Adele Parks
Louise Patten
Alice Peterson
Karen Quinn
Victoria Routledge
Annie Sanders
Patricia Scanlan
Kirsty Scott
Kathleen Gilles Seidel
Robyn Sisman
Kate Thompson
Sarah Tucker
Jane Elizabeth Varley
Arabella Weir
Sue Welfare
Julia Williams
Polly Williams
Isabel Wolff
Cathy Woodman

Paranormal

Almost anything paranormal or unexplained by natural causes is included in this genre, especially vampires and werewolves. Settings can be either historical or contemporary and the beings can be the embodiment of either good and evil.

Kelley Armstrong	Mary Janice Davidson	Richelle Mead
Keri Arthur	Christine Feehan	Stephenie Meyer
Patricia Briggs	Laurell K Hamilton	Kim Newman
Jim Butcher	Lori Handeland	Anne Rice
Rachel Caine	Charlaine Harris	Phil Rickman
Mike Carey	Kim Harrison	Michelle Rowen
P C & Kristin Cast	Barb & J C Hendee	Lilith Saintcrow
Karen Chance	Sherrilyn Kenyon	Darren Shan
Cassandra Clare	Katie MacAlister	Susan Sizemore
Justin Cronin	Suzanne McLeod	J R Ward

Saga

A popular genre, frequently set against an historical background, telling the story of two or more generations of a family, with the plot often revolving around the purchase of property or the development of a family business.

Lyn Andrews	Dilly Court	Elizabeth Gill
Diana Appleyard	Josephine Cox	Rosie Goodwin
Aileen Armitage	Amanda Craig	Iris Gower
Trisha Ashley	Maggie Craig	Pip Granger
Judy Astley	Tania Crosse	Hilary Green
Anne Baker	Glenice Crossland	Annie Groves
Tessa Barclay	Janet Dailey	Ruth Hamilton
Lily Baxter	Elizabeth Daish	Beverley Harper
Anne Bennett	Doris Davidson	Rosie Harris
Maeve Binchy	Margaret Thomson Davis	Sarah Harrison
Charlotte Bingham	Domenica de Rosa	Lilian Harry
Emma Blair	Frank Delaney	Meg Henderson
Jessica Blair	Barbara Delinsky	Ann Hood
Barbara Taylor Bradford	Margaret Dickinson	Evelyn Hood
Rita Bradshaw	Annabel Dilke	Rachel Hore
Amanda Brookfield	Anne Doughty	Una Horne
Benita Brown	Rose Doyle	Eve Houston
Julia Bryant	Jessica Duchen	Audrey Howard
Elizabeth Buchan	Elizabeth Edmondson	Sandra Howard
Anita Burgh	Elizabeth Elgin	Harriet Hudson
Helen Cannam	Pamela Evans	Meg Hutchinson
Amelia Carr	Patricia Fawcett	Sara Hylton
Sarah Challis	Kate Fenton	Sarah Jackman
Clare Chambers	Leah Fleming	Anna Jacobs
Lucy Clare	Katie Flynn	Margaret James
Victoria Clayton	Jess Foley	Elizabeth Jeffrey
Marika Cobbold	June Francis	Jeannie Johnson
Catrin Collier	Jean Fullerton	Joan Jonker
Alexandra Connor	Patricia Gaffney	Penny Jordan
Catherine Cookson	Adèle Geras	Margaret Kaine

Sheelagh Kelly
Catherine King
Beryl Kingston
Gwen Kirkwood
Mary A Larkin
Maureen Lee
Prue Leith
Judith Lennox
Freda Lightfoot
Elizabeth Lord
Ken McCoy
Sara MacDonald
Betty McInnes
Mary Mackie
Tamara McKinley
Gwen Madoc
Beryl Matthews
Margaret Mayhew
Connie Monk
Charlotte Moore
Di Morrissey
Elizabeth Murphy
Annie Murray
Kitty Neale
Sheila Newberry
Judy Nunn
Geraldine O'Neill

Gilda O'Neill
Joan O'Neill
Pamela Oldfield
Sharon Owens
Lynda Page
Lesley Pearse
Victor Pemberton
Robin Pilcher
Rosamunde Pilcher
Belva Plain
D M Purcell
Alexandra Raife
Eileen Ramsay
Miss Read
Elvi Rhodes
Carol Rivers
Denise Robertson
Wendy Robertson
Liz Ryan
Susan Sallis
Kate Saunders
Judith Saxton
Rebecca Shaw
Jack Sheffield
Anne Rivers Siddons
Linda Sole
Mary Jane Staples

Danielle Steel
Kay Stephens
Sally Stewart
Jessica Stirling
Rowena Summers
Janet Tanner
June Tate
Michael Taylor
Rosie Thomas
Grace Thompson
Nicola Thorne
Margaret Thornton
Rachael Treasure
Adriana Trigiani
Joanna Trollope
Janet MacLeod Trotter
Elizabeth Waite
Jeanne Whitmee
Barbara Whitnell
Madeleine Wickham
Marcia Willett
Dee Williams
Audrey Willsher
Mary Withall
Valerie Wood
Janet Woods
Sally Worboyes

Science Fiction

Although Science Fiction (SF) and Fantasy are often mixed, SF deals with the possible, and is based (often tenuously) on scientific knowledge obeying the laws of nature in the universe — however fantastic some of the stories may seem. The literature of SF is substantial and we have used five subgenres to help you find the type of author you want to read: **Near future** – stories concerning all pervasive technologies, their use and misuse, normally set within the next hundred years; **Space opera** – space adventure stories of extravagant dimensions, often involving galactic empires and space battles; **Space and time** – travel into either the past or the future, exploring history as it might have been, or the future as the author sees it; **Technical** – SF novels with an overriding emphasis on the technical and scientific achievement, usually involving flight into outer space; **Humour** – authors whose books highlight the humorous aspects of SF.

Humour

Douglas Adams
Rob Grant

Harry Harrison

Robert Rankin

Near future

Neal Asher
Tony Ballantyne
John Birmingham

Cory Doctorow
Greg Egan
Jaine Fenn

William Gibson
Jon Courtenay Grimwood
James Lovegrove

Science Fiction (continued)

Near future (continued)

Richard Powers
Kim Stanley Robinson
Justina Robson
Geoff Ryman

Robert J Sawyer
Michael Marshall Smith
Neal Stephenson
Karen Traviss

Tad Williams
David Wingrove
John Wyndham

Space and time

Brian W Aldiss
Isaac Asimov
Ray Bradbury
Philip K Dick
Harlan Ellison
Christie Golden
Anne McCaffrey

Todd McCaffrey
Jack McDevitt
Ian McDonald
Ian R MacLeod
Ken MacLeod
Larry Niven

Christopher Priest
Kristine Kathryn Rusch
Robert Silverberg
Jeff Vandermeer
Kurt Vonnegut
David Zindell

Space opera

Dan Abnett
Kevin J Anderson
Iain M Banks
Lois McMaster Bujold
Orson Scott Card
Michael Cobley
Alan Dean Foster

Gary Gibson
Colin Greenland
Joe Haldeman
Peter F Hamilton
Brian Herbert
Frank Herbert

Philip Palmer
Alastair Reynolds
John Scalzi
Dan Simmons
Charles Stross
Tricia Sullivan

Technical

J G Ballard
Stephen Baxter
Greg Bear

Gregory Benford
Arthur C Clarke

Paul J McAuley
Linda Nagata

Sea

A popular category where many authors have gained a well-deserved reputation for writing about the sea, either in an historical or a modern setting. Many novelists in this genre might equally be found under **Adventure/Thriller** or **War stories**.

Historical

Tom Connery
David Donachie
C S Forester
Seth Hunter
Alexander Kent

Jonathan Lunn
James L Nelson
Patrick O'Brian
Sean Thomas Russell
John Stack

Julian Stockwin
Peter Smalley
G S Beard
Philip McCutchan
Dudley Pope

Modern

Brian Callison
James H Cobb

Duncan Harding
Douglas Reeman

Patrick Robinson
Peter Tonkin

Authors who have written widely but not exclusively about war, generally within the 19th and 20th centuries. Many books about war will also be found under **Adventure/Thriller** and also under **Sea stories**. Some **General** novelists have also written individual books about war.

Patrick Bishop	Matt Lynn	Guy Walters

Historical

Joy Chambers	Allan Mallinson	Garry Kilworth C19th
Bernard Cornwell	Grant Sutherland	Patrick Mercer C19th
George Macdonald Fraser	Adrian Goldsworthy C19th	John Wilcox C19th
Iain Gale		

Modern

Francis Cottam	James Holland	Derek Robinson
Elizabeth Darrell	Andy McNab	Alan Savage
David Fiddimore	Robert Radcliffe	Terence Strong
W E B Griffin		

Characters and Series

This section lists all the Characters, Series and Family names which appear in the main A-Z sequence of the guide.

A

44 Scotland Street	Alexander McCall Smith
Abbess of Meaux	Cassandra Clark
Bea Abbot	Veronica Heley
Ben Abbott	Justin Scott
Abdouf	Jean-Christophe Grangé
Simon Abelard	Bill James
Jack Absolute	C C Humphreys
Laura Ackroyd	Patricia Hall
Eleanor of Acquitaine	Sharon Penman
The Hon Barnaby Adair	Stephanie Laurens
Adams Family	Mary Jane Staples
Commissaire Adamsberg	Fred Vargas
Aelric	Richard Blake
Adelia Aguiler	Ariana Franklin
Captain Alatriste	Arturo Pérez-Reverte
Alexander the Great	Paul Doherty, Valerio Massimo Manfredi
Alfred the Great	Bernard Cornwell
DS Khalid Ali	Lesley Horton
Dante Alighieri	Giulio Leoni
Gabriel Allon	Daniel Silva
Alpiew	Fidelis Morgan
DI Enrique Alvarez	Roderic Jeffries
Amerotke	Paul Doherty
Simon Ames	Patricia Finney
Robert Amiss	Ruth Dudley Edwards
Sophie Anderson	P D Martin
Fitzroy Maclean Angel	Mike Ripley
DI Michael Angel	Roger Silverwood
Anno Dracula Series	Kim Newman
Father Anselm	William Brodrick
Callie Anson	Kate Charles
DI John Appleby	Michael Innes
April Grove Series	Lilian Harry
Marcus Valerius Aquila	Anthony Riches
Lew Archer	Ross Macdonald
Owen Archer	Candace Robb
Kate Ardleigh	Robin Paige
Comm Jan Argand	Julian Rathbone
Jonathan Argyll	Iain Pears
Israel Armstrong	Ian Sansom
Sheriff Spenser Arrowood	Sharyn McCrumb
King Arthur	Bernard Cornwell
Countess Ashby-de-la-Zouche	Fidelis Morgan
Peter Ashton	Clive Egleton
DI Carol Ashton	Claire McNab

Characters & Series

Askham Family	Nicola Thorne
Demetrios Askiates	Tom Harper
Brother Athelstan	Paul Doherty
Attila the Hun	William Napier
Jack Aubrey	Patrick O'Brian
Kurt Austin	Clive Cussler
Mick Axbrewder	Stephen Donaldson

B

Bad Hair Day Mysteries	Nancy Cohen
Badge of Honour Series	W E B Griffin
DS Geoffrey Bailey	Frances Fyfield
Bill Bailey	Catherine Cookson
Jonathan Bale	Edward Marston
Frank Balenger	David Morrell
Jessica Balzano	Richard Montanari
CI Alan Banks	Peter Robinson
Chief Holly Barker	Stuart Woods
Barleybridge Series	Rebecca Shaw
DCI Tom Barnaby	Caroline Graham
Alexandra Barnaby	Janet Evanovich
Harry Barnett	Robert Goddard
Smoky Barrett	Cody McFadyen
Stone Barrington	Stuart Woods
Matthew Bartholomew	Susanna Gregory
Lee Bartholomew	Hope McIntyre
Lily Barton	Di Morrissey
Dorina Basarab	Karen Chance
Frank Bascombe	Richard Ford
Charlie Bassett	David Fiddimore
Bastion Club	Stephanie Laurens
Mark Beamon	Kyle Mills
Det J P Beaumont	J A Jance
Martin Beck	Maj Sjöwall & Per Wahlöö
David Becket	Patricia Finney
Det Sam Becket	Hilary Norman
Dr Jo Beckett	Meg Gardiner
Holly Beckman	Jessica Stirling
Frank Behr	David Levien
Isaac Bell	Clive Cussler
Beloved People Trilogy	Denise Robertson
Alex Benedict	Jack McDevitt
Annika Bengtzon	Liza Marklund
Det David 'Kubu' Bengu	Michael Stanley
Det Michael Bennett	James Patterson
Sgt Francis Benton-Smith	P D James
Det Rick Bentz	Lisa Jackson
DI Ernest Best	Joan Lock
Mirabelle Bevan	Sara Sheridan
Ashraf Bey	Jon Courtenay Grimwood
Captain Isaac Biddlecomb	James L Nelson
Big Stone Gap Series	Adriana Trigiani
Jim Bishop	Andrew Klavan
Lucrezia 'Cree' Black	Daniel Hecht

Tom Black	Elizabeth Darrell
Sam Blackman	Mark de Castrique
Oz Blackstone	Quintin Jardine
Insp Sam Blackstone	Sally Spencer
Mike Blackwood	Douglas Reeman
Det Sonora Blair	Lynn Hightower
Anita Blake	Laurell K Hamilton
Natasha Blake	Fiona Mountain
Naomi Blake	Jane Adams
DS Lucy Blake	J M Gregson
Vicky Bliss	Elizabeth Peters
Mikael Blomkvist	Stieg Larsson
Becky Bloomwood	Sophie Kinsella
Blotto	Simon Brett
Alec Blume	Conor Fitzgerald
Body Farm Series	Jefferson Bass
Sgt Lou Boldt	Ridley Pearson
Myron Bolitar	Harlan Coben
Richard Bolitho	Alexander Kent
Adam Bolitho	Alexander Kent
Napoleon Bonaparte	Simon Scarrow
James Bond	Jeffery Deaver, Ian Fleming
Theodore Boone	John Grisham
Harry Bosch	Michael Connelly
Sgt Bottomley	Norman Russell
Boudica	Manda Scott
Sister Agnes Bourdillon	Alison Joseph
Jason Bourne	Robert Ludlum, Eric Van Lustbader
Samuel Bowater	James L Nelson
Eva Bower	Aileen Armitage
Lucifer Box	Mark Gatiss
DS Tina Boyd	Simon Kernick
Billy Boyle	James Benn
Nicholas Bracewell	Edward Marston
Sheriff Joanna Brady	J A Jance
Kate Brannigan	Val McDermid
DS Brant	Ken Bruen
Andy Brazil	Patricia D Cornwell
Breadmakers Series	Margaret Thomson Davis
Brenda	Paul Magrs
Dr Temperance Brennan	Kathy Reichs
DI Philip Brennan	Tania Carver
Gervase Bret	Edward Marston
Brethren of the Coast Trilogy	James L Nelson
Dr Solomon Brightman	Alex Gray
PI Nicholas Brisbane	Deanna Raybourn
DCI Harry Brock	Graham Ison
DCI David Brock	Barry Maitland
Dr Bill Brockton	Jefferson Bass
Det Jackson Brodie	Kate Atkinson
Chris Bronson	James Becker
Brotherhood of War Series	W E B Griffin

Richard Browning	Peter Corris
Commissario Guido Brunetti	Donna Leon
Giordano Bruno	S J Parris
Arthur Bryant	Christopher Fowler
Ren Bryce	Alex Barclay
Tam Buchanan	Joyce Holms
Kate Burkholder	Linda Castillo
DI Kate Burrows	Martina Cole
Dr Clare Burtonall	Jonathan Gash
Buryin' Barry Mystery Series	Mark de Castrique
Kevin Byrne	Richard Montanari
Johannes Cabal	Jonathan L Howard
Brother Cadfael	Ellis Peters
Julius Caesar	Conn Iggulden
DI Jack Caffery	Mo Hayder
Alex Cahill	G J Moffat
Hailey Cain	Jodi Compton
Keith Calder	Gerald Hammond
Alex Calder	Michael Ridpath
Calder Family	Janet Dailey
Camel Club	David Baldacci
Sgt Anna Cameron	Karen Campbell
Donald Cameron	Philip McCutchan
Fiona Cameron	Val McDermid
Margaret Campbell	Peter May
Sgt Liam Campbell	Dana Stabenow
Campion Family	Annie Groves
Camulod Series	Jack Whyte
Caper Court Series	Caro Fraser
Det John Cardinal	Giles Blunt
Det Steve Carella	Ed McBain
Sam 'Mad' Carew	Ken McCoy
Sir Robert Carey	P F Chisholm
Neal Carey	Don Winslow
Carlotta Carlyle	Linda Barnes
Liz Carlyle	Stella Rimington
Tommy Carmellini	Stephen Coonts
Insp James Carrick	Margaret Duffy
Annie Carter	Jessie Keane
Samuel Carver	Tom Cain
DCI Casey	Geraldine Evans
Felix Castor	Mike Carey
Quintus Licinus Cato	Simon Scarrow
Thomas Catt	Geraldine Evans
Sandro Cellini	Christobel Kent
Chadwick Family	Marcia Willett
Insp Hal Challis	Garry Disher
Thomas Chaloner	Susanna Gregory
Lindsay Chamberlain	Beverly Connor
Champagne Series	Nicola Thorne
Det Mike Chapman	Linda Fairstein
Eddie Chase	Andy McDermott

C

Characters & Series

Tom Chatto	Philip McCutchan
Jim Chee	Tony Hillerman
Insp Chen	Qiu Xiaolong
DCI Henry Christie	Nick Oldham
Winston Churchill	Michael Dobbs
Cicero	Robert Harris
Robert Clark	Lis Howell
DC Siobhan Clarke	Ian Rankin
Claudia	Paul Doherty
Barry Clayton	Mark de Castrique
Joe Clayton	Tom Bale
Denise Cleever	Claire McNab
Frank Clemons	Thomas H Cook
Artie Cohen	Reggie Nadelson
Insp Robert Colbeck	Edward Marston
Elvis Cole	Robert Crais
Lewis Cole	Brendan Dubois
Hap Collins	Joe R Lansdale
DI Stacey Collins	Kevin Lewis
Insp Mario Conde	Leonardo Padura
Harper Connelly	Charlaine Harris
Conquest Trilogy Series	Jack Ludlow
The Continental Op	Dashiell Hammett
Conway Family	Jessica Stirling
DC Ben Cooper	Stephen Booth
Alexandra Cooper	Linda Fairstein
Jenny Cooper	M R Hall
Det Emmanuel Cooper	Malla Nunn
PC Den Cooper	Rebecca Tope
Coppins Bridge Series	Elizabeth Daish
Sir Hugh Corbett	Paul Doherty
Corduroy Mansion Series	Alexander McCall Smith
Cordwainer Series	Iris Gower
Det John Corey	Nelson DeMille
Corps Series	W E B Griffin
Frank Corso	G M Ford
Corvill Family	Tessa Barclay
Marcus Corvinus	David Wishart
Det Nic Costa	David Hewson
Peter Cotton	Aly Monroe
Capt Bruno Courrèges	Martin Walker
Thomas Covenant	Stephen Donaldson
Covert-One Series	Robert Ludlum
Lt Dick Coward	James Delingpole
Melissa Craig	Betty Rowlands
Craigallan Family	Tessa Barclay
Alan Craik	Gordon Kent
Francis Crawford of Lymond	Dorothy Dunnett
Ray Crawley	Peter Corris
Sgt Cribb	Peter Lovesey
Dr Anya Crichton	Kathryn Fox
DI Mike Croft	Jane Adams

	DS Crosby	Catherine Aird
	Det Alex Cross	James Patterson
	Sgt 'Fancy' Jack Crossman	Garry Kilworth
	DI John Crow	Roy Lewis
	Crowner John	Bernard Knight
	Gabriel Crowther	Imogen Robertson
	Hew Cullan	Shirley McKay
	Gil Cunningham	Pat McIntosh
	John Cunningham	Gerald Hammond
	Richard Cypher	Terry Goodkind
D	Josse D'Acquin	Alys Clare
	Supt Adam Dalgliesh	P D James
	Isabel Dalhousie	Alexander McCall Smith
	Eve Dallas	J D Robb
	Dalriada Trilogy	Jules Watson
	Daisy Dalrymple	Carola Dunn
	Quintilian Dalrymple	Paul Johnston
	DI Dalziel	Reginald Hill
	Kathryn Dance	Jeffery Deaver
	Supt Theo Daquin	Dominique Manotti
	Antonia Darcy	R T Raichev
	Mr & Mrs Darcy Series	Carrie Bebris
	The Dark Tower Series	Stephen King
	Lucas Davenport	John Sandford
	'Dangerous' Davies	Leslie Thomas
	Leo Davies	Caro Fraser
	Sgt de Gier	Janwillem van de Wetering
	Hugh de Lac	James Patterson
	Comm De Luca	Carlo Lucarelli
	Flavia de Luce	Alan Bradley
	Commd't Michel de Palma	Xavier-Marie Bonnot
	Justin de Quincey	Sharon Penman
	Andre de Roland	A L Berridge
	Hugh de Verdon	Simon Acland
	Sir John de Wolfe	Bernard Knight
	DeBeers Family Series	Virginia Andrews
	Decipherer's Chronicles	Grant Sutherland
	Lt Pete Decker	Faye Kellerman
	Officer Cindy Decker	Faye Kellerman
	Jade del Cameron	Suzanne Arruda
	Evan Delaney	Meg Gardiner
	DI Jack Delaney	Mark Pearson
	Alex Delaware	Jonathan Kellerman
	Ralph Delchard	Edward Marston
	Det Alex Delillo	Scott Frost
	John Delmas	Raymond Chandler
	Captain Carmine Delmonico	Colleen McCullough
	Det Lisa Delorme	Giles Blunt
	Joe DeMarco	Mike Lawson
	Leo Demidov	Tom Rob Smith
	Denton	Kenneth Cameron
	Deravenel Series	Barbara Taylor Bradford

Harry Devlin	Martin Edwards
Insp Benedict Devlin	Brian McGilloway
Georgia Dew	Amy Myers
Jacques Deza	Javier Marias
Det Hermes Diaktoros	Anne Zouroudi
Det Serena Dial	Brian Freeman
Peter Diamond	Peter Lovesey
Auguste Didier	Amy Myers
Diesel	Janet Evanovich
Sean Dillon	Jack Higgins
Diogenes Club Series	Kim Newman
Discworld	Terry Pratchett
Maisie Dobbs	Jacqueline Winspear
Charlie Doig	James Fleming
Trixie Dolan	Marian Babson
DS Cal Donovan	Jo Bannister
DS Sam Donovan	Elena Forbes
John Dortmunder	Donald Westlake
Alistair Douglas	Grant Sutherland
Harry Dresden	Jim Butcher
Drovers Series	Iris Gower
Drummond Family	Emma Blair
Philip Dryden	Jim Kelly
Mike Dukas	Gordon Kent
Steven Dunbar	Ken McClure
Vanessa Duncan	Catherine Shaw
Eve Duncan	Iris Johansen
Dune Saga	Frank Herbert (creator) continued by son Brian Herbert with Kevin J Anderson
Gus Dury	Tony Black
Noah Dyson	James McCreet
Easter Empire	Beryl Kingston
Effie	Paul Magrs
Tam Eildor	Alanna Knight
Eisdalsa Island Trilogy	Mary Withall
John Eisenmenger	Keith McCarthy
DC Frank Elder	John Harvey
Emma	Elizabeth Daish
Empire of the Moghul Series	Alex Rutherford
Empress Orchid Series	Anchee Min
Harry Erskine	Graham Masterton
Elena Estes	Tami Hoag
Nicholas Everard	Alexander Fullerton
Det Jan Fabel	Craig Russell
Fairacre	Miss Read
Marcus Didius Falco	Lindsey Davis
Insp Javier Falcon	Robert Wilson
William Falconer	Ian Morson
Diane Fallon	Beverly Connor
Erast Fandorin	Boris Akunin
DI Joe Faraday	Graham Hurley
Fargo Series	Clive Cussler

E

F

DI Jeremy Faro	Alanna Knight
Brodie Farrell	Jo Bannister
Feeney Family	Sheelagh Kelly
Gerry Fegan	Stuart Neville
CI George Felse	Ellis Peters
Dave Fenner	James Hadley Chase
DCI Andrew Fenwick	Elizabeth Corley
Chief Sup Ferrara	Michele Giuttari
'Fiarlyden' Series	Gwen Kirkwood
Sister Fidelma	Peter Tremayne
Kit Fielding	Dick Francis
Mary Finch	Rose Melikan
DCI Jack Finch	June Thomson
Logan Finch	G J Moffat
Finn	Alex Dryden
Firebird Series	Iris Gower
First North American Series	Kathleen O'Neal Gear
Hon Phryne Fisher	Kerry Greenwood
Ginny Fistoulari	Stephen Donaldson
Fizz Fitzgerald	Joyce Holms
Henry Fitzroy	Tanya Huff
Sir Harry Flashman	George Macdonald Fraser
DI Marjory Fleming	Aline Templeton
Helena Flemming	Keith McCarthy
Shannon Flinder	Denise Ryan
Nicolas Le Floch	Jean François Parot
DS Ray Flowers	Jane Adams
Det Virgil Flowers	John Sandford
Zelda Fluck	Pip Granger
Capt Simon Fonthill	John Wilcox
Forrest Family	Julia Bryant
Lily Forrester	Nancy Taylor Rosenberg
Michael Forsythe	Adrian McKinty
Socrates Fortlow	Walter Mosley
Sarah Fortune	Frances Fyfield
44 Scotland Street	Alexander McCall Smith
DI Foster	Margaret Murphy
Artemis Fowl	Eoin Colfer
Father Anthony Fowler	Juan Gómez-Jurado
Charlie Fox	Zoë Sharp
Malcolm Fox	Ian Rankin
Foxearth Trilogy	Pamela Oldfield
Jill Francis	Andrew Taylor
Max Freeman	Jonathon King
Sister Frevisse	Margaret Frazer
Kinky Friedman	Kinky Friedman
DI Jack Frost	R D Wingfield
DS Diane Fry	Stephen Booth
Det Joe Frye	P J Parrish
Sir Baldwin Furnshill	Michael Jecks
John Fury	G S Beard
Sheriff Matt Gabriel	Paula Gosling

G

Ethan Gage	William Dietrich
Jimmy Gage	Robert Ferrigno
Det Galileo	Keigo Higashino
DI John Gallan	Simon Kernick
Dr Ruth Galloway	Elly Griffiths
CI Armand Gamache	Louise Penny
Det Lena Gamble	Robert Ellis
Winston Garano	Patricia D Cornwell
Com Amanda Lee Garrett	James H Cobb
Jack Garrett	Neil White
Nora Gavin	Erin Hart
Riley Gavin	Adrian Magson
Angie Gennaro	Dennis Lehane
Merry Gentry	Laurell K Hamilton
Insp Ghote	H R F Keating
Annie Gibson	Anna Jacobs
Gideon	Eric Jerome Dickey
Patrick Gillard	Margaret Duffy
Rosie Gilmour	Anna Smith
Dandy Gilver	Catriona McPherson
Mark Girland	James Hadley Chase
Mariana Givens	Thalassa Ali
Alison Glasby	James Brownley
Abe Glitsky	John T Lescroart
The Godfather	Mario Puzo
Tom Goodfellow	Michael Dobbs
DC Gary Goodhew	Alison Bruce
Gordianus the Finder	Steven Saylor
Lindsay Gordon	Val McDermid
DS Roy Grace	Peter James
Rear Admiral Jake Grafton	Stephen Coonts
DI Liz Graham	Jo Bannister
Grail Quest Series	Bernard Cornwell
Patrick Grant	Margaret Yorke
Cordelia Gray	P D James
DI Will Grayson	John Harvey
Alan Gregory	Stephen White
Det Insp Ewert Grens	Roslund and Hellström
Lady Julia Grey	Deanna Raybourn
Lord John Grey	Diana Gabaldon
Paula Grey	Colin Forbes
Det Bernie Griessel	Deon Meyer
Lew Griffin	James Sallis
Adjutant Grijpstra	Janwillem van de Wetering
Marshal Guarnaccia	Magdalen Nabb
Thora Gudmundsdottir	Yrsa Sigurdardottir
Guido Guerrieri	Gianrico Carofiglio
Martha Gunn	Priscilla Masters
Bernard Gunther	Philip Kerr
Lt Joe Gunther	Archer Mayor
Nathaniel Gye	Derek Wilson
Insp Hackett	Benjamin Black

H

Jack Haldean	Dolores Gordon-Smith
St Vincent Halfhyde	Philip McCutchan
Mickey Haller	Michael Connelly
Sid Halley	Dick Francis
Emma Hamilton	Sinead Moriarty
Hamilton Family	Anne Doughty
Judy Hammer	Patricia D Cornwell
Francis Hancock	Barbara Nadel
DI Handford	Lesley Horton
Sigrid Harald	Margaret Maron
DI Hardcastle	Graham Ison
Cliff Hardy	Peter Corris
Dismas Hardy	John T Lescroart
Sgt Timo Harjunpaa	Matti Joensuu
Robert Harland	Henry Porter
DS Frances Harman	Judith Cutler
Steve Harmas	James Hadley Chase
DCI Colin Harpur	Bill James
DCI Harrison	Charlie Owen
Emma Harte	Barbara Taylor Bradford
Scot Harvath	Brad Thor
Harvey Series	Gloria Cook
Det Ellie Hatcher	Alafair Burke
DS Barbara Havers	Elizabeth George
Alexander Hawke	Ted Bell
Det Al Hawkin	Laurie R King
Hawksmoor Series	Aileen Armitage
Matthew Hawkwood	James McGee
Lieut Charles Hayden	Sean Thomas Russell
DS Roger Hayes	Vivien Armstrong
Lieut James Hayter	Peter Smalley
Heart of Gold Series	Catrin Collier
Det Patrik Hedstrom	Camilla Läckberg
Abbess Helewise	Alys Clare
Nick Heller	Joseph Finder
DCI Hennessy	Peter Turnbull
Henry II	Sharon Penman
Heron Saga	Pamela Oldfield
Matthew Hervey	Allan Mallinson
DI Andrew Hicks	Steve Mosby
Dr Tony Hill	Val McDermid
Hillsbridge Family	Janet Tanner
Kate Hilton	Margaret Dickinson
Hitch-Hikers Guide to the Galaxy Series	Douglas Adams
Dido Hoare	Marianne MacDonald
DI Harry Hole	Jo Nesbo
Billy-Bob Holland	James Lee Burke
PC Jonas Holly	Belinda Bauer
Sherlock Holmes	Arthur Conan Doyle
Sherlock Holmes	Laurie R King
Sebastian Holmes	Brian Freemantle
Max Holt	Janet Evanovich

	Robin Hood	Angus Donald
	Det Bert Hook	J M Gregson
	Sam Hooker	Janet Evanovich
	Ben Hope	Scott Mariani
	Alison Hope	Susan B Kelly
	DS Lloyd Hopkins	James Ellroy
	Ward Hopkins	Michael Marshall
	John Ray Horn	Edward Wright
	Horatio Hornblower	C S Forester
	DI Andy Horton	Pauline Rowson
	Dep Sheriff Carl Houseman	Donald Harstad
	Jack Howard	David Gibbins
	Robin Hudson	Sparkle Hayter
	DI Lorraine Hunt	Sheila Quigley
	Dr David Hunter	Simon Beckett
	Joe Hunter	Matt Hilton
	Det Robert Hunter	Chris Carter
I	Cetin Ikmen	Barbara Nadel
	ACC Desmond Iles	Bill James
	Iliona	Marilyn Todd
	Cal Innes	Ray Banks
	Jack Irish	Peter Temple
	Dr Maura Isles	Tess Gerritsen
	Kate Ivory	Veronica Stallwood
J	DI Saul Jackson	Norman Russell
	DS Ken Jackson	Anthea Fraser
	DCI Jacobson	Iain McDowall
	Det Karin Jacobsson	Mari Jungstedt
	CI Daniel Jacquot	Martin O'Brien
	Amanda Jaffe	Phillip Margolin
	DI Gemma James	Deborah Crombie
	Jeeves	P G Wodehouse
	Sgt '352' Jenkins	John Wilcox
	Riley Jensen	Keri Arthur
	Sarah Jensen	Linda Davies
	Sonchai Jitpleecheep	John Burdett
	Det Kimmo Joentaa	Jan Costin Wagner
	John the Eunuch	Mary Reed and Eric Mayer
	Joliffe Players Series	Margaret Frazer
	Bridget Jones	Helen Fielding
	Sam Jones	Lauren Henderson
	D J Jones	Chris Kuzneski
	Constable Sunset Jones	Joe R Lansdale
	Fearless Jones	Walter Mosley
	Magnus Jonson	Michael Ridpath
	DCI Carol Jordan	Val McDermid
	Insp Daniel Journa	Nick Brownlee
	Judge of Egypt	Christian Jacq
	Miss Julia	Ann B Ross
	Jimm Juree	Colin Cotterill
	DCI Richard Jury	Martha Grimes

K

Det Andreas Kaldis	Jeffrey Siger
Dmitri Kameron	Michael Pearce
India Kane	Caroline Carver
Kane Family	Frank Delaney
Roger 'Butch' Karp	Robert K Tanenbaum
DI Frank Kavanagh	David Armstrong
George Keene	Derek Wilson
John Keller	Lawrence Block
Irene Kelly	Jan Burke
Michael Kelly	Michael Harvey
Clare Kelso	Jessica Stirling
Commodore Kemp	Philip McCutchan
Kylie Kendall	Claire McNab
DI Christy Kennedy	Paul Charles
Patrick Kenzie	Dennis Lehane
Harry Keogh	Brian Lumley
Kevin Kerney	Michael McGarrity
DS Kerr	Iain McDowall
Margaret Kerr	Candace Robb
Kershaw Sisters	Anna Jacobs
Insp Khalifa	Paul Sussman
Genghis Khan	Conn Iggulden
Kidd	John Sandford
Nolan Kilkenny	Tom Grace
Sal Kilkenny	Cath Staincliffe
Kit Killigrew	Jonathan Lunn
Ben Kincaid	William Bernhardt
DDA Samantha Kincaid	Alafair Burke
DS Duncan Kincaid	Deborah Crombie
Det Louis Kincaid	P J Parrish
Kineas	Christian Cameron
Sean King	David Baldacci
Willow King	Natasha Cooper
King Arthur	M K Hume
Tom Kirk	James Twining
Frieda Klein	Nicci French
Louie Knight	Malcolm Pryce
Knights Templar	Robyn Young
Deborah Knott	Margaret Maron
Daniel Knox	Will Adams
CI Anders Knutas	Mari Jungstedt
DS Kathy Kolla	Barry Maitland
DS Mike Korpanski	Priscilla Masters
Det Sam Kovac	Tami Hoag
Thomas Paine Kydd	Julian Stockwin

L

Tim Lacy	Derek Wilson
Peter Lamb	Iain Gale
Det John Lambert	J M Gregson
Locke Lamora	Scott Lynch
Lampitt Chronicles	A N Wilson
Arnold Landon	Roy Lewis
Daisy Lane	June Hampson

Liberty Lane	Caro Peacock
Professor Robert Langdon	Dan Brown
Ingrid Langley	Margaret Duffy
DCI James Langton	Lynda La Plante
DCI Mark Lapsie	Nigel McCrery
Lilac Larkin	Katie Flynn
Dr Samantha Laschen	Nicci French
Capt William Laurence	Naomi Novik
Commissaire Laviolette	Pierre Magnan
Rina Lazarus	Faye Kellerman
Joe Leaphorn	Tony Hillerman
Dr Hannibal Lecter	Thomas Harris
Aimée Leduc	Cara Black
Victor Legris	Claude Izner
Thorgils Leiffson	Tim Severin
Insp Denis Lennon	Andrew Nugent
Lennox	Craig Russell
Det Supt Sholto Lestrade	M J Trow
Billy Liar	Keith Waterhouse
Sarjeant Libby	Lesley Cookman
Libertus	Rosemary Rowe
Abe Lieberman	Stuart M Kaminsky
Dr Max Liebermann	Frank Tallis
Jack Liffey	John Shannon
PI Gemma Lincoln	Gabrielle Lord
Insp Ann Lindell	Kjell Eriksson
Nicholas Linnear	Eric Van Lustbader
Sara Linton	Karin Slaughter
Tinks Liska	Tami Hoag
Sgt D Llewellyn	Geraldine Evans
Ryan Lock	Sean Black
Paul Lomax	Raymond Haigh
London Sequence	Margaret Pemberton
DCI William Lorimer	Alex Gray
Loveday Series	Kate Tremayne
Lovejoy	Jonathan Gash
Gretchen Lowell	Chelsea Cain
Ed Loy	Declan Hughes
Det Joe Lucchesi	Alex Barclay
Harry Ludlow	David Donachie
LuEllen	John Sandford
Hector Lynch	Tim Severin
DCI Thomas Lynley	Elizabeth George
Lyons Corner House Series	Lilian Harry
Lytton Trilogy	Penny Vincenzi

M

PC Hamish MacBeth	M C Beaton
Terry McCaleb	Michael Connelly
Jay McCaulay	Caroline Carver
Sharon McCone	Marcia Muller
CSI Darby McCormick	Chris Mooney
Jack McEvoy	Michael Connelly
DC Laura McGanity	Neil White

Leonid McGill	Walter Mosley
Joanna Mackenzie	Margaret Duffy
Peter Macklin	Loren D Estleman
Alex McKnight	Steve Hamilton
Patrick McLanahan	Dale Brown
Brodie MacLennan	Grace Monroe
Rhona MacLeod	Lin Anderson
Insp James McLevy	David Ashton
Andrina McPherson	Margaret Thomson Davis
Elizabeth McPherson	Sharyn McCrumb
Rose McQuinn	Alanna Knight
DS Logan McRae	Stuart MacBride
Lucius Cornelius Macro	Simon Scarrow
Insp John Madden	Rennie Airth
Det Cassie Maddox	Tana French
Paul Madriani	Steve Martini
Trish Maguire	Natasha Cooper
Commissaire Jules Maigret	Georges Simenon
Reuben Maitland	John Macken
Sgt Kathleen Mallory	Carol O'Connell
Vic Malloy	James Hadley Chase
Cotton Malone	Steve Berry
Chief Cuddy Mangum	Michael Malone
Det Johnny Mann	Lee Weeks
Judge Mara	Cora Harrison
Daniel Marchant	Jon Stock
Captain Quentin Margont	Armand Cabasson
DI Tom Mariner	Chris Collett
Mariner Series	Peter Tonkin
Det Supt Alan Markby	Ann Granger
George Markham	Tom Connery
Philip Marlowe	Raymond Chandler
Thomas Marlowe	James L Nelson
Miss Marple	Agatha Christie
DS Charles Marriott	Graham Ison
Peter Marsh	Amy Myers
DS Harriet Martens	H R F Keating
Saz Martin	Stella Duffy
Lizzie Martin	Ann Granger
Det Kate Martinelli	Laurie R King
Henrietta (Harry) Martinez	Ava McCarthy
Rebecka Martinsson	Åsa Larsson
DS Mary Mary	Jasper Fforde
Det Harry Mason	Richard Kunzmann
Masters of Rome Series	Colleen McCullough
Mathilde of Westminster	Paul Doherty
Daphne Matthews	Ridley Pearson
Stephen Maturin	Patrick O'Brian
Alex Mavros	Paul Johnston
Peter Maxwell	M J Trow
Michelle Maxwell	David Baldacci
John May	Christopher Fowler

Caroline Maybry	Jess Walter
Kate Mayfield	Nelson DeMille
Supt Gil Mayo	Marjorie Eccles
Lois Meade	Ann Purser
Bruce Medway	Robert Wilson
Paddy Meehan	Denise Mina
DI Jim Meldrum	Frederic Lindsay
Patrick Melrose	Edward St Aubyn
Decius Caecilius Metellus the younger	John Maddox Roberts
David Middleton-Brown	Kate Charles
Alec Milius	Charles Cumming
Millenium Trilogy	Stieg Larsson
Kinsey Millhone	Sue Grafton
Milo Milodragovitch	James Crumley
Det Minami	David Peace
PI Max Mingus	Nick Stone
Paris MInton	Walter Mosley
Miranda	Jefferson Bass
DI Kate Miskin	P D James
Meredith Mitchell	Ann Granger
Mitchell Family	Kimberley Chambers
Mitford Series	Jan Karon
Captain Eberhard Mock	Marek Krajewski
Adrian Mole	Sue Townsend
Tess Monaghan	Laura Lippman
Insp William Monk	Anne Perry
Hester Monk	Anne Perry
Monkton Family	Margaret Thomson Davis
Insp Salvo Montalbano	Andrea Camilleri
Dr Laurie Montgomery	Robin Cook
Det Reuben Montoya	Lisa Jackson
Monty (dog)	Iris Johansen
DI Abigail Moon	Marjorie Eccles
DS Stella Mooney	David Lawrence
Jake Moore	Nick Brownlee
Det Carl Mørck	Jussi Adler-Olsen
Rachel Morgan	Kim Harrison
Dexter Morgan	Jeff Lindsay
Admiral Arnold Morgan	Patrick Robinson
Antony Morgan	Patrick Mercer
Morland Dynasty	Cynthia Harrod-Eagles
Christine Morris	Maureen Jennings
DC Alex Morrow	Denise Mina
DI Morse	Colin Dexter
Whit Mosley	Jeff Abbott
DS Angus Mott	Clare Curzon
Evadne Mount	Gilbert Adair
Charlie Muffin	Brian Freemantle
Det William Murdoch	Maureen Jennings
Tom Musgrave	Peter Tonkin
Mystery Man Series	Bateman
N Nefertiti	Michelle Moran

	Insp Grazia Negro	Carlo Lucarelli
	Vicki Nelson	Tanya Huff
	DCI Harry Nelson	Elly Griffiths
	Insp Nergui	Michael Walters
	Net Force Explorers	Tom Clancy
	Bob Newman	Colin Forbes
	DI Albert Newsome	James McCreet
	Thursday Next	Jasper Fforde
	Neyler Family	Judith Saxton
	Nicholson Family	Jessica Stirling
	Pierre Niemans	Jean-Christophe Grangé
	Jack Nightingale	Stephen Leather
	The No 1 Ladies' Detective Agnecy	Alexander McCall Smith
	Noble Dead Series	Barb & J C Hendee
	Les Norton	Robert G Barrett
	Numa Files Series	Clive Cussler
O	Det Petra O'Connor	Jonathan Kellerman
	Maggie O'Dell	Alex Kava
	Maureen O'Donnell	Denise Mina
	O'Hara Family	Kimberley Chambers
	Joseph O'Loughlin	Michael Robotham
	Kit O'Malley	Lindy Cameron
	Oathsworn Series	Robert Low
	Oceania Series	Tamara McKinley
	Det Supt Oddie	Robert Barnard
	Odysseus	Glyn Iliffe
	Capt James Ogilvie	Philip McCutchan
	Sigurdur Oli	Arnaldur Indridason
	Billy Oliphant	Alan Dunn
	Oregon Files Series	Clive Cussler
	Michael Osbourne	Daniel Silva
	Mysteries of Osiris	Christian Jacq
	Otter House Vets Series	Cathy Woodman
	Rev Francis Oughterard	Suzette Hill
	Outlander Series	Diana Gabaldon
	Gareth Owen (The Mamur Zapt)	Michael Pearce
P	P Division	Peter Turnbull
	Sam Packer	Geoffrey Archer
	Lena Padgett	Lynn Hightower
	Lorraine Page	Lynda La Plante
	Christopher Paget	Richard North Patterson
	Dr Siri Paiboun	Colin Cotterill
	Palace Theatre Series	Iris Gower
	Cassandra Palmer	Karen Chance
	Harry Palmer	Len Deighton
	Frank Palmer	Adrian Magson
	George & Molly Palmer-Jones	Ann Cleeves
	DCI Monika Panatowski	Sally Spencer
	Mrs Pargeter	Simon Brett
	Charles Paris	Simon Brett
	Jack Paris	Richard Montanari
	PC Nick Parish	Nicholas Rhea

Rona Parish	Anthea Fraser
Ruby Parker	Rowan Coleman
Charlie 'Bird' Parker	John Connolly
Henry Parker	Jason Pinter
Parker	Richard Stark
Jack Parlabane	Christopher Brookmyre
DS Pascoe	Reginald Hill
Kamil Pasha	Jenny White
Sarah Patrick	Iris Johansen
Patterson Family	Jessica Stirling
Jonathon Payne	Chris Kuzneski
Hugh Payne	R T Raichev
Amelia Peabody	Elizabeth Peters
DC Charlie Peace	Robert Barnard
DCI Percy Peach	J M Gregson
Nathan Peake	Seth Hunter
Pearce	Allan Guthrie
John Pearce	David Donachie
Insp Pekkala	Sam Eastland
Sister Pelagia	Boris Akunin
John Pellam	Jeffery Deaver
DS Mark Pemberton	Nicholas Rhea
Aloysius Pendergast	Douglas Preston
Pendragon Island Series	Grace Thompson
Pengarron Series	Gloria Cook
Det Jimmy Perez	Ann Cleeves
Douglas Perkins	Marian Babson
DS Lou Perlman	Campbell Armstrong
Gianni Peroni	David Hewson
Reginald Perrin	David Nobbs
Toby Peters	Stuart M Kaminsky
DS Wesley Peterson	Kate Ellis
Vlado Petric	Dan Fesperman
Det Porfiry Petrovich	R N Morris
Primavera Phillips	Quintin Jardine
Joe Pickett	C J Box
DI Joanna Piercy	Priscilla Masters
Joe Pike	Robert Crais
Pinarius Family	Steven Saylor
Leonard Pine	Joe R Lansdale
Dirk Pitt	Clive Cussler
Insp Thomas Pitt	Anne Perry
Charlotte Pitt	Anne Perry
DI Joe Plantagenet	Kate Ellis
DI Montague Pluke	Nicholas Rhea
Stephanie Plum	Janet Evanovich
DS Romulus Poe	Faye Kellerman
Hercule Poirot	Agatha Christie
Poldark Series	Winston Graham
DS Poole	Graham Ison
Harry Potter	J K Rowling
DS Kate Power	Judith Cutler

Sgt Molly Power	Andrew Nugent
Lord Francis Powerscourt	David Dickinson
Sgt Prentice	Vivien Armstrong
DI Ian Preston	Vivien Armstrong
Prey Series	John Sandford
Det Sarah Pribek	Jodi Compton
Sgt Tom Price	James Delingpole
Pride Family	Annie Groves
DI Charlie Priest	Stuart Pawson
Prince Family	Sheelagh Kelly
Princess Mia Diaries Series	Meg Cabot
Prior's Ford Series	Evelyn Hood and Eve Houston
DS Judith Pullen	Vivien Armstrong
Vish Puri	Tarquin Hall
Simon Puttock	Michael Jecks
Pyke	Andrew Pepper

Q

Queen of Freedom Trilogy	Christian Jacq
Samantha Quest	Raymond Haigh
Ellie Quicke	Veronica Heley
Pierce Quincy	Lisa Gardner
Kimberly Quincy	Lisa Gardner
Jonathan Quinn	Brett Battles
Terry Quinn	George P Pelecanos
Quinn Family	Nora Roberts
Quinsigamond Series	Jack O'Connell
Quirke	Benjamin Black
Francis Quoynt	Christie Dickason
Imogen Quy	Jill Paton Walsh

R

DI Joe Rafferty	Geraldine Evans
Alexandra Rafferty	James W Hall
Rai Rahotep	Nick Drake
John Rain	Barry Eisler
Det Barrett Raines	Darryl Wimberley
Agatha Raisin	M C Beaton
Rambo	David Morrell
Precious Ramotswe	Alexander McCall Smith
DI Stephen Ramsay	Ann Cleeves
Ramses	Christian Jacq
Sunny Randall	Robert B Parker
Mitch Rapp	Vince Flynn
Raven Series	Giles Kristian
Ravenscar Series	Barbara Taylor Bradford
John Rawlings	Deryn Lake
Easy Rawlins	Walter Mosley
Captain Daniel Rawson	Edward Marston
Jack Reacher	Lee Child
DI John Rebus	Ian Rankin
Red Riding Quartet	David Peace
Christopher Redmayne	Edward Marston
Clio Rees	Jo Bannister
Regan Reilly	Carol Higgins Clark
Nina Reilly	Perri O'Shaughnessy

Insp Arkady Renko	Martin Cruz Smith
Capt William Rennie	Peter Smalley
Republic Series	Jack Ludlow
DI Charlie Resnick	John Harvey
Retallick Family	E V Thompson
Nick Revill	Philip Gooden
Revolution at Sea Saga	James L Nelson
Sukey Reynolds	Betty Rowlands
Alison Reynolds	J A Jance
DI Oskar Rheinhardt	Frank Tallis
Bernie Rhodenbarr	Lawrence Block
Lincoln Rhyme	Jeffery Deaver
Alice Rice	Gillian Galbraith
DI Tom Richmonds	Marjorie Eccles
Major Jason Richter	Dale Brown
DI Rickman	Margaret Murphy
Maximum Ride	James Patterson
Tom Ripley	Patricia Highsmith
Rising Family	Susan Sallis
Sophie Rivers	Judith Cutler
Leo Rivers	Robert Edric
Det Jane Rizzoli	Tess Gerritsen
Robert the Bruce	Robyn Young
DCI Roberts	Ken Bruen
Dave Robicheaux	James Lee Burke
Insp Lucas Rocco	Adrian Magson
Roger the Chapman	Kate Sedley
Helga Rolfe	James Hadley Chase
Jean Rombaud	C C Humphreys
Jim Rook	Graham Masterton
Rosato & Associates	Lisa Scottoline
Rose Saga	Linda Sole
Insp Ben Ross	Ann Granger
Insp Porfiry Rostnikov	Stuart M Kaminsky
Roth Trilogy	Andrew Taylor
Billy Rucher	Adam Baron
Horace Rumpole	John Mortimer
Rune	Jeffery Deaver
Gaius Petreius Ruso	R S Downie
John Russell	David Downing
Mary Russell	Laurie R King
Insp Ian Rutledge	Charles Todd
Finn Ryan	Paul Christopher
Jack Ryan	Tom Clancy
Det Rob Ryan	Tana French
Blackie Ryan	Andrew M Greeley
Sam Ryan	Nigel McCrery
Max Rydal	Elizabeth Darrell
Det Carson Ryder	J A Kerley
Harry Ryder	A L Berridge
Jonah Said	Simon Conway
Lisbeth Salander	Stieg Larsson

S

DC Jane Salt	David Armstrong
Gerald Samper	James Hamilton-Paterson
Bernard Samson	Len Deighton
Insp Joe Sandilands	Barbara Cleverly
Lucky Santangelo	Jackie Collins
Det Justin Savile	Michael Malone
DCI Hannah Scarlett	Martin Edwards
Kay Scarpetta	Patricia D Cornwell
Det Karin Schaeffer	Katia Lief
Capt Shane Schofield	Matthew Reilly
Matthew Scudder	Lawrence Block
Det Shane Scully	Stephen J Cannell
Carole Seddon	Simon Brett
Lucy Sedgwick	Clare Curzon
Claudia Seferius	Marilyn Todd
Insp Konrad Sejer	Karin Fossum
Gerhard Self	Bernhard Schlink
Sara Selkirk	Morag Joss
DCI Simon Serrailler	Susan Hill
Seymour	Michael Pearce
Kate Shackleton	Frances Brody
John Shakespeare	Rory Clements
Alex Shanahan	Lynne Heitman
Deets Shanahan	Ronald Tierney
DCI Frank Shapiro	Jo Bannister
Dr Matthew Shardlake	C J Sansom
Nick Sharman	Mark Timlin
DC Karen Sharpe	John Connor
Richard Sharpe	Bernard Cornwell
Mary Ann Shaughnessy	Catherine Cookson
DI Peter Shaw	Jim Kelly
Jack Sheffield	Jack Sheffield
Dan 'Spider' Shepherd	Stephen Leather
Archie Sheridan	Chelsea Cain
Sir Charles Sheridan	Robin Paige
Sheridan Family	Elizabeth Darrell
Shopaholic Series	Sophie Kinsella
Kate Shugak	Dana Stabenow
Sigma Force	James Rollins
Harry Silver	Tony Parsons
Evangeline Sinclair	Marian Babson
Insp Singh	Shamini Flint
Sisterhood Series	Fern Michaels
Joe Sixsmith	Reginald Hill
Jacob Skarre	Karin Fossum
DS Bob Skinner	Quintin Jardine
DI Bill Slider	Cynthia Harrod-Eagles
DI Sloan	Catherine Aird
Drew Slocombe	Rebecca Tope
Lieut Viktor Slutsky	Andrey Kurkov
Henry Smart	Roddy Doyle
George Smiley	John Le Carré

Grace Smith	Liz Evans
Sam Spade	Dashiell Hammett
Suzy Spencer	Lis Howell
Spenser	Robert B Parker
DI Jon Spicer	Chris Simms
DI Jack Spratt	Jasper Fforde
Srayanka	Christian Cameron
Sebastian St Cyr	C S Harris
Sookie Stackhouse	Charlaine Harris
DI Vera Stanhope	Ann Cleeves
Staples Family	Mary Jane Staples
Dr Jack Stapleton	Robin Cook
Nathaniel Starbuck	Bernard Cornwell
Jeanna Stark	Marcia Muller
Dan Starkey	Colin Bateman
Clarice Starling	Thomas Harris
Insp Starrett	Paul Charles
Lt Jack Steel	Iain Gale
Nick Stefanos	George P Pelecanos
Kellen Stewart	Manda Scott
Hanno Stiffeniis	Michael Gregorio
Nick Stone	Andy McNab
Chief Jesse Stone	Robert B Parker
Stone of Light Trilogy	Christian Jacq
Stonemoor Series	Kay Stephens
Serge Storms	Tim Dorsey
Derek Strange	George P Pelecanos
John Stratton	Duncan Falconer
DI Ted Stratton	Laura Wilson
Pearl Street	Maureen Lee
Leo Street	Pauline McLynn
Det Jonathan Stride	Brian Freeman
DS Jim Stringer	Andrew Martin
Whilbert Stroop	Clio Gray
Lt Jack Stryker	Paula Gosling
Supt Yngvar Stubo	Anne Holt
Det Milo Sturgis	Jonathan Kellerman
C W Sughrue	James Crumley
Sheriff John Victor Sully	Boston Teran
Supt Gregory Summers	Susan B Kelly
Sunday Philosophy Club Series	Alexander McCall Smith
Det Sven Sunkist	Roslund and Hellström
Sutton Family	Elizabeth Elgin
Insp Erlendur Sveinsson	Arnaldur Indridason
Cassie Swann	Susan Moody
Kyle Swanson	Jack Coughlin
Sweet Rosie Series	Iris Gower
Hannah Swensen	Joanne Fluke
Jack Swyteck	James Grippando
Yashim Tagalu	Jason Goodwin
Laetitia Talbot	Barbara Cleverly
Tales of the City	Armistead Maupin

T

Paul Tallis	E V Seymour
Sgt Jack Tanner	James Holland
DI Mark Tartaglia	Elena Forbes
Gerry Tate	Marian Babson
Harry Tate	Adrian Magson
Betsy Taylor	Mary Janice Davidson
Jack Taylor	Ken Bruen
Karen Taylor	Natasha Cooper
Telamon	Paul Doherty
Temeraire	Naomi Novik
Templar Series	Paul Christopher
Templar Trilogy	Jack Whyte
The Templars	Paul Doherty
DCI Jane Tennison	Lynda La Plante
Frank Terrell	James Hadley Chase
Josephine Tey	Nicola Upson
DCI Michael Thackeray	Patricia Hall
PC Thackeray	Peter Lovesey
Elsie Thirkettle	L C Tyler
Odd Thomas	Dean R Koontz
Mercy Thompson	Patricia Briggs
Barney Thomson	Douglas Lindsay
Rosa Thorn	Vena Cork
Thorn	James W Hall
DI Tom Thorne	Mark Billingham
DI Richard Thornhill	Andrew Taylor
Charles Thoroughgood	Alan Judd
Three Sisters Island Trilogy	Nora Roberts
Thrush Green	Miss Read
Tilla	R S Downie
Leslie Titmus	John Mortimer
Tokyo Trilogy	David Peace
Jeffrey Tolliver	Karin Slaughter
Tom and Matt Series	Anna Maxted
Lina Townend	Judith Cutler
C J Townsend	Jilliane Hoffman
Tramont Family	Tessa Barclay
Det Anna Travis	Lynda La Plante
Will Trent	Karin Slaughter
Ethelred Tressider	L C Tyler
Supt Perry Trethowan	Robert Barnard
DCI Nick Trevellyan	Susan B Kelly
Prof Kate Trevorne	Paula Gosling
Tilly Trotter	Catherine Cookson
Baroness Troutbeck	Ruth Dudley Edwards
CDS Frederick Troy	John Lawton
DS Troy	Caroline Graham
CI Trubshawe	Gilbert Adair
Capt Trujillo	José Latour
Jacob Tshabalala	Richard Kunzmann
Lizzy Tucker	Janet Evanovich
John Turner	James Sallis

Turnham Malpas Series	Rebecca Shaw
Tweed	Colin Forbes
Twilight Saga	Stephenie Meyer
Twinks	Simon Brett
DI Tom Tyler	Maureen Jennings
Francis Urquhart Trilogy	Michael Dobbs
Lilly Valentine	Helen Black
DS George Valentine	Jim Kelly
Valley Series	Grace Thompson
Vampire Chronicles	Anne Rice
Zatopek 'Zed' van Heerden	Deon Meyer
Insp Van Veeteren	Häkan Nesser
Harriet Vane	Jill Paton Walsh
Fran Varady	Ann Granger
Daniel Vartanian	Karen Rose
Vengeance of the Gods	Christian Jacq
DI Charles Vignoles	Stephen Done
Johanna Vik	Anne Holt
Lord Miles Vorkosigan	Lois McMaster Bujold
Prof Dr Moritz-Maria von Igelfeld	Alexander McCall Smith
Jason Wade	Rick Mofina
DI Will 'Staffe' Wagstaffe	Adam Creed
Zack Walker	Linwood Barclay
Amos Walker	Loren D Estleman
Supt Mike Walker	Lynda La Plante
DS Helen Walker	John Harvey
Insp Kurt Wallander	Henning Mankell
Bella Wallis	Brian Thompson
Penny Wanawake	Susan Moody
War Torn Series	Andy McNab
Eric Ward	Roy Lewis
Ward Family	Elizabeth Murphy
Det Sgt D D Warren	Lisa Gardner
V I Warshawski	Sara Paretsky
Simon Waterhouse	Sophie Hannah
Leo Waterman	G M Ford
Merrily Watkins	Phil Rickman
Dr John Watson	Arthur Conan Doyle
Anne Waverley	Laurie R King
Benjamin Weaver	David Liss
Milo Weaver	Olen Steinhauer
DCI David Webb	Anthea Fraser
Insp Decimus Webb	Lee Jackson
Webster Family	Beryl Matthews
Scott Weiss	Andrew Klavan
Duke of Wellington	Simon Scarrow
John Wells	Alex Berenson
Matt Wells	Paul Johnston
Heather Wells Series	Meg Cabot
Werner Family	Belva Plain
Helen West	Frances Fyfield
Jack West Jr	Matthew Reilly

	Harriet Westerman	Imogen Robertson
	CI George Wexford	Ruth Rendell
	Murray Whelan	Shane Maloney
	Jane Whitefield	Thomas Perry
	Wideacre Trilogy	Philippa Gregory
	Oscar Wilde	Gyles Brandreth
	Nina Wilde	Andy McDermott
	Hamish Williams	Adrian Goldsworthy
	Sgt George Williamson	James McCreet
	Henry Wilt	Tom Sharpe
	Lord Peter Wimsey	Dorothy L Sayers, Jill Paton Walsh
	Erik Winter	Ake Edwardson
	DC Paul Winter	Graham Hurley
	'Women's Murder Club'	James Patterson
	C F Wong	Nury Vittachi
	DCI Charlie Woodend	Sally Spencer
	Bertie Wooster	P G Wodehouse
	World War 1 Series	Anne Perry
	Supt Wycliffe	W J Burley
Y	Bubbles Yablonsky	Sarah Strohmeyer
	Det Li Yan	Peter May
	Yaotl	Simon Levack
	Supt Mike Yeadings	Clare Curzon
	DS Yellich	Peter Turnbull
	Omar Yussef	Matt Rees
Z	Charlie Zailer	Sophie Hannah
	Faith Zanetti	Anna Blundy
	The Mamur Zapt (Gareth Owen)	Michael Pearce
	Aurelio Zen	Michael Dibdin
	Nathan Zuckerman	Philip Roth
	Miss Zukas	Jo Dereske
	Nick Zuliani	Ian Morson

Environments

Listed here are the geographical and/or environmental settings used by a range of novelists - countries, counties and towns - as well as dates where appropriate. Authors' names are appended alongside each location.

'Adensfield', Yorkshire	Nicholas Rhea
'Algonquin Bay', Canada	Giles Blunt
'Ballydown', Ireland	Anne Doughty
'Blackwater Bay', Michigan	Paula Gosling
'Bradfield', Yorkshire	Patricia Hall
'Broadshire', Home Counties	Anthea Fraser
'Burracombe' village, Devon	Lilian Harry
'Calleshire'	Catherine Aird
'Crowby', Midlands	Iain McDowall
'Denton'	R D Wingfield
'Eborby', North Yorkshire	Kate Ellis
'Fethering', Sussex	Simon Brett
'Greater Birchester'	H R F Keating
'Handstead New Town', Manchester	Charlie Owen
'Hawkenlye Abbey' - C12th Kent	Alys Clare
'Heartsdale', Georgia	Karin Slaughter
'Hillston', North Carolina	Michael Malone
'Isola' Police Department - 87th Precinct	Ed McBain
'Kingsmarkham'	Ruth Rendell
'Lafferton'	Susan Hill
'Long Farnden'	Ann Purser
'Lydmouth', 1950s Welsh Borders	Andrew Taylor
'Midsomer Worthy'	Caroline Graham
'Moorlands', Staffordshire	Priscilla Masters
'Oakwood', Canada	Linwood Barclay
'Painter's Creek', Ohio	Linda Castillo
'Paradise', Mass	Robert B Parker
'Paradise', Michigan	Steve Hamilton
'Priorton', NE England	Wendy Robertson
'Rapstone Valley'	John Mortimer
'Round Ringford'	Ann Purser
'Saddlestring', Wyoming	C J Box
'Santa Teresa', California	Sue Grafton
'Seatoun', South Coast, England	Liz Evans
'Strattenburg'	John Grisham
'Talyton', Devon	Cathy Woodman
1920s	Carola Dunn
1930s	Simon Brett, Nicola Upson
1950s	Alan Bradley

Environments

	87th Precinct, 'Isola' Police Department	Ed McBain
A	Abbot Agency	Veronica Heley
	Aberdeen	Stuart MacBride
	Aberystwyth	Malcolm Pryce
	Afghanistan	Andy McNab
	Afghanistan - C19th	Thalassa Ali
	Africa 1920s	Suzanne Arruda
	Alaska	Dana Stabenow
	American Civil War	Bernard Cornwell, James L Nelson
	Amsterdam	Janwillem van de Wetering
	Ancient	Colleen McCullough
	Ancient Egypt	Paul Doherty
	Ancient Greece	Glyn Iliffe, Steven Pressfield, Marilyn Todd
	Ancient Roman navy	John Stack
	Ancient Rome	Lindsey Davis, Douglas Jackson, Ben Kane, Jack Ludlow, Steven Saylor, Harry Sidebottom, Marilyn Todd, David Wishart
	Ancient Rome - C11th	Paul Doherty
	Ancient Rome - Politics	John Maddox Roberts
	Appalachians, East Tennessee	Sharyn McCrumb
	Arizona	J A Jance
	Art world	Derek Wilson
	Asia	Shamini Flint
	Atlanta	Karin Slaughter
	Australia	Caroline Carver, Garry Disher, Claire McNab
	Australia - Melbourne	Lindy Cameron, Shane Maloney, Peter Temple
	Australia - Melbourne, 1920s	Kerry Greenwood
	Australia - Sydney	Robert G Barrett, Peter Corris, Gabrielle Lord
	Aviation	Dale Brown, Lynne Heitman
B	Baltimore	Laura Lippman
	Bari	Gianrico Carofiglio
	Bath	Margaret Duffy, Morag Joss
	Bath - C20th	Peter Lovesey
	Belfast	Colin Bateman, Stuart Neville
	Birmingham	Anne Bennett, Chris Collett, Judith Cutler, Meg Hutchinson, Annie Murray
	Bisbee, Arizona	J A Jance
	Blackpool	Nick Oldham, Margaret Thornton
	Boer War	John Wilcox
	Bologna - Fascist period	Carlo Lucarelli
	Bombay	H R F Keating
	Bosnia	Dan Fesperman
	Boston, Mass	Lisa Gardner, William Landay, Linda Barnes, Dennis Lehane, Robert B Parker
	Botswana	Alexander McCall Smith, Michael Stanley
	Boulder, Colorado	Stephen White
	Bradford, Yorkshire	Lesley Horton
	Brattleboro, Vermont	Archer Mayor
	Brighton	Peter James
	British Secret Service	Stephanie Laurens

Environments

	Denver	Michael Connelly
	Destroyer USS Cunningham	James H Cobb
	Detroit	Loren D Estleman
	Devon	Rebecca Tope
	Devon - 'Burracombe' village	Lilian Harry
	Devon - 'Talyton'	Cathy Woodman
	Devon - C12th	Bernard Knight
	Devon - C14th	Michael Jecks
	Dorset - C19th	Janet Woods
	Dragon Air Force C19th	Naomi Novik
	Dublin	Declan Hughes, Gene Kerrigan, Ava McCarthy, Pauline McLynn, Andrew Nugent
	Dublin - 1950s	Benjamin Black
	Dublin - Garda police force	Tana French
E	**East Lancashire**	J M Gregson
	Edinburgh	David Ashton, Tony Black, Gillian Galbraith, Allan Guthrie, Quintin Jardine, Alexander McCall Smith, Grace Monroe, Ian Rankin, Joyce Holms
	Edinburgh - C19th	Alanna Knight
	Edinburgh - C21st	Paul Johnston
	Egypt	Michelle Moran, Elizabeth Peters, Wilbur Smith
	Egypt - early C20th	Michael Pearce
	Ely, Cambridgeshire	Jim Kelly
	England	Anthony Riches
	England - 1900	Robin Paige
	England - 1920s	Charles Todd, Dolores Gordon-Smith
	England - C11th	Edward Marston
	England - C12th	Sharon Penman
	England - C13th	Paul Doherty
	England - C14th	Paul Doherty
	England - C14th & C17th	Susanna Gregory
	England - C15th	Dorothy Dunnett, Kate Sedley, Margaret Frazer
	England - C16th and C18th	C C Humphreys
	England - C16th, theatre	Edward Marston
	England - C17th	Edward Marston
	England - C18th	Imogen Robertson
	England - C18th/19th	Julian Stockwin, C S Forester
	England - C19th	M J Trow, Peter Lovesey, Anne Perry
	England - C20th	Amy Myers, Anne Perry
	England - Early C20th	Clare Curzon
	England - Edwardian	Kenneth Cameron, David Dickinson, Mark Gatiss
	England - Elizabethan	Patricia Finney
	England, South Coast	Jo Bannister
	Erde	L E Modesitt Jr
	Essex	June Thomson
	Europe	Adrian Magson
	Europe - C18th & C19th	Simon Scarrow
	Europe - C19th	Amy Myers
	Europe & Near East	Jack Whyte
	Exmoor	Belinda Bauer
F	**Far East**	Nury Vittachi

	FBI	Thomas Harris, Kyle Mills
	FBI - Special Operations Unit	Dale Brown
	Finland	Jan Costin Wagner
	Finland - Helsinki	Matti Joensuu
	Florida	Lee Child, Tim Dorsey, James W Hall, Carl Hiaasen, Jonathon King, Darryl Wimberley, Stuart Woods
	France - 1960s	Adrian Magson
	France - C12th	Sharon Penman
	France - C17th & C18th	Edward Marston
	France - Medieval	James Patterson
	France - Marseilles	Xavier-Marie Bonnot, Martin O'Brien
	France - Paris	Cara Black, Dominique Manotti, Fred Vargas, Georges Simenon
	France - Paris, C18th	Jean François Parot
	France - Paris, C19th	Claude Izner
	France - Périgord	Martin Walker
	France - Provence	Pierre Magnan
G	**Georgia**	Beverly Connor
	Georgia - 'Heartsdale'	Karin Slaughter
	Germany	Philip Kerr, Bernhard Schlink
	Germany - Hamburg	Craig Russell
	Germany - Regensburg	Alexander McCall Smith
	Germany - WW2	David Downing
	Glasgow	Lin Anderson, Campbell Armstrong, Karen Campbell, Alex Gray, Val McDermid, Pat McIntosh, Denise Mina, G J Moffat, Caro Ramsay, Craig Russell, Manda Scott, Anna Smith, Jessica Stirling, Peter Turnbull
	Glasgow - 1940s	Gordon Ferris
	Gosport, Hampshire	June Hampson
	Great Yarmouth	Vivien Armstrong
	Greece	Paul Johnston, Jeffrey Siger, Anne Zouroudi
	Greece - C3rd BC	Paul Doherty
H	**Harvard University**	Dan Brown
	Hayling Island	Pauline Rowson
	Hollywood	Jonathan Kellerman
	Hollywood - 1940s	Stuart M Kaminsky
	Hollywood - C20th	Megan Abbott
	Horse racing	Dick Francis, John Francome, Lyndon Stacey
	Hull	Robert Edric
I	**Iceland**	Arnaldur Indridason, Michael Ridpath
	India	Tarquin Hall
	India - C19th	Thalassa Ali
	India - 1920s	Barbara Cleverly
	Indian Mutiny	Patrick Mercer
	Indianapolis	Ronald Tierney
	Ireland	Maeve Binchy, Benjamin Black, Erin Hart, Andrew Nugent, Joan O'Neill, D M Purcell, Liz Ryan, Kate Thompson
	Ireland - 'Ballydown'	Anne Doughty
	Ireland - Burren	Cora Harrison
	Ireland - C7th	Peter Tremayne
	Ireland - Galway	Ken Bruen
	Irish Serious Crime Unit	Paul Charles

Environments

	Isle of Wight	Elizabeth Daish
	Israeli Secret Service	Daniel Silva
	Istanbul	Jason Goodwin, Barbara Nadel, Orhan Pamuk
	Istanbul - C19th	Jenny White
	Italy	Andrea Camilleri, Michael Dibdin, Conor Fitzgerald, David Hewson, Donna Leon, Carlo Lucarelli
	Italy - C16th	Marina Fiorato
	Italy - Florence	Michele Giuttari, Christobel Kent, Giulio Leoni, Magdalen Nabb
	Italy - Tuscany	James Hamilton-Paterson
J	Japan	Eric Van Lustbader
	Johannesburg	Richard Kunzmann
K	Kent	Judith Cutler, Pamela Oldfield, Sally Worboyes
	Kenya	Nick Brownlee, Barbara & Stephanie Keating
	Knights Templar	Robyn Young
L	Lake District	Martin Edwards
	Lake Tahoe, California	Perri O'Shaughnessy
	Lancashire	Alexandra Connor, Anna Jacobs, Sally Spencer, Neil White
	Lancashire & Liverpool	Ruth Hamilton, Audrey Howard
	Laos	Colin Cotterill
	Las Vegas	Faye Kellerman
	Lehigh, Pennsylvania	Sarah Strohmeyer
	Leicester	Lynda Page
	Leicestershire	Audrey Willsher
	Light Dragoons - C19th	Allan Mallinson
	Lincolnshire	Margaret Dickinson
	Lincolnshire	Mary Mackie
	Liverpool	Anne Baker, Martin Edwards, Katie Flynn, June Francis, Annie Groves, Joan Jonker, Maureen Lee, Margaret Murphy, Denise Ryan
	Liverpool & Lancashire	Ruth Hamilton, Audrey Howard
	Liverpool & Wales	Rosie Harris
	Liverpool Irish	Lyn Andrews
	London	Marian Babson, Robert Barnard, Adam Baron, Mark Billingham, Ken Bruen, Paul Charles, P F Chisholm, Natasha Cooper, Adam Creed, Deborah Crombie, Elizabeth Daish, Stella Duffy, Pamela Evans, Gordon Ferris, Christopher Fowler, Nicci French, Frances Fyfield, Jonathan Gash, Elizabeth George, Ann Granger, Martha Grimes, Cynthia Harrod-Eagles, Mo Hayder, Lauren Henderson, Patricia Highsmith, Michael Innes, Graham Ison, Lee Jackson, P D James, Paul Johnston, Simon Kernick, Beryl Kingston, Lynda La Plante, David Lawrence, John Lawton, Stephen Leather, Elizabeth Lord, Marianne MacDonald, Hope McIntyre, Barry Maitland, John Mortimer, Mark Pearson, Victor Pemberton, Mike Ripley, Mary Jane Staples, Brian Thompson, Mark Timlin, Elizabeth Waite, Jeanne Whitmee, Audrey Willsher, Sally Worboyes
	London - 1940s	Laura Wilson
	London - C17th	Fidelis Morgan
	London - C18th	Deryn Lake
	London - C19th	Edward Marston, Sally Spencer
	London - C20th	Laurie R King

Environments

	London - East End	Kimberley Chambers, Martina Cole, Jean Fullerton, Jessie Keane, Barbara Nadel, Gilda O'Neill, Dee Williams
	London - Henrician	C J Sansom
	London - Isle of Dogs	Carol Rivers
	London - North	Andrew Taylor
	London - Soho, 1940s	Pip Granger
	London - Victorian	Joan Lock, James McCreet
	London - West	Elena Forbes
	London & Glasgow	Denise Mina
	London & Kent - WW1 & onwards	Jacqueline Winspear
	London Inner Temple Legal Chambers	Caro Fraser
	Londonderry	Brian McGilloway
	Los Angeles	Chris Carter, Raymond Chandler, Michael Connelly, Robert Crais, James Ellroy, Robert Ferrigno, Scott Frost, Faye Kellerman, Jonathan Kellerman, Lynda La Plante, Claire McNab, Walter Mosley, John Shannon, Edward Wright
	Los Angeles Police Dept (LAPD)	Stephen J Cannell, Robert Ellis, Joseph Wambaugh
	Louisiana	Rebecca Wells
	Luton	Reginald Hill
	Luxor, Egypt	Paul Sussman
M	**Mallorca**	Roderic Jeffries
	Manchester	Mandasue Heller, Freda Lightfoot, Val McDermid, Chris Simms, Cath Staincliffe
	Manchester - 'Handstead New Town'	Charlie Owen
	MANIAC Special Forces	Chris Kuzneski
	Marblehead	Janet Evanovich
	Marseilles	Xavier-Marie Bonnot, Martin O'Brien
	Mass - 'Paradise'	Robert B Parker
	Merchant Navy	Philip McCutchan
	Metropolitan Police	Kevin Lewis
	Mexico	Simon Levack
	MI6	Geoffrey Archer, Brian Freemantle
	Miami, Florida	James Grippando, Jilliane Hoffman, Nick Stone, P J Parrish
	Michigan - 'Blackwater Bay'	Paula Gosling
	Michigan - 'Paradise'	Steve Hamilton
	Midlands	Marjorie Eccles
	Midlands - 'Crowby'	Iain McDowall
	Milan	Carlo Lucarelli
	Minneapolis	Jodi Compton, John Sandford
	Minneapolis Police Dept	Tami Hoag
	Minnesota	Joanne Fluke, Brian Freeman, John Sandford
	Mississippi	John Sandford
	Missouri	Carol Higgins Clark
	Mongolia	Ian Morson, Michael Walters
	Montana	James Lee Burke, James Crumley
	Montreal	Kathy Reichs
	Moscow	Stuart M Kaminsky
N	**Napoleonic Wars**	Bernard Cornwell, David Donachie, Adrian Goldsworthy, Sean Thomas Russell

	Nation County, Iowa	Donald Harstad
	Navajo Reservation, Arizona	Tony Hillerman
	NE England	Rita Bradshaw, Catherine Cookson, Alan Dunn, Una Horne, Ken McCoy, Denise Robertson, Janet MacLeod Trotter
	NE England - 'Priorton'	Wendy Robertson
	Nelson's navy	G S Beard
	Netherlands	Janwillem van de Wetering
	Nevada	Don Winslow
	New England	John Connolly
	New Iberia, Louisiana	James Lee Burke
	New Mexico	Michael McGarrity
	New Orleans	Lisa Jackson, James Sallis
	New York	Sean Black, Lawrence Block, Harlan Coben, Robin Cook, Jeffery Deaver, Linda Fairstein, Tess Gerritsen, Sparkle Hayter, Walter Mosley, Reggie Nadelson, Carol O'Connell, Jason Pinter, Douglas Preston, Stuart Woods, Kinky Friedman, Robert K Tanenbaum
	New York - future	J D Robb
	New York Police Dept (NYPD)	Alex Barclay, Alafair Burke, Margaret Maron
	Newark, New Jersey	Janet Evanovich
	Newcastle	Roy Lewis
	Norbridge Chronicles	Lis Howell
	Norfolk	Jane Adams, Elly Griffiths, Jim Kelly, Mary Mackie
	North Carolina	Margaret Maron, Kathy Reichs
	North Carolina - 'Hillston'	Michael Malone
	North Yorkshire - 'Eborby'	Kate Ellis
	Northern Ireland	Mary A Larkin
	Northumberland	Ann Cleeves
	Northumberland police	Roy Lewis
	Nottingham	John Harvey
	Norway - Oslo	Karin Fossum, Anne Holt, Jo Nesbo
O	**Ohio - 'Painter's Creek'**	Linda Castillo
	Oklahoma	William Bernhardt
	Oxford	Colin Dexter, Veronica Stallwood
	Oxford University	Ian Morson
	Oxfordshire	Vivien Armstrong
	Ozark Mountains - Missouri	Daniel Woodrell
P	**Palestine**	Matt Rees
	Peak District	Stephen Booth
	Philadelphia	W E B Griffin, Lisa Scottoline
	Politics - Ancient Rome	John Maddox Roberts
	Pontypridd, Wales	Catrin Collier
	Portland, Oregon	Alafair Burke
	Portsmouth	Julia Bryant, Lilian Harry, Graham Hurley
	Portugal	Robert Wilson
	Preston	Annie Groves
	Prussia - C19th	Michael Gregorio
Q	**Quebec**	Louise Penny
	Queen's Own Royal Strathspeys	Philip McCutchan
R	**Railways - 1940s**	Stephen Done
	Railways of C19th England	Edward Marston

	Reading Police Dept	Jasper Fforde
	Reykjavik	Arnaldur Indridason
	Roman and Celtic Britain	Jules Watson
	Roman Britain	Rosemary Rowe, Manda Scott
	Roman Empire	Richard Blake, R S Downie, Paul Waters
	Roman Europe - C1st AD	Simon Scarrow
	Rome	Conor Fitzgerald, David Hewson
	Royal Military Police	Elizabeth Darrell
	Royal Navy	Philip McCutchan
	Russia	Alex Dryden, Sam Eastland, R N Morris, Martin Cruz Smith
	Russia - 1950s	Tom Rob Smith
	Russia & Ukraine	Andrey Kurkov
	Russian Revolution	James Fleming
S	**San Diego**	Steve Martini
	San Francisco	Meg Gardiner, Dashiell Hammett, Andrew Klavan, John T Lescroart, Marcia Muller, James Patterson, Richard North Patterson, Laurie R King
	Santa Barbara, California	Meg Gardiner
	Saudi Arabia	Zoë Ferraris
	Scotland	M C Beaton, Emma Blair, Christopher Brookmyre, Maggie Craig, Doris Davidson, Margaret Thomson Davis, Evelyn Hood, Eve Houston, Gwen Kirkwood, Douglas Lindsay, Frederic Lindsay, Betty McInnes, Alexandra Raife, Eileen Ramsay, Jessica Stirling, Aline Templeton, Mary Withall
	Scotland - 1920s	Catriona McPherson
	Scotland - C13th	Candace Robb, Robyn Young
	Scotland - Jacobean	Alanna Knight
	Scottish Borders	Gerald Hammond
	Scottish Grenadiers	Iain Gale
	Seattle	G M Ford, J A Jance, Rick Mofina, Ridley Pearson
	Severn Vale District	M R Hall
	Shanghai	Qiu Xiaolong
	Shetland Isles	Ann Cleeves
	Shrewsbury	Priscilla Masters
	Shropshire	David Armstrong
	Shropshire - C13th	Ellis Peters
	Siberia - 1950s	Sam Eastland
	Sicily	Andrea Camilleri
	SIS	Colin Forbes, Andy McNab
	Somerset	Janet Tanner
	South Africa	Richard Kunzmann, Deon Meyer Michael Stanley
	South Africa, 1950s	Malla Nunn
	South London	Kitty Neale
	South Wales	Iris Gower
	Southern States	J A Kerley, Ann B Ross
	Southern USA	Carson McCullers
	South-west USA	Cormac McCarthy
	Spain	Roderic Jeffries
	Spain - C17th	Arturo Pérez-Reverte
	St Agatha's College, Cambridge	Jill Paton Walsh
	St Andrews	Shirley McKay

Environments

	St Botolphs 'Molehill'	Suzette Hill
	St Petersburg - C19th	R N Morris
	Staffordshire - 'Moorlands'	Priscilla Masters
	Staffordshire potteries - 1950s	Margaret Kaine
	Sunderland	Sheila Quigley
	Surrey	Rennie Airth
	Sussex	Simon Brett, Elizabeth Corley
	Swansea	Gwen Madoc
	Sweden	Kjell Eriksson, Åsa Larsson, Häkan Nesser, Leif J W Persson, Roslund and Hellström
	Sweden - Fjällbacka	Camilla Läckberg
	Sweden - Gothenburg	Ake Edwardson
	Sweden - Gotland	Mari Jungstedt
	Sweden - Öland	Johan Theorin
	Sweden - Stockholm	Liza Marklund, Maj Sjöwall & Per Wahlöö
	Sweden - Ystad	Henning Mankell
	Swindon	Jasper Fforde
T	Tennessee	Jefferson Bass, James Sallis
	Texas	Jeff Abbott, James Lee Burke, James Crumley
	Texas & 1930s Texas	Joe R Lansdale
	Thailand	Colin Cotterill
	Thames Valley	Clare Curzon, Susan B Kelly
	Theatre - C16th England	Edward Marston
	Thebes, Ancient Egypt	Nick Drake
	Tokyo	David Peace
	Toronto	Maureen Jennings
	Tsarist Russia	Michael Pearce
	Turkey	Barbara Nadel
	Tyneside	Roy Lewis
	Tyneside - C19th	Benita Brown
U	Ukraine & Russia	Andrey Kurkov
	Ulaan Bataan - Serious crime squad	Michael Walters
	USA	Matt Hilton, Jan Karon, James L Nelson, Belva Plain
	US Marine Corps	Matthew Reilly
	US Naval Intelligence	Gordon Kent
	US Navy Seal	Tom Grace
	US Southern States	P D Martin
	USSR	Martin Cruz Smith
V	Vatican	Juan Gómez-Jurado
	Venice	Donna Leon
	Venus (Venice)	Tanith Lee
	Victoria	Garry Disher
	Vienna, early 1900s	Frank Tallis
	Vikings	Giles Kristian, Robert Low
	Virginia	Patricia D Cornwell, Adriana Trigiani
W	Wales	Bill James, Leslie Thomas, Grace Thompson
	Wales and Liverpool	Rosie Harris
	Warwickshire, England	Norman Russell
	Washington DC	David Baldacci, Joseph Finder, James Patterson, George P Pelecanos

	Washington State	Jo Dereske
	Washington State - Spokane	Jess Walter
	Welsh Borders - 'Lydmouth' 1950s	Andrew Taylor
	West Africa	Robert Wilson
	West Country	Kate Ellis, Connie Monk, Susan Sallis, Rowena Summers
	West Yorkshire	John Connor
	Whitby	Paul Magrs
	Wisconsin	Lori Handeland
	WW1 & onwards, London & Kent	Jacqueline Winspear
	WW2	Patrick Bishop, James Delingpole, Iain Gale, Hilary Green, James Holland, Sheila Newberry, June Tate
	WW2 - Germany	David Downing
	WWI - London	Graham Ison
	Wyoming - 'Saddlestring'	C J Box
Y	**York**	Cassandra Clark, Peter Turnbull
	York - C14th	Candace Robb
	Yorkshire	Aileen Armitage, Robert Barnard, Frances Brody, Marjorie Eccles, Elizabeth Elgin, Reginald Hill, Sheelagh Kelly, Stuart Pawson, David Peace, Peter Robinson, Jack Sheffield, Kay Stephens
	Yorkshire - 'Adensfield'	Nicholas Rhea
	Yorkshire - 'Bradfield'	Patricia Hall
	Yorkshire - C19th	Jessica Blair
	Yorkshire Moors	Deanna Raybourn

Environments

Literary Prizes and Awards

There are over 250 literary prizes and awards available in the United Kingdom. Thirty-five of those that relate to fiction are listed in this section with a brief description of each award followed by the names of the winning authors and titles, generally from 2005 or when the award commenced. Earlier winners and discontinued prizes can be found at www.whoelsewriteslike.com.

Authors' Club First Novel Award

This is awarded to the most promising First Novel written by a British author and published in the UK during the calendar year preceding the year in which the award is presented.

2005	Henry Shukman	*Sandstorm*
2006	Neil Griffiths	*Betrayal in Naples*
2007	Nicola Monaghan	*The Killing Jar*
2008	Segun Afolabi	*Goodbye Lucille*
2009	Laura Beatty	*Pollard*
2010	Anthony Quinn	*The Rescue Man*
2011	Jonathan Kemp	*London Triptych*
2012	Kevin Barry	*City of Bohane*

James Tait Black Memorial Prizes

www.ed.ac.uk/about/people/tait-black/about

The James Tait Black Memorial Prizes, founded in memory of a partner in the publishing house A & C Black Ltd, were instituted in 1919. Two prizes are awarded annually for the best work of fiction and the best biography published in the previous year. The prizes are the UK's oldest continuous book awards.

2005	Ian McEwan	*Saturday*
2006	Cormac McCarthy	*The Road*
2007	Rosalind Belben	*Our Horses in Egypt*
2008	Sebastian Barry	*The Secret Scripture*
2009	A S Byatt	*The Children's Book*
2010	Tatjana Soli	*The Lotus Eaters*
2011	Padgett Powell	*You and I*

Prizes

Bollinger Everyman Wodehouse Prize

www.experiencebollinger.co.uk/thearts

Established in 2000 and named in honour of P G Wodehouse, this prize is awarded for comic writing. The winner is announced at the annual Hay Festival in May. In addition to the main prize a Gloucester Old Spot pig is also named after the winning novel.

2005	Marina Lewycka	*A Short History of Tractors in Ukrainian*
2006	Christopher Brookmyre	*All Fun and Games until Somebody Loses an Eye*
2007	Paul Torday	*Salmon Fishing in the Yemen*
2008	Will Self	*The Butt*
2009	Geoff Dyer	*Jeff in Venice, Death in Varanasi*
2010	Ian McEwan	*Solar*
2011	Gary Shteyngart	*Super Sad True Love Story*
2012	Terry Pratchett	*Snuff*

Harry Bowling Prize for New Writing

www.harrybowlingprize.co.uk

The Harry Bowling Prize was set up in 2000 in memory of the author. From 2010 it has been renamed The Harry Bowling Prize for New Writing in partnership with the Romantic Novelists' Association. It is awarded every two years and the prize is given for the first chapter and synopsis of a novel written by anyone who has not previously published an adult novel.

2006	Jean Fullerton	*No Cure for Love*
2008	Kathie Highley	*Falling*
2010	Debbie Johnson	*Fear No Evil*
2012	Natalie Lloyd-Evans	*A Dark Flowering*

British Fantasy Awards

www.britishfantasysociety.co.uk/british-fantasy-awards

The British Fantasy Society, founded in 1971, sponsors a number of awards including the August Derleth Award for the best novel of the year. Winners are selected by members of the Society at their annual Fantasy Convention.

2005	Stephen King	*Dark Tower VII, the Dark Tower*
2006	Neil Gaiman	*Anansi Boys*
2007	Tim Lebbon	*Dusk*
2008	Ramsey Campbell	*The Grin of the Dark*
2009	William Heaney (aka Graham Joyce)	*Memoirs of a Master Forger*
2010	Conrad Williams	*One*
2011	Sam Stone	*Demon Dance*
2012	Adam Nevill (best horror novel)	*The Ritual*
	Jo Walton (best fantasy novel)	*Among Others*

British Science Fiction Association Awards

www.bsfa.co.uk/bsfa-awards

Awarded annually after a ballot of members, by the British Science Fiction Association (BSFA). Winners of the Best Novel prize are listed below.

2005	Geoff Ryman	Air
2006	Jon Courtenay Grimwood	End of the World Blues
2007	Ian McDonald	Brasyl
2008	Ken MacLeod	The Night Sessions
2009	China Miéville	The City and the City
2010	Ian McDonald	The Dervish House
2011	Christopher Priest	The Islanders

Arthur C Clarke Award

www.clarkeaward.com

Established in 1986 the Arthur C Clarke Award is supported and judged jointly by the British Science Fiction Association, the Science Fiction Foundation and the Science Museum. It is for a Science Fiction novel receiving its first British publication. Horror and Fantasy are excluded unless there is a strong Science Fiction element in the book.

2005	China Miéville	Iron Council
2006	Geoff Ryman	Air
2007	M John Harrison	Nova Swing
2008	Richard Morgan	Black Man
2009	Ian R MacLeod	Song of Time
2010	China Miéville	The City and the City
2011	Lauren Beukes	Zoo City
2012	Jane Rogers	The Testament of Jessie Lamb

Commonwealth Writers' Prize

www.commonwealthfoundation.com/Howwedeliver/Prizes/CommonwealthBookPrize

Established in 1987 by the Commonwealth Foundation in association with the Book Trust and the Royal Overseas League, the award is administered annually within one of four regions of the Commonwealth. Entries submitted by publishers must be novels or short stories in English.

2005	Andrea Levy	Small Island
2006	Kate Grenville	The Secret River
2007	Lloyd Jones	Mister Pip
2008	Lawrence Hill	The Book of Negroes
2009	Christos Tsiolkas	The Slap
2010	Rana Dasgupta	Solo
2011	Aminatta Forna	The Memory of Love
2012	Shehan Karunatilaka	Chinaman: The Legend of Pradeep Mathew

Prizes

Costa Book Awards

(formerly the Whitbread Book of the Year and Literary Awards) www.costabookawards.com

Established in 1971, the Whitbread plc prizes were ultimately awarded to five categories: Novel; First Novel; Children's Novel; Poetry and Biography. From 2006 sponsorship passed to the Costa Coffee Co, a subsidiary of Whitbread plc with the format of the awards unchanged.

Whitbread

2005	First Novel	Tash Aw	*The Harmony Silk Factory*
	Novel	Ali Smith	*The Accidental*

Costa

2006	First Novel & 'Book of the Year'	Stef Penney	*The Tenderness of Wolves*
	Novel	William Boyd	*Restless*
2007	First Novel	Catherine O'Flynn	*What Was Lost*
	Novel & 'Book of the Year'	A L Kennedy	*Day*
2008	First Novel	Sadie Jones	*The Outcast*
	Novel & 'Book of the Year	Sebastian Barry	*The Secret Scripture*
2009	First Novel	Raphael Selbourne	*Beauty*
	Novel	Colm Toibin	*Brooklyn*
2010	First Novel	Kishwar Desai	*Witness the Night*
	Novel	Maggie O'Farrell	*The Hand That First Held Mine*
2011	First Novel	Christie Watson	*Tiny Sunbirds Far Away*
	Novel & 'Book of the Year'	Andrew Miller	*Pure*

Crime Writers' Association

www.thecwa.co.uk/daggers/index.html

The first meeting of the Association was convened by John Creasey in November 1953 and awards have been presented since 1955.

The **Dagger of Daggers** was a special award given to John Le Carré for *The Spy Who Came in From the Cold* in 2005 to celebrate the CWA's Golden Jubilee. All books that had previously won the CWA Gold Dagger for Best Crime Novel of the Year were eligible, and the purpose was to select "the best of the best".

John Creasey (New Blood) Dagger

For the best crime novel by an author who has not previously published a full-length work of fiction (formerly *JCMA*, known as *New Blood* 2006-2008).

2005	Dreda Say Mitchell	*Running Hot*
2006	Louise Penny	*Still Life*
2007	Gillian Flynn	*Sharp Objects*
2008	Matt Rees	*The Bethlehem Murders*
2009	Johan Theorin	*Echoes from the Dead*
2010	Ryan David Jahn	*Acts of Violence*
2011	S J Watson	*Before I Go To Sleep*

Prizes

Dagger in the Library

For "the author of crime fiction whose work has given most pleasure to readers" as nominated by UK libraries.

2005 Jake Arnott
2006 Jim Kelly
2007 Stuart MacBride
2008 Craig Russell
2009 Colin Cotterill
2010 Ariana Franklin
2011 Mo Hayder
2012 Steve Mosby

Debut Dagger

A new-writing competition open to anyone writing in the English language whose work has not been published before. First awarded 1998.

2005	Ruth Dugdall	*The Woman Before Me*
2006	Otis Twelve	*Imp: Being the Lost Notebooks of Rufus Wilmot Griswold in the Matter of the Death of Edgar Allan Poe*
2007	Alan Bradley	*The Sweetness at the Bottom of the Pie*
2008	Amer Anwar	*Western Fringes*
2009	Catherine O'Keefe	*The Pathologist*
2010	Patrick Eden	*A Place of Dying*
2011	Michele Rowe	*What Hidden Lies*
2012	Sandy Gingras	*Beached*

Diamond Dagger

For outstanding contribution to the genre of crime writing (known as *Cartier Diamond Dagger* 1986-2011).

2005 Ian Rankin
2006 Elmore Leonard
2007 John Harvey
2008 Sue Grafton
2009 Andrew Taylor
2010 Val McDermid
2011 Lindsey Davis
2012 Frederick Forsyth

Crime Writers' Association (continued)

Gold Dagger

For the best thriller, suspense novel or spy fiction published in the UK in the English language (known as *Duncan Lawrie Dagger* 2006-2008).

2005	Arnaldur Indridason	*Silence of the Grave*
2006	Ann Cleeves	*Raven Black*
2007	Peter Temple	*The Broken Shore*
2008	Frances Fyfield	*Blood From Stone*
2009	William Brodrick	*A Whispered Name*
2010	Belinda Bauer	*Blacklands*
2011	Tom Franklin	*Crooked Letter, Crooked Letter*

International Dagger

For the best crime novel translated into English (known as *Duncan Lawrie International Dagger* 2006-2008).

2006	Fred Vargas	*The Three Evangelists*
2007	Fred Vargas	*Wash This Blood Clean From My Hand*
2008	Dominique Manotti	*Lorraine Connection*
2009	Fred Vargas	*The Chalk Circle Man*
2010	Johan Theorin	*The Darkest Room*
2011	Roslund and Hellström	*Three Seconds*
2012	Andrea Camilleri	*The Potter's Field*

Ellis Peters Historical Dagger

Some years known as *Ellis Peters Award*.

2005	C J Sansom	*Dark Fire*
2006	Edward Wright	*Red Sky Lament*
2007	Ariana Franklin	*Mistress of the Art of Death*
2008	Laura Wilson	*Stratton's War*
2009	Philip Kerr	*If the Dead Rise Not*
2010	Rory Clements	*Revenger*
2011	Andrew Martin	*The Somme Stations*
2012	Aly Monroe	*Icelight*

Silver Dagger

For the runner-up (1969-2005).

2005	Barbara Nadel	*Deadly Web*

Steel Dagger

The Ian Fleming Steel Dagger for best thrillers.

2005	Henry Porter	*Brandenburg*
2006	Nick Stone	*Mr Clarinet*
2007	Gillian Flynn	*Sharp Objects*
2008	Tom Robb Smith	*Child 44*
2009	John Hart	*The Last Child*
2010	Simon Conway	*A Local Spy*
2011	Steve Hamilton	*The Lock Artist*

Desmond Elliott Prize

www.desmondelliottprize.org

Named after the literary agent and publisher, the prize was launched in 2007 as a biennial award for a first novel published in the UK. Following the good reception of the first winning entry in 2008, the trustees changed the award to an annual event. The panel of three judges look for a first novel with wide appeal and star quality.

2008	Nikita Lalwani	*Gifted*
2009	Edward Hogan	*Blackmoor*
2010	Ali Shaw	*The Girl with Glass Feet*
2011	Anjali Joseph	*Saraswati Park*
2012	Grace McCleen	*Land of Decoration*

Encore Award

www.encoreaward.com

Awarded to the best second novel of the year published in that calendar year. The winner is chosen by a panel of judges from entries submitted by publishers.

2005	Nadeem Aslam	*Maps For Lost Lovers*
2007	M J Hyland	*Carry Me Down*
2009	Julia Leigh	*Disquiet*
2011	Adam Foulds	*The Quickening Maze*
2012	Joe Dunthorne	*Wild Abandon*

Geoffrey Faber Memorial Prize

As a memorial to the founder and first Chairman of the firm, Faber and Faber Limited established the prize in 1963. Awarded annually, it is given in alternate years for a volume of verse and for a volume of prose fiction published originally in this country by writers who are under 40 years of age.

2005	David Mitchell	*Cloud Atlas*
2007	Edward Docx	*Self Help*
2009	David Szalay	*London and the South-East*
2011	Belinda McKeon	*Solace*

Foster Grant Romantic Novel of the Year

See Romantic Novel of the Year (page 342)

Miles Franklin Award

www.milesfranklin.com.au

The Miles Franklin Literary Award is an annual literary prize for the best Australian published novel or play portraying Australian life in any of its phases. The award was set up according to the will of Stella Miles Franklin, the renowned Australian author, three years after her death in 1957.

2005	Andrew McGahan	*The White Earth*
2006	Roger McDonald	*The Ballad of Desmond Kale*
2007	Alexis Wright	*Carpentaria*
2008	Steven Carroll	*The Time We Have Taken*
2009	Tim Winton	*Breath*
2010	Peter Temple	*Truth*
2011	Kim Scott	*That Deadman Dance*
2012	Anna Funder	*All That I Am*

Guardian First Book Award

This award succeeded the Guardian Fiction Prize in 1999. It now recognises and rewards new writing by honouring an author's first book, which may be fiction or non-fiction.

2005	Alexander Masters	*Stuart: a Life Backwards*
2006	No award to fiction	
2007	Dinaw Mengestu	*Children of the Revolution*
2009	Petina Gappah	*An Elegy for Easterly*
2010 & 2011	No award to fiction	

Hawthornden Prize

Founded in 1919 by Miss Alice Warrender and along with the James Tait Black Award, it is one of the UK's oldest literary prizes. Awarded annually to an English writer for the best work of imaginative literature, it is especially designed to encourage young authors, and the word 'imaginative' is given a broad interpretation.

2005	Justin Cartwright	*The Promise of Happiness*
2006	Alexander Masters	*Stuart: a Life Backwards*
2007	M J Hyland	*Carry Me Down, Carry Me Down*
2008	Nicola Barker	*Darkmans*
2009-2011	No award to fiction	

Prizes

Independent Foreign Fiction Award

Funded by the Arts Council & Champagne Taittinger and promoted by *The Independent* newspaper, an annual prize for the best contemporary work of prose fiction translated into English from any other tongue and published between 1 January and 31 December each year, since 2001.

2005	Frédéric Beigbeder	*Windows on the World*
		translated from the French by Frank Wynne
2006	Per Petterson	*Out Stealing Horses*
		translated from the Norwegian by Anne Born
2007	José Eduardo Agualusa	*The Book of Chameleons*
		translated from the Portuguese by Daniel Hahn
2008	Paul Verhaeghen	*Omega Minor*
		translated from the Dutch by the author
2009	Evelia Rosero	*The Armies*
		translated from the Spanish by Anne McLean
2010	Philippe Claudel	*Brodeck's Report*
		translated from the French by John Cullen
2011	Santiago Roncagliolo	*Red April*
		translated from the Peruvian by Edith Grossman
2012	Aharon Appelfeld	*Blooms of Darkness*
		translated from the Hebrew by Jeffrey M Green

International IMPAC Dublin Literary Award

www.impacdublinaward.ie

Established in 1996 and awarded to a work of fiction written and published in the English language or written in a language other than English and published in English translation. Nominations are submitted by public libraries worldwide.

2005	Edward P Jones	*The Known World*
2006	Colm Toibin	*The Master*
2007	Per Petterson	*Out Stealing Horses*
2008	Rawi Hage	*De Niro's Game*
2009	Michael Thomas	*Man Gone Down*
2010	Gerbrand Bakker	*The Twin*
		translated from the original Dutch by David Colmer
2011	Colum McCann	*Let the Great World Spin*
2012	Jon McGregor	*Even the Dogs*

Prizes

Jewish Quarterly/Wingate Literary Prize for Fiction

Established in 1977 by the late Harold Hyman Wingate, this prize is the only award in the UK to recognise major works by Jewish or non-Jewish authors that stimulate an interest in and awareness of themes of Jewish concern among a wider reading public.

2005	David Besmozgis	*Natasha and Other Stories*
2006	Imre Kertesz	*Fatelessness*
2007	Howard Jacobson	*Katooki Nights*
2008	Etgar Keret	*Missing Kissinger*
2009	Fred Wander	*The Seventh Well*
2010	No award to fiction	
2011	David Grossman	*To the End of the Land*

John Llewellyn Rhys Prize

www.booktrust.org.uk/prizes-and-awards/3

This prize is awarded in honour of the writer John Llewellyn Rhys, who was killed in action in World War II. It was founded by his young widow to honour and celebrate his life. It rewards the best work of literature (fiction, non-fiction, poetry, drama) by a UK or Commonwealth writer aged 35 or under. From 1987 to 2003 it was funded by *The Mail on Sunday;* the prize is now run by Booktrust. At the time of going to press, this prize was on hold, although the Booktrust website states It will be brought back in the very near future.

2005	Uzodinma Iweala	*Beasts of No Nation*
2006-07	Sarah Hall	*The Carhullan Army*
2009	Evie Wyld	*After the Fire, a Still Small Voice*
2010	Amy Sackville	*The Still Point*

Man Booker International Prize

www.themanbookerprize.com/prize

Awarded every two years from 2005 to an author writing fiction in the English language or whose work is widely translated into English. It will celebrate English language fiction as a major cultural force in the modern world.

2005	Ismail Kadare
2007	Chinua Achebe
2009	Alice Munro
2011	Philip Roth

Prizes

Man Booker Prize for Fiction

www.themanbookerprize.com/prize

Established in 1968 by Booker McConnell Ltd. Eligible novels must be written in English by a citizen of Britain, the Commonwealth or the Republic of Ireland. Since 2002 sponsorship has been by the Man Group and the prize is now known as the Man Booker Prize.

The *Man Booker Best of Beryl* was a special prize created in 2011 to honour the work of Dame Beryl Bainbridge, who died in 2010. She had been short-listed for the prize five times but never won. The public voted on their favourite of five short-listed titles.

2005	John Banville	*The Sea*
2006	Kiran Desai	*The Inheritance of Loss*
2007	Anne Enright	*The Gathering*
2008	Aravind Adiga	*The White Tiger*
2009	Hilary Mantel	*Wolf Hall*
2010	Howard Jacobson	*The Finkler Question*
2011	Julian Barnes	*The Sense of an Ending*
Best of Beryl	Beryl Bainbridge	*Master Georgie*
2012	Hilary Mantel	*Bring up the Bodies*

In 2008, to celebrate the 40th anniversary of this award, Salman Rushdie's *Midnight's Children* was crowned the Best of the Booker.

Somerset Maugham Awards

www.societyofauthors.org/somerset-maugham

The purpose of these annual awards is to encourage young writers to travel, and the emphasis of the founder is on originality and promise. Authors must be under 35 years of age, a British subject by birth, and ordinarily resident in the United Kingdom. Poetry, fiction and non-fiction are all eligible.

joint winners	2005	Justin Hill	*Passing Under Heaven*
		Maggie O'Farrell	*The Distance Between Us*
joint winners	2006	Chris Cleave	*Incendiary*
		Zadie Smith	*On Beauty*
	2007	James Scudamore	*The Amnesia Clinic*
joint winners	2008	Gwendoline Riley	*Joshua Spassky*
		Steven Hall	*The Raw Shark Texts*
	2009	Adam Foulds	*The Broken Word*
	2010	Jacob Polley	*Talk of the Town*
	2011	No award to fiction	

McKitterick Prize

www.societyofauthors.org/mckitterick

Endowed by the late Tom McKitterick the award is made to a first novel (published or unpublished) by an author over the age of 40.

2005	Lloyd Jones	*Mr Vogel*
2006	Peter Pouncey	*Rules for Old Men Waiting*
2007	Reina James	*This Time of Dying*
2008	Jennie Walker	*24 for 3*
2009	Chris Hannan	*Missy*
2010	Raphael Selbourne	*Beauty*
2011	Emma Henderson	*Grace Williams Says It Loud*
2012	Ginny Baily	*Africa Junction*

Melissa Nathan Award for Comedy Romance

www.melissanathan.com/Award/Index.asp

This award was set up by Melissa's husband in 2007 honouring the criteria that she drew up herself very shortly before she died of cancer in 2006. She wanted to encourage and reward writers who can combine in a novel the magical, life-enhancing elements of humour and love.

2007	Marian Keyes	*Anybody Out There*
2008	Lisa Jewell	*31 Dream Street*
2009	Farahad Zama	*The Marriage Bureau for Rich People*
2010	Janet Skeslien Charles	*Moonlight in Odessa*
2011	Helen Simonson	*Major Pettigrew's Last Stand*
2012	Jenny Colgan	*Meet Me at the Cupcake Cafe*

Ondaatje Prize

www.rslit.org/rsl-ondaatje-prize

The Royal Society of Literature launched in 2004 this new award for writing 'that evokes the spirit of a place'. It has been funded by businessman and philanthropist Christopher Ondaatje with extra backing from *Conde Nast Traveller* magazine. It is open to fiction and non-fiction works and was presented for the first time in May 2004. This award is a successor to the Winifred Holtby prize for regional fiction which has been discontinued.

2005	No award to fiction	
2006	James Meek	*The People's Act of Love*
2007	Hisham Matar	*In the Country of Men*
2008-11	No award to fiction	
2012	Rahul Bhattacharya	*The Sly Company of People Who Care*

This prize was created in 2005 and ran for six years until 2010. Open to any first work of fiction by a woman of any nationality and published in the UK in the preceding year. Novels could be entered for both the new Award and the main Orange Prize.

2005	Diana Evans	*26a*
2006	Naomi Alderman	*Disobedience*
2007	Karen Connelly	*The Lizard Cage*
2008	Joanna Kavenna	*Inglorious*
2009	Francesca Kay	*An Equal Stillness*
2010	Irene Sabatini	*The Boy Next Door*

This prize has now been discontinued.

Orange Prize

www.orangeprize.co.uk

Founded in 1996, this award is open to women authors of any nationality, provided that entries have been published in the United Kingdom. Administered by Booktrust.

2005	Lionel Shriver	*We Need to Talk About Kevin*
2006	Zadie Smith	*On Beauty*
2007	Chimamanda Ngozi Adichie	*Half of a Yellow Sun*
2008	Rose Tremain	*The Road Home*
2009	Marilynne Robinson	*Home*
2010	Barbara Kingsolver	*The Lacuna*
2011	Téa Obreht	*The Tiger's Wife*
2012	Madeline Miller	*The Song of Achilles*

Prizes

Pulitzer Prize for Fiction

www.pulitzer.org/bycat/Fiction

Joseph Pulitzer, reporter, editor, publisher and a founder of the Graduate School of Journalism at Columbia University, established in 1903 a system of prizes to encourage 'public service, public morals, American literature and the advancement of education'. The Fiction Prize was first awarded in 1948.

2005	Marilynne Robinson	*Gilead*
2006	Geraldine Brooks	*March*
2007	Cormac McCarthy	*The Road*
2008	Junot Diaz	*The Brief Wondrous Life of Oscar Wao*
2009	Elizabeth Strout	*Olive Kitteridge*
2010	Paul Harding	*Tinkers*
2011	Jennifer Egan	*A Visit from the Goon Squad*
2012	No award	

Romantic Novel of the Year

www.romanticnovelistsassociation.org/index.php/awards/romantic_novel_of_the_year

Established in 1960 and administered by The Romantic Novelists Association, the award is for the best romantic novel of the year by a United Kingdom citizen.

2005	Katharine Davies	*A Good Voyage*
2006	Erica James	*Gardens of Delight*
2007	Rosie Thomas	*Iris & Ruby*
2008	Freya North	*Pillow Talk*
2009	Julia Gregson	*East of the Sun*
2010	Lucy Dillon	*Lost Dogs and Lonely Hearts*
2011	Jojo Moyes	*The Last Letter from your Lover*
2012	Jane Lovering	*Please Don't Stop the Music*

Saltire Society Scottish Book of the Year Award

www.saltiresociety.org.uk/3705

This Award is given to a book by a living author(s) of Scottish descent or residing in Scotland or the book subject must be the work or life of a Scot or with a Scottish question, event or situation.

2005	Kate Atkinson	*Case Histories*
2006	No award to fiction	
2007	A L Kennedy	*Day*
2008	James Kelman	*Kieron Smith, Boy*
2009	No award to fiction	
2010	James Robertson	*And the Land Lay Still*
2011	No award to fiction	

Theakston's Old Peculier Crime Novel of the Year

http://harrogateinternationalfestivals.com/crime/award/award-winners

This award is open to British and Irish Crime Fiction published for the first time in paperback. It is sponsored by Theakston's Old Peculier, in partnership with Asda, and in association with the *Daily Mirror*. The winner is selected from a short list issued in March and the prize is presented in July at the Harrogate Crime Writing Festival. First awarded in 2005.

2005	Mark Billingham	*Lazy Bones*
2006	Val McDermid	*The Torment of Others*
2007	Allan Guthrie	*Two-Way Split*
2008	Stef Penney	*The Tenderness of Wolves*
2009	Mark Billingham	*Death Message*
2010	R J Ellory	*A Simple Act of Violence*
2011	Lee Child	*61 Hours*
2012	Denise Mina	*The End of the Wasp Season*

Prizes

Theakston's Old Peculier Outstanding Contribution to Crime Fiction Award

This award honours writers who have made a lasting and distinct impression on the genre over the span of their careers, and are often people who have provided inspiration for other great authors who have followed in their wake. First awarded in 2010.

2010	Reginald Hill
2011	P D James
2012	Colin Dexter

Betty Trask Awards

www.societyofauthors.org/betty-trask

Started in 1984 and administered by the Society of Authors, the awards are for the benefit of young authors (under 35), and are given on the strength of the manuscript of a first novel of a romantic or traditional - rather than experimental - nature. The winners are required to use the money for foreign travel. The principal winners are:

2005	Susan Fletcher	*Eve Green*
2006	Nick Laird	*Utterly Monkey*
2007	Will Davis	*My Side of the Story*
2008	David Szalay	*London & the South East*
2009	Samantha Harvey	*The Wilderness*
2010	Nadifa Mohamed	*Black Mamba Boy*
2011	Anjali Joseph	*Saraswati Park*
2012	David Whitehouse	*Bed*

Patrick White Award

Prizes

This is an annual literary prize established by Patrick White, Australian author and winner of the 1973 Nobel Prize in Literature.

A cash award is given to an Australian writer who has been highly creative over a long period but has not necessarily received adequate recognition. Writers are automatically eligible without the necessity for submissions.

2005	Fay Zwicky
2006	Morris Lurie
2007	David Rowbotham
2008	John Romeril
2009	Beverley Farmer
2010	David Foster
2011	Robert Adamson

Classic Authors

The following 'classic' and 'modern classic' authors appeared in the 6th edition but do not feature in the 7th. However, they remain well worth seeking out, and this list also includes recommended titles for each author.

Kingsley Amis	*Lucky Jim* *The Old Devils*
Jane Austen	*Pride and Prejudice* *Sense and Sensibility*
Saul Bellow	*Herzog* *Humboldt's Gift*
John Buchan	*The Thirty-Nine Steps* *Greenmantle*
Joseph Conrad	*Lord Jim* *Nostromo*
Charles Dickens	*David Copperfield* *Little Dorritt*
William Faulkner	*The Sound and the Fury* *Absalom! Absalom!*
John Galsworthy	*The Forsyte Saga* (Trilogy)
Elizabeth Gaskell	*Cranford* *North and South*
Thomas Hardy	*The Mayor of Casterbridge* *Far From the Madding Crowd*
Joseph Heller	*Catch-22* *Something Happened*
Ernest Hemingway	*A Farewell to Arms* *For Whom the Bell Tolls*
Aldous Huxley	*Brave New World* *Eyeless in Gaza*
Henry James	*Portrait of a Lady* *The Ambassadors*
James Joyce	*A Portrait of the Artist as a Young Man* *Ulysses*

D H Lawrence	*Sons and Lovers* *Women in Love*
Harper Lee	*To Kill a Mockingbird*
C S Lewis	*The Chronicles of Narnia* (7-Book Series)
Norman Mailer	*The Naked and the Dead*
W Somerset Maugham	*Of Human Bondage* *The Razor's Edge*
Vladimir Nabokov	*Lolita*
George Orwell	*1984* *Coming Up For Air*
Anthony Powell	*A Dance to the Music of Time* (12-Book Series)
J B Priestley	*The Good Companions* *Angel Pavement*
Erich Maria Remarque	*All Quiet on the Western Front*
J D Salinger	*The Catcher in the Rye*
Robert Louis Stevenson	*Kidnapped* *Catriona*
Anthony Trollope	*Barchester Towers* *Can You Forgive Her?*
Jules Verne	*20,000 Leagues Under the Sea* *Journey to the Centre of the Earth*
H G Wells	*Kipps* *The History of Mr Polly*
Edith Wharton	*The House of Mirth* *Ethan Frome*
Virginia Woolf	*To the Lighthouse* *Mrs Dalloway*

Crossover Authors

Selecting suitable books for Young Adults, i.e. the 16+ age group is not easy. The right book for the right person at this stage can vary enormously. One author may write just one title which appeals or maybe every book by that author will be devoured. Where these authors have written books for children these are indicated with a ☺ as the children's books are written for a much younger age range. The list is certainly not exhaustive for several other authors in **Who Else Writes Like ...?** will be enjoyed by young adults. The suggestions here are subjective but, in our opinion, offer a reliable selection of authors to introduce older teenagers to adult fiction.

Recommended authors are indicated by ⌒ in the main listing.

Viv Warren and Mary Yardley

Chinua Achebe
Peter Ackroyd
Douglas Adams
Cecelia Ahern
Brian W Aldiss
Monica Ali
Isabel Allende
Martin Amis
Kevin J Anderson ☺
Virginia Andrews
Jeffrey Archer
Keri Arthur
Sherry Ashworth ☺
Isaac Asimov
Kate Atkinson
Margaret Atwood
Jean M Auel
David Baddiel
Beryl Bainbridge
David Baldacci
J G Ballard
Iain Banks
Iain M Banks
Clive Barker ☺
Pat Barker
Raffaella Barker ☺
Bateman ☺
Colin Bateman ☺
Stephen Baxter ☺
Greg Bear
M C Beaton
Alan Bennett
Maeve Binchy

Sam Bourne
William Boyd
T C Boyle
John Boyne ☺
Malcolm Bradbury
Ray Bradbury
Alan Bradley
Marion Zimmer Bradley
Ann Brashares ☺
Simon Brett
Anita Brookner
Terry Brooks
Dan Brown
Candace Bushnell
A S Byatt
Armand Cabasson
Meg Cabot ☺
Rachel Caine ☺
Trudi Canavan ☺
Orson Scott Card
Peter Carey
Isobelle Carmody ☺
P C & Kristin Cast ☺
Raymond Chandler
Tracy Chevalier
Lee Child ☺
Agatha Christie
Tom Clancy
Mary Higgins Clark
Arthur C Clarke
Susanna Clarke
Ann Cleeves
Harlan Coben ☺

Jonathan Coe
Paulo Coelho
J M Coetzee
Martina Cole
Eoin Colfer ☺
Jenny Colgan
Michael Connelly
Joseph Conrad
Jilly Cooper
Louise Cooper ☺
Bernard Cornwell
Patricia D Cornwell
Douglas Coupland
Michael Crichton
Michael Cunningham
Clive Cussler
Mary Janice Davidson
Lindsey Davis
Louis de Bernières
Jeffery Deaver
Len Deighton
Anita Desai
Colin Dexter
Philip K Dick
Cory Doctorow ☺
Stephen Donaldson
Jennifer Donnelly ☺
Arthur Conan Doyle
Roddy Doyle ☺
Margaret Drabble
Daphne Du Maurier
Helen Dunmore ☺
David Eddings

Clive Egleton
Ben Elton
Barbara Erskine
Janet Evanovich
Nicholas Evans
Sebastian Faulks
Christine Feehan
Jasper Fforde ☺
Helen Fielding
Anne Fine ☺
F Scott Fitzgerald
Ian Fleming ☺
James Follett
Ken Follett
C S Forester
E M Forster
Margaret Forster
Frederick Forsyth
John Fowles
Clare Francis
Dick Francis
Jonathan Franzen
George Macdonald Fraser
Michael Frayn
Nicci French
Esther Freud
Stephen Fry
Carlos Fuentes
Alexander Fullerton
Kate Furnivall
Jostein Gaarder ☺
Neil Gaiman ☺
Patrick Gale
Gabriel Garcia Márquez
Jane Gardam ☺
Alex Garland
Mark Gatiss
David Gemmell
Elizabeth George
Adèle Geras ☺
Nicci Gerrard
Tess Gerritsen
William Gibson
Robert Goddard
William Golding
Terry Goodkind
Sue Grafton
Caroline Graham
Winston Graham
Rob Grant

Jane Green
Graham Greene
Philippa Gregory ☺
John Grisham ☺
David Guterson
Mark Haddon ☺
Laurell K Hamilton
Joanne Harris ☺
Robert Harris
Thomas Harris
Zoë Heller
Frank Herbert
Georgette Heyer
Carl Hiaasen ☺
Jack Higgins ☺
Patricia Highsmith
Charles Higson ☺
Reginald Hill
Susan Hill
Victoria Hislop
Robin Hobb
Peter Hoeg
Alice Hoffman
Wendy Holden
Tom Holt
Nick Hornby ☺
Khaled Hosseini
Elizabeth Jane Howard
Conn Iggulden
John Irving
Kazuo Ishiguro
P D James
Peter James
Lisa Jewell
Ruth Prawer Jhabvala
Robert Jordan
Cathy Kelly
Thomas Keneally
Alexander Kent
Sherrilyn Kenyon
Jack Kerouac
Katharine Kerr
Marian Keyes
Garry Kilworth ☺
Stephen King
Sophie Kinsella
Dean R Koontz
Elizabeth Kostova
Hanif Kureishi
Lynda La Plante

John Lanchester
Stephen R Lawhead
John Le Carré
Ursula K Le Guin ☺
Stephen Leather
Tanith Lee ☺
Elmore Leonard
Doris Lessing
Andrea Levy
Marina Lewycka
Toby Litt
Penelope Lively ☺
Sam Llewellyn ☺
David Lodge
Robert Ludlum
Anne McCaffrey
Alexander McCall Smith ☺
Val McDermid
Ross Macdonald
Ian McEwan ☺
Alistair MacLean
Larry McMurtry
Andy McNab ☺
Allan Mallinson
Henning Mankell ☺
Jill Mansell
Hilary Mantel
Yann Martel
Armistead Maupin
Stephenie Meyer ☺
Santa Montefiore
Michael Moorcock
Toni Morrison
John Mortimer
Kate Mosse
Iris Murdoch
David Nicholls
William Nicholson ☺
Garth Nix ☺
Freya North
Patrick O'Brian
Edna O'Brien
Joseph O'Connor
Joan O'Neill ☺
Joyce Carol Oates ☺
Michael Ondaatje
Sara Paretsky
Tony Parsons
James Patterson ☺
Elizabeth Peters

Ellis Peters
Jodi Picoult
Christopher Pike ☺
Terry Pratchett ☺
Philip Pullman ☺
Mario Puzo
Ian Rankin
Robert Rankin
Kathy Reichs
Ruth Rendell
Anne Rice
Meg Rosoff ☺
Rosemary Rowe
Salman Rushdie ☺
Edward Rutherfurd
Chris Ryan ☺
Lilith Saintcrow
Dorothy L Sayers
Alex Scarrow ☺
Simon Scarrow ☺
Bernhard Schlink
Alice Sebold
Will Self
Vikram Seth

Darren Shan ☺
Tom Sharpe
Lionel Shriver
Nevil Shute
Georges Simenon
Ali Smith
Martin Cruz Smith
Zadie Smith
Muriel Spark
John Steinbeck
Mary Stewart
Patrick Suskind
Graham Swift
Paul Theroux
Kate Thompson ☺
J R R Tolkien ☺
Sue Townsend ☺
P J Tracy
Rose Tremain
Joanna Trollope
Christos Tsiolkas
Anne Tyler
Barry Unsworth
Salley Vickers

Kurt Vonnegut
Alice Walker
Fiona Walker
Minette Walters
Keith Waterhouse
Evelyn Waugh
Alison Weir
Margaret Weis
Fay Weldon
Irvine Welsh
Kim Wilkins
Tad Williams
R D Wingfield
Jacqueline Winspear
Jeanette Winterson ☺
P G Wodehouse
Tom Wolfe
Chris Wooding ☺
John Wyndham
Xinran
Robyn Young
Carlos Ruiz Zafón ☺
Markus Zusak ☺

Further Reading

Many long-standing reference guides to fiction are no longer being updated. However, the following list provides a worthwhile selection of reference books which can be used alongside *Who Else Writes Like...?*. The Bloomsbury and Rough Guides featured in the 6th edition of this guide have generally not been updated for a few years, but are still well worth seeking out.

Crime Fiction Since 1800 by Stephen Knight - Palgrave MacMillan, 2010

Death in a Cold Climate: a guide to Scandinavian crime fiction by Barry Forshaw - Palgrave MacMillan, 2012

100 Must-read Classic Novels by Nick Rennison - A & C Black, 2006

100 Must-read Crime Novels by Nick Rennison and Richard Shephard - A & C Black, 2006

100 Must-read Science Fiction Novels by Stephen E Andrews and Nick Rennison - A & C Black 2006

The Reader's Advisory Guide to Mystery by John Charles et al - ALA editions, 2nd rev. edition, 2011

A Reference Guide to Crime Fiction by Gabrielle Dantz - Webster's Digital Services, 2012

Snobbery With Violence: English crime stories and their audience by Colin Watson - Faber Finds, 2009

1000 Books to Change Your Life - Time Out Guides, 2007

1001 Books You Must Read Before You Die General Editor Peter Boxall - Cassell, 2008

The Ultimate Teen Book Guide edited by Daniel Hahn and Leonie Flynn - A & C Black, 2010

Who Next...? a guide to children's authors edited by Viv Warren and Mary Yardley - LISU, Loughborough University, 4th edition, 2011

Who's Who of Twentieth Century Novelists edited by Tim Woods - Routledge, 2001

Websites

As the power of the internet grows ever stronger, so the number of book-related websites continues to expand. The following list was accurate at the time of going to print and includes a selection of UK, Australian and international resources.

General Interest
www.thebookbag.co.uk
www.bookclubforum.co.uk
www.thebookexplorer.com
www.bookstoreread.com
www.booktrust.org.uk/books-and-reading
http://literature.britishcouncil.org/writers
www.fantasticfiction.co.uk
www.gnod.net
www.thegoodbookguide.com
www.goodreadingmagazine.com.au
www.goodreads.com
www.guardian.co.uk/books
www.librarything.com
www.literaryfestivals.co.uk
www.lovereading.co.uk
www.meettheauthor.co.uk
www.packabook.com
www.rtbookreviews.com
www.shelfari.com
www.welovethisbook.com
www.whatshouldireadnext.com
www.whichbook.net

Chick Lit
www.chicklit.co.uk
www.chicklitreviewsandnews.com

Crime
www.austcrimefiction.org/authors_australian
www.crimedownunder.com
www.crimetime.co.uk
www.thecwa.co.uk
www.eurocrime.co.uk
www.nedkellyawards.com
www.reviewingtheevidence.com
www.sistersincrime.org.au
www.stopyourekillingme.com
www.thrillingdetective.com
www.twbooks.co.uk

Historical Fiction
www.historical-fiction.com
www.historicalnovelsociety.org

Horror
www.horrorworld.org
www.australianhorror.com

Romance
www.likesbooks.com
www.outbackromances.com
www.rna-uk.org
www.romanceaustralia.com
www.theromancereader.com